RUTH HALL

and Other Writings

AMERICAN WOMEN WRITERS SERIES

Joanne Dobson, Judith Fetterley, and Elaine Showalter, series editors

ALTERNATIVE ALCOTT
Louisa May Alcott
Elaine Showalter, editor

MOODS
Louisa May Alcott
Sarah Elbert, editor

STORIES FROM THE COUNTRY OF LOST BORDERS
Mary Austin
Marjorie Pryse, editor

CLOVERNOOK SKETCHES AND OTHER STORIES
Alice Cary
Judith Fetterley, editor

HOBOMOK AND OTHER WRITINGS ON INDIANS
Lydia Maria Child
Carolyn L. Karcher, editor

"HOW CELIA CHANGED HER MIND" AND SELECTED STORIES
Rose Terry Cooke
Elizabeth Ammons, editor

THE LAMPLIGHTER
Maria Susanna Cummins
Nina Baym, editor

RUTH HALL AND OTHER WRITINGS
Fanny Fern
Joyce Warren, editor

THE ESSENTIAL MARGARET FULLER
Jeffrey Steele, editor

GAIL HAMILTON: SELECTED WRITINGS
Susan Coultrap-McQuin, editor

A NEW HOME, WHO'LL FOLLOW?
Caroline M. Kirkland
Sandra A. Zagarell, editor

QUICKSAND AND *PASSING*
Nella Larsen
Deborah E. McDowell, editor

HOPE LESLIE
Catharine Maria Sedgwick
Mary Kelley, editor

THE HIDDEN HAND
E.D.E.N. Southworth
Joanne Dobson, editor

"THE AMBER GODS" AND OTHER STORIES
Harriet Prescott Spofford
Alfred Bendixen, editor

OLDTOWN FOLKS
Harriet Beecher Stowe
Dorothy Berkson, editor

WOMEN ARTISTS, WOMEN EXILES: "MISS GRIEF" AND OTHER STORIES
Constance Fenimore Woolson
Joan Myers Weimer, editor

AMERICAN WOMEN POETS OF THE NINETEENTH CENTURY: AN ANTHOLOGY
Cheryl Walker, editor

RUTH HALL
and Other Writings

FANNY FERN

Edited and with an Introduction by

JOYCE W. WARREN

RUTGERS UNIVERSITY PRESS

New Brunswick, New Jersey

Seventh paperback printing, 1996

Manufactured in the United States of America

Library of Congress Cataloging-in-Publication Data
Fern, Fanny, 1811–1872.
Ruth Hall and other writings.
(American women writers series)
Bibliography: p.
I. Warren, Joyce W. II. Fern, Fanny, 1811–1872.
Ruth Hall. 1986. III. Title. IV. Series.
PS2523.P9A6 1986 813'.3 86–3682
ISBN 0–8135–1167–4
ISBN 0–8135–1168–2 (pbk)

CONTENTS

ACKNOWLEDGMENTS

I want to thank the librarians at the many libraries at which I have conducted research for this volume, especially the staffs at the Sophia Smith Collection at Smith College, the American Antiquarian Society in Worcester, Massachusetts, the Watkinson Library in Hartford, the New York Public Library, the Philadelphia Public Library, the Butler Library at Columbia University, the Barnard College Library, and the Paul Klapper Library at Queens College. I am also grateful to James Parton II, the great-grandson of Fanny Fern, for his interest and help in providing me with information about his family. And most of all, I want to thank Leslie Mitchner, senior editor at Rutgers University Press, whose response to my suggestion several years ago that the press reprint Fanny Fern's *Ruth Hall* has made this edition possible and whose informed counsel and support have made the undertaking so rewarding.

INTRODUCTION

> If Fanny Fern were a man,—a man who believed that the gratification of revenge were a proper occupation for one who has been abused, and that those who have injured us are fair game, *Ruth Hall* would be a natural and excusable book. But we confess that we cannot understand how a delicate, suffering woman can hunt down even her persecutors so remorselessly. We cannot think so highly of [such] an author's womanly gentleness.

So read a lengthy review of Fanny Fern's novel *Ruth Hall* in the *New York Times* on December 20, 1854. Overall the review was favorable, but like almost every other review of the novel—whether favorable or unfavorable—the *Times* was baffled by one terrible question: how could a *woman* write such a book?

In spite of her flowery pseudonym (and even that was partially intended as a satirical comment on popular literature),[1] Fanny Fern was in many ways out of place in nineteenth-century America. At a time when the "cult of the lady" urged women to be gentle, "feminine," and submissive, Fern's writing was satirical, outspoken, polemical—even outrageous. To be sure, she could also write traditionally, and her traditional "sentimental" pieces gave her respectability, perhaps enabling her work to be published in the first place. The editors of her first books put in an inordinate number of sentimental pieces and toned down some of her satirical writing.

Until very recently, twentieth-century critics have contemptuously characterized Fanny Fern as nothing more than a tear-drenched sentimentalist. They may have made this judgment partly because her first collection, *Fern Leaves from Fanny's Portfolio* (1853), by which she was most widely known, contained a disproportionate number of her sentimental writings. This is not the only reason, however. That such a false assessment could have been allowed to persist tells us a great deal about the prejudices that have determined official literary judgments: twentieth-century critics have simply equated "popular nineteenth-century American woman writer" with "sentimental nonentity" and, without bothering to read her work, have dismissed the popular Fanny Fern as the "grandmother of all sob sisters" (Pattee 110–18, Ross 39, James D. Hart 97). Certainly Fred Lewis Pattee, whose book *The Feminine Fifties* (1940) did much to promulgate this distorted view of Fern's work, could not have read further in her works than the first part of *Fern Leaves* or he would never have been so far off the mark as to call the satirical Fanny Fern the "most tearful and convulsingly 'female' moralizer" of the period (110). Anyone who reads her work today knows how absurd this judgment is, yet this opinion has prevailed.

Fanny Fern's contemporaries would not have recognized her in this twentieth-century portrait. The majority of her writings were far from sentimental; they were regarded as unfeminine by her contemporaries. As one anonymous review of *Ruth Hall* "by a lady" stated, Fern's early newspaper work had demonstrated that the "author was not sufficiently endowed with female delicacy." Praising her sentimental writing, the reviewer lamented that "while a perfect sketch, artistically wrought out, and disfigured by no defects of style or coarse innuendoes, partially filled a column, the same column often contained another article, full of those blemishes" (OB 12/30/54).

Those "blemishes" are the very features that make her work so interesting today. The coarse innuendos were her satirical portrayals of the hypocrisy and cant behind the facade of some of society's most sacred institutions—particularly marriage. And the down-to-earth language and straightforward writing that conservative critics regarded as defects of style were, in fact, innovations marking a significant shift away from the verbose gentility of much popular writing of the time. Thus *Harper's* in July 1854 heralded Fanny Fern as the welcome harbinger of a new writing style, which showed "that the day for stilted rhetoric, scholastic refinements, and big dictionary words, the parade and pomp, and the pageantry of literature, is declining."

The name Fanny Fern first came before the public in 1851. Short, satirical pieces signed with that name were published first in the Boston *Olive Branch*, then in the *True Flag*, and were immediately copied—pirated—by newspapers all over the country and across the Atlantic. "Who is Fanny Fern?" became the question of the day. Was "she" a man (surely no woman could write so "indelicately"), or was she a woman (some of her pieces spoke directly to "a woman's heart")?

It was four years before the public learned that Fanny Fern was Sara Payson Willis, the daughter of Nathaniel and Hannah Willis, and the sister of N. P. Willis, New York poet and journalist.[2] She was born in Portland, Maine, on July 9, 1811, the fifth of nine children. Six weeks after her birth, the family moved to Boston, where in 1816 Nathaniel Willis founded *The Recorder*, the first religious newspaper in the United States, and eleven years later, the first juvenile newspaper, *The Youth's Companion*. He was a strict Calvinist and deacon of the Park Street Church, called "Brimstone Corner" in part because of the fiery sermons that issued from its pulpit. Deacon Willis, as he was commonly called, frowned on dancing and other "ungodly" pursuits, and worried that his spirited daughter Sara was not sufficiently serious or fearful of God's wrath. In later years she wrote: "The God *my eyes* see, is not a tyrant, driving his creatures to heaven through fear of hell" (*New Story Book* 20). Her God was a nurturing maternal figure rather than a wrathful patriarch. "Who but God can comfort like a mother?" she wrote; "there is no word save God which is so . . . heart-satisfying" (*New Story Book* 26; NYL 4/29/71). Hannah Willis, Sara's mother, was as warm and cheerful in her disposition as Deacon Willis was sober and distant. As a child, Sara was closer to her mother in temperament as well as in religious feeling, and throughout her life she remembered her mother with admiration and longing. In 1864, she wrote in "A Story about Myself":

> If there is any poetry in my nature, from my mother I inherited it. . . . Had my mother's time not been so constantly engrossed by a fast-increasing family, had she found time for literary pursuits, I am confident she would have distinguished herself. Her hurried letters, written with one foot upon the cradle, give ample evidence of this. She *talked poetry unconsciously*! (*New Story Book* 10-13)

In her newspaper articles Fanny Fern refers often to her mother. Her writings reveal not only how strong were her ties with her mother, but also how her perceptions of her mother's life helped shape her later rebellion against masculine authority (e.g., *New Story Book* 10-13; NYL 6/23/66).

Sara's older brother, Nathaniel P. Willis, experienced a religious conversion when he was only fifteen, but she never did. A few years later, however, while a student at Yale and rapidly making a name for himself as a poet, N. P. Willis began the religious backsliding that ultimately led to his being expelled from the Congregational Church. The elder Willis, worried about his son's religious defection, became even more concerned about Sara's seeming lack of piety and determined to send her to Catharine Beecher's Female Seminary in Hartford, where students were known to respond positively to Beecher's religious influence. It was the young Sara's third boarding school, and she did not want to go. Nor was the school able to effect the religious improvement that her father had hoped for.

Fortunately, Catharine Beecher's methods were not repressive, and the youthful Sara remained unsubdued. Fifteen years later, she met Catharine Beecher in Boston, and in response to her former student's query, Beecher replied: "Not remember *you*, Sara Willis. You were the worst behaved girl in my school!" Then after a significant pause she added: "And I loved you the best" (EP 98). Harriet Beecher Stowe, who was a pupil-teacher in her sister's school, later remembered Sara as a "bright, laughing witch of a half saint half sinner. . . . The girl with a head of light crêpe curls—with a jaunty little bonnet tipped on one side, & laughing light blue eyes—writing always good compositions & fighting off your Arithmetic lessons" (SSC).

Sara Willis's compositions were sought by the editor of a local newspaper who often came to the seminary to ask for "Miss Willis's latest" (EP 70). The only composition that survives from her school days, however, is a description of her struggle to learn arithmetic, written for the school's Annual Exhibition Day in July 1829. It is rich in satire and the clever wordplay that would later gain recognition for Fanny Fern (SSC).

In 1830 or 1831, Sara Willis came home to Boston, as she later said, to "learn the 'Lost Arts' of bread-making and button-hole stitching" (NYL 2/26/70). She also read proof and wrote articles for her father's newspapers when needed, something she had done since she was twelve years old, without remuneration and with no thought of a professional career. After several years at home, on May 4, 1837, she married Charles Harrington Eldredge, a cashier at the Merchants' Bank in Boston, who was called Handsome Charlie by his friends. The years of their marriage are fictionalized in

Ruth Hall. Their first child, Mary, was born in 1838, and Grace was born three years later. For seven years Sara was happy as wife and mother. Then in 1844 began a series of tragedies that were to change her life forever. In February, her youngest sister, Ellen, died of complications after the birth of her first child. Six weeks later, her mother died, leaving a void that she felt for the rest of her life. And in March 1845, six months after the birth of her third daughter, named Ellen for her dead sister, her firstborn was dead of brain fever. This death is graphically described in *Ruth Hall*.

But her troubles were not over. The following year, Charles Eldredge died of typhoid fever. That experience is recorded also in *Ruth Hall*, with the same result for the widow in real life as in fiction. Eldredge had been involved in a lengthy lawsuit which was decided against him, and after his death, when his creditors had been satisfied, there was nothing left for his widow and children. Sara's father, who had soon remarried, reluctantly contributed a small portion of her support, and the Eldredges, equally reluctant, supplied the rest. Deacon Willis resented having to support a daughter whom he had supposed well settled, and he tactlessly blamed Charles Eldredge for handling his affairs so poorly. The Eldredges, on the other hand, blamed their daughter-in-law, maintaining that if she had been more economical, her husband would have had more money to leave her. Together they conferred, as she once said bitterly, "to decide which family need do the least" (EP 101).

Meanwhile, the deacon urged his daughter to remarry as the best means of supporting herself, and, after her own attempts to earn money were unsuccessful, she capitulated, agreeing to a marriage of convenience with Samuel P. Farrington, a widower who had pressed his suit in spite of her previous refusal and her honest assertion that she did not love him. They were married on January 15, 1849. As her daughter Ellen later wrote, the marriage was "a terrible mistake" (SSC). Farrington was violently jealous of his wife's appearance, her friends, his friends, even of her dead husband's memory. Although she conscientiously tried to be a good mother to his two little girls, he made them into spies against their stepmother. Finally, she took a desperate step, unprecedented in her family and shocking to her contemporaries: in January 1851 she contacted a law firm and left her husband, moving into the Marlboro Hotel in Boston. Farrington spread malicious rumors about her, rumors denied by his own brother (SSC). Farrington left Boston, escaping the necessity of supporting his wife, and two years later obtained a divorce in Chicago on grounds of desertion. In later years, Fanny Fern never spoke of the Farrington episode in her life; she used it, however, in her second novel, *Rose Clark*, as the basis for the disastrous marriage of Gertrude Dean.

When she left her husband, Sara's family was scandalized at the disgrace her unconventional behavior had brought upon them, and refused to resume her support. She took the examination to become a teacher in the Boston public schools, but did not obtain a position. She worked as a seamstress, but could never earn more than seventy-five cents a week, no matter how hard she worked. Unable to support both children, she had been forced to let the Eldredges take her elder daughter, Grace, while she and Ellen lived on bread and milk in cheap boarding houses. This period of her life is vividly portrayed in *Ruth Hall*. Finally, in desperation, she decided to try writing for the newspapers. Her first piece was published in the *Olive Branch* on June 28, 1851. She was paid fifty cents for it.[3] She did not begin using the Fanny Fern signature until September, and it was probably that summer that she sent several sample articles to her brother, N. P. Willis, editor of the New York *Home Journal*, and asked for his help. Although he had helped to establish other women writers, notably Fanny Forrester and Grace Greenwood, he refused to help his sister. He wrote that he was ashamed to have any editor know that a sister of his had written anything so "vulgar" and "indecent" and advised her to write for the religious papers (SSC).

Angry and bitter at her brother's betrayal, she could not forgive him. Her article "Apollo Hyacinth" (included here) appeared in the New York *Musical World and Times* on June 18, 1853, and its satirical portrait of Willis caused a minor sensation. Then in 1855 *Ruth Hall* appeared with its picture of Willis as the pretentious dandy, Hyacinth Ellet, Ruth's brother, who "recognizes only the drawing-room side of human nature. Sorrow in satin he can sympathize with, but sorrow in rags is too plebeian for his exquisite organization" (ch. 88). Willis's contemporaries apparently had no trouble recognizing him in the portrait, and, although Fanny Fern was widely criticized for her "unsisterly" treatment of Willis, many readers felt that her portrayal was true. As one British review dryly stated: "The book contains one undoubted portrait, which will be recognized by every literary man, but in the present state of our information, we decline condemning its introduction" (*Tait's* 199).

Undeterred by her brother's failure to help her, Fanny Fern persevered on her own. Soon she was writing several articles a week for both the *Olive Branch* and the *True Flag* at two dollars a column, two columns for the *Olive Branch* and one for the *True Flag*, for a total of six dollars a week. To earn this amount, she had to write between five and ten articles a week. One of the many newspapers pirating copies of her articles was her brother's paper, the *Home Journal*, in New York. When Willis found out, he demanded that his editor, James Parton, stop clipping his sister's articles. But Parton admired Fanny Fern's work and had previously sent a note to the unknown writer advising her to come to New York. When Parton argued against dropping the articles, Willis insisted, and Parton resigned.

In September 1852 Oliver Dyer—publisher of the New York *Musical World and Times*, which was edited by Fanny Fern's other brother, Richard Willis—contacted her through the Boston papers, proposing that she write exclusively for his paper, one article a week for double the combined payments by the *Olive Branch* and *True Flag*, which, he felt, were exploiting her. To his amazement, Dyer found that the columnist was his editor's sister. Richard Willis did not share his brother's animosity toward their sister and on September 25, 1852, the *Musical World* announced that Fanny Fern would soon write exclusively for that paper. Two weeks later her first article appeared under the heading "Fanny Fern's Column." Thus she became the first woman columnist in the United States. Other women—among them Lydia Maria Child and Margaret Fuller—had been correspondents or editors, but Fanny Fern was the first to be a columnist in the twentieth-century sense of the word: a professional journalist paid a salary to write a regular column expressing the author's personal opinions on social and political issues.

For several weeks Fern's articles did not appear in the *Olive Branch* and *True Flag*. The editors of those papers were devastated at the loss of their star contributor, and they reluctantly agreed to increase the amount they were paying her so that ultimately she was earning a total of thirteen dollars a week from the two Boston papers. Dyer graciously released her from the exclusivity of their agreement, and on December 11, 1852, the editor of the *True Flag* announced that Fanny Fern had agreed to write a regular column for his paper as well.

Early in 1853, James Derby of the Derby and Miller publishing firm, wrote to Fanny Fern in care of the *True Flag* proposing that he publish a book of her newspaper articles. He offered her ten cents a copy in royalties or one thousand dollars to purchase the copyright.[4] She chose the royalties, which later proved to be a wise decision. *Fern Leaves from Fanny's Portfolio* was published in June 1853, and seventy thousand copies were sold in less than a year. Another twenty-nine thousand copies were sold in England. Within a year Fanny Fern had earned almost ten thousand dollars from that book alone. Later in 1853 Derby and Miller brought out a collection for children, *Little Ferns for Fanny's Little Friends*, and in 1854, *Fern Leaves*, Second Series. By June of 1854, 180,000 copies of the three books had been sold (John Hart 472).

With the money from her recently published book, Fanny Fern left Boston for New York with her daughter Ellen in June 1853, and soon afterward she was able to reclaim Grace. Although she was no longer writing for the Boston papers, she continued to write for the *Musical World* until November 1853, when the Philadelphia *Saturday Evening Post* announced that Fanny Fern would soon begin writing for that paper. She wrote for the *Post* for only a few months, however. On February 16, 1854, she signed a preliminary agreement with Mason Brothers to write "a novel or tale" of four hundred pages, and agreed that she would not engage in any other literary activities until the novel was completed. On their part, Mason Brothers agreed to pay her fifteen cents a copy, as opposed to Derby's ten cents, and promised extraordinary measures to promote the book.

Mason Brothers were true to their word. In November 1854, they launched a mammoth advertising campaign. They inundated the newspapers with advertisements, and when the novel appeared in December 1854, they responded boldly to an unfavorable review of *Ruth Hall* which had claimed that "almost any educated girl" could write such a book: they offered to award $10,000 to every "'well educated' girl (or other person for that matter) who will furnish us for publication the manuscript of a tale equal to *Ruth Hall*."

That Fanny Fern's name was well known already made Mason Brothers' task easier, of course. And then on December 30, 1854, something happened that, although catastrophic for Fern personally, dramatically increased the sale of the book. The editor of the *True Flag*, William U. Moulton, angered by his loss of Fanny Fern's columns and incensed at her unflattering portrait of him in *Ruth Hall* (Mr. Tibbetts of *The Pilgrim*), began a series of spiteful articles revealing the carefully guarded secret of her identity. Having written the book in the belief that her incognita was safe, Fanny Fern had based the story of Ruth Hall on her own life, using real models for many characters, who, though fictionalized, were easily recognizable once her identity was known. Sales of *Ruth Hall* climbed to 70,000. The book became a roman à clef, with readers particularly eager to see the author's portrait of her famous brother, N. P. Willis. But the critics castigated Fanny Fern for her negative treatment of her father, brother, and in-laws, whose uncharitableness toward her when she and her children were living in poverty she had sharply satirized in the novel. However unkind her relatives may have been, the critics insisted, it was not proper in a woman to be so unfeminine as to criticize them. Fern was compared to Goneril and Regan, and the book was described as "abominable," "monstrous," "overflowing with an unfemininely bitter wrath and spite."[5] The primary reason behind this violent reaction to Fern's satirical portraits of her male relatives probably was the one openly stated by the New Orleans *Crescent City* in a review of *Ruth Hall* in January of 1855: "As we wish no sister of ours, nor no female relative to show toward us, the ferocity she has displayed toward her nearest relatives we take occasion to censure this book that might initiate such a possibility."

The threat to male self-esteem by Fanny Fern's "ferocity" can be further seen in the vituperative pseudo-biography that appeared anonymously in March 1855. The author of *The Life and Beauties of Fanny Fern* was apparently Moulton, the editor of the *True Flag* who had revealed her identity. The book contained the articles already printed in the *True Flag*, along with other criticism, and a selection of her most satirical and unconventional articles, which, the author pointed out, had been left out of *Fern Leaves*, but which he erroneously believed would discredit her in the eyes of the public. The book was a vindictive attempt to injure Fanny Fern's reputation, and was filled with innuendoes and false statements designed to cast doubts on her morals, character, and integrity.

Throughout all of the blistering criticism, Fanny Fern, the writer and public woman, never faltered. But, for Sara Willis Eldredge Farrington, the private person, the criticism was devastating. Many years later she wrote:

> And how I *did* cry if an editor reviewed *me* personally, instead of my book, in his book notices. How I used to wish I were Tom Hyer, or Jack Sayers, or some high and mighty muscular pugilist, to make mincemeat of the coward, who wouldn't have dared to "hit one of his own size" in that sneaking fashion. (NYL 11/26/64)

After her arrival in New York, Fanny Fern's constant companion and escort had been James Parton, her early champion in the editorial offices of her brother, N. P. Willis, and the prototype of Horace Gates in *Ruth Hall*. Parton, after leaving Willis's *Home Journal*, had written *The Life of Horace Greeley*, which was published the same month as *Ruth Hall*, and which was to be the first in a long line of distinguished biographies. The two were married on January 5, 1856, after signing a prenuptial agreement stating that Fanny Fern's property was hers alone, ultimately to become her children's. She was forty-four, Parton thirty-three. In July 1856 they moved into a house on Oxford Street in Brooklyn which she had purchased with her earnings. Her article in the *New York Ledger* on July 19, "My Old Ink-stand and I" (reprinted here), reflects the satisfaction she felt at her independently won success. They lived in Brooklyn for three years, but in 1859 they moved into a brownstone on East Eighteenth Street in Manhattan that she also purchased.

In 1855 Fanny Fern had signed a contract with Robert Bonner, editor of the weekly *New York Ledger*, agreeing to write a story for his paper. Bonner, after acquiring an obscure businessman's newspaper in 1851, set out to make it a newspaper giant. His first move was to sign a contract with Lydia Sigourney to write for his paper, his second to obtain the services of Fanny Fern—then the most touted name in journalism. He began by offering her twenty-five dollars a column to write a story for his paper. When she refused, he raised his offer until she finally accepted at a hundred dollars a column—which made Fanny Fern the highest paid newspaper writer of her time. This was such an outrageous amount that Bonner, who was fast becoming a master of advertising, notified his readers of the fact; when the first of ten installments of the famous "hundred dollar a column story"—"Fanny Ford"—appeared in June 1855, its success showed Bonner the way to make his *Ledger* the most popular newspaper in the country. He signed an exclusive contract with Fanny Fern, and her columns began appearing on January 5, 1856, her wedding day. By the end of 1856, the *Ledger*, which put out 2500 copies when Bonner acquired it, had a circulation of 180,000.

Fanny Fern realized the value of her name and in July 1856 went to court to stop publication of a book that had been fraudulently published under it. She won the case and the exclusive right to the pseudonym's use. On August 2, 1856, she wrote about the suit in the *Ledger*, urging women to assert their rights. Interestingly enough, the name Fanny Fern had gradually become her own in private as well as in public life. Her husband called her Fanny, her friends wrote to her as Fanny Fern Parton, and she signed her letters Fanny Fern.

In 1856 she also published a second novel, *Rose Clark*. After the criticism she had received for portraying herself in Ruth Hall, she was careful in her second novel to dissociate herself from her protagonist. Rose is a more traditional heroine, gentle and delicate. The secondary character, Gertrude Dean, is self-sustaining, however—"strong-minded" and "clear-headed," an "independent thinker" like her creator (219). Gertrude Dean's experiences also parallel Fanny Fern's: left a widow, she marries a widower with two children who proves to be jealous and who spreads ugly rumors about her. Her relatives refuse to defend her because they do not want to support her, and she is forced to support herself. There are some interesting satirical portraits in the novel: Mrs. Markham, the matron at the orphanage; Mrs. Howe, Rose's cousin; Mr. Finels, the parasitical poet. The novel does not have the strength of *Ruth Hall* however, partly because the plot, which relies on too many unlikely coincidences, lacks the realism of the former novel, and partly because the heroine is not as interesting. *Rose Clark* was well received and sold well, though not so well as *Fern Leaves* and *Ruth Hall*. Between 1857 and 1872, Fern also published six more collections of her newspaper articles. Unlike *Fern Leaves*, her later collections for adults contained few sentimental articles; the sentimental pieces were printed primarily in three collections for children.

Fanny Fern's column appeared in the *New York Ledger* regularly for sixteen years. Grace Greenwood, who wrote a short biography of her in

1868, noted with amazement that in all the time she had been writing for the *Ledger* she had never missed a week (Parton, *Eminent Women* 80). On October 10, 1872, Fanny Fern died of cancer. But until the very end she did not tell even her close friends of her impending death. When she lost the use of her right arm, she wrote with her left hand, and when that became impossible, she dictated her columns to her daughter or her husband. Her last column appeared two days after her death.

Ruth Hall

When conservative critics reacted violently to *Ruth Hall*, they did so with reason: it was a revolutionary book. They did not, however, criticize it on its own terms but focused instead on issues connected with the author's identity as a woman; in writing such a book, she had deviated from the role prescribed for women at the time. *Ruth Hall* was attacked on five counts: the author's lack of femininity in seeking revenge (a woman was expected to be gentle and submissive); her self-portrayal in heroic terms (a woman was supposed to be selfless and self-effacing); her failure to show filial piety because she criticized her father, brother, and in-laws (a woman must be respectful of and deferential toward her male relatives); her vulgarity (a woman should never be lacking in female delicacy); and her sacrilege in satirizing devout people (the crowning glory of any woman was her religious piety and respect for religion).

These criticisms were all directed at the author, not the book. Although the critics were right in seeing the danger of these unconventional qualities in a woman (without them, Fanny Fern could never have written *Ruth Hall*), by focusing on them, they missed the book's revolutionary message. The real threat posed by the novel was its insistence that a woman should be independent. And, for Fanny Fern, true independence could come only with financial freedom. The role of the American individualist, she was saying (contrary to popular thought at the time), should not be reserved for male Americans only; women too could be self-reliant and self-sufficient. Like the male heroes of countless "rags-to-riches" novels, Ruth Hall realizes the American Dream. She gains wealth and success by her own talents and industry.

The term "revolutionary" clearly does not apply here to a radical change in the economic structure of society, but rather to a rearrangement of the power alignments associated with the control of wealth. Fanny Fern did not question the basis of capitalism, although she was critical of its abuses and satirized the selfishness of an uncontrolled individualism. With her awareness of social injustice, moreover, she knew that self-reliance would not always work. She had seen too many people—particularly working women—struggling against impossible odds. She felt a kinship with suffering humanity and believed that society had a responsibility to help "life's unfortunates." But if women were to gain power in a money-oriented society, they must have a share in the wealth. Ultimately, then, *Ruth Hall* was revolutionary because it threatened to subvert the male-dominated power structure of society by suggesting that women get some money for themselves. To the criticism directed at a woman sculptor who had received a federal commission, Fern replied in the *New York Ledger* on April 10, 1869: "I would like to ask, amid the crowd of lobbying *men*, whose paws are in the national basket, after the loaves and fishes—should not this little woman's cunning white hand have slily drawn some out?" (reprinted here).

For Fanny Fern, then, financial independence, even more than the vote, was the key to women's rights:

> When you can, achieve financial independence. Freedom from subjection may be gotten by the fruits of your own labors, and by your own efforts you can learn to conquer yourselves. When you have done all this, you may rightfully demand—even the right to vote, as vote you certainly will some day. (Adams 23)

Thus Fern's "Modern Old Maid" (included here) does not live with her married sister and tend her nine children. Instead, she supports herself:

> She teaches, or she lectures, or she writes books, or poems, or she is a book-keeper, or she sets types, or she does anything but hang on to the skirts of somebody else's husband. . . . She lives in a nice house, earned by herself, . . . and has a bank-book and dividends.

Her widows are equally self-reliant. Even in her works for children, she insists on the necessity for female independence. In "Cicely Hunt," published in *Little Ferns for Fanny's Little Friends* in 1853, Cicely and her mother refuse to accept a friend's offer to help them further than to get them started; after that "they supported *themselves*" (206). As she wrote in 1861 in "A Bit of Injustice" (reprinted here), there is "no crust so tough as the grudged bread of dependence."

Nor in Fanny Fern's view should a woman be quick to exchange financial independence for marriage. In her 1869 article "Women's Salaries" (included in this volume), she insisted that no woman should give up "independent dollars" to become the "serf" of a selfish man. And in 1870 she advised women not to be in a hurry to marry; in other employments, she said, a woman has two advantages: first, she is earning wages, and second she can change masters "if the situation don't suit" (NYL 9/3/70). Finally, in a remarkably daring article in 1857, "A Word on the Other Side" (reprinted here), she urged women to leave their husbands if necessary, asserting that the "toil of self-support" could never be more degrading than a dehumanizing marriage.

The career of Ruth Hall—and incidentally of Fanny Fern herself—provided a rare role model for nineteenth-century women: the example of a woman who had achieved financial independence solely on her own. Fern realized that not every woman could have the opportunity or the ability to succeed, but, as she states in her preface, she saw her novel as a means of providing hope and inspiration for women all over America. *Ruth Hall* was far more than the momentary aberration of an individual woman; it was a call to arms to women everywhere, for whom the conventional formula for feminine success (submissive dependency) had not worked.

Ruth Hall is nearly unique in that, unlike other nineteenth-century American novels in which an impoverished woman is forced to support herself, it does not end with the heroine's marriage and the renunciation of her career. In many novels, a woman might find she is quite able to support herself, but this is seen as only a temporary measure. At the end of the novel, the woman finds a husband and gives up her career for what she and the author and society see as her true calling: submerging herself in love and marriage.

The principal attribute of nineteenth-century American woman's fiction is its portrayal of a heroine who, although she may not engage in the heroic activities of Catharine Sedgwick's spirited protagonist in *Hope Leslie*

(1827), is nevertheless a strong, independent central character. *Ruth Hall* follows this tradition, but also diverges from it in three important respects. First, Fanny Fern takes her heroine farther into independence than any other heroine of the period. Hester Prynne in *The Scarlet Letter* (1850) is, like Ruth Hall, totally self-sustaining to the end of the novel, but Fanny Fern does not have the ambivalence toward her character's self-assertion that Hawthorne has. In many novels written by women, the heroine is spirited and self-sustaining, sometimes self-supporting for a time, but even the most aggressively independent heroine of all these novels, the lively Capitola in E.D.E.N. Southworth's *Hidden Hand* (1859), marries at the end of the novel. Similarly, Fleda Ringgen in Susan Warner's *Queechy* (1852) and Edna Earl in Augusta Jane Evans's *St. Elmo* (1866) support themselves with admirable grit and determination, but at the conclusion of the novels they give up their economic independence. In these novels marriage is seen as a refuge from the world, and the heroine is rescued from the necessity of supporting herself. As St. Elmo says to Edna in the last chapter of Evans's novel:

> To-day I snap the fetters of your literary bondage. There shall be no more books written! No more study, no more toil, no more anxiety, no more heartaches! And that dear public you love so well, must even help itself, and whistle for a new pet. You belong solely to me now, and I shall take care of the life you nearly destroyed in your inordinate ambition.

All of these heroines are quite young when they begin to support themselves, and the implication is that they have not come to their true vocation until they marry.[6] Ruth Hall, however, has already tried love and marriage, and although for her it was good while it lasted, it did not last. Ruth realizes that she cannot depend on others; even a loving husband can die. Her goal becomes independence, and Fanny Fern portrays this as a necessary and desirable goal for women, just as Americans already believed it was a necessary and desirable goal for men.

Second, Fanny Fern's heroine diverges from the norm in mid-nineteenth-century woman's fiction in the scope of her power. As Nina Baym points out in *Woman's Fiction*, the heroine traditionally manages, in the course of the novels, to gain power and control over her environment

(35). Although she might "belong" to her husband, as St. Elmo said, he would look to her for moral and spiritual guidance, and she would rule the domestic sphere. These novels celebrate the home values of love and harmony over the pragmatic values of the marketplace; their heroines build domestic strongholds where those superior feminine values can prevail. Since the home was seen as a training center for the world, as Baym notes, to grant the heroine the home was to give her considerable power (48–49). Jane Tompkins describes the process thus in *Sensational Designs*: "the sentimental novelist elaborated a myth that gave women the central position of power and authority in their culture" (125).

Like the heroines of these novels, Ruth Hall gains power and control over her environment, but her influence extends into the world outside the home. The domestic values of love and harmony which seem to be extolled at the beginning of the novel gradually give way to a cynical realism as the heroine evolves from a trusting innocent into a hard-headed businesswoman. Instead of retreating from the marketplace into a domestic paradise, Ruth leaves a domestic paradise—which proves to be a fool's paradise—enters, and prevails in the competitive male world. Although Ruth retains her deep attachment to her children and keeps the feminine values of love and harmony, she discovers that by themselves these values are worthless; they must be joined to a realistic understanding of the world outside the home. She learns that if she is to survive, she cannot retreat from the unpleasantness of a moneyed society, but must adapt herself to it. Fanny Fern was impatient with her society's double standard of financial success and wrote on June 8, 1861:

> There are few people who speak approbatively of a woman who has a smart business talent or capability. No matter how isolated or destitute her condition, the majority would consider it more "feminine" would she unobtrusively gather up her thimble, and, retiring into some out-of-the-way place, gradually scoop out her coffin with it, than to develop that smart turn for business which would lift her at once out of her troubles; and which, in a man so situated, would be applauded as exceedingly praiseworthy. (reprinted here)

Finally, Fanny Fern's portrayal of her heroine departs from most woman's fiction in her encouragement of self-assertion as a positive virtue.

In these novels self-assertion is often depicted as a character flaw. Although the heroine is strong, she has to learn to curb her will and suppress her anger, rebellion, or defiance—all the qualities that spur Ruth Hall on to success. Whereas Ellen Montgomery in Susan Warner's novel *The Wide, Wide World* (1851) and Gerty in Maria Cummins's novel *The Lamplighter* (1854) are successful because they are able to conquer the self, Ruth's success is possible only through her assertion of the self. Once she enters the male world of competition, she needs that individualistic self-assertion American society encouraged in men. Religion too is used differently in Fern's novel. In *The Wide, Wide World* and *The Lamplighter*, religion helps the heroine to gain a victory over self. But Ruth Hall finds in religion the encouragement she needs to continue her struggle for independence in defiance of her male relatives (ch. 60).

Since economic independence for women is a central concept in *Ruth Hall*, it will be useful to trace Fanny Fern's development of the theme, both in her protagonist's career and in the novel's important subplots. At the beginning of the story, Ruth Hall is dependent upon her father, and when she marries she rejoices in her "new freedom." But her in-laws infringe upon this freedom until, moving away from them, she rejoices again in her "new-found freedom" in her own home. Still, she is dependent upon her husband, and she discovers to what extent when he dies and she is unable to support herself. She remains dependent—this time upon her father and father-in-law—until, stung by her father's grudging charity, she decides to try writing for the newspapers: "She would so gladly support herself, so cheerfully toil day and night, if need be, could she only win an independence" (ch. 56). Then, rebuffed by her brother when she asks for his help, she determines to succeed on her own: "I *can* do it, I *feel* it, I *will* do it." (ch. 56). The three successive "I" clauses emphasize her self-assertion. Her goal throughout the rest of the novel is to maintain that course, and the author describes Ruth metaphorically as a ship "steering with straining sides, and a heart of oak, for the nearing port of Independence" (ch. 64).

Ruth Hall tramps the streets and endures rudeness and hardship, but her eye is always on her goal. She has no time even for romance, and her success at the end of the novel is marked, not by the acquisition of a husband, but by the acquisition of ten thousand dollars in bank stock—a very American ending (paralleling that of *Tom Sawyer*, for example), but not one for a nineteenth-century novel with a female protagonist.

This struggle for independence is counterpointed by the very different stories of two other women in the novel: the comic history of Mrs. Skiddy and the tragedy of Mary Leon. Mrs. Skiddy, whose husband deserts her to go to California, successfully manages her own business for a year, and when he finally writes and asks her to send him the passage money to come home, she looks at her purse filled with "her own honest earnings," and hisses through her teeth, "like ten thousand serpents, the word 'N—e—v—e—r!'" (ch. 53). By itself, the story of Mrs. Skiddy—based on an earlier article (see "Family Jars" in this volume)—is an amusing anecdote. But within the context of the novel, it provides an important touchstone for Ruth and the reader.

Mrs. Skiddy, although a comic figure, is clearly better off than Mary Leon, Ruth's alter ego. We are told that Ruth did not have many female friends, but from the beginning she feels a kinship with Mary Leon, who like her despises such "air bubbles" as the "common female employments and recreations." Mrs. Leon is a passionate, intelligent woman. Her husband, however, does not regard her as a person, but simply as a possession. He buys her fine clothes and jewels, but, as she tells Ruth, "they, equally with myself, are necessary appendages to Mr. Leon's establishment" (ch. 25). When he tires of her, he has her committed to an insane asylum where she dies alone, like other women there, "forgotten by the world and him in whose service her bloom had withered, insane—only in that her love had outlived his patience" (ch. 54). The story of Mary Leon, who had warned Ruth that a woman should not marry only for economic security, is based on Fanny Fern's earlier article "Mary Lee" (TF 5/8/52). Mary Lee's husband was patterned after Fern's second husband in what was a marriage of convenience. But Ruth, with Mary Leon's tragic fate as an example, will not seek economic support in a second marriage; instead she determines to support herself.

If *Ruth Hall* was a revolutionary book in its major theme, stylistically it also departed radically from nineteenth-century popular fiction. It begins as a sentimental novel: a young girl, mistreated by her family, finds a strong, protective male figure. Guided by religion and the beauty of nature, she endures countless trials, including the death of a beloved child. In the first part of the novel, the prose often takes on the sentimental rhetoric of the period: such phrases as "death's dark wing," "most blessed of all hours," "velvet cheek nestled up to as velvet a bosom," "the bounteous Giver" remind us that the novel was written in the mid-nineteenth century. Yet after Ruth's husband dies and she is thrust out on her own, these phrases disappear, and Fanny Fern consistently uses the sharp staccato prose that characterized her satirical newspaper articles. The earlier prose reflects the young heroine's state of mind—innocent and trusting in her idyllic bower—whereas the later writing conforms to her disillusionment and realistic determination to succeed on her own.

Despite this clear stylistic shift, however, the book from the beginning shows its resistance to convention. First of all, marriage, which is the culmination of the action in many novels, here takes place at the opening. Like Hester Prynne, Ruth is already married when the major action takes place; the title of the novel is her married name. Also, a cynical undertone constantly undercuts the sentiment. In the first chapter, on the eve of her wedding, Ruth is thinking not of the happiness before her, but of possible disillusionment: "Would the step whose lightest footfall now made her heart leap, ever sound in her ear like a death-knell?" But, most important, the tone of the novel shifts constantly and suddenly; each description of Ruth's early happiness is immediately undercut by a satirical scene portraying the other characters' sour comments or unfeeling behavior. Early in the story Ruth's marriage is seen through the selfish eyes of her dilettante brother Hyacinth, and her happiness in her new home is prefaced by her jealous mother-in-law's interior monologue. Her joy at her first child's birth is balanced against her in-laws' cynical attitude and against the portrait of her unctuous profiteering baby nurse. Even the deaths in the novel are not presented in purely sentimental terms; Ruth's sorrow is only one factor amid the coarse, hypocritical, or mercenary comments or actions of the other characters. When Ruth lies prostrate after her husband's death, for example, her brother thinks: "Somebody ought to tell her, when she comes to, that her hair is parted unevenly and needs brushing badly" (ch. 29). Thus each time the author seems to indulge in a tender description of family life or death, the reader is immediately snapped back to a harsher reality by an opposing scene. It is almost as if the first part of the book were written from two points of view: the perspective of the young Ruth and that of the cynical realist, Fanny Fern (or the disillusioned Ruth Hall indirectly commenting on her own prior innocence). With Ruth's growing disillusionment, the realistic and satirical scenes gradually increase in number and length until they finally take over the book.

Fanny Fern's strength did not lie in the creation of fully-developed characters of great psychological depth and emotional intensity. Ruth Hall herself is the novel's only complex character. But Fern's genius for observation enabled her to capture her characters' personalities with very specific details of gesture and expression. She put this talent to good use in her satirical portrayals in *Ruth Hall*. Hyacinth Ellet, the Halls, the Millets (particularly "the wooden man"), Ruth's father, and the minor characters that appear on the scene—the mantua maker, the boardinghouse loungers, Mrs. Waters, the editors Tibbetts and Lescom—are skillfully drawn portraits that simultaneously create a character and make a social comment.

Significantly, Fanny Fern, unlike less sensitive writers who made minority groups and the uneducated classes the butt of their humor, always directed her satire at pretentiousness and pomp. Her sympathy is with decent people, whatever their race, religion, or social status. Robert Bonner described her as "one of the most democratic and catholic of women."[7] The sympathetic characters in *Ruth Hall*—other than Ruth herself, her children, Mary Leon, John Walter, and Horace Gates—are the black servants, Irish laborers, simple farm women, Johnny Galt, and the "unhonored" firemen. Although her relatives and former friends never visit Ruth in her poverty, the farm boy Johnny Galt brings her apples and a bouquet of flowers. And Ruth's inhuman treatment by her cousins, the Millets, is contrasted with the sympathetic attitude of their black maid and white cook, who provide a kind of choric comment on their employers' cruelty. These sympathies are apparent throughout Fern's writing, from the 1852 article "The Model Grandmamma" which states that one of her characteristics is that she does not teach her grandchildren racial prejudice (OB 8/7/52), to the 1872 article "Theological Nuts" (included here), which criticizes doctrinaire clergymen and urges tolerance and understanding of other religions. This latter article was so controversial that, although the editor allowed it to be printed, he appended an editorial comment emphasizing the importance of doctrine.

Fanny Fern's sympathy for common people carries over in the abundance of detail from everyday life. In this regard her writing is linked most clearly to other novels written by women at the mid-century. We read about where Ruth Hall lives and shops, where she keeps her milk, the cost of a train ticket to visit Katy at the Halls, her interviews with the editors, the letters she receives, the phrenological exam, the chores and specific delights of child raising. We are not simply told that she becomes wealthy and famous; we follow her chronicle step by step. By integrating the demands of everyday life and relationships with the details of Ruth's individual struggle, Fanny Fern combines the realism of woman's fiction with the self-determining theme of the American male writers of the period.

Finally, an important aspect of Fanny Fern's style is its terseness. The novel is written in a brisk, off-hand style, which includes the vernacular when necessary, and except in the early sections, seldom reaches for effect. Fern writes more dialogue than description and is particularly effective in her use of understatement. At the end of Chapter 3, for example, Ruth, in her new apartment after her marriage, looks around and sees her husband's things in "unrebuked proximity" to her own. The author says simply, "Ruth liked it."

At times, however, the novel, with its short chapters and lack of transition between them, seems to carry terseness too far. Fern won fame for her short newspaper sketches, and at first glance the novel seems to be simply a succession of independent sketches. Once one understands Fern's method, however, one can see that the short chapters and lack of transition clearly contribute to the effectiveness of the novel. First, the constant shifts in tone which are so important in the first part of the book are possible primarily because of the abrupt chapter breaks. Second, several seemingly unrelated chapters presented in rapid succession are used to provide different aspects of the same point. When Ruth becomes poor, for instance, the cumulative effect of chapters 35 to 51 provides an effective picture of the treatment she will receive in her newly vulnerable position. The Halls and her father haggle about who will pay for her support; the boardinghouse loungers plan an assault on the unprotected widow; Tom Develin takes advantage of her ignorance of the law; two women friends will not call because they do not wish to be seen in such a poor neighborhood; and the Millets, her cousins, refuse to help her. This accumulation of cruelty and selfishness is relieved only by a short section in the middle: Chapter 42 portrays the sympathy of the Millets' servants, and Chapter 43 brings the apples and bouquet of Johnny Galt.

The structure of the chapters also enables Fanny Fern to order the events without commenting overtly on the action. She juxtaposes chapters that comment on each other, either by contrast (as in the case of the satirical scenes following the sentimental scenes) or by reinforcement and clarification, as in the portrayal of the hotel fire toward the end of the novel. The fire is given minimal description and seems to function principally to praise the firemen. It gains significance, however, when we see that sandwiched between the references to the fire are four chapters depicting respectively the Millets, Mrs. Hall, Mr. Ellet, and Tom Develin and their various reactions to Ruth's success. By juxtaposing these chapters with the story of Johnny Galt, who unselfishly has just saved Ruth from the fire, and whose simple flowers and basket of apples "saved her life" in another way when she was shunned by everyone else, Fern indirectly comments on the selfishness of the other characters.

The fire also has an important relationship to the major theme of the novel, functioning as an ironic comment on the nineteenth-century reader's expectations that so unconventional a heroine would surely be punished, perhaps even killed, by the censorious author. This latter was the fate of Mark Twain's transgressing heroine, Laura Hawkins in *The Gilded Age* (1873), for example, and of Cooper's self-assertive heroines, Isabella, Cora, and Judith in *The Spy* (1821), *The Last of the Mohicans* (1826), and *The Deerslayer* (1846). Fanny Fern, however, refuses to censor Ruth, and in order to make her position wholly clear, allows her triumphant heroine to survive a major catastrophe unscathed.

The hotel fire is the closest we come to a hair-breadth escape in *Ruth Hall*. As Fanny Fern stated in her preface, *Ruth Hall* is "at variance with all set rules for novel-writing": there are no "startling developments," no transitions (she "enters unceremoniously and unannounced into people's houses"), and no long passages of "description." In some ways *Ruth Hall* seems disconnected and too spare in its development of plot and character. But with her talents as a writer of short, pointed newspaper articles—her true forte—Fanny Fern has ordered the short chapters into a well-structured contrapuntal pattern. Writing from her own experience and developing her theme with characteristic sharpness and vitality, she has created in *Ruth Hall* an original and effective novel of extraordinary power.

The Newspaper Articles

Fanny Fern was a professional journalist for twenty-one years. During that time she wrote on many subjects, all of which are represented in this collection. In content, her articles are related to the socially conscious articles written by Lydia Maria Child and Margaret Fuller in the 1840s. However, the language and style of Fern's articles are very different.

By far the most common subject in Fanny Fern's newspaper work is the subject of women and women's rights. She was not an active member of the women's rights movement: she never made a speech nor did she participate in a meeting until late in her career. Her feminism was practical, deriving from the exigencies of her life experience. Similarly, she was not part of any reform movement, yet she had a sympathy for the oppressed and a hatred of injustice that caused her to deal often with social issues. She also wrote on people, events, literature, and religion. Some articles are sentimental, some autobiographical. The main feature of all her essays is their depth of commitment.

Fanny Fern, of course, was not unique in the goals she advocated for women and in the other social concerns she expressed. What was unique was that she was so popular, even though many of her ideas were not. For years readers mobbed the offices of the *Ledger* on the day the paper came out, eager to be the first to see what Fanny Fern had to say. And throughout her career she was deluged with fan mail far beyond the expectations for any writer of the period. Nor was she forgotten by the literati. In 1855 at the opening of the Crystal Palace in New York to which the most distinguished literary people of the time were invited, Fanny Fern was included in the "gathering of immortals" presided over by the president of the Publishers' Association. In 1864, responding to criticism that a lady should not be so "egotistical" as to refer to herself as famous, she wrote:

"When a lady has had a mud-scow and a hand-cart, a steamboat and a hotel, a perfume and a score of babies, not to mention a tobacco and music named for her," she has a right to call herself famous (NYL 12/10/64).

This immense popularity can be attributed to Fanny Fern's original style and the vivid rendering of ideas. Almost as important as the ideas themselves, is her presentation of them in plain language. Her talent lay in her ability to give life to the flaws she saw in society. The popularity of her columns, of course, also derived from her pungent satire. She stripped people—particularly men—of their grandiose airs and pompous self-complacency, and she satirized folly and pretention in all facets of life. Antiromantic and often cynical, Fanny Fern was the originator of the now-famous phrase, "The way to a man's heart is through his stomach." Fern's humor is not in the tradition of the sprightly playfulness of Grace Greenwood. It is sharp and cutting. Her closest rival was Gail Hamilton, who began contributing to the newspapers some years after her, and whose barbs Fern praised in her 1868 biographical sketch of Hamilton. The seriousness behind Fern's wit is apparent in her reply to a reader who wanted to meet her because of her articles' humor: "You labor under the hallucination that I felt *merry* when I wrote all that nonsense! *Not a bit of it*; it's a way I have when I can't find a razor handy to cut my throat!" (OB 1/31/52)

Male and female critics of the day spoke of her lack of "delicacy," while her sentimental writings were seen as a saving grace. In 1856 she wrote a daring review unqualifiedly praising Walt Whitman's *Leaves of Grass*, which had been almost universally condemned for its "vulgarity" and explicit "sensuality"; the *New York Ledger* printed the review, but on the same page the editor reprinted her 1853 sentimental article, "Little Benny" (both are included in this volume). Most contemporary critics agreed with the *New York Tribune*, which wrote on May 26, 1854, that fortunately Fanny Fern's "taste for satire" was "tempered by warm womanly sympathies." Many of her sentimental articles reflect the depth of feeling that she considered to be an essential part of any human life. In the 1858 article "What Came of a Violet" (reprinted here) she indicates this attitude in describing the person who goes through life so unfeelingly that "she leaves reflections to her mirror, and is never reminded of her heart save by her corset-lacings."

Fanny Fern was sympathetic to the "treadmill lives" of many women of her day. She was also critical of women's pettiness, however, their affectations and their cruelties to one another. She urged women to broaden their experience when they could, through education and a career or simply by reading and writing. She advocated practical, comfortable dress for women and plenty of fresh air and exercise. Her ideal woman was independent, vital, and energetic, not bound by convention and not limited to marriage as a goal. Her view of marriage was realistic and critical. She undercut the idealized portrait of happy submissive wives and satirized pompous selfish husbands. Writing fearlessly on subjects then considered taboo, particularly for women, she deplored the sexual double standard, approved divorce if necessary, and urged family planning. Women must look out for themselves, she said, and refuse to allow themselves to be victimized by the misuse of masculine authority. "Look after No. 1," she advised women in the *New York Ledger* on September 4, 1869. Fern's own experience as a seamstress working long hours for a pittance gave her a lifelong sympathy with working women, and throughout her journalistic career she advocated equal pay and more opportunities for women. She first publicly urged the vote for women in the *Ledger* on May 29, 1858. Prior to that time she had advocated a more subtle approach (see, for example her 1852 article "A Little Bunker Hill" in this volume). But she always insisted on a mother's right to her children and a woman's right to any and all privileges and rights belonging to men. In 1868 she helped form the Sorosis Society (the first women's club) in reaction to the New York Press Club's refusal to invite women journalists to the farewell dinner for Charles Dickens.

In addition to women's rights, Fanny Fern wrote often on other social issues of the day: poverty, crime, prostitution, venereal disease, prison reform. She felt strongly about the suffering she saw and believed society had a responsibility to the poor. A particularly daring aspect of her social comment—one that appears in *Ruth Hall* as well—is her sympathy with and understanding of women who had turned to prostitution because of the lack of adequately paying jobs and the failure of platitudinous reformers to offer real help. "Where's the marvel?" she wrote in 1853 (TF 1/29/53). Another taboo subject that she brought into her columns was venereal disease. Forty years before Ibsen's *Ghosts* appeared, Fern was writing on the tragedy of congenital syphilis. She also deplored the incidence of "respectable" husbands infecting their wives and condemned the double standard that made this possible.

Another important subject in Fanny Fern's columns was the question of children's rights. Her ideas on education and child rearing were far in advance of her day. In *Ruth Hall* the satirical portrayal of the teachers' examination and the discussion of school committees reflect Fern's disgust with the pettiness that caused educational authorities to disregard the children's welfare. And the Halls' treatment of Katy and the oppressive school to which they send her constitute Fern's criticism of a too-common practice at the time. She advocated less repressive educational methods, smaller classes, physical exercise, and cheerful, comfortable classrooms. She also cautioned parents to appreciate the individuality of each child, urged fathers to take an active role in child rearing, and demanded an end to the practice of giving favored treatment to the boys in a family.

Many of Fanny Fern's columns are on literature and publishing. Ruth Hall's experiences with Tibbetts and Lescom, and Horace Gates's dissatisfaction with the *Irving Magazine* give some idea of her criticism of editorial practice—the tendency of reviewers to praise books for other than their literary merit or to review them without even reading them, for example. She was particularly critical of reviewers' unfair treatment of women writers and in 1857 satirized their condescending attitude in a review (included here) of her own book, *Fresh Leaves*. She admired originality and boldness in writing, as is apparent in her review of Whitman's *Leaves of Grass* and her satirical 1853 article, "Borrowed Light" (reprinted here).

Finally, throughout her lifetime her columns were sprinkled with essentially autobiographical articles. Criticized for being "egotistical" because it was not considered proper for a woman to write about herself, she nevertheless continued to provide her public with amusing and moving glimpses into her own life. Not only are these articles interesting for what they tell us about Fanny Fern, they present useful insights into the common problems of women of the day. Such articles as "Tom Pax's Conjugal Soliloquy" and "A Voice from Bedlam" (both included here) illustrate the problems facing a woman who attempted to combine a career with marriage and a family. But most of all, these autobiographical articles emphasize how much of the author was in her work. One cannot read them without feeling that one knows her, and the depth and strength of her personality.

Fanny Fern's independent stance on social issues and her unconventional writing style were courageous—particularly for a woman—and she was criticized for them. Yet some critics recognized that the strength of her writing derived from her not being bound by the conventions of femininity which restricted many American women. A British review of *Fern Leaves* in 1853 praised her work because she was "totally without that affectation of extreme propriety which is popularly attributed to the ladies of the New World" (*Living Age* 485). And Nathaniel Hawthorne, also writing from abroad, wrote to his publisher in February 1855 that after reading *Ruth Hall* he wanted to qualify his earlier criticism of the "mob of scribbling women":

> In my last, I recollect, I bestowed some vituperation on female authors. I have since been reading "Ruth Hall"; and I must say I enjoyed it a good deal. The woman writes as if the devil was in her; and that is the only condition under which a woman ever writes anything worth reading. Generally women write like emasculated men, and are only distinguished from male authors by greater feebleness and folly; but when they throw off the restraints of decency, and come before the public stark naked, as it were—then their books are sure to possess character and value. Can you tell me anything about this Fanny Fern? If you meet her, I wish you would let her know how much I admire her. (*Letters to Ticknor* 1:78)

Although critics have been eager to quote Hawthorne's comments on "scribbling women" (so much so that the phrase has become a part of our national literary vocabulary), they have been puzzled by his later comments on Fanny Fern.[8] The statement itself is quite clear. Hawthorne is saying that women writers were hampered by conventions imposed by society and that those restrictions prevented them from writing as powerfully as they otherwise could have. The strength of *Ruth Hall*, he believed, was possible exactly because Fanny Fern had thrown off the straitjacket of convention, which, he said, was the only way a woman could write anything worthwhile.

One wonders why critics have not been as interested in this latter point as in Hawthorne's earlier comments. His statements denigrating women writers were so eagerly taken up, I believe, because they did just that—denigrated women writers. They have been used to confirm the official attitude toward nineteenth-century women writers. Conversely, critics have been puzzled by or have not taken up Hawthorne's comments praising Fanny Fern because they did not understand, or did not wish to understand, why Hawthorne would praise a woman writer—particularly one whom they had decided was worthless. To consider seriously Hawthorne's comment would be to reexamine good writing in America, where a major criterion was that the writer must be a man. "Let him write like a man," Herman Melville advised the writer in 1851, "for then he will be sure to write like an American" (545–46). In an August 1853 review of *Fern Leaves*, the *United States Review* betrayed the same bias:

> Why do we regret Fanny's popularity?
>
> Because we naturally ask, when we see such a book *the* book of the day, where is American genius? Where are the original, the brilliant, the noble works, in whose publication we might take a lasting and national pride, from whose perusal we might derive delight, instruction, and elevation?
>
> Where are the men to write them? . . .
>
> American authors, be men and heroes! Make sacrifices, . . . but *publish books* . . . for the hope of the future and the honor of America. Do not leave its literature in the hands of a few industrious females.

The logical outcome of this thinking is that nothing valuable can be written by a woman—even a woman who is not hamstrung by convention—unless, perhaps, that woman forgets that she is a woman, and writes from the point of view of a man. As Nina Baym concludes in "Melodramas of Beset Manhood," literary criticism in America has not recognized women writers because it has assumed that the "matter of American experience is inherently male" (70). Fanny Fern was often told that her writing was masculine or manly because she took a strong independent stance and was not afraid to say what she thought. "Isn't it the funniest thing in life," she wrote in exasperation in the *New York Ledger* on November 19, 1870, "that a woman can't be vital and energetic, without being thought masculine?" But although her independence may have been called masculine, she always wrote from the *perspective* of a woman. If that perspective is perceived to have no value, then the same is true for Fern's writing, and a reason, perhaps, that her work has been consigned to oblivion in American literature. If, however, the woman's voice is considered valuable—as most modern critics would, I think, concede—one cannot ignore Fanny Fern, whose independent thinking and innovative style make her one of the most significant voices to come out of nineteenth-century America. Writing from the perspective of a woman and yet able to transcend the conventions society imposed on women, she writes from within her culture, giving an accurate and realistic portrayal of people and events. Yet she also brings to her assessment a critical eye, a sense of humor, and a fearlessness that provide us with unusual insights into the thought and customs of her time.

NOTES TO INTRODUCTION

1. In "Borrowed Light," written in 1853, Fern commented on these writers: "In choosing your signature, bear in mind that nothing goes down, now-a-days, but *alliteration*. For instance, Delia Daisy, Fanny Foxglove, Harriet Honeysuckle" (reprinted here). Although she is ridiculing writers who have copied her, she, in taking the alliterative pseudonym in 1851, was also following the lead of Grace Greenwood and Fanny Forrester, two of her brother's protégées. Her tone in this article suggests that the name was intended satirically, at least at first. Later in her career, after the name had become her own, she said that she thought the reason that she chose "Fern" was because she remembered picking ferns for her mother when she was a child (*New Story Book* 7). The idea for the first name may have come from her friend Fanny Osgood, who died the year before the name Fanny Fern was born (see the article on Osgood, MWT 6/4/53). For the period after Fanny Fern became the writer's professional name I have used it rather than her maiden name (Willis) or her third husband's name (Parton) because it was the name by which she was known and the name she preferred. In 1856 she went to court to win exclusive rights to her pseudonym; her friends called her Fanny Fern; her husband called her Fanny; and all of her works were published under that name.

2. The spelling of her first name appears variously as Sarah and Sara. The birth records in Portland, Maine, record it as Sarah, but in Fanny Fern's private papers it appears more often as Sara.

3. Fern did not begin using the "Fanny Fern" signature until September 6, 1851, with "The Little Sunbeam" in the *Olive Branch*. I have been able to identify with certainty seven articles that appeared before that date, however. The style and tone of the earlier articles are Fern's, and there are similarities between them and her later articles. "The Model Husband" (reprinted here) appeared in the *Olive Branch* on June 28, 1851, signed "Clara," and is the first article I can find that is clearly by Fanny Fern. The second identifiable article prior to the Fern signature is "Thoughts on Dress" (reprinted here), the first of five articles signed "Tabitha," a persona that Fern used occasionally in her later articles (e.g., "Tabitha Tompkins' Soliloquy" MWT 10/8/53 and "Tabitha Trot's Soliloquy" NYL 5/2/57). Fern's comments about men's dress are similar to those she makes elsewhere (e.g., OB 1/7/52 and TF 7/10/52). The other Tabitha articles are "The Model Wife" (OB 8/2/51); an untitled article written as a letter to the editor about an unlucky woman (OB 8/2/51); "Deacons' Daughters and Ministers' Sons" (reprinted here), a clearly autobiographical essay; and an untitled article about the unamiability of women (OB 8/16/51) which includes many comments she made in later articles. On August 30 she published with no signature "Little May" in the Youth's Department of the *Olive Branch*. This article is very similar to "Where Is Little Nelly?" in *Little Ferns for Fanny's Little Friends*, and is reminiscent of the description in *Ruth Hall* of little Daisy, who similarly allows a yellow caterpillar to climb upon her without revulsion because, she says, "God made it."

In later years, it was said that Fern's first article was "The Model Minister," and that it had been published in either the *Olive Branch* or the *Mother's Assistant* in July 1851 (see JP 52, EP 111, John S. Hart 410, Ross 40–41). "The Model Minister" appeared in the *Olive Branch* on April 24, 1852, however, after she had been writing with the signature of Fanny Fern for seven months. And the only article by Fern in the *Mother's Assistant* was "Maternal Influence," which appeared in December 1851. What was erroneously remembered as "The Model Minister" probably was "The Model Husband," and the date was June 28, rather than July, 1851. The editor wrote an introductory note to this article, which he seldom did, suggesting that he was introducing a new contributor. That another article by Fern did not appear for three weeks might be explained by her having had to call several times before she was paid; she may have wanted to be sure of remuneration before submitting a new article (see EP 112).

Many similarities exist between "The Model Husband" and later Fern articles—her characteristic style and several specific references that come up again later (see, for example, "Family Jars" (reprinted here). Moreover, "The Model Husband" is the first in a series of "model" articles that became a Fern trademark—"The Model Wife" (OB 8/2/51), "The Model Minister" (OB 4/24/52), "The Model Lady" (OB 4/24/52), "The Model Editor" (OB 5/22/52), "The Model Doctor" (OB 6/26/52), "The Model Step-Mother" (OB 8/7/52).

4. Different figures have been given for the amount Derby offered to Fern. In *Fifty Years among Authors, Books and Publishers*, he says he offered her a thousand dollars (208–09). James Parton in *Fanny Fern, A Memorial Volume*, states that the sum offered was six hundred (58).

5. Some examples are *Putnam's Monthly* 5 (February 1855): 216; *Protestant Episcopal Quarterly Review* 2 (April 1855): 301; *True Flag* (January 13, 1855): 3; *Southern Quarterly* 27 (April 1855): 449; *National Era* 9 (April 5, 1855): 55.

6. An interesting exception to this pattern is Hagar in *The Deserted Wife* by E.D.E.N. Southworth (1855) who is deserted by her husband and pursues a profitable career as a singer. At the end of the novel, however, she is reunited with her husband, and, although she no longer "worships" him, the author tells us, she does not continue with her career.

7. NYL 2/16/56. The only exceptions to this ecumenical spirit that I have found in Fern's work have to do with money. In *Ruth Hall* there are two references to the term "Jew" as a synonym for greed (chs. 46 and 69). I have found no similar references in all of her newspaper articles except for an 1853 article which uses the term "Scot" as a synonym for someone who is tightfisted. Although modern readers are aware of the prejudice inherent in such stereotypes, unfortunately they were common in Fern's day. Harriet Beecher Stowe, for example, uses the same stereotype in a letter to Fanny Fern in 1868, where she describes a publisher with whom she "had a long haggling battle the other night in which he cheapened literary wares in the style of a Jew peddler" (SSC).

8. Pattee (111, 115, 120), for example, struggles to explain what he calls Hawthorne's "infatuation" with Fanny Fern and concludes that Hawthorne did not know about Fern's anger at her family and thus could not judge the novel accurately—which is no explanation at all. And in fact, when Hawthorne did learn of Fern's family problems with her brother and father, he only reiterated his praise of the novel (EP 128).

SELECTED BIBLIOGRAPHY

ARCHIVAL WORKS

The following are referred to in the Introduction and Notes by the designated initials:

EP	Ethel Parton, "Fanny Fern, An Informal Biography." Unpublished manuscript in the Sophia Smith Collection at Smith College.
MWT	New York *Musical World and Times*, 1853–54. New York Public Library.
NYL	*New York Ledger*, 1855–72. The Watkinson Library, Trinity College, Hartford.
OB	Boston *Olive Branch*, 1851–55. American Antiquarian Society, Worcester, MA.
SEP	*Saturday Evening Post*, 1853–54. Philadelphia Public Library.
SSC	Documents in the Sophia Smith Collection at Smith College.
TF	Boston *True Flag*, 1851–55. American Antiquarian Society, Worcester, MA.

WORKS BY FANNY FERN

Caper-Sauce. New York: G. W. Carleton, 1872.
Fern Leaves from Fanny's Portfolio. Auburn: Derby and Miller, 1853.

Fern Leaves from Fanny's Portfolio. Second Series. Auburn and Buffalo: Miller, Orton, and Mulligan, 1854.
Folly As It Flies. New York: G. W. Carleton, 1868.
Fresh Leaves. New York: Mason Brothers, 1857.
Ginger-Snaps. New York: G. W. Carleton, 1870.
Little Ferns for Fanny's Little Friends. Auburn: Derby and Miller, 1853.
A New Story Book for Children. New York: Mason Brothers, 1864.
The Play-Day Book. New York: Mason Brothers, 1857.
Rose Clark. New York: Mason Brothers, 1856.
Ruth Hall. New York: Mason Brothers, 1855.

SECONDARY SOURCES

Adams, Florence Bannard. *Fanny Fern, or a Pair of Flaming Shoes*. West Trenton, NJ: Hermitage, 1966.
Anon. *The Life and Beauties of Fanny Fern*. New York: H. Long, and Brother, 1855.
Baym, Nina. "Melodramas of Beset Manhood: How Theories of American Fiction Exclude Women Authors." *The New Feminist Criticism*. Ed. Elaine Showalter. New York: Pantheon, 1985. 63–80.
———. *Woman's Fiction: A Guide to Novels by and about Women in America, 1820–1870*. Ithaca: Cornell UP, 1978.
Breslaw, Elaine Gellis. "Popular Pundit: Fanny Fern and the Emergence of the American Newspaper Columnist." Master's Thesis, Smith Coll., 1956.
Derby, James C. *Fifty Years among Authors, Books and Publishers*. New York: G. W. Carleton, 1884.
Eckert, Robert P., Jr. "Friendly, Fragrant Fanny Ferns." *The Colophon* 18 (September 1934).
Hart, James D. *The Popular Book*. New York: Oxford UP, 1950.
Hart, John S. *The Female Prose Writers of America*. Philadelphia: E. H. Butler, 1857.
Hawthorne, Nathaniel. *The Letters of Hawthorne to William Ticknor, 1851–1869*. 1910. Edited by C. E. Frazer Clark, Jr. 2 vols. Repr. Newark, NJ: Carteret Book Club, Inc., 1972.

Huf, Linda. *A Portrait of the Artist as a Young Woman: The Writer as Heroine in American Literature*. New York: Ungar, 1983.

Kelley, Mary. *Private Women, Public Stage: Literary Domesticity in Nineteenth-Century America*. New York: Oxford UP, 1984.

Living Age, The. 3 (November 19, 1853): 485. Reprint of a British review.

McGinnis, Patricia. "Fanny Fern, American Novelist." *Biblion* 2 (1969): 2–37.

Melville, Herman. "Hawthorne and His Mosses." Reprinted in *Moby-Dick*, Norton Critical Edition. Ed. Harrison Hayford and Hershel Parker. New York: Norton, 1967. 535–51.

Parton, Ethel. "Fanny Fern at the Hartford Female Seminary." *New England Magazine* 24 (March 1901): 94–98.

———. "A Little Girl and Two Authors." *The Horn Book Magazine* 17 (March–April 1941): 81–86.

———. "A New York Childhood: The Seventies in Stuyvesant Square." *New Yorker* (June 13, 1936): 32–39.

Parton, James, ed. *Eminent Women of the Age*. Hartford: S. M. Betts, 1868.

———. *Fanny Fern, A Memorial Volume*. New York: G. W. Carleton, 1873.

Pattee, Fred Lewis. *The Feminine Fifties*. D. Appleton-Century, 1940.

Ross, Ishbel. *Ladies of the Press*. New York: Harper, 1936.

Schlesinger, Elizabeth Bancroft. "Fanny Fern: Our Grandmother's Mentor." *New York Historical Society Quarterly* 38 (October 1954): 501–19.

———. "Proper Bostonians as Seen by Fanny Fern." *New England Quarterly* 27 (March 1954): 97–102.

Tait's Magazine. Review of *Ruth Hall*. Reprinted in *The Eclectic Magazine* 35 (June 1855): 196–200.

Tompkins, Jane. *Sensational Designs: The Cultural Work of American Fiction, 1790–1860*. New York: Oxford UP, 1985.

Wood, Ann Douglas. "Scribbling Women and Fanny Fern: Why Women Wrote." *American Quarterly* 23 (September 1971): 3–14.

Zlotnik, Mae Weintraub. "Fanny Fern: A Biography." Master's Thesis, Columbia, 1939.

A NOTE ON THE TEXT

The text of *Ruth Hall* is taken from the original 1855 edition published by Mason Brothers. For the newspaper articles, I have followed as closely as possible the original newspaper texts, retained spelling and punctuation, and have modified only the capitalization of initial words for the sake of consistency. I have arranged the newspaper articles chronologically by date of original publication.

RUTH HALL
and Other Writings

RUTH HALL

A Domestic Tale

of the Present Time

PREFACE

TO THE READER

I PRESENT YOU with my first continuous story. I do not dignify it by the name of "A novel." I am aware that it is entirely at variance with all set rules for novel-writing. There is no intricate plot; there are no startling developments, no hair-breadth escapes. I have compressed into one volume what I might have expanded into two or three. I have avoided long introductions and descriptions, and have entered unceremoniously and unannounced, into people's houses, without stopping to ring the bell. Whether you will fancy this primitive mode of calling, whether you will like the company to which it introduces you, or—whether you will like the book at all, I cannot tell. Still, I cherish the hope that, somewhere in the length and breadth of the land, it may fan into a flame, in some tried heart, the fading embers of hope, well-nigh extinguished by wintry fortune and summer friends.

Fanny Fern

CONTENTS

Ruth Hall

CHAPTER I

THE OLD CHURCH CLOCK rang solemnly out on the midnight air. Ruth started. For hours she had sat there, leaning her cheek upon her hand, and gazing through the open space between the rows of brick walls, upon the sparkling waters of the bay, glancing and quivering 'neath the moon-beams. The city's busy hum had long since died away; myriad restless eyes had closed in peaceful slumber; Ruth could not sleep. This was the last time she would sit at that little window. The morrow would find her in a home of her own. On the morrow Ruth would be a bride.

Ruth was not sighing because she was about to leave her father's roof, (for her childhood had been anything but happy,) but she was vainly trying to look into a future, which God has mercifully veiled from curious eyes. Had that craving heart of her's at length found its ark of refuge? Would clouds or sunshine, joy or sorrow, tears or smiles, predominate in her future? Who could tell? The silent stars returned her no answer. Would a harsh word ever fall from lips which now breathed only love? Would the step whose lightest footfall now made her heart leap, ever sound in her ear like a death-knell? As time, with its ceaseless changes, rolled on, would love flee affrighted from the bent form, and silver locks, and faltering footstep? Was there no talisman to keep him?

"Strange questions," were they, "for a young girl!" Ah, but Ruth could remember when she was no taller than a rosebush, how cravingly her little heart cried out for love! How a careless word, powerless to wound one less sensitive, would send her, weeping, to that little room for hours; and, young as she was, life's pains seemed already more to her than life's pleasures. Would it *always* be so? Would she find more thorns than roses in her *future* pathway?

Then, Ruth remembered how she used to wish she were beautiful,—not that she might be admired, but that she might be loved. But Ruth was "very plain,"—so her brother Hyacinth told her, and "awkward," too; she had heard that ever since she could remember; and the recollection of it dyed her cheek with blushes, whenever a stranger made his appearance in the home circle.

So, Ruth was fonder of being alone by herself; and then, they called her "odd," and "queer," and wondered if she would "ever make anything;" and Ruth used to wonder, too; and sometimes she asked herself why a sweet strain of music, or a fine passage in a poem, made her heart thrill, and her whole frame quiver with emotion?

The world smiled on her brother Hyacinth. He was handsome, and gifted. He could win fame, and what was better, love. Ruth wished he would love her a little. She often used to steal into his room and "right" his papers, when the stupid housemaid had displaced them; and often she would prepare him a tempting little lunch, and carry it to his room, on his return from his morning walk; but Hyacinth would only say, "Oh, it is you, Ruth, is it? I thought it was Bridget;" and go on reading his newspaper.

Ruth's mother was dead. Ruth did not remember a great deal about her—only that she always looked uneasy about the time her father was expected home; and when his step was heard in the hall, she would say in a whisper, to Hyacinth and herself, "Hush! hush! your father is coming;" and then Hyacinth would immediately stop whistling, or humming, and Ruth would run up into her little room, for fear she should, in some unexpected way, get into disgrace.

Ruth, also, remembered when her father came home and found company to tea, how he frowned and complained of headache, although he always ate as heartily as any of the company; and how after tea he would stretch himself out upon the sofa and say, "I think I'll take a nap;" and then, he would close his eyes, and if the company commenced talking, he would start up and say to Ruth, who was sitting very still in the corner, "*Ruth*, don't make such a noise;" and when Ruth's mother would whisper gently in his ear, "Wouldn't it be better, dear, if you laid down up stairs? It is quite comfortable and quiet there," her father would say, aloud, "Oh yes, oh yes, you want to get rid of me, do you?" And then her mother would say, turning to the company, "How very fond Mr. Ellet is of a joke!" But Ruth remembered that her mother often blushed when she said so, and that her laugh did not sound natural.

After her mother's death, Ruth was sent to boarding-school, where she shared a room with four strange girls, who laid awake all night, telling the most extraordinary stories, and ridiculing Ruth for being such an old maid that she could not see "where the laugh came in." Equally astonishing to the unsophisticated Ruth, was the demureness with which they would bend over their books when the pale, meek-eyed widow, employed as duenna, went the rounds after tea, to see if each inmate was preparing the next day's lessons, and the coolness with which they would jump up, on her departure, put on their bonnets and shawls, and slip out at the side-street door to meet expectant lovers; and when the pale widow went the rounds again at nine o'clock, she would find them demurely seated, just where she left them, apparently busily conning their lessons! Ruth wondered if *all* girls were as mischievous, and if fathers and mothers ever stopped to think what companions their daughters would have for room-mates and bed-fellows, when they sent them away from home. As to the Principal, Madame Moreau, she contented herself with sweeping her flounces, once a day, through the recitation rooms; so it was not a difficult matter, in so large an establishment, to pass muster with the sub-teachers at recitations.

Composition day was the general bugbear. Ruth's madcap room-mates were struck with the most unqualified amazement and admiration at the facility with which "the old maid" executed this frightful task. They soon learned to put her services in requisition; first, to help them out of this slough of despond; next, to save them the necessity of wading in at all, by writing their compositions for them.

In the all-absorbing love affairs which were constantly going on between the young ladies of Madame Moreau's school and their respective admirers, Ruth took no interest; and on the occasion of the unexpected reception of a bouquet, from a smitten swain, accompanied by a copy of amatory verses, Ruth crimsoned to her temples and burst into tears, that any one could be found so heartless as to burlesque the "awkward" Ruth. Simple child! She was unconscious that, in the freedom of that atmosphere where a "prophet out of his own country is honored," her lithe form had rounded into symmetry and grace, her slow step had become light and elastic, her eye bright, her smile winning, and her voice soft and melodious. Other bouquets, other notes, and glances of involuntary admiration from passers-by, at length opened her eyes to the fact, that she was "plain, awkward Ruth" no longer. Eureka! She had arrived at the first epoch in a young girl's life,—she had found out her power! Her manners became assured and self-possessed. *She*, Ruth, could inspire love! Life became dear to her. There was something worth living for—something to look forward to. She had a motive—an aim; she should *some* day make somebody's heart glad,—somebody's hearth-stone bright; somebody should be proud of her; and oh, how she *could* love that somebody! History, astronomy, mathematics, the languages, were all pastime now. Life wore a new aspect; the skies were bluer, the earth greener, the flowers more fragrant;—her twin-soul existed somewhere.

When Ruth had been a year at school, her elegant brother Hyacinth came to see her. Ruth dashed down her books, and bounded down three stairs at a time, to meet him; for she loved him, poor child, just as well as if he were worth loving. Hyacinth drew languidly back a dozen paces, and holding up his hands, drawled out imploringly, "kiss me if you insist on it, Ruth, but for heaven's sake, don't tumble my dickey." He also remarked, that her shoes were too large for her feet, and that her little French apron was "slightly askew;" and told her, whatever else she omitted, to be sure to learn "to waltz." He was then introduced to Madame Moreau, who remarked to Madame Chicchi, her Italian teacher, what a very *distingué* looking person he was; after which he yawned several times, then touched his hat gracefully, praised "the very superior air of the establishment," brushed an imperceptible atom of dust from his beaver, kissed the tips of his fingers to his demonstrative sister, and tip-toed Terpsichoreally over the academic threshold.

In addition to this, Ruth's father wrote occasionally when a term-bill became due, or when his tradesmen's bills came in, on the first of January; on which occasion an annual fit of poverty seized him, an almshouse loomed up in perspective, he reduced the wages of his cook two shillings, and advised Ruth either to get married or teach school.

Three years had passed under Madame Moreau's roof; Ruth's schoolmates wondering the while why she took so much pains to bother her head with those stupid books, when she was every day growing prettier, and all the world knew that it was quite unnecessary for a pretty woman to be clever. When Ruth once more crossed the paternal threshold, Hyacinth levelled his eye-glass at her, and exclaimed, "'Pon honor, Ruth, you've positively had a narrow escape from being handsome." Whether old Mr. Ellet was satisfied with her physical and mental progress, Ruth had no means of knowing.

AND NOW, as we have said before, it is the night before Ruth's bridal; and there she sits, though the old church bell has long since chimed the midnight hour, gazing at the moon, as she cuts a shining path through the waters; and trembling, while she questions the dim, uncertain future. Tears, Ruth? Have phantom shapes of terror glided before those gentle prophet eyes? Has death's dark wing even now fanned those girlish temples?

CHAPTER II

"*IT WAS SO ODD* in Ruth to have no one but the family at the wedding. It was just one of her queer freaks! Where was the use of her white satin dress and orange wreath? what the use of her looking handsomer than she ever did before, when there was nobody there to see her?"

"Nobody to see her?" Mark that manly form at her side; see his dark eye glisten, and his chiselled lip quiver, as he bends an earnest gaze on her who realizes all his boyhood dreams. Mistaken ones! it is not admiration which that young beating heart craves; it is love.

"A very fine-looking, presentable fellow," said Hyacinth, as the carriage rolled away with his new brother-in-law. "Really, love is a great beautifier. Ruth looked quite handsome to-night. Lord bless me! how immensely tiresome it must be to sit opposite the same face three times a day, three hundred and sixty-five days in a year! I should weary of Venus herself. I'm glad my handsome brother-in-law is in such good circumstances. Duns *are* a bore. I must keep on the right side of him. Tom, was that tailor here again yesterday? Did you tell him I was out of town? Right, Tom."

CHAPTER III

"*WELL,* I *hope* Harry will be happy," said Ruth's mother-in-law, old Mrs. Hall, as she untied her cap-strings, and seated herself in the newly-furnished parlor, to await the coming of the bride and bridegroom. "I can't say, though, that I see the need of his being married. I always mended his socks. He has sixteen bran new shirts, eight linen and eight cotton. I made them myself out of the Hamilton long-cloth. Hamilton long-cloth is good cotton, too; strong, firm, and wears well. Eight cotton and eight linen shirts! Can anybody tell what he got married for? *I* don't know. If he tired of his boarding-house, of course he could always come home. As to Ruth, I don't know anything about her. Of course she is perfect in *his* eyes. I remember the time when he used to think *me* perfect. I suppose I shall be laid on the shelf now. Well, what beauty he can find in that pale, golden hair, and those blue-gray eyes, I don't know. I can't say I fancy the family either. Proud as Lucifer, all of 'em. Nothing to be proud of, either. The father next to nothing when he began life. The son, a conceited jackanapes, who divides his time between writing rhymes and inventing new ties for his cravat. Well, well, we shall see; but I doubt if this bride is anything but a well-dressed doll. I've been peeping into her bureau drawers to-day. What is the use of all those ruffles on her under-clothes, I'd like to know? Who's going to wash and iron them? *Presents* to her! Well, why don't people make *sensible* presents,—a dozen of dish towels, some crash rollers, a ball of wick-yarn, or the like of that?"

"O-o-oh d-e-a-r! there's the carriage! Now, for one month to come, to say the least, I shall be made perfectly sick with their billing and cooing. I shouldn't be surprised if Harry didn't speak to me oftener than once a day. Had he married a practical woman I wouldn't have cared—somebody who looked as if God made her for something; but that little yellow-haired simpleton—umph!"

Poor Ruth, in happy ignorance of the state of her new mother-in-law's feelings, moved about her apartments in a sort of blissful dream. How odd it seemed, this new freedom, this being one's own mistress. How odd to see that shaving-brush and those razors lying on *her* toilet table! then that saucy looking smoking-cap, those slippers and that dressing-gown, those fancy neckties, too, and vests and coats, in unrebuked proximity to her muslins, laces, silks and de laines!

Ruth liked it.

CHAPTER IV

"GOOD MORNING, RUTH; *Mrs. Hall* I suppose *I should* call you, only that I can't get used to being shoved one side quite so suddenly," said the old lady, with a faint attempt at a laugh.

"Oh, pray don't say Mrs. Hall to *me*," said Ruth, handing her a chair; "call me any name that best pleases you; I shall be quite satisfied."

"I suppose you feel quite lonesome when Harry is away, attending to business, and as if you hardly knew what to do with yourself; don't you?"

"Oh, no," said Ruth, with a glad smile, "not at all. I was just thinking whether I was not glad to have him gone a little while, so that I could sit down and think how much I love him."

The old lady moved uneasily in her chair. "I suppose you understand all about housekeeping, Ruth?"

Ruth blushed. "No," said she, "I have but just returned from boarding school. I asked Harry to wait till I had learned house-keeping matters, but he was not willing."

The old lady untied her cap-strings, and patted the floor restlessly with her foot.

"It is a great pity you were not brought up properly," said she. "I learned all that a girl should learn, before I married. Harry has his fortune yet to make, you know. Young people, now-a-days, seem to think that money comes in showers, whenever it is wanted; that's a mistake; a penny at a time—that's the way we got ours; that's the way Harry and you will have to get yours. Harry has been brought up sensibly. He has been taught economy; he is, like me, naturally of a very generous turn; he will occasionally offer you pin-money. In those cases, it will be best for you to pass it over to me to keep; of course you can always have it again, by telling me how you wish to spend it. I would advise you, too, to lay by all your handsome clothes. As to the silk stockings you were married in, of course you will never be so extravagant as to wear them again. I never had a pair of silk stockings in my life; they have a very silly, frivolous look. Do you know how to iron, Ruth?"

"Yes," said Ruth; "I have sometimes clear-starched my own muslins and laces."

"Glad to hear it; did you ever seat a pair of pantaloons?"

"No," said Ruth, repressing a laugh, and yet half inclined to cry; "you forget that I am just home from boarding-school."

"Can you make bread? When I say *bread* I *mean* bread—old fashioned, yeast riz bread; none of your sal-soda, salæratus, sal-volatile poisonous mixtures, that must be eaten as quick as baked, lest it should dry up; *yeast* bread—do you know how to make it?"

"No," said Ruth, with a growing sense of her utter good-for-nothingness; "people in the city always buy baker's bread; my father did."

"Your father! land's sake, child, you mustn't quote your father now you're married; you haven't any father."

I never had, thought Ruth.

"To be sure; what does the Bible say? 'Forsaking father and mother, cleave to your wife,' (or husband, which amounts to the same thing, I take it;) and speaking of that, I hope you won't be always running home, or running anywhere in fact. Wives should be keepers at home. Ruth," continued the old lady after a short pause, "do you know I should like your looks better, if you didn't curl your hair?"

"I don't curl it," said Ruth, "it curls naturally."

"That's a pity," said the old lady, "you should avoid everything that looks frivolous; you must try and pomatum it down. And Ruth, if you should feel the need of exercise, don't gad in the streets. Remember there is nothing like a broom and a dust-pan to make the blood circulate."

"You keep a rag bag, I suppose," said the old lady; "many's the glass dish I've peddled away my scissors-clippings for. 'Waste not, want not.' I've got that framed somewhere. I'll hunt it up, and put it on your wall. It won't do you any harm to read it now and then."

"I hope," continued the old lady, "that you don't read novels and such trash. I have a very select little library, when you feel inclined to read, consisting of a treatise on 'The Complaints of Women,' an excellent sermon on Predestination, by our old minister, Dr. Diggs, and Seven Reasons why John Rogers, the martyr, must have had *ten* children instead of *nine* (as is *generally* supposed); any time that you stand in need of *rational* reading come to me;" and the old lady, smoothing a wrinkle in her black silk apron, took a dignified leave.

CHAPTER V

POOR RUTH! her sky so soon overcast! As the door closed on the prim, retreating figure of her mother-in-law, she burst into tears. But she was too sensible a girl to weep long. She wiped her eyes, and began to consider what was to be done. It would never do to complain to Harry—dear Harry. He would have to take sides; oh no, that would never do; she could never complain to him of his *own* mother. But why did he bring them together? knowing, as he must have known, how little likely they were to assimilate. This thought she smothered quickly, but not before it had given birth to a sigh, close upon the heels of which love framed this apology: It was so long since Harry had lived under the same roof with his mother he had probably forgotten her eccentricities; and then she was so dotingly fond of him, that probably no points of collision ever came up between the two.

In the course of an hour, what with cold bathing and philosophy, Ruth's eyes and equanimity were placed beyond the suspicion even of a newly-made husband, and when she held up her lips to him so temptingly, on his return, he little dreamed of the self-conquest she had so tearfully achieved for his sake.

CHAPTER VI

HARRY'S FATHER began life on a farm in Vermont. Between handling ploughs, hoes, and harrows, he had managed to pick up sufficient knowledge to establish himself as a country doctor; well contented to ride six miles on horseback of a stormy night, to extract a tooth for some distracted wretch, for twenty-five cents. Naturally loquacious, and equally fond of administering jalap and gossip, he soon became a great favorite with the "women folks," which every aspiring Esculapius, who reads this, knows to be half the battle. They soon began to trust him, not only in drawing teeth, but in cases involving the increase of the village census. Several successes in this line, which he took no pains to conceal, put him behind a gig of his own, and enabled his practice to overtake his fame as far as the next village.

Like many other persons, who revolve all their life in a peck measure, the doctor's views of the world in general, and its denizens in particular, were somewhat circumscribed. Added to this, he was as persevering as a fly in the dog-days, and as immovable as the old rusty weather-cock on the village meeting-house, which for twenty years had never been blown about by any whisking wind of doctrine. "When he opened his mouth, no dog must bark;" and any dissent from his opinion, however circumspectly worded, he considered a personal insult. As his wife entertained the same liberal views, occasional conjugal collisions, on this narrow track, were the consequence; the interest of which was intensified by each reminding the other of their Calvinistic church obligations to keep the peace. They had, however, one common ground of undisputed territory—their "*Son Harry*," who was as infallible as the Pope, and (until he got married) never did a foolish thing since he was born. On this last point, their "Son Harry" did not exactly agree with them, as he considered it decidedly the most delightful negotiation he had ever made, and one which he could not even think of without a sudden acceleration of pulse.

Time wore on, the young couple occupying their own suite of apartments, while the old people kept house. The doctor, who had saved enough to lay his saddle-bags with his medical books on the shelf, busied himself, after he had been to market in the morning, in speculating on what Ruth was about, or in peeping over the balustrade, to see who called when the bell rang; or, in counting the wood-pile, to see how many sticks the cook had taken to make the pot boil for dinner. The second girl (a supernumerary of the bridal week) had long since been dismissed; and the doctor and his wife spent their evenings with the cook, to save the expense of burning an extra lamp. Consequently, Betty soon began to consider herself one of the family, and surprised Ruth one day by modestly requesting the loan of her bridal veil "to wear to a little party;" not to speak of sundry naps to which she treated herself in Ruth's absence, in her damask rocking chair, which was redolent, for some time after, of a strong odor of dish-water.

Still, Ruth kept her wise little mouth shut; moving, amid these discordant elements, as if she were deaf, dumb, and blind.

Oh, love! that thy silken reins could so curb the spirit and bridle the tongue, that thy uplifted finger of warning could calm that bounding pulse, still that throbbing heart, and send those rebellious tears, unnoticed, back to their source.

Ah! could we lay bare the secret history of many a wife's heart, what martyrs would be found, over whose uncomplaining lips the grave sets its unbroken seal of silence.

But was Harry blind and deaf? Had the bridegroom of a few months grown careless and unobservant? Was he, to whom every hair of that sunny head was dear, blind to the inward struggles, marked only by fits of feverish gaiety? Did he never see the sudden *ruse* to hide the tell-tale blush, or starting tear? Did it escape his notice, that Ruth would start, like a guilty thing, if a sudden impulse of tenderness betrayed her into laying her hand upon his forehead, or leaning her head upon his shoulder, or throwing her arms about his neck, when the jealous mother was by? Did not his soul bend the silent knee of homage to that youthful self-control that could repress its own warm emotions, and stifle its own sorrows, lest *he* should know a heart-pang?

Yes; Ruth read it in the magnetic glance of the loving eye as it lingeringly rested on her, and in the low, thrilling tone of the whispered,

"God bless you, my wife;" and many an hour, when alone in his counting room, was Harry, forgetful of business, revolving plans for a separate home for himself and Ruth.

This was rendered every day more necessary, by the increased encroachments of the old people, who insisted that no visitors should remain in the house after the old-fashioned hour of nine; at which time the fire should be taken apart, the chairs set up, the lights extinguished, and a solemn silence brood until the next morning's cock-crowing. It was also suggested to the young couple, that the wear and tear of the front entry carpet might be saved by their entering the house by the back gate, instead of the front door.

Meals were very solemn occasions; the old people frowning, at such times, on all attempts at conversation, save when the doctor narrated the market prices he paid for each article of food upon the table. And so time wore on. The old couple, like two scathed trees, dry, harsh, and uninviting, presenting only rough surfaces to the clinging ivy, which fain would clothe with brightest verdure their leafless branches.

CHAPTER VII

HARK! to that tiny wail! Ruth knows that most blessed of all hours. Ruth is a *mother!* Joy to thee, Ruth! Another outlet for thy womanly heart; a mirror, in which thy smiles and tears shall be reflected back; a fair page, on which thou, God-commissioned, mayst write what thou wilt; a heart that will throb back to thine, love for love.

But Ruth thinks not of all this now, as she lies pale and motionless upon the pillow, while Harry's grateful tears bedew his first-born's face. She cannot even welcome the little stranger. Harry thought her dear to him before; but now, as she lies there, so like death's counterpart, a whole life of devotion would seem too little to prove his appreciation of all her sacrifices.

The advent of the little stranger was viewed through very different spectacles by different members of the family. The doctor regarded it as a little automaton, for pleasant Æsculapian experiments in his idle hours; the old lady viewed it as another barrier between herself and Harry, and another tie to cement his already too strong attachment for Ruth; and Betty groaned, when she thought of the puny interloper, in connection with washing and ironing days; and had already made up her mind that the first time its nurse used her new saucepan to make gruel, she would strike for higher wages.

Poor, little, unconscious "Daisy," with thy velvet cheek nestled up to as velvet a bosom, sleep on; thou art too near heaven to know a taint of earth.

CHAPTER VIII

RUTH'S NURSE, Mrs. Jiff, was fat, elephantine, and unctuous. Nursing agreed with her. She had "tasted" too many bowls of wine-whey on the stairs, tipped up too many bottles of porter in the closet, slid down too many slippery oysters before handing them to "her lady," not to do credit to her pantry devotions. Mrs. Jiff wore an uncommonly stiff gingham gown, which sounded, every time she moved, like the rustle of a footfall among the withered leaves of autumn. Her shoes were new, thick, and creaky, and she had a wheezy, dilapidated-bellowsy way of breathing, consequent upon the consumption of the above-mentioned port and oysters, which was intensely crucifying to a sick ear.

Mrs. Jiff always "forgot to bring" her own comb and hair brush. She had a way, too, of opening drawers and closets "by mistake," thereby throwing her helpless victim into a state of profuse perspiration. Then she would go to sleep between the andirons, with the new baby on the edge of her knee, in alarming proximity to the coals; would take a pinch of snuff over the bowl of gruel in the corner, and knock down the shovel, poker, and tongs, every time she went near the fire; whispering—sh—sh—sh—at the top of her lungs, as she glanced in the direction of the bed, as if its demented occupant were the guilty cause of the accident.

Mrs. Jiff had not nursed five-and-twenty years for nothing. She particularly affected taking care of young mothers, with their first babies;

knowing very well that her chairt shortened, with every after addition to maternal experience: she considered herself, therefore, quite lucky in being called upon to superintend little Daisy's advent.

It *did* occasionally cross Ruth's mind as she lay, almost fainting with exhaustion, on the pillow, while the ravenous little Daisy cried, "give, give," whether it took Mrs. Jiff two hours to make *one* cup of tea, and brown *one* slice of toast; Mrs. Jiff solacing herself, meanwhile, over an omelette in the kitchen, with Betty, and pouring into her ready ears whole histories of "gen'lemen as wasn't gen'lemen, whose ladies she nursed," and how "nobody but herself knew how late they *did* come home when their wives were sick, though, to be sure, she'd scorn to tell of it!" Sometimes, also, Ruth innocently wondered if it was necessary for the nurse to occupy the same bed with "her lady;" particularly when her circumference was as Behemoth-ish, and her nose as musical as Mrs. Jiff's; and whether there would be any impropriety in her asking her to take the babe and keep it quiet *part* of the night, that she might occasionally get a nap. Sometimes, too, she considered the feasibility of requesting Mrs. Jiff not to select the time when she (Ruth) was sipping her chocolate, to comb out her "false front," and polish up her artificial teeth; and sometimes she marvelled why, when Mrs. Jiff paid such endless visits to the kitchen, she was always as fixed as the North Star, whenever dear Harry came in to her chamber to have a conjugal chat with her.

CHAPTER IX

"*HOW DO YOU DO* this morning, Ruth?" said the old lady, lowering herself gradually into a softly-cushioned arm chair. "How your sickness *has* altered you! You look like a ghost? I shouldn't wonder if you lost all your hair; it is no uncomon thing in sickness; or your teeth either. How's the baby? She don't favor our side of the house at all. She is quite a plain child, in fact. Has she any symptoms, yet, of a sore mouth? I hope not, because she will communicate it to your breast, and then you'll have a time of it. I knew a poor, feeble thing once, who died of it. Of course, you intend, when Mrs. Jiff leaves, to take care of the baby yourself; a nursery girl would be very expensive."

"I believe Harry has already engaged one," said Ruth.

"I don't think he has," said the old lady, sitting up very straight, "because it was only this morning that the doctor and I figured up the expense it would be to you, and we unanimously came to the conclusion to tell Harry that you'd better take care of the child yourself. I always took care of my babies. You oughtn't to have mentioned a nursery girl, at all, to Harry."

"He proposed it himself," replied Ruth; "he said I was too feeble to have the care of the child."

"Pooh! pshaw! stuff! no such thing. You are well enough, or will be, before long. Now, there's a girl's board to begin with. Servant girls eat like boa-constrictors. Then, there's the soap and oil she'll waste;—oh, the thing isn't to be thought of; it is perfectly ruinous. If you hadn't made a fool of Harry, he never could have dreamed of it. You ought to have sense enough to check him, when he would go into such extravagances for you, but some people *haven't* any sense. Where would all the sugar, and starch, and soap, go to, I'd like to know, if we were to have a second girl in the house? How long would the wood-pile, or pitch-kindlings, or our new copper-boiler last? And who is to keep the back gate bolted, with such a chit flying in and out?"

"Will you please hand me that camphor bottle?" said Ruth, laying her hand upon her throbbing forehead.

"*HOW'S MY LITTLE* snow-drop to-day?" said Harry, entering Ruth's room as his mother swept out; "what ails your eyes, Ruth?" said her husband, removing the little hands which hid them.

"A sudden pain," said Ruth, laughing gaily; "it has gone now; the camphor was too strong."

Good Ruth! brave Ruth! Was Harry deceived? Something ails *his* eyes, now; but Ruth has too much tact to notice it.

Oh Love! thou skilful teacher! learned beyond all the wisdom of the schools.

CHAPTER X

"*YOU WILL BE HAPPY* here, dear Ruth," said Harry; "you will be your own mistress."

Ruth danced about, from room to room, with the careless glee of a happy child, quite forgetful that she was a wife and a mother; quite unable to repress the flow of spirits consequent upon her new-found freedom.

Ruth's new house was about five miles from the city. The approach to it was through a lovely winding lane, a little off the main road, skirted on either side by a thick grove of linden and elms, where the wild grapevine leaped, clinging from branch to branch, festooning its ample clusters in prodigal profusion of fruitage, and forming a dense shade, impervious to the most garish noon-day heat; while beneath, the wild brier-rose unfolded its perfumed leaves in the hedges, till the bees and humming-birds went reeling away, with their honeyed treasures.

You can scarce see the house, for the drooping elms, half a century old, whose long branches, at every wind-gust, swept across the velvet lawn. The house is very old, but Ruth says, "All the better for that." Little patches of moss tuft the sloping roof, and swallows and martens twitter round the old chimney. It has nice old-fashioned beams, running across the ceiling, which threaten to bump Harry's curly head. The doorways, too, are low, with honeysuckle, red and white, wreathed around the porches; and back of the house there is a high hill (which Ruth says must be terraced off for a garden), surmounted by a gray rock, crowned by a tumble-down old summer-house, where you have as fine a prospect of hill and valley, rock and river, as ever a sunset flooded with rainbow tints.

It was blessed to see the love-light in Ruth's gentle eyes; to see the rose chase the lily from her cheek; to see the old spring come back to her step; to follow her from room to room, while she draped the pretty white curtains, and beautified, unconsciously, everything her fingers touched.

She could give an order without having it countermanded; she could kiss little Daisy, without being called "silly;" she could pull out her comb, and let her curls flow about her face, without being considered "frivolous;" and, better than all, she could fly into her husband's arms, when he came home, and kiss him, without feeling that she had broken any penal statute. Yes; she was free as the golden orioles, whose hanging nests swayed to and fro amid the glossy green leaves beneath her window.

But not as thoughtless.

Ruth had a strong, earnest nature; she could not look upon this wealth of sea, sky, leaf, bud, and blossom; she could not listen to the little birds, nor inhale the perfumed breath of morning, without a filling eye and brimming heart, to the bounteous Giver. Should she revel in all this loveliness,—should her heart be filled to its fullest capacity for earthly happiness, and no grateful incense go up from its altar to Heaven?

And the babe? Its wondering eyes had already begun to seek its mother's; its little lip to quiver at a harsh or discordant sound. An unpracticed hand must sweep that harp of a thousand strings; trembling fingers must inscribe, indelibly, on that blank page, characters to be read by the light of eternity: the maternal eye must never sleep at its post, lest the enemy rifle the casket of its gems. And so, by her child's cradle, Ruth first learned to pray. The weight her slender shoulders could not bear, she rolled at the foot of the cross; and, with the baptism of holy tears, mother and child were consecrated.

CHAPTER XI

TIME FLEW ON; seasons came and went; and still peace brooded, like a dove, under the roof of Harry and Ruth. Each bright summer morning, Ruth and the little Daisy, (who already partook of her mother's love for nature,) rambled, hand in hand, through the woods and fields, with a wholesome disregard of those city bugbears, sun, dew, bogs, fences, briers, and cattle. Wherever a flower opened its blue eye in the rock cleft; wherever the little stream ran, babbling and sparkling, through the emerald meadow; where the golden moss piled up its velvet cushion in the cool woods; where the pretty clematis threw the graceful arms of youth 'round the gnarled trunk of decay; where the bearded grain swaying to and fro, tempted to its death the reaper; where the red and white clover dotted the meadow grass; or where, in the damp marsh, the whip-poor-will moaned, and the crimson lobelia nodded its regal crown; or where the valley smiled in its beauty 'neath the lofty hills, nestling 'mid its foliage the snow-white cottages; or where the cattle dozed under the broad, green branches, or bent to the glassy lake to drink; or where, on the breezy hill-tops, the voices of childhood came up, sweet and clear, as the far-off hymning of angels,—there, Ruth and her soul's child loved to linger.

It was beautiful, yet fearful, to mark the kindling eye of the child; to see the delicate flush come and go on her marble cheek, and to feel the silent pressure of her little hand, when this alone could tell the rapture she had no words to express.

Ah, Ruth! gaze not so dotingly on those earnest eyes. Know'st thou not,

> The rose that sweetest doth awake,
> Will soonest go to rest?

CHAPTER XII

"WELL," said the doctor, taking his spectacles from his nose, and folding them up carefully in their leathern case; "I hope you'll be easy, Mis. Hall, now that we've toted out here, bag and baggage, to please you, when I supposed I was settled for the rest of my life."

"*Fathers* can't be expected to have as much natural affection, or to be as self-sacrificing as *mothers*," said the old lady. "Of course, it was some trouble to move out here; but, for Harry's sake, I was willing to do it. What does Ruth know about house-keeping, I'd like to know? A pretty muss she'll make of it, if *I'm* not around to oversee things."

"It strikes me," retorted the doctor, "that you won't get any thanks for it—from *one* side of the house, at least. Ruth never *says* anything when you vex her, but there's a look in her eye which—well, Mis. Hall, it tells the whole story."

"I've seen it," said the old lady, while her very cap-strings fluttered with indignation, "and it has provoked me a thousand times more than if she had thrown a brick-bat at my head. That girl is no fool, doctor. She knows very well what she is about: but diamond cut diamond, *I* say. Doctor, doctor, there are the hens in the garden. I want that garden kept nice. I suppose Ruth thinks that nobody can have flowers but herself. Wait till my china-asters and sweet peas come up. I'm going over to-day to take a peep round her house; I wonder what it looks like? Stuck full of gimcracks, of all sorts, I'll warrant. Well, I shan't furnish my best parlor till I see what she has got. I've laid by a little money, and—"

"Better give it to the missionaries, Mis. Hall," growled the doctor; "I tell you Ruth don't care a pin what you have in your parlor."

"Don't you believe it," said the old lady.

"Well, anyhow," muttered the doctor, "you can't get the upper hand of *her* in that line; i.e., if she has a mind that you shall not. Harry is doing a very good business; and you know very well, it is no use to try to blind your eyes to it, that if she wanted Queen Victoria's sceptre, he'd manage to get it for her."

"That's more than I can say of *you*," exclaimed the old lady, fanning herself violently; "for all that I used to mend your old saddle-bags, and once, made, with my own hands, a pair of leather small-clothes to ride horse-back in. Forty years, doctor, I've spent in your service. I don't look much as I did when you married me. I was said then to have 'woman's seven beauties,' including the 'dimple in the chin,' which I see still remains;" and the old lady pointed to a slight indentation in her wrinkled face. "I might have had him that was Squire Smith, or Pete Packer, or Jim Jessup. There wasn't one of 'em who had not rather do the chores on *our* farm, than on any other in the village."

"Pooh, pooh," said the doctor, "don't be an old fool; that was because your father kept good cider."

Mrs. Hall's cap-strings were seen flying the next minute through the sitting-room door; and the doctor was heard to mutter, as she banged the door behind her, "*that* tells the whole story!"

CHAPTER XIII

"*A SUMMER HOUSE,* hey!" said the old lady, as with stealthy, cat-like steps, she crossed a small piece of woods, between her house and Ruth's; "a summer house! that's the way the money goes, is it? What have we here? a book;" (picking up a volume which lay half hidden in the moss at her feet;) "poetry, I declare! the most frivolous of all reading; all pencil marked;—and here's something in Ruth's own hand-writing—*that's* poetry, too: worse and worse."

"Well, we'll see how the *kitchen* of this poetess looks. I will go into the house the back way, and take them by surprise; that's the way to find people out. None of your company faces for me." And the old lady peered curiously through her spectacles, on either side, as she passed along towards the kitchen door, and exclaimed, as her eye fell on the shining row, "*six* milkpans!—wonder if they *buy* their milk, or keep a cow. If they buy it, it must cost them something; if they keep a cow, I've no question the milk is half wasted."

The old lady passed her skinny forefinger across one of the pans, examining her finger very minutely after the operation; and then applied the tip of her nose to the interior of it. There was no fault to be found with that milkpan, if it was Ruth's; so, scrutinizing two or three dish towels, which were hanging on a line to dry, she stepped cautiously up to the kitchen door. A tidy, respectable-looking black woman met her on the threshold; her woolly locks bound with a gay-striped bandanna, and her ebony face shining with irresistible good humor.

"Is Ruth in?" said the old lady.

"Who, Missis?" said Dinah.

"Ruth."

"Missis Hall lives *here*," answered Dinah, with a puzzled look.

"Exactly," said the old lady; "she is my son's wife."

"Oh! I beg your pardon, Missis," said Dinah, curtseying respectfully. "I never heard her name called Ruth afore: massa calls her 'bird,' and 'sunbeam.'"

The old lady frowned.

"Is she at home?" she repeated, with stately dignity.

"No," said Dinah, "Missis is gone rambling off in the woods with little Daisy. She's powerful fond of flowers, and things. She climbs fences like a squir'l! it makes this chil' laf' to see the ol' farmers stare at her."

"You must have a great deal to do, here;" said the old lady, frowning; "Ruth isn't much of a hand at house-work."

"Plenty to do, Missis, and willin' hands to do it. Dinah don't care how hard she works, if she don't work to the tune of a lash; and Missis Hall goes singing about the house so that it makes time fly."

"She don't ever *help* you any, does she?" said the persevering old lady.

"Lor' bless you! yes, Missis. She comes right in and makes a pie for Massa Harry, or cooks a steak jess' as easy as she pulls off a flower; and when Dinah's cooking anything new, she asks more questions how it's done than this chil' kin answer."

"You have a great deal of company, I suppose; that must make you extra trouble, I should think; people riding out from the city to supper, when you are all through and cleared away: don't it tire you?"

"No; Missis Hall takes it easy. She laf's merry, and says to the company, 'you get *tea* enough in the city, so I shan't give you any; we had tea long ago; but here's some fresh milk, and some raspberries and cake; and if you can't eat *that*, you ought to go hungry.'"

"She irons Harry's shirts, I suppose?" said the old lady.

"She? s'pose dis chil' let her? when she's so careful, too, of ol' Dinah's bones?"

"Well," said the old lady, foiled at all points, "I'll walk over the house a bit, I guess; I won't trouble you to wait on me, Dinah;" and the old lady started on her exploring tour.

CHAPTER XIV

"*THIS IS THE PARLOR,* hey?" soliloquized old Mrs. Hall, as she seated herself on the sofa. "A few dollars laid out here, I guess."

Not so fast, my dear madam. Examine closely. Those long, white curtains, looped up so prettily from the open windows, are plain, cheap muslin; but no artist could have disposed their folds more gracefully. The chairs and sofas, also, Ruth covered with her own nimble fingers: the room has the fragrance of a green-house, to be sure; but if you examine the flowers, which are scattered so profusely round, you will find they are *wild* flowers, which Ruth, basket in hand, climbs many a stone fence every morning to gather; and not a country boy in the village knows their hiding-places as well as she. See how skilfully they are arranged! with what an eye to the blending of colors! How dainty is that little tulip-shaped vase, with those half opened wild-rose buds! see that little gilt saucer, containing only a few tiny green leaves; yet, mark their exquisite shape and finish. And there are some wood anemonies; some white, with a faint blush of pink at the petals; and others blue as little Daisy's eyes; and see that velvet moss, with its gold-star blossoms!

"Must take a deal of time to gather and fix 'em," muttered the old lady.

Yes, my dear madam; but, better pay the shoemaker's than the doctor's bill; better seek health in hunting live flowers, than ruining it by manufacturing those German worsted abortions.

You should see your son Harry, as he ushers a visitor in through the low door-way, and stands back to mark the surprised delight with which he gazes upon Ruth's little fairy room. You should see how Harry's eyes glisten, as they pass from one flower vase to another, saying, "Who but Ruth would ever have spied out *that* tiny little blossom?"

And little Daisy has caught the flower mania, too; and every day she must have *her* vase in the collection; now withdrawing a rose and replacing it with a violet, and then stepping a pace or two back and looking at it with her little head on one side, as knowingly as an artist looks at the finishing touches to a favorite picture.

But, my dear old lady, we beg pardon; we are keeping you too long from the china closet, which you are so anxious to inspect; hoping to find a flaw, either in crockery or cake. Not a bit! You may draw those prying fingers across the shelves till you are tired, and not a particle of dust will adhere to them. Neither cups, saucers, tumblers, nor plates, stick to your hands; the sugar-bowl is covered; the cake, in that tin pail, is fresh and light; the preserves, in those glass jars, tied down with brandy papers, are clear as amber; and the silver might serve for a looking-glass, in which you could read your own vexation.

Never mind! A great many people keep the *first* floor spick and span; mayhap you'll find something wrong *up* stairs. Walk in; 'tis the "best chamber." A gilt arrow is fastened to the wall, and pretty white lace curtains are thrown (tent fashion) over it; there is a snow-white quilt and a pair of plump, tempting pillows; the furniture and carpet are of a light cream color; and there is a vase of honeysuckle on the little light-stand. Nothing could be more faultless, you see.

Now, step into the nursery; the floor is strewed with play-things; thank God, there's a child in the house! There is a broken doll; a torn picture-book; a little wreath of oak leaves; a dandelion chain; some willow tassels; a few acorns; a little red shoe, full of parti-colored pebbles; the wing of a little blue-bird; two little, speckled eggs, on a tuft of moss; and a little orphan chicken, nestling in a basket of cotton wool, in the corner. Then, there is a work-basket of Ruth's with a little dress of Daisy's, partly finished, and a dickey of Harry's, with the needle still sticking in it, which the little gypsey wife intends finishing when she comes back from her wood ramble.

The old lady begins to think she must give it up; when, luckily, her eye falls on a crouching "Venus," in the corner. Saints and angels! why, she has never been to the dress-makers! There's a text, now! What a pity there is no appreciative audience to see the glow of indignation with which those half averted eyes regard the undraped goddess!

"Oh, Harry! is this the end of all my teachings? Well, it is all *Ruth's* doings—*all* Ruth's doings. Harry is to be pitied, not blamed;" and the old lady takes up, at length, her *triumphant* march for home.

CHAPTER XV

"*HALLO!* what are you doing there?" exclaimed the doctor, looking over the fence at a laborer, at work in one of Harry's fields.

"Ploughing this bit o' ground, sir. Mr. Hall told me to be sure and get it finished before he came home from the city this afternoon."

"Nonsense!" replied the doctor, "I was born sometime before my son Harry; put up your plough, and lay that bit of stone wall yonder; that needs to be done first."

"I'm thinking Masther Hall won't be afther liking it if I do, sir," said Pat; "I had my orders for the day's work before masther went to the city, sir, this morning."

"Pooh, pooh," said the old man, unchaining the horse from the plough, and turning him loose in the pasture; "young folks *think* old folks are fools; old folks *know* young folks to be so."

Pat eyed the doctor, scratched his head, and began slowly to lay the stone wall.

"What's *that* fellow doing over yonder?" said the doctor to Pat.

"Planting corn, yer honor."

"Corn? ha! ha! city farming! Good. Corn? That's just the spot for potatoes. H-a-l-l-o there! Don't plant any more corn in that spot, John; it never'll come to anything—never."

"But, Mr. Hall?" said John, hesitatingly, leaning on his hoe-handle.

"Harry? Oh, never mind him. He has seen more ledgers than corn. Corn? Ha! that's good. You can go cart that load of gravel up the hill. What a fortunate thing for Harry, that I am here to oversee things. This amateur farming is pretty play enough; but the way it sinks the money is more curious than profitable. I wonder, now, if that tree is grafted right. I'll take off the ligatures and see. That hedge won't grow, I'm certain; the down-east cedars thrive the best for hedges. I may as well pull these up, and tell Harry to get some of the other kind;" and the doctor pulled them up by the roots, and threw them over the fence.

CHAPTER XVI

"*TIME* for papa to come," said little Daisy, seating herself on the low door-step; "the sun has crept way round to the big apple-tree;" and Daisy shook back her hair, and settling her little elbows on her knees, sat with her chin in her palms, dreamily watching the shifting clouds. A butterfly alights on a blade of grass near her: Daisy springs up, her long hair floating like a veil about her shoulders, and her tiny feet scarce bending the clover blossoms, and tiptoes carefully along in pursuit.

He's gone, Daisy, but never mind; like many other coveted treasures, he would lose his brilliancy if caught. Daisy has found something else; she closes her hand over it, and returns to her old watch-post on the door-step. She seats herself again, and loosing her tiny hold, out creeps a great, bushy, yellow caterpillar. Daisy places him carefully on the back of her little, blue-veined hand, and he commences his travels up the polished arm, to the little round shoulder. When he reaches the lace sleeve, Daisy's laugh rings out like a robin's carol; then she puts him back, to retravel the same smooth road again.

"Oh, Daisy! Daisy!" said Ruth, stepping up behind her, "what an *ugly* playfellow; put him down, do darling; I cannot bear to see him on your arm."

"Why—*God* made him," said little Daisy, with sweet, upturned eyes of wonder.

"True, darling," said Ruth, in a hushed whisper, kissing the child's brow, with a strange feeling of awe. "Keep him, Daisy, dear, if you like."

CHAPTER XVII

"PLEASE, SIR, I'll be afther leaving the night," said John, scraping out his hind foot, as Harry drew rein on Romeo, and halted under a large apple-tree.

"Leave?" exclaimed Harry, patting Romeo's neck; "you seemed a contented fellow enough when I left for the city this morning. Don't your wages suit? What's in the wind now? out with it, man."

John scratched his head, kicked away a pebble with the toe of his brogan, looked up, and looked down, and finally said, (lowering his voice to a confidential whisper, as he glanced in the direction of the doctor's cottage;) "It's the ould gintleman, sir, savin' yer presence. It is not *two* masthers Pat would be afther having;" and Pat narrated the affair of the plough.

Harry bit his lip, and struck Romeo a little quick cut with his riding-whip. Harry was one of the most dutiful of sons, and never treated his father with disrespect; he had chosen a separate home, that he might be master of it; and this old annoyance in a new shape was very provoking. "Pat," said he at length, "there is only one master here; when *I* give you an order, you are to stick to it, till you get a different one from me. D'ye understand?"

"By the Holy Mother, I'll do it," said Pat delightedly, resuming his hoe with fresh vigor.

CHAPTER XVIII

"*THAT'S* the fourth gig that has been tied to Harry's fence, since dinner," said the old lady. "I hope Harry's business will continue to prosper. Company, company, company. And there's Ruth, as I live, romping round that meadow, without a bit of a bonnet. Now she's climbing a cherry-tree. A *married woman* climbing a cherry-tree! Doctor, do you hear that?"

"Shoot 'em down," said the doctor, abstractedly, without lifting his eyes from the Almanac.

"Shoot *who* down?" said the old lady, shaking him by the shoulder. "I said that romp of a Ruth was up in a cherry-tree."

"Oh, I thought you were talking of those thievish robins stealing the cherries," said the doctor; "as to Ruth I've given her up long ago; *she* never will settle down to anything. Yesterday, as I was taking a walk over Harry's farm to see if things were not all going to the dogs, I saw her down in the meadow yonder, with her shoes and stockings off, wading through a little brook to get at some flowers, which grew on the other side. Half an hour after she came loitering up the road, with her bonnet hanging on the back of her neck, and her apron crammed full of grasses, and herbs, and branches, and all sorts of green trash. Just then the minister came along.

I was glad of it. Good enough for her, thinks I to myself; she'll blush for once. Well, what do you think she did, Mis. Hall?"

"*What?*" said the old lady, in a sepulchral whisper, dropping her knitting-needles and drawing her rocking-chair within kissing distance of the doctor.

"Why, she burst out a-laughing, perched herself on top of a stone wall, took a great big leaf to fan herself, and then invited the minister to sit down 'long side of her, *jest* as easy as if her hair wasn't all flying round her face like a wild Arab's."

"I give up now," said the old lady, dropping her hands in an attitude of the extremest dejection; "there's no hope of her after that; and what is worse, it is no use talking to Harry; she's got him so bewitched that he imagines everything she does is right. How she did it, passes me. I'm sure she has no beauty. I've no patience to see Harry twisting those yellow curls of hers round his fingers, and calling them 'threads of gold;' threads of fiddlesticks! She'd look a deal more proper like, if she'd wear her hair smooth behind her ears, as I do."

"But your hair is false," said the literal doctor.

"Doctor," said the old lady, snapping her eyes, "I never can argue with you but you are sure to get off the track, sooner or later; there is no need of your telling all, you know. Suppose I was always alluding to your wig, how would you like it?"

CHAPTER XIX

WINTER had set in. The snow in soft, white piles, barred up the cottage door, and hung shelving over the barn-roof and fences; while every tiny twig and branch bent heavily, with its soft fleecy burthen. "Papa," was to go to the city that morning in a sleigh. Daisy had already heard the bells tinkling at the barn-door, as Pat necklaced Romeo, who stood pawing and snorting, as if it were fine fun to plough five miles of unbroken road into the city. Daisy had turned Papa's over-coat sleeves inside out, and warmed them thoroughly at the fire; she had tied on his moccasins, and had thrown his fur collar round his neck; and now she stood holding his warm cap and furred gloves, while he and mamma were saying their usual good-bye.

"Take care of that cough, Daisy," said Harry; "don't come to the door, darling, to breathe in this keen air. Kiss your hand to papa, from the window;" and Harry scratched the frost away with his finger nails from the window-pane, that Daisy might see him start.

"Oh, how pretty!" exclaimed the child, as Pat tossed the bright, scarlet-lined buffalo robe into the sleigh, and tucked the corners snugly over his master's feet, and Romeo, inspirited by the merry tinkle of the bells and the keen frosty air, stood on his hind legs and playfully held up his fore feet; "Oh, how pretty!" Harry turned his head as he gathered the reins in his hand; his cap was crowded down so snugly over his forehead, and his fur collar turned up so closely about his chin, that only a glimpse of his dark eye and fine Roman nose was visible. One wave of the hand, and the light, feathery snow flew, on either side, from under Romeo's flying heels—and Papa was out of sight.

CHAPTER XX

"*WHY IN THE WORLD,* Ruth, are you wandering about there, like a ghost, in the moonlight?" said Harry, rubbing open his sleepy eyes.

"Hist, Harry! listen to Daisy's breathing; it sounds as if it came through a brazen tube. She must be ill."

"Little wife, don't torment yourself. She has only a bad cold, which, of course, appears worse at night. Her breathing is irregular, because her head is too low. Give her this pillow: there; now she's comfortable. What a frightened little puss you are! Your hand trembles as if you had the palsy; now go to sleep; it must be near two o'clock; you'll be sick yourself to-morrow:" and Harry, wearied out with an annoying day of business, was soon fast asleep.

Only the eye of God watches like a mother's. Ruth could not sleep. She was soon again at Daisy's side, with her fingers upon her wrist, and her eye fixed upon the child's face; marking every contortion of feature, noting every change of posture.

"What is it, darling?" asked her mother, as Daisy grasped her throat with both hands.

"It hurts," said the child.

Ruth glanced at Harry. He was so weary, it were a pity to wake him needlessly. Perhaps her fears were groundless, and she was over-anxious; and then, perhaps, Daisy really needed *immediate* medical aid.

Ruth's fears preponderated.

"Dear Harry," said she, laying her hand softly on his forehead, "do call up Pat, and send for the doctor."

"Certainly, if you think best," said Harry, springing up; "but it is a cold night for the old man to come out; and really, Ruth, Daisy has only a stuffed cold."

"*Please* let Pat go," said Ruth, pleadingly; "I shall feel happier, Harry."

It was a venturous undertaking to rouse Pat suddenly, as his bump of destructiveness generally woke first; and a fight seemed always with him a necessary preliminary to a better understanding of things.

"Hold! hold!" said Harry, seizing his brawny, belligerent fists; "not quite so fast man; open your eyes, and see who I am."

"Did I sthrike yer honor?" said Pat; "I hope yer'll forgive me; but you see, I was jist born with my fists doubled up."

All right," said his master, laughing; "but get on your clothes as soon as possible; harness Romeo, and bring the old gentleman up here. Mrs. Hall feels very uneasy about Daisy, and wants him to prescribe for her."

"I'll bring him back in a flash," said Pat; "but what'll I do if he won't come?"

"*WHO'S THERE?* what do you want? Speak quick, if you've anything to say, for I'm catching the rheumatiz' in my head;" said the doctor, as he poked his bald poll out the cottage window, into the frosty night air. Who are you? and what on earth do you want?"

"It's me," said Pat.

"Who's me?" said the Doctor.

"Botheration," growled Pat; "don't the ould owl know the voice of me?—It's Pat Donahue; the childer is sick, and Misthress Ruth wants you to come wid me, and give her something to betther her."

"Pooh! pooh! is that all you woke me up for? The child was well enough this noon, except a slight cold. Ruth is full of notions. Go home and take that bottle, and tell her to give Daisy half a teaspoonful once in two hours; and I'll come over in the morning. She's always a-fussing with that child, and thinking, if she sneezes, that she is going to die. It's a wonder if I don't die myself, routed out of a warm bed, without my wig, this time of night. There—there—go along, and mind you shut the gate after you. Ten to one he'll leave it open," soliloquized the doctor, slamming down the window with a jerk. "I hate an Irishman as I do a rattlesnake. An Irishman is an incomplete biped—a human tower of Babel; he was finished up to a certain point, and there he was left."

"Mis. Hall! Mis. Hall! if you've no objection, I should like you to stop snoring. I should like to sleep, if the village of Glenville will let me. Dear, dear, what a thing it is to be a doctor!"

CHAPTER XXI

"IF de las' day *has* come, dis chil' ought to know it," said Dinah, springing to her feet and peering out, as she scratched away the frost from the window; "has de debbel broke loose? or only de horse? Any way, 'tis about de same ting;" and she glanced in the direction of the barn. "Massy sakes! dere's Pat stealing off in de night wid Romeo; no he ain't neider—he's putting him up in de barn. Where you s'pose he's been dis time o' night? *Courting* p'r'aps! Well, dis chil' dunno. And dere's a bright light shining on de snow, from Massa Harry's window. Dinah can't sleep till she knows what's to pay, dat's a fac';" and tying a handkerchief over her woolly head, and throwing on a shawl, she tramped down stairs. "Massy sakes!" said she, stopping on the landing, as Daisy's shrill cough fell on her ear; "Massy! jes' hear dat!" and opening the chamber-door, Dinah stood staring at the child, with distended eye-balls, then looking from Harry to Ruth, as if she thought them both under the influence of night-mare. "For de *Lord's* sake, Massa Harry, send for de doctor," said Dinah, clasping her hands.

"We have," said Harry, trying to coax Daisy to swallow another spoonful of the medicine, "and he said he'd be here in the morning."

"*She won't*," said Dinah, in a low, hoarse whisper to Harry, as she pointed to Daisy. "Don't you *know*, Massa, it's de croup! de croup; de *wu'st* way, Massa! *Oh* Lor'!"

Harry was harnessing Romeo in an instant, and on his way to the doctor's cottage. In vain he knocked, and rang, and thumped. The old man, comfortably tucked up between the blankets, was far away in the land of dreams.

"What is to be done?" said Harry; "I must tie Romeo to the post and climb in at the kitchen-window."

"Father! father!" said he, shaking the old gentleman by the shoulders, "Daisy is worse, and I want you to go right home with me."

"Don't believe it," said the old man; "you are only frightened; it's an awful cold night to go out."

"I know it," said Harry; "but I brought two buffaloes; hurry, father. Daisy is *very* sick."

The old doctor groaned; took his wig from the bed post, and put it on his head; tied a woollen muffler, with distressing deliberation, over his unbelieving ears, and, returning four times to tell "Mis. Hall to be sure and bolt the front door after him," climbed into the sleigh. "I shall be glad if I don't get a sick spell myself," said the doctor, "coming out this freezing night. Ruth has frightened you to death, I s'pose. Ten to one when I get up there, nothing will ail the child. Come, come, don't drive so fast; my bones are old, and I don't believe in these gay horses of yours, who never make any use of their fore-legs, except to hold them up in the air. Whoa, I say—Romeo, whoa!"

"*GET OUT DE WAY,* Pat!" said Dinah; "your Paddy fingers are all thumbs. Here, put some more water in dat kettle dere; now stir dat mustard paste; now run quick wid dat goose-grease up to Missus, and tell her to rub de chil's troat wid it; 't ain't no use, though. Oh, Lor'! dis nigger knew she wouldn't live, ever since she said dat 'bout de caterpillar. De Lord wants de chil', dat's a fac'; she nebber played enough to suit Dinah."

CHAPTER XXII

STAMPING THE SNOW from his feet, the doctor slowly untied his woollen muffler, took off his hat, settled his wig, hung his overcoat on a nail in the entry, drew from his pocket a huge red handkerchief, and announcing his arrival by a blast, loud enough to arouse the seven sleepers, followed Harry up stairs to the sick chamber.

The strong fire-light fell upon Ruth's white figure, as she sat, pale and motionless, in the corner, with Daisy on her lap, whose laborious breathing could be distinctly heard in the next room. A dark circle had settled round the child's mouth and eyes, and its little hands hung helplessly at its side. Dinah was kneeling at the hearth, stirring a fresh mustard paste, with an air which seemed to say, "it is no use, but I must keep on doing something."

The doctor advanced, drew his spectacles from their leathern case, perched them astride the end of his nose, and gazed steadily at Daisy without speaking.

"*Help her*," said Ruth, imploringly.

"Nothing to be done," said the doctor, in an unmoved tone, staring at Daisy.

"Why didn't you come afore, den?" said Dinah, springing to her feet and confronting the doctor. "Don't you see you've murdered *two* of 'em?" and she pointed to Ruth, whose head had dropped upon her breast.

"I tell you, Harry, it's no use to call another doctor," said his father, shaking off his grasp; "the child is struck with death; let her drop off quietly; what's the sense of tormenting her?"

Harry shuddered, and drew his father again to Daisy's side.

"Help her," said Ruth; "don't talk; try *something*."

"Well, I can put on these leeches, if you insist," said the old man, uncorking a bottle; "but I tell you, it is only tormenting the dying."

Dinah cut open the child's night dress, and bared the fair, round chest, to which the leeches clung eagerly; Daisy, meanwhile, remaining motionless, and seemingly quite insensible to the disagreeable pricking sensation they caused.

"*THE OTHER DOCTOR* is below," whispered Pat, thrusting his head in at the door.

"Bring him up," said the old gentleman.

An expression of pain passed over the young man's features as his eye fell upon the child. As yet, he had not become so professionally hardened, as to be able to look unmoved upon the group before him, whose imploring eyes asked vainly of him the help no mortal hand could give.

A few questions he asked to avoid being questioned himself; a few remedies he tried, to appease the mother's heart, whose mournful eyes were on him like a spell.

"Water," said Daisy, faintly, as she languidly opened her eyes.

"God be thanked," said Ruth, overcome by the sound of that blessed little voice, which she never expected to hear again, "God be thanked."

The young doctor returned no answering smile, as Ruth and Harry grasped his hand; but he walked to the little window and looked out upon the gray dawn, with a heavy sigh, as the first faint streak of light ushered in the new-born day.

Still the fire-light flashed and flickered—now upon the old doctor, who had fallen asleep in his arm chair; now upon Ruth's bowed head; now upon Daisy, who lay motionless in her mother's lap, (the deadly paleness of her countenance rendered still more fearful by the dark blood-stains on her night dress;) then upon Harry, who, kneeling at Daisy's side, and stifling his own strong heart, gazed alternately at mother and child; then upon Dinah, who, with folded arms, stood like some grim sentinel, in the shadow of the farther corner; the little mantle clock, meanwhile, ticking, ticking on—numbering the passing moments with startling distinctness.

Oh, in such an hour, when wave after wave of anguish dashes over us, where are the infidel's boasted doubts, as the tortured heart cries out, instinctively, "save, Lord; or we perish!"

Slowly the night waned, and the stars paled. Up the gray east the golden sun slowly glided. One beam penetrated the little window, hovering like a halo over Daisy's sunny head. A quick, convulsive start, and with one wild cry (as the little throat filled to suffocation), the fair white arms were tossed aloft, then dropped powerless upon the bed of Death!

CHAPTER XXIII

"*THERE CAN BE* no sorrow greater than this sorrow," sobbed Ruth, as the heavy sod fell on Daisy's little breast.

In after years, when bitterer cups had been drained to the dregs, Ruth remembered these, her murmuring words. Ah! mourning mother! He who seeth the end from the beginning, even in this blow "remembered mercy."

"*YOUR DAUGHTER-IN-LAW* is quite crushed by her affliction, I hear," said a neighbor to old Mrs. Hall.

"Yes, Mrs. Jones, I think she is," said the old lady complacently. "It has taken right hold of her."

"It died of croup, I believe," said Mrs. Jones.

"Well, they *say* so," said the old lady. "It is *my* opinion the child's death was owing to the thriftlessness of the mother. I don't mourn for it, because I believe the poor thing is better off."

"You surprise me," said Mrs. Jones. "I always had the impression that young Mrs. Hall was a pattern mother."

"People differ," said the old lady, raising her eyebrows, compressing her lips, and looking mysteriously at the ceiling, as if she *could* tell a tale, were she not too charitable.

"Well, the amount of it is," said the garrulous old doctor, emerging from the corner; "the amount of it is, that the mother always thought she knew better than anybody else how to manage that child. Now, you know, Mis. Jones, I'm a physician, and *ought* to know something about the laws that govern the human body, but you'll be astonished to hear that she frequently acted directly contrary to my advice, and this is the result; that tells the whole story. However, as Mis. Hall says, the child is better off; and as to Ruth, why the Lord generally sends afflictions where they are *needed*;" and the doctor returned to his corner.

"It looks very lonely at the Glen since they moved away," remarked Mrs. Jones. "I suppose they don't think of coming back."

"How?" replied the doctor, re-appearing from his corner.

"I suppose your son and his wife have no idea of returning to the Glen," said Mrs. Jones.

"No—no. Ruth is one of the uneasy kind; it's coming and going—coming and going with her. She fancied everything in doors and out reminded her of Daisy, and kept wandering round, trying to be rid of herself. Now that proves she didn't make a sanctifying use of her trouble. It's no use trying to dodge what the Lord sends. We've just got to stand and take it; if we don't, he'll be sending something else. Them's my sentiments, and I consider 'em scripteral. I shouldn't be surprised if *Harry* was taken away from her;—a poor, miserable thing she'd be to take care of herself, if he was. She couldn't earn the salt to her porridge. Thriftless, Mis. Jones, thriftless—come of a bad stock—can't expect good fruit off a wild apple tree, at least, not without grace is grafted on; that tells the whole story."

"Well; my heart aches for her," said the kind Mrs. Jones. "Mrs. Hall is very delicately organized,—one of those persons capable of compressing the happiness or misery of a lifetime into a few moments."

"Stuff," said the doctor, "stuff; don't believe it. *I'm* an example to the contrary. I've been through everything, and just look at me;" and the doctor advanced a pace or two to give Mrs. Jones a better view of his full-blown peony face, and aldermanic proportions; "don't believe it, Mis. Jones; stuff! Fashion to be sentimental; nerves a modern invention. Ridiculous!"

"But," said the persistent Mrs. Jones, "don't you think, doctor that—"

"Don't think anything *about* it," said the doctor. "Don't want to *hear* anything about it. Have no patience with any woman who'd let a husband sell a farm at such a sacrifice as Harry's was sold, merely because there was a remote chance she would become insane if she staid there. Now, I've enough to do—plenty to do, but, still, I was willing to superintend that farm a little, as my doing so was such a help to Harry. Well, well; they'll both go to the dogs, that's the amount of it. A rolling stone gathers no moss. Harry was good for something before he married Ruth; had a mind of his own. Ruth ain't the wife for him."

"He did not appear to think so," replied the obstinate Mrs. Jones. "Everybody in the village says, 'what a happy couple they are.'"

"*O-o-h*—my!" hissed the old lady, "did you *ever*, doctor? Of course,

Mrs. Jones, you don't suppose Harry would be such a fool as to tell people how miserable he was; but *mothers*, Mrs. Jones, *mothers* are keen-sighted; can't throw dust in a *mother's* eyes."

"*Nor in mine*," retorted the independent Mrs. Jones, with a mock courtesy to the old lady, as she walked out the door, muttering as she went down the road, "Sally Jones will tell her the truth if nobody else will."

"Mis. Hall," said the doctor, drawing himself up so straight as to snap off his waist-band button, "this is the last time that woman ever crosses *my* threshold. I shall tell Deacon Smith that I consider her a proper subject for church discipline; she's what the bible calls 'a busy body in other men's matters;' a character which both you and I despise and abominate, Mis. Hall."

CHAPTER XXIV

THE first-born! Oh, other tiny feet may trip lightly at the hearth-stone, other rosy faces may greet us round the board; with tender love we soothe their childish pains and share their childish sports; but "Benjamin is not," is written in the secret chamber of many a bereaved mother's heart, where never more the echo of a childish voice may ring out such liquid music as death hath hushed.

Spring had garlanded the earth with flowers, and Autumn had withered them with his frosty breath. Many a Summer's sun, and many a Winter's snow, has rested on Daisy's grave, since the date of our last chapter.

At the window of a large hotel in one of those seaport towns, the resort alike of the invalid and pleasure-seeker, sat Ruth; the fresh sea-breeze lifting her hair from temples thinner and paler than of yore, but stamped with a holier beauty. From the window might be seen the blue waters of the bay leaping to the bright sunlight; while many a vessel outward and inward bound, spread its sails, like some joyous white-winged sea bird. But Ruth was not thinking of the sapphire sky, though it were passing fair; nor of the blue sea, decked with its snowy sails; for in her lap lay a little half-worn shoe, with the impress of a tiny foot, upon which her tears were falling fast.

A little half-worn shoe! And yet no magician could conjure up such blissful visions; no artist could trace such vivid pictures; no harp of sweetest sounds could so fill the ear with music.

Eight years since the little Daisy withered! And yet, to the mother's eye, she still blossomed fair as Paradise. The soft, golden hair still waved over the blue-veined temples; the sweet, earnest eyes still beamed with their loving light; the little fragile hand was still outstretched for maternal guidance, and in the wood and by the stream they still lingered. Still, the little hymn was chanted at dawn, the little prayer lisped at dew-fall; still, that gentle breathing mingled with the happy mother's star-lit dreams.

A little, bright-eyed creature, crept to Ruth's side, and lifting a long, wavy, golden ringlet from a box on the table near her, laid it beside her own brown curls.

"Daisy's in heaven," said little Katy, musingly. "Why do you cry, mamma? Don't you like to have God keep her for you?"

A tear was the only answer.

"*I* should like to die, and have you love *my* curls as you do Daisy's, mother."

Ruth started, and looked at the child; the rosy flush had faded away from little Katy's cheek, and a tear stole slowly from beneath her long lashes.

Taking her upon her lap, she severed one tress of her brown hair, and laid it beside little Daisy's golden ringlet.

A bright, glad smile lit up little Katy's face, and she was just throwing her arms about her mother's neck, to express her thanks, when, stopping suddenly, she drew from her dimpled foot one little shoe, and laid it in her mother's palm.

'Mid smiles and tears Ruth complied with the mute request; and the little sister shoes lay with the twin ringlets, lovingly side by side.

Blessed childhood! the pupil and yet the teacher; half infant, half sage, and whole angel! what a desert were earth without thee!

CHAPTER XXV

HOTEL LIFE is about the same in every latitude. At Beach Cliff there was the usual number of vapid, fashionable mothers; dressy, brainless daughters; half-fledged wine-bibbing sons; impudent, whisker-dyed roués; bachelors, anxious to give their bashfulness an airing; bronchial clergymen, in search of health and a text; waning virgins, languishing by candle-light; gouty uncles, dyspeptic aunts, whist-playing old ladies, flirting nursery maids and neglected children.

Then there were "hops" in the hall, and sails upon the lake; there were nine-pin alleys, and a gymnasium; there were bathing parties, and horse-back parties; there were billiard rooms, and smoking rooms; reading rooms, flirtation rooms,—room for everything but—thought.

There could be little or nothing in such an artificial atmosphere congenial with a nature like Ruth's. In all this motley crowd there was but one person who interested her, a Mrs. Leon, upon whose queenly figure all eyes were bent as she passed; and who received the homage paid her, with an indifference which (whether real or assumed) became her passing well. Her husband was a tall, prim, proper-looking person, who dyed his hair and whiskers every Saturday, was extremely punctilious in all points of etiquette, very particular in his stated inquiries as to his wife's and his horse's health, very fastidious in regard to the brand of his wine, and the quality of his venison; maintaining, under all circumstances, the same rigidity of feature, the same immobility of the cold, stony, gray eye, the same studied, stereotyped, conventionalism of manner.

Ruth, although shunning society, found herself drawn to Mrs. Leon by an unaccountable magnetism. Little Katy, too, with that unerring instinct with which childhood selects from the crowd, an unselfish and loving nature, had already made rapid advances toward acquaintance. What road to a mother's heart so direct, as through the heart of her children? With Katy for a "medium," the two ladies soon found themselves in frequent conversation. Ruth had always shrunk from female friendship. It might be that her boarding-school experience had something to do in effecting this wholesale disgust of the commodity. Be that as it may, she had never found any woman who had not misunderstood and misinterpreted her. For the common female employments and recreations, she had an unqualified disgust. Satin patchwork, the manufacture of German worsted animals, bead-netting, crotchet-stitching, long discussions with milliners, dress-makers, and modistes, long forenoons spent in shopping, or leaving bits of paste-board, party-giving, party-going, prinking and coquetting, all these were her aversion. Equally with herself, Mrs. Leon seemed to despise these air bubbles. Ruth was sure that, under that faultless, marble exterior, a glowing, living, loving heart lay slumbering; waiting only the enchanter's touch to wake it into life. The more she looked into those dark eyes, the deeper seemed their depths. Ruth longed, she scarce knew why, to make her life happy. Oh, if she *had* a soul!

Ruth thought of *Mr.* Leon and shuddered.

Mrs. Leon was often subject to severe and prostrating attacks of nervous headache. On these occasions, Ruth's magnetic touch seemed to woo coy slumber, like a spell; and the fair sufferer would lie peacefully for hours, while Ruth's fingers strayed over her temples, or her musical voice, like David's harp, exorcised the demon Pain.

"You are better now," said Ruth, as Mrs. Leon slowly opened her eyes, and looked about her; "you have had such a nice sleep, I think you will be able to join us at the tea table tonight. I will brush these long dishevelled locks, and robe these dainty limbs; though, to my eye, you look lovelier just as you are. You are very beautiful, Mary. I heard a couple of young ladies discussing you, in the drawing-room, the other evening, envying your beauty and your jewels, and the magnificence of your wardrobe."

"Did they envy me my *husband?*" asked Mary, in a slow, measured tone.

"That would have been useless," said Ruth, averting her eyes; "but they said he denied you nothing in the way of dress, equipage or ornament."

"Yes," said Mary; "I have all those pretty toys to satisfy my heart-cravings; they, equally with myself, are necessary appendages to Mr. Leon's establishment. Oh, Ruth!" and the tears streamed through her jewelled fingers—"love me—pity me; you who are so blessed. I too *could* love; that is the drop of poison in my cup. When *your* daughters stand at the altar, Ruth, never compel them to say words to which the heart yields no response. The chain is none the less galling, because its links are golden. God bless you, Ruth; 'tis long since I have shed such tears. You have touched the rock; forget that the waters have gushed forth."

CHAPTER XXVI

OCTOBER HAD COME! coy and chill in the morning, warm and winning at noon, veiling her coat of many colors in a fleecy mist at evening, yet lovely still in all her changeful moods. The gay butterflies of fashion had already spread their shrivelled wings for the warmer atmosphere of the city. Harry and Ruth still lingered;—there was beauty for them in the hill-side's rainbow dyes, in the crimson barberry clusters, drooping from the wayside hedges; in the wild grape-vine that threw off its frost-bitten leaves, to tempt the rustic's hand with its purple clusters; in the piles of apples, that lay gathered in parti-colored heaps beneath the orchard trees; in the yellow ears of Indian corn, that lay scattered on the seedy floor of the breezy barn; in the festoons of dried apples, and mammoth squashes, and pumpkins, that lay ripening round the thrifty farmers' doors; and in the circling leaves, that came eddying down in brilliant showers on the Indian summer's soft but treacherous breath.

"*YOU ARE ILL,* Harry," said Ruth, laying her hand upon his forehead.

"Slightly so," replied Harry languidly; "a pain in my head, and—"

A strong ague chill prevented Harry from finishing the sentence.

Ruth, who had never witnessed an attack of this kind, grew pale as his teeth chattered, and his powerful frame shook violently from head to foot.

"Have you suffered much in this way?" asked the physician who was summoned.

"I had the fever and ague very badly, some years since, at the west," said Harry. "It is an unpleasant visitor, doctor; you must rid me of it as soon as you can, for the sake of my little wife, who, though she can endure pain herself like a martyr, is an arrant little coward whenever it attacks me.

Don't look so sober, Ruth, I shall be better to-morrow. I can not afford time to be sick long, for I have a world of business on hand. I had an important appointment this very day, which it is a thousand pities to postpone; but never mind, I shall certainly be better to-morrow."

But Harry was not "better to-morrow;" nor the next day; nor the next; the doctor pronouncing his case to be one of decided typhus fever.

Very reluctantly the active man postponed his half-formed plans, and business speculations, and allowed himself to be placed on the sick list. With a sigh of impatience, he saw his hat, and coat, and boots, put out of sight; and watched the different phials, as they came in from the apothecary; and counted the stroke of the clock, as it told the tedious hours; and marvelled at the patience with which (he now recollected) Ruth bore a long bed-ridden eight-weeks' martyrdom, without a groan or complaint. But soon, other thoughts and images mixed confusedly in his brain, like the shifting colors of a kaleidoscope. He was floating—drifting—sinking—soaring, by turns;—the hot blood coursed through his veins like molten lava; his eye glared deliriously, and the hand, never raised but in blessing, fell, with fevered strength, upon the unresisting form of the loving wife.

"You must have a nurse," said the doctor to Ruth; "it is dangerous for you to watch with your husband alone. He might injure you seriously, in one of these paroxysms."

"But Harry has an unconquerable dislike to a hired nurse," said Ruth; "his reason may return at any moment, and the sight of one will trouble him. I am not afraid," replied Ruth, between a tear and a smile.

"But you will wear yourself out; you must remember that you owe a duty to your children."

"My *husband* has the *first* claim," said Ruth, resuming her place by the bed-side; and during the long hours of day and night, regardless of the lapse of time—regardless of hunger, thirst or weariness, she glided noiselessly about the room, arranged the pillows, mixed the healing draught, or watched with a silent prayer at the sufferer's bed-side; while Harry lay tossing from side to side, his white teeth glittering through his unshorn beard, raving constantly of her prolonged absence, and imploring her in heart-rending tones to come to his side, and "bring Daisy from the Glen."

Many a friendly voice whispered at the door, "How is he?" The Irish waiters crossed themselves and stept softly through the hall, as they went on their hasty errands; and many a consultation was held among warm-hearted gentlemen friends, (who had made Harry's acquaintance at the hotel, during the pleasant summer,) to decide which should first prove their friendship by watching with him.

Ruth declined all these offers to fill her place. "I will never leave him," she said; "his reason may return, and his eye seek vainly for me. No—no; I thank you all. Watch *with* me, if you will, but do not ask me to leave him."

IN THE STILL MIDNIGHT, when the lids of the kind but weary watchers drooped heavily with slumber, rang mournfully in Ruth's ear the sad plaint of Gethsemane's Lord, "Could ye not watch with me one hour?" and pressing her lips to the hot and fevered hand before her, she murmured, "I will never leave thee, nor forsake thee."

CHAPTER XXVII

"*HAVE YOU GOT* the carpet-bag, doctor? and the little brown bundle? and the russet-trunk? and the umberil? and the demi-john, and the red band-box, with my best cap in it? one—two—three—four; yes—that's all right. Now, mind those thievish porters. Goodness, how they charge here for carriage hire! I never knew, before, how much money it took to journey. Oh dear! I wonder if Harry *is* worse? There now, doctor, you've put your foot right straight through that band-box. Now, where, for the land's sake, are my spectacles? 'Tisn't possible you've left them behind? I put them in the case, as you stood there in the chayna closet, drinking your brandy and water, and asked you to put them in your side-pocket, because my bag was full of orange-peels, scissors, camphor, peppermint-drops, and seed-cakes. I wouldn't have left 'em for any money. Such a sight of trouble as it was to get them focussed right to my eyes. How *could* you, doctor, be so blundering? I declare it is enough to provoke a saint."

"If that's the case, there's no immediate call for *you* to get vexed," said the doctor, tartly.

"IS THAT THE HOUSE?" asked the old lady, her curiosity getting the better of her indignation; "what a big hotel! I wonder if Harry *is* worse? Mercy me, I'm all of a quiver. I wonder if they will take us right into the drawing-room? I wonder if there's many ladies in it—my bonnet is awfully jammed: beside, I'm so powdered with dust, that I look as if I had had an ash barrel sifted over me. Doctor! doctor! don't go on so far ahead. It looks awk'ard, as if I had no protector."

"HOW'S HARRY?" said the doctor, to a white-jacketted waiter, who stood gossiping on the piazza steps with a comrade.

"Funny old chap!" said the waiter, without noticing the doctor's query; "I say, Bill, look how his hair is cut!"

"'Taint hair," said Tom, "it is a wig."

"Bless my eyes! so it is; and a red one, too! Bad symptoms; red wigs are the cheapest; no extra fees to be got out of *that* customer, for blacking boots and bringing hot beafsteaks. Besides, just look at his baggage; you can always judge of a traveler, Bill, by his trunks; it never fails. Now, *I* like to see a trunk thickly studded with brass nails, and covered with a linen overall; then I know, if it is a lady's, that there's diamond rings inside, and plenty of cash; if 'tis a gentleman's, that he knows how to order sherry-cobblers in the forenoon, and a bottle of old wine or two with his dinner; and how to fee the poor fellow who brings it, too, who lives on a small salary, with large expectations."

"How's Harry?" thundered the doctor again, (after waiting what he considered a reasonable time for an answer,) "or if *you* are too lazy to tell, you whiskered jackanapes, go call your employer."

The word "employer" recalled the rambling waiter to his senses, and great was his consternation on finding that "the old chap with the red wig" was the father of young Mr. Hall, who was beloved by everything in the establishment, down to old Neptune the house-dog.

"I told you so," said the doctor, turning to his wife; "Harry's no better—consultation this morning—very little hope of him;—so much for *my* not being here to prescribe for him. Ruth shouldered a great responsibility when she brought him away out of reach of *my* practice. You go into that room, there, Mis. Hall, No. 20, with your traps and things, and take off your bonnet and keep quiet, while I go up and see him."

CHAPTER XXVIII

"*HUMPH!*" said the doctor, "humph!" as Ruth drew aside the curtain, and the light fell full upon Harry's face. "Humph! it is all up with *him*; he's in the last stage of the complaint, won't live two days;" and stepping to the table, the doctor uncorked the different phials, applied them to the end of his nose, examined the labels, and then returned to the bed-side, where Ruth stood bending over Harry, so pallid, so tearless, that one involuntarily prayed that death, when he aimed his dart, might strike down both together.

"Humph!" said the doctor again! "when did he have his reason last?"

"A few moments, day before yesterday," said Ruth, without removing her eyes from Harry.

"Well; he has been *murdered*,—yes murdered, just as much as if you had seen the knife put to his throat. That tells the whole story, and I don't care who knows it. I have been looking at those phials,—wrong course of treatment altogether for typhoid fever; fatal mistake. His death will lie heavy at *somebody's* door," and he glanced at Ruth.

"Hush! he is coming to himself," said Ruth, whose eyes had never once moved from her husband.

"Then I must tell him that his hours are numbered," said the doctor, thrusting his hands in his pockets, and pompously walking round the bed.

"No, no," whispered Ruth, grasping his arm with both hands; "you will kill him. The doctor said it might destroy the last chance for his life. *Don't* tell him. You know he is not afraid *to die*; but oh, spare him the parting with me! it will be so hard; he loves me, father."

"Pshaw!" said the doctor, shaking her off; "he ought to settle up his affairs while he can. I don't know how he wants things fixed. Harry! Harry!" said he, touching his shoulder, "I've come to see you; do you know me?"

"Father!" said Harry, languidly, "yes, I'm—I'm sick. I shall be better soon; don't worry about me. Where's my wife? where's Ruth?"

"You'll *never* be better, Harry," said the doctor, bluntly, stepping between him and Ruth; "you may not live the day out. If you have got anything to say, you'd better say it now, before your mind wanders. You are a dead man, Harry; and you know that when I say *that*, I know what I'm talking about."

The sick man gazed at the speaker, as if he were in a dream; then slowly, and with a great effort, raising his head, he looked about the room for Ruth. She was kneeling at the bedside, with her face buried in her hands. Harry reached out his emaciated hand, and placed it upon her bowed head.

"Ruth? wife?"

Her arm was about his neck in an instant—her lips to his; but her eyes were tearless, and her whole frame shook convulsively.

"Oh, how *can* I leave you? who will care for you? Oh God, in mercy spare me to her;" and Harry fell back on his pillow.

The shock was too sudden; reason again wandered; he heard the shrill whistle of the cars, recalling him to the city's whirl of business; he had stocks to negotiate; he had notes to pay; he had dividends due. Then the scene changed;—he could not be carried on a hearse through the street, surrounded by a gaping crowd. Ruth must go alone with him, by night;—why *must* he die at all? He would take anything. Where was the doctor? Why did they waste time in talking? Why not do something more for him? How cruel of Ruth to let him lie there and die?

"We will try this new remedy," said one of the consulting physicians to Harry's father; "it is the only thing that remains to be done, and I confess I have no faith in its efficacy in this case."

"He rallies again!" said Ruth, clasping her hands.

"The children!" said Harry; "bring me the children."

"Presently," said the new physician; "try and swallow this first;" and he raised his head tenderly.

They were brought him. Little Nettie came first,—her dimpled arms and rosy face in strange contrast to the pallid lips she bent, in childish glee, to kiss. Then little Katy, shrinking with a strange awe from the dear papa she loved so much, and sobbing, she scarce knew why, at his whispered words, "Be kind to your mother, Katy."

Again Harry's eyes sought Ruth. She was there, but a film—a mist had come between them; he could not see her, though he felt her warm breath.

And now, that powerful frame collected all its remaining energies for the last dread contest with death. So fearful—so terrible was the struggle, that friends stood by, with suppressed breath and averted eyes, while Ruth alone, with a fearful calmness, hour after hour, wiped the death damp from his brow, and the oozing foam from his pallid lips.

"*HE IS GONE,*" said the old doctor, laying Harry's hand down upon the coverlid.

"No; he breathes again."

"Ah; that's his last!"

"Take her away," said the doctor, as Ruth fell heavily across her husband's body; and the unresisting form of the insensible wife was borne into the next room.

Strange hands closed Harry's eyes, parted his damp locks, straightened his manly limbs, and folded the marble hands over as noble a heart as ever lay cold and still beneath a shroud.

CHAPTER XXIX

"*IT IS REALLY* quite dreadful to see her in this way," said Hyacinth, as they chafed Ruth's hands and bathed her temples; "it is really quite dreadful. Somebody ought to tell her, when she comes to, that her hair is parted unevenly and needs brushing sadly. Harry's finely-chiseled features look quite beautiful in repose. It is a pity the barber should have been allowed to shave off his beard after death; it looked quite oriental and picturesque. But the sight of Ruth, in this way, is really dreadful; it quite unnerves me. I shall look ten years older by to-morrow. I must go down and take a turn or two on the piazza." And Hyacinth paced up and down, thinking—not of the bereaved sister, who lay mercifully insensible to her loss, nor yet of the young girl whose heart was to throb trustfully at the altar, by his side, on the morrow,—but of her broad lands and full coffers, with which he intended to keep at bay the haunting creditors, who were impertinent enough to spoil his daily digestion by asking for their just dues.

ONE O'CLOCK! The effect of the sleeping potion administered to Ruth had passed away. Slowly she unclosed her eyes and gazed about her. The weary nurse, forgetful of her charge, had sunk into heavy slumber.

Where was Harry?

Ruth presses her hands to her temples. Oh God! the consciousness that *would* come! the frantic out-reaching of the arms to clasp—a vain shadow!

Where had they lain him?

She crossed the hall to Harry's sick room; the key was in the lock; she turned it with trembling fingers. Oh God! the dreadful stillness of that outlined form! the calm majesty of that marble brow, on which the moonbeams fell as sweetly as if that peaceful sleep was but to restore him to her widowed arms. That half-filled glass, from which his dying lips had turned away;—those useless phials;—that watch—*his* watch—moving—and *he* so still!—the utter helplessness of human aid;—the dreadful might of Omnipotence!

"Harry!"

Oh, when was he ever deaf before to the music of that voice? Oh, how could Ruth (God forgive her!) look upon those dumb lips and say, "Thy will be done!"

"Horrible!" muttered Hyacinth, as the undertaker passed him on the stairs with Harry's coffin. "These business details are very shocking to a sensitive person. I beg your pardon; did you address me?" said he, to a gentleman who raised his hat as he passed.

"I wished to do so, though an entire stranger to you," said the gentleman, with a sympathizing glance, which was quite thrown away on Hyacinth. "I have had the pleasure of living under the same roof, this summer, with your afflicted sister and her noble husband, and have become warmly attached to both. In common with several warm friends of your brother-in-law, I am pained to learn that, owing to the failure of parties for whom he had become responsible, there will be little or nothing for the widow and her children, when his affairs are settled. It is our wish to make up a purse, and request her acceptance of it, through you, as a slight token of the estimation in which we held her husband's many virtues. I understand you are to leave before the funeral, which must be my apology for intruding upon you at so unseasonable an hour."

With the courtliest of bows, in the blandest of tones, Hyacinth assured, while he thanked Mr. Kendall, that himself, his father, and indeed, all the members of the family, were abundantly able, and most solicitous, to supply every want, and anticipate every wish of Ruth and her children; and that it was quite impossible she should ever suffer for anything, or be obliged in any way, at any future time, to exert herself for her own, or their support; all of which good news for Ruth highly gratified Mr. Kendall, who grasped the velvet palm of Hyacinth, and dashed away a grateful tear, that the promise to the widow and fatherless was remembered in heaven.

CHAPTER XXX

"*THEY ARE VERY ATTENTIVE* to us here," remarked the doctor, as one after another of Harry's personal friends paid their respects, for his sake, to the old couple at No. 20. "Very attentive, and yet, Mis. Hall, I only practiced physic in this town six months, five years ago. It is really astonishing how long a good physician will be remembered," and the doctor crossed his legs comfortably, and tapped on his snuff-box.

"Ruth's brother, Hyacinth, leaves before the funeral, doctor," said the old lady. "I suppose you see through *that*. He intends to be off and out of the way, before the time comes to decide where Ruth shall put her head, after Harry is buried; and there's her father, just like him; he has been as uneasy as an eel in a frying-pan, ever since he came, and this morning *he* went off, without asking a question about Harry's affairs. I suppose he thinks it is *our* business, and he owning bank stock. I tell you, doctor, that Ruth may go a-begging, for all the help she'll get from *her* folks."

"Or from me, either," said the doctor, thrusting his thumbs into the arm-holes of his vest, and striding across the room. "She has been a spoiled baby long enough; she will find earning her living a different thing from sitting with her hands folded, with Harry chained to her feet."

"What did you do with that bottle of old wine, Mis. Hall, which I told you to bring out of Harry's room? He never drank but one glass of it, after that gentleman sent it to him, and we might as well have it as to let those lazy waiters drink it up. There were two or three bunches of grapes, too, he didn't eat; you had better take them, too, while you are about it."

"Well, it don't seem, after all, as if Harry was dead," said the doctor, musingly; "but the Lord's will be done. Here comes your dress-maker, Mis. Hall."

"*GOOD AFTERNOON,* ma'am, good afternoon, sir," said Miss Skinlin, with a doleful whine, drawing down the corners of her mouth and eyes to suit the occasion. "Sad affliction you've met with. As our minister says, 'man is like the herb of the field; blooming to-day, withered to-morrow.' Life is short: will you have your dress gathered or biased, ma'am?"

"Quite immaterial," said the old lady, anxious to appear indifferent; "though you may as well, I suppose, do it the way which is worn the most."

"Well, some likes it one way, and then again, some likes it another. The doctor's wife in the big, white house yonder—do you know the doctor's wife, ma'am?"

"No," said the old lady.

"Nice folks, ma'am; open-handed; never mind my giving 'em back the change, when they pay me. *She* was a Skefflit. Do you know the Skefflits? Possible? why they are our first folks. Well, la, where was I? Oh! the doctor's wife has *her* gowns biased; but then she's getting fat, and wants to look slender. I'd advise you to have yourn gathered. Dreadful affliction you've met with, ma'am. Beautiful corpse your son is. I always look at corpses to remind me of my latter end. Some corpses keep much longer than others; don't you think so, ma'am? They tell me your son's wife is most crazy, because they doted on one another so."

The doctor and his wife exchanged meaning looks.

"*Do tell?*" said Miss Skinlin, dropping her shears. "Well, I never! 'How desaitful the heart is,' as our minister says. Why, everybody about here took 'em for regular turtle-doves."

"'All is not gold that glitters,'" remarked the old lady. "There is many a heart-ache that nobody knows anything about, but He who made the heart. In my opinion our son was not anxious to continue in this world of trial longer."

"You don't?" said Miss Skinlin. "Pious?"

"*Certainly*," said the doctor. "Was he not *our* son? Though, since his marriage, his wife's influence was very worldly."

"Pity," whined Miss Skinlin; "professors should let their light shine. *I* always try to drop a word in season, wherever business calls *me*. Will you have a cross-way fold on your sleeve, ma'am? I don't think it would be out of place, even on this mournful occasion. Mrs. Tufts wore one when her eldest child died, and she was dreadful grief-stricken. I remember she gave me (poor dear!) a five-dollar note, instead of a two; but that was a thing I hadn't the heart to harass her about at such a time. I respected her grief too much, ma'am. Did I understand you that I was to put the cross-way folds on your sleeve, ma'am?"

"You may do as you like," whined the old lady; "people *do* dress more at hotels."

"Yes," said Miss Skinlin; "and I often feel reproved for aiding and abetting such foolish vanities; and yet, if I refused, from conscientious scruples, to trim dresses, I suppose somebody else *would*; so you see, it wouldn't do any good. Your daughter-in-law is left rich, I suppose. I always think that's a great consolation to a bereaved widow."

You needn't *suppose* any such thing," said the doctor, facing Miss Skinlin; "she hasn't the first red cent."

"Dreadful!" shrieked Miss Skinlin. "What *is* she going to do?"

"That tells the whole story," said the doctor; "sure enough, what *is* she going to do?"

"I suppose she'll live with *you*," said Miss Skinlin, suggestively.

"You needn't suppose *that*, either," retorted the doctor. "It isn't every person, Miss Skinlin, who is agreeable enough to be taken into one's house; besides, she has got folks of her own."

"Oh,—ah!"—said Miss Skinlin; "rich?"

"Yes, very," said the doctor; "unless some of their poor relatives turn up, in which case, they are always dreadfully out of pocket."

"I un-der-stand," said Miss Skinlin, with a significant nod. "Well; I don't see anything left for her to do, but to earn her living, like some other folks."

"P-r-e-c-i-s-e-l-y," said the doctor.

"Oh—ah,"—said Miss Skinlin, who had at last possessed herself of "the whole story."

"I forgot to ask you how wide a hem I should allow on your black crape veil," said Miss Skinlin, tying on her bonnet to go. "Half a yard width is not considered too much for the *deepest* affliction. Your daughter, the widow, will probably have that width," said the crafty dress-maker.

"In my opinion, Ruth is in no deeper affliction than we are," said the doctor, growing very red in the face; "although she makes more fuss about it; so you may just make the hem of Mis. Hall's veil half-yard deep too, and send the bill into No. 20, where it will be footed by Doctor Zekiel Hall, who is not in the habit of ordering what he can't pay for. *That* tells the whole story."

"Good morning," said Miss Skinlin, with another doleful whine. "May the Lord be your support, and let the light of His countenance shine upon you, as our minister says."

CHAPTER XXXI

SLOWLY the funeral procession wound along. The gray-haired gate-keeper of the cemetery stepped aside, and gazed into the first carriage as it passed in. He saw only a pale woman veiled in sable, and two little wondering, rosy faces gazing curiously out the carriage window. All about, on either side, were graves; some freshly sodded, others green with many a summer's verdure, and all treasuring sacred ashes, while the mourners went about the streets.

"Dust to dust."

Harry's coffin was lifted from the hearse, and laid upon the green sward by the side of little Daisy. Over him waved leafy trees, of his own planting; while through the branches the shifting shadows came and went, lending a mocking glow to the dead man's face. Little Katy came forward, and gazed into the yawning grave till her golden curls fell like a veil over her wondering eyes. Ruth leaned upon the arm of her cousin, a dry, flinty, ossified man of business; a man of angles—a man of forms—a man with veins of ice, who looked the Almighty in the face complacently, "thanking God he was not as other men are;" who gazed with stony eyes upon the open grave, and the orphan babes, and the bowed form at his side, which swayed to and fro like the young tree before the tempest blast.

"Dust to dust!"

Ruth shrinks trembling back, then leans eagerly forward; now she takes the last lingering look at features graven on her memory with lines of fire; and now, as the earth falls with a hard, hollow sound upon the coffin, a lightning thought comes with stunning force to little Katy, and she sobs out, "Oh, they are covering my papa up; I can't ever see papa any more."

"Dust to dust!"

The sexton smooths the moist earth carefully with his reversed spade; Ruth's eyes follow his movements with a strange fascination. Now the carriages roll away one after another, and the wooden man turns to Ruth and says, "Come." She looks into his stony face, then at the new-made mound, utters a low, stifled cry, and staggers forth with her crushing sorrow.

Oh, Earth! Earth! with thy mocking skies of blue, thy placid silver streams, thy myriad, memory-haunting odorous flowers, thy wheels of triumph rolling—rolling on, over breaking hearts and prostrate forms—maimed, tortured, crushed, yet not destroyed. Oh, mocking Earth! snatching from our frenzied grasp the life-long coveted treasure! Most treacherous Earth! are these thy unkept promises?

Oh, hadst thou no Gethsemane—no Calvary—no guarded tomb—no risen Lord!

CHAPTER XXXII

"AND IS IT because Biddy M'Pherson don't suit yer, that ye'd be afther sending her away?" said Ruth's nursery maid.

"No, Biddy," replied Ruth; "you have been respectful to me, and kind and faithful to the children, but I cannot afford to keep you now since—" and Ruth's voice faltered.

"If that is all, my leddy," said Biddy, brightening up, "then I'll not be afther laving, sure."

"Thank you," said Ruth, quite moved by her devotion; "but you must not work for me without wages. Besides, Biddy, I could not even pay your board."

"And the tears not dry on your cheek; and the father of him and you with plenty of the siller. May the divil fly away wid 'em! Why, Nettie is but a babby yet, and Masther used to say you must walk every day, to keep off the bad headaches; and it's coming could weather, and you can't take Nettie out, and you can't lave her with Katy; and anyhow it is n't Biddy M'Pherson that'll be going away intirely."

The allusion to Harry's tender care of Ruth's health opened the wound afresh, and she wept convulsively.

"I say it's a shame," said Biddy, becoming more excited at the sight of her tears; "and you can't do it, my leddy; you are as white as a sheet of paper."

"I *must*," said Ruth, controlling herself with a violent effort; "say no more, Biddy. I don't know where I am going; but wherever it may be I shall always be glad to see you. Katy and Nettie shall not forget their kind nurse; now, go and pack your trunk," said Ruth, assuming a composure she was far from feeling. "I thank you for your kind offer, though I cannot accept it."

"May the sowls of 'em niver get out of purgatory; that's Biddy's last word to 'em," said the impetuous Irish girl; "and if the priest himself should say that St. Peter wouldn't open the gate for your leddyship, I wouldn't believe him." And unclasping little Nettie's clinging arms from her neck, and giving a hurried kiss to little Katy, Biddy went sobbing through the door, with her check apron over her broad Irish face.

CHAPTER XXXIII

"*WHO'S THAT* coming up the garden-walk, doctor?" said the old lady; "Ruth's father, as true as the world. Ah! I understand, we shall see what we shall see; mind you keep a stiff upper lip, doctor."

"Good morning, doctor," said Mr. Ellet.

"Good morning, sir," said the doctor, stiffly.

"Fine place you have here, doctor."

"Very," replied the doctor.

"I have just come from a visit to Ruth," said Mr. Ellet.

The imperturbable doctor slightly nodded to his visitor, as he took a pinch of snuff.

"She seems to take her husband's death very hard."

"Does she?" replied the doctor.

"I'm sorry to hear," remarked Mr. Ellet, fidgeting in his chair, "that there is nothing left for the support of the family."

"So am I," said the doctor.

"I suppose the world will talk about us, if nothing is done for her," said the non-committal Mr. Ellet.

"Very likely," replied the doctor.

"Harry was *your* child," said Mr. Ellet, suggestively.

"Ruth is yours," said the doctor.

"Yes, I know," said Mr. Ellet; "but you are better off than I am, doctor."

"I deny it—I deny it," retorted the doctor, fairly roused; "you own the house you live in, and have a handsome income, or *ought* to have," said he, sneeringly, "at the rate you live. If you have brought up your daughter in extravagance, so much the worse for *her;* you and Ruth must settle that between you. I wash *my* hands of her. I have no objection to take Harry's *children*, and try to bring them up in a sensible manner; but, in that case, I'll have none of the mother's interference. Then her hands will be free to earn her own living, and she's none too good for it, either. I don't believe in your doll-baby women; she's proud, you are all proud, all your family—that tells the whole story."

This was rather plain Saxon, as the increased redness of Mr. Ellet's ears testified; but pecuniary considerations helped him to swallow the bitter pill without making a wry face.

"I don't suppose Ruth could be induced to part with her children," said Mr. Ellet, meditatively.

"Let her try to support them then, till she gets starved out," replied the doctor. "I suppose you know, if the mother's inability to maintain them is proved, the law obliges each of the grand-parents to take one."

This was a new view of the case, and one which immediately put to flight any reluctance Mr. Ellet might have had to force Ruth to part with her children; and remarking that he thought upon reflection, that the children *would* be better off with the doctor, Mr. Ellet took his leave.

"I thought that stroke would tell," said the doctor, laughing, as Mr. Ellet closed the door.

"Yes, you hit the right nail on the head that time," remarked the old lady; "but those children will be a sight of trouble. They never sat still five minutes at a time, since they were born; but I'll soon cure them of that. I'm determined Ruth shan't have them, if they fret me to fiddling-strings; but what an avaricious old man Mr. Ellet is. We ought to be thankful we have more of the gospel spirit. But the clock has struck nine, doctor. It is time to have prayers, and go to bed."

CHAPTER XXXIV

THE DAY was dark and gloomy. Incessant weeping and fasting had brought on one of Ruth's most violent attacks of nervous headache. Ah! where was the hand which had so lately charmed that pain away? where was the form that, with uplifted finger and tiptoe tread, hushed the slightest sound, excluded the torturing light, changed the heated pillow, and bathed the aching temples? Poor Ruth! nature had been tasked its utmost with sad memories and weary vigils, and she sank fainting to the floor.

Well might the frightened children huddle breathless in the farther corner. The coffin, the shroud, and the grave, were all too fresh in their childish memory. Well might the tearful prayer go up to the only Friend they knew,—"Please God, don't take away our mamma, too."

Ruth heard it not; well had she *never* woke, but the bitter cup was not yet drained.

"Good morning, Ruth," said her father, (a few hours after,) frowning slightly as Ruth's pale face, and the swollen eyes of her children, met his view. "Sick?"

"One of my bad headaches," replied Ruth, with a quivering lip.

"Well, that comes of excitement; you shouldn't get excited. I never allow myself to worry about what can't be helped; this is the hand of God, and you ought to see it. I came to bring you good news. The doctor has very generously offered to take both your children and support them. It will be a great burden off your hands; all he asks in return is, that he shall have the entire control of them, and that you keep away. It is a great thing, Ruth, and what I didn't expect of the doctor, knowing his avaricious habits. Now you'll have something pleasant to think about, getting their things ready to go; the sooner you do it the better. How soon, think?"

"I can *never* part with my children," replied Ruth, in a voice which, though low, was perfectly clear and distinct.

"Perfect madness," said her father, rising and pacing the floor; "they will have a good home, enough to eat, drink, and wear, and be taught—"

"To disrespect their mother," said Ruth, in the same clear, low tone.

"Pshaw," said her father impatiently; "do you mean to let such a trifle as that stand in the way of their bread and butter? I'm poor, Ruth, or at least I *may* be tomorrow, who knows? so you must not depend on me; I want you to consider that, before you refuse. Perhaps you expect to support them yourself; you can't do it, that's clear, and if you should refuse the doctor's offer, and then die and leave them, he wouldn't take them."

"Their *Father in Heaven* will," said Ruth. "He says, 'Leave thy fatherless children with me.'"

"Perversion of Scripture, perversion of Scripture," said Mr. Ellet, foiled with his own weapons.

Ruth replied only with her tears, and a kiss on each little head, which had nestled up to her with an indistinct idea that she needed sympathy.

"It is of no use getting up a scene, it won't move me, Ruth," said Mr. Ellet, irritated by the sight of the weeping group before him, and the faint twinges of his own conscience; "the doctor *must* take the children, there's nothing else left."

"Father," said Ruth, rising from her couch and standing before him; "my children are all I have left to love; in pity do not distress me by urging what I can never grant."

"As you make your bed, so lie in it," said Mr. Ellet, buttoning up his coat, and turning his back upon his daughter.

It was a sight to move the stoutest heart to see Ruth that night, kneeling by the side of those sleeping children, with upturned eyes, and clasped hands of entreaty, and lips from which no sound issued, though her heart was quivering with agony; and yet a pitying Eye looked down upon those orphaned sleepers, a pitying Ear bent low to list to the widow's voiceless prayer.

CHAPTER XXXV

"WELL, Mis. Hall, you have got your answer. Ruth won't part with the children," said the doctor, as he refolded Mr. Ellet's letter.

"I believe you have lived with me forty years, come last January, haven't you, doctor?" said his amiable spouse.

"What of that? I don't see where that remark is going to fetch up, Mis. Hall," said the doctor. "You are not as young as you might be, to be sure, but I'm no boy myself."

"There you go again, off the track. I didn't make any allusion to my age. It's a thing I *never* do. It's a thing I never wish *you* to do. I repeat, that I have lived with you these forty years; well, did you ever know me back out of anything I undertook? Did you ever see me foiled? That letter makes no difference with me; Harry's children I'm determined to have, sooner or later. What can't be had by force, must be had by stratagem. I propose, therefore, a compromise, (*pro-tem*). You and Mr. Ellet had better agree to furnish a certain sum for awhile, for the support of Ruth and her children, giving her to understand that it is discretionary, and may stop at any minute. That will conciliate Ruth, and will *look* better, too.

"The fact is, Miss Taffety told me yesterday that she heard some hard talking about us down in the village, between Mrs. Rice and Deacon Gray (whose child Ruth watched so many nights with, when it had the scarlet fever). Yes, it will have a better look, doctor, and we can withdraw the allowance whenever the 'nine days' wonder' is over. These people have something else to do than to keep track of poor widows."

"I never supposed a useless, fine lady, like Ruth, would rather work to support her children than to give them up; but I don't give her any credit for it now, for I'm quite sure it's all sheer obstinacy, and only to spite us," continued the old lady.

"Doctor!" and the old lady cocked her head on one side, and crossed her two forefingers, "whenever—you—see—a—blue-eyed—soft-voiced—gentle—woman,—look—out—for—a—hurricane. I tell you that placid Ruth is a smouldering volcano."

"That tells the whole story," said the doctor. "And speaking of volcanoes, it won't be so easy to make Mr. Ellet subscribe anything for Ruth's support; he thinks more of one cent than of any child he ever had. I am expecting him every moment, Mis. Hall, to talk over our proposal about Ruth. Perhaps you had better leave us alone; you know you have a kind of irritating way if anything comes across you, and you might upset the whole business. As to my paying anything towards Ruth's board unless he does his full share, you needn't fear."

"Of course not; well, I'll leave you," said the old lady, with a sly glance at the china closet, "though I doubt if *you* understand managing him alone. Now I could wind him round my little finger in five minutes if I chose, but I hate to stoop to it, I so detest the whole family."

"I'll shake hands with you there," said the doctor; "but that puppy of a Hyacinth is my *especial* aversion, though Ruth is bad enough in her way; a mincing, conceited, tip-toeing, be-curled, be-perfumed popinjay—faugh! Do you suppose, Mis. Hall, there *can* be anything in a man who wears fancy neck-ties, a seal ring on his little finger, and changes his coat and vest a dozen times a day? No; he's a sensuous fop, that tells the whole story; ought to be picked up with a pair of sugartongs, and laid carefully on a rose-leaf. Ineffable puppy!"

"They made a great fuss about his writings," said the old lady.

"*Who* made a fuss? Fudge—there's that piece of his about 'The Saviour'; he describes him as he would a Broadway dandy. That fellow is all surface, I tell you; there's no depth in him. How should there be? Isn't he an Ellet? but look, here comes his father."

"GOOD DAY, doctor. My time is rather limited this morning," said Ruth's father nervously; "was it of Ruth you wished to speak to me?"

"Yes," said the doctor; "she seems to feel so badly about letting the children go, that it quite touched my feelings, and I thought of allowing her something for awhile, towards their support."

"Very generous of you," said Mr. Ellet, infinitely relieved; "very."

"Yes," continued the doctor, "I heard yesterday that Deacon Gray and Mrs. Rice, two very influential church members, were talking hard of you and me about this matter; yes, as you remarked, Mr. Ellet, I *am* generous, and I am *willing* to give Ruth a small sum, for an unspecified time, provided you will give her the same amount."

"*Me?*" said Mr. Ellet; "*me?*—I am a poor man, doctor; shouldn't be surprised any day, if I had to mortgage the house I live in: you wouldn't have me die in the almshouse, would you?"

"No; and I suppose you wouldn't be willing that Ruth should?" said the doctor, who could take her part when it suited him to carry a point.

"Money is tight, money is tight," said old Mr. Ellet, frowning; "when a man marries his children, they ought to be considered off his hands. I don't know why I should be called upon. Ruth went out of my family, and went into yours, and there she was when her trouble came. Money is tight, though, of course, *you* don't feel it, doctor, living here on your income with your hands folded."

"Yes, yes," retorted the doctor, getting vexed in his turn; "that all sounds very well; but the question is, what *is* my 'income'? Beside, when a man has earned his money by riding six miles of a cold night, to pull a tooth for twenty-five cents, he don't feel like throwing it away on other folks' children."

"Are not those children as much your grand-children as they are mine?" said Mr. Ellet, sharply, as he peered over his spectacles.

"Well, I don't know about that," said the doctor, taking an Aesculapian view of the case; "shouldn't think they were—blue eyes—sanguine temperament, like their mother's—not much Hall blood in 'em I fancy; more's the pity."

"It is no use being uncivil," said Mr. Ellet, reddening. "*I* never am uncivil. I came here because I thought you had something to say; if you have not, I'll go; my time is precious."

"You have not answered my question yet," said the doctor; "I asked you, if you would give the same that I would to Ruth for a time, only a *short* time?

"The fact is, Mr. Ellet," continued the doctor, forced to fall back at last upon his reserved argument; "we are both church members; and the churches to which we belong have a way (which I think is a wrong way, but that's neither here nor there) of meddling in these little family matters. It would not be very pleasant for you or me to be catechised, or disciplined by a church committee; and it's my advice to you to avoid such a disagreeable alternative; they say hard things about us. We have a Christian reputation to sustain, brother Ellet," and the doctor grew pietistic and pathetic.

Mr. Ellet looked anxious. If there was anything he particularly prided himself upon, it was his reputation for devoted piety. Here was a desperate struggle—mammon pulling one way, the church the other. The doctor saw his advantage, and followed it.

"Come, Mr. Ellet, what will you give? here's a piece of paper; put it down in black and white," said the vigilant doctor.

"Never put anything on paper, never put anything on paper," said Mr. Ellet, in a solemn tone, with a ludicrously frightened air; "parchments, lawyers, witnesses, and things, make me nervous."

"Ha! ha!" chuckled the old lady from her hiding-place in the china-closet.

"Well, then, if you won't put it on paper, *tell* me what you will give," said the persistent doctor.

"I'll *think* about it," said the frenzied Mr. Ellet, seizing his hat, as if instant escape were his only safety.

The doctor followed him into the hall.

"*DID YOU* make him do it?" asked the old lady, in a hoarse whisper, as the doctor entered.

"Yes; but it was like drawing teeth," replied the doctor. "It is astonishing how avaricious he is; he may not stick to his promise now, for he would not put it on paper, and there was no witness."

"Wasn't there though?" said the old lady, chuckling. "Trust me for that."

CHAPTER XXXVI

IN A DARK, narrow street, in one of those heterogeneous boarding-houses abounding in the city, where clerks, market-boys, apprentices, and sewing-girls, bolt their meals with railroad velocity; where the maid-of-all-work, with red arms, frowzy head, and leathern lungs, screams in the entry for any boarder who happens to be inquired for at the door; where one plate suffices for fish, flesh, fowl, and dessert; where soiled table-cloths, sticky crockery, oily cookery, and bad grammar, predominate; where greasy cards are shuffled, and bad cigars smoked of an evening, you might have found Ruth and her children.

"*JIM,* what do you think of her?" said a low-browed, pig-faced, thick-lipped fellow, with a flashy neck-tie and vest, over which several yards of gilt watch-chain were festooned ostentatiously; "prettyish, isn't she?"

"Deuced nice form," said Jim, lighting a cheap cigar, and hitching his heels to the mantel, as he took the first whiff; "I shouldn't mind kissing her."

"*You?*" said Sam, glancing in an opposite mirror; "I flatter myself you would stand a poor chance when your humble servant was round. If I had not made myself scarce, out of friendship, you would not have made such headway with black-eyed Sue, the little milliner."

"Pooh," said Jim, "Susan Gill was delf, this little widow is porcelain; I say it is a deuced pity she should stay up stairs, crying her eyes out, the way she does."

"Want to marry her, hey?" said Sam, with a sneer.

"Not I; none of your ready-made families for me; pretty foot, hasn't she? I always put on my coat in the front entry, about the time she goes up stairs, to get a peep at it. It is a confounded pretty foot, Sam, bless me if it isn't; I should like to drive the owner of it out to the race-course, some pleasant afternoon. I must say, Sam, I like widows. I don't know any occupation more interesting than helping to dry up their tears; and then the little dears are so grateful for any little attention. Wonder if my swallow-tailed coat won't be done to-day? that rascally tailor ought to be snipped with his own shears."

"*WELL, NOW,* I wonder when you gentlemen intend taking yourselves off, and quitting the drawing-room," said the loud-voiced landlady, perching a cap over her disheveled tresses; "this parlor is the only place I have to dress in; can't you do your talking and smoking in your own rooms? Come now—here's a lot of newspapers, just take them and be off, and give a woman a chance to make herself beautiful."

"Beautiful!" exclaimed Sam, "the old dragon! she would make a good scarecrow for a corn-field, or a figure-head for a piratical cruiser; beautiful!" and the speaker smoothed a wrinkle out of his flashy yellow vest; "it is my opinion that the uglier a woman is, the more beautiful she thinks herself; also, that any of the sex may be bought with a yard of ribbon, or a breastpin."

"Certainly," said Jim, "you needn't have lived to this time of life to have made that discovery; and speaking of that, reminds me that the little widow is as poor as Job's turkey. My washerwoman, confound her for ironing off my shirt-buttons, says that she wears her clothes rough-dry, because she can't afford to pay for both washing and ironing."

"She does?" replied Sam; "she'll get tired of that after awhile. I shall request 'the dragon' to-morrow, to let me sit next her at the table. I'll begin by helping the children, offering to cut up their victuals, and all that sort of thing—that will please the mother, you know; hey? But, by Jove! it's three o'clock, and I engaged to drive a gen'leman down to the steamboat landing; now some other hackney coach will get the job. Confound it!"

CHAPTER XXXVII

COUNTING HOUSES, like all other spots beyond the pale of female jurisdiction, are comfortless looking places. The counting-room of Mr. Tom Develin was no exception to the above rule; though we will do him the justice to give in our affidavit, that the ink-stand, for seven consecutive years, had stood precisely in the same spot, bounded on the north by a box of letter stamps, on the south by a package of brown business envelopes, on the east by a pen wiper, made originally in the form of a butterfly, but which frequent ink dabs had transmuted into a speckled caterpillar, on the west by half sheets of blank paper, rescued economically from business letters, to save too prodigal consumption of foolscap.

It is unnecessary to add that Mr. Tom Develin was a bachelor; perpendicular as a ram-road, moving over *terra firma* as if fearful his joints would unhinge, or his spinal column slip into his boots; carrying his *arms* with military precision; supporting his ears with a collar, never known by "the oldest inhabitant" to be limpsey; and stepping circumspectly in boots of mirror-like brightness, never defiled with the mud of the world.

Perched on his apple-sized head, over plastered wind-proof locks, was the shiniest of hats, its wearer turning neither to the right nor the left; and, although possessed of a looking-glass, laboring under the hallucination that *he*, of all masculine moderns, was most dangerous to the female heart.

Mr. Develin's book store was on the west side of Literary Row. His windows were adorned with placards of new theological publications of the blue-school order, and engravings of departed saints, who with their last breath had, with mock humility, requested brother somebody to write their obituaries. There was, also, to be seen there an occasional oil painting "for sale," selected by Mr. Develin himself, with a peculiar eye to the greenness of the trees, the blueness of the sky, and the moral "tone" of the picture.

Mr. Develin congratulated himself on his extensive acquaintance with clergymen, professors of colleges, students, scholars, and the literati generally. By dint of patient listening to their desultory conversations, he had picked up threads of information on literary subjects, which he carefully wound around his memory, to be woven into his own tête-à-têtes, where such information would "tell;" always, of course, omitting quotation marks, to which some writers, as well as conversationists, have a constitutional aversion. It is not surprising, therefore, that his tête-à-têtes should be on the *mosaic* order; the listener's interest being heightened by the fact, that he had not, when in a state of pinafore, cultivated Lindley Murray too assiduously.

Mr. Develin had fostered his bump of caution with a truly praiseworthy care. He meddled very gingerly with new publications; in fact, transacted business on the old fogy, stage-coach, rub-a-dub principle; standing back with distended eyes, and suppressed breath, in holy horror of the whistle, whiz-rush and steam of modern publishing houses. "A penny saved, is a penny gained," said this eminent financier and stationer, as he used *half a wafer* to seal his business letters.

"ANY LETTERS this morning?" said Mr. Develin to his clerk, as he deposited his umbrella in the northwest corner of his counting-room, and re-smoothed his unctuous, unruffled locks; "any letters?" and taking a package from the clerk's hand, he circumspectly lowered himself between his coat-tails into an arm-chair, and leisurely proceeded to their inspection.

"MR. DEVELIN:—

"Sir,—I take the liberty, knowing you to be one of the referees about our son's estate, which was left in a dreadful confusion, owing probably to his wife's thriftlessness, to request of you a small favor. When our son died, he left a great many clothes, vests, coats, pants, &c., which his wife, no doubt, urged his buying, and which, of course, can be of no use to her now, as she never had any boys, which we always regretted. I take my pen in hand to request you to send the clothes to me, as they will save my tailor's bill; please send, also, a circular broadcloth cloak, faced with velvet, his cane, hats, and our son's Bible, which Ruth, of course, never looks into—we wish to use it at family prayers. Please send them all at your earliest convenience. Hoping you are in good health, I am yours to command,

"ZEKIEL HALL"

Mr. Develin re-folded the letter, crossed his legs and mused. "The law allows the widow the husband's wearing apparel, but what can Ruth do with it? (as the doctor says, she has no boys,) and with her *peculiar notions*, it is not probable she would sell the clothes. The law is on her side, undoubtedly, but luckily she knows no more about law than a baby; she is poor, the doctor is a man of property; Ruth's husband was my friend to be sure, but a man must look out for No. 1 in this world, and consider a little what would be for his own interest. The doctor may leave me a little slice of property if I keep on the right side of him, who knows? The clothes must be sent."

CHAPTER XXXVIII

"'TISN'T a pretty place," said little Katy, as she looked out the window upon a row of brick walls, dingy sheds, and discolored chimneys; "'tisn't a pretty place, mother, I want to go home."

"Home!" Ruth started! the word struck a chord which vibrated—oh how painfully.

"Why *don't* we go home, mother?" continued Katy; "won't papa ever, ever, come and take us away? there is something in my throat which makes me want to cry all the time, mother," and Katy leaned her curly head wearily on her mother's shoulder.

Ruth took the child on her lap, and averting her eyes, said with a forced smile:

"Little sister don't cry, Katy."

"Because she is a little baby, and don't know anything," replied Katy; "she used to stay with Biddy, but papa used to take me to walk, and toss me up to the wall when he came home, and make rabbits with his fingers on the wall after tea, and take me on his knee and tell me about little Red Riding Hood, and—oh, I want papa, I want papa," said the child, with a fresh burst of tears.

Ruth's tears fell like rain on Katy's little up-turned face. Oh, how could she, who so much needed comfort, speak words of cheer? How could her tear-dimmed eyes and palsied hand, 'mid the gloom of so dark a night, see, and arrest a sunbeam?

"Katy, dear, kiss me; you *loved* papa—it grieved you to see him sick and suffering. Papa has gone to heaven, where there is no more sickness, no more pain. Papa is happy now, Katy."

"Happy? without *me*, and *you*, and *Nettie*," said Katy, with a grieved lip?

OH, FAR-REACHING—questioning childhood, who is sufficient for thee? How can lips, which so stammeringly repeat, 'thy will be done,' teach *thee* the lesson perfect?

CHAPTER XXXIX

"*GOOD MORNING,* Mrs. Hall," said Mr. Develin, handing Ruth the doctor's letter, and seating himself at what he considered a safe distance from a female; "I received that letter from the doctor this morning, and I think it would be well for you to attend to his request as soon as possible."

Ruth perused the letter, and handed it back with a trembling hand, saying, "'tis true the clothes are of no use, but it is a great comfort to me, Mr. Develin, to keep everything that once belonged to Harry." Then pausing a moment, she asked, "have they a *legal* right to demand those things, Mr. Develin?"

"I am not very well versed in law," replied Mr. Develin, dodging the unexpected question; "but you know the doctor doesn't bear thwarting, and your children—in fact—" Here Mr. Develin twisted his thumbs and seemed rather at a loss. "Well, the fact is, Mrs. Hall, in the present state of your affairs, you cannot afford to refuse."

"True," said Ruth, mournfully, "true."

Harry's clothes were collected from the drawers, one by one, and laid upon the sofa. Now a little pencilled memorandum fluttered from the pocket; now a handkerchief dropped upon the floor, slightly odorous of cologne, or cigars; neck-ties there were, shaped by his full round throat, with the creases still in the silken folds, and there was a crimson smoking cap, Ruth's gift—the gilt tassel slightly tarnished where it had touched the moist dark locks; then his dressing-gown, which Ruth herself had often playfully thrown on, while combing her hair—each had its little history, each its tender home associations, daguerreotyping, on tortured memory, sunny pictures of the past.

"Oh, I cannot—I cannot," said Ruth, as her eye fell upon Harry's wedding-vest; "oh, Mr. Develin, I cannot."

Mr. Develin coughed, hemmed, walked to the window, drew off his gloves, and drew them on, and finally said, anxious to terminate the interview, "I can fold them up quicker than you, Mrs. Hall."

"If you please," replied Ruth, sinking into a chair; "*this* you will leave me, Mr. Develin," pointing to the white satin vest.

"Y-e-s," said Mr. Develin, with an attempt to be facetious. "The old doctor can't use that, I suppose."

The trunk was packed, the key turned in the lock, and the porter in waiting, preceded by Mr. Develin, shouldered his burden, and followed him down stairs, and out into the street.

And there sat Ruth, with the tears dropping one after another upon the wedding vest, over which her fingers strayed caressingly. Oh, where was the heart which had throbbed so tumultuously beneath it, on that happy bridal eve? With what a dirge-like echo fell upon her tortured ear those bridal words,—"till death do us part."

CHAPTER XL

"TOM HERBERT, are you aware that this is the sixth spoonful of sugar you have put in that cup of tea? and what a forlorn face! I'd as lief look at a tombstone. Now look at *me*. Did you ever see such a fit as that boot? Is not my hair as smooth and as glossy as if I expected to dine with some other gentleman than my husband? Is not this jacket a miracle of shapeliness? Look what a foil you are to all this loveliness; lack-lustre eyes—mouth drawn down at the corners: you are a dose to contemplate."

"Mary," said her husband, without noticing her raillery; "do you remember Mrs. Hall?"

"Mrs. Hall," replied Mary; "oh, Ruth Ellet? yes; I used to go to school with her. She has lost her husband, they say."

"Yes, and a fine noble fellow he was too, and very proud of his wife. I remember he used to come into the store, and say, with one of his pleasant smiles, 'Herbert, I wonder if you have anything here handsome enough for my wife to wear.' He bought all her clothes himself, even to her gloves and boots, and was as tender and careful of her as if she were an infant. Well, to-day she came into my store, dressed in deep mourning, leading her two little girls by the hand, and asked to see me. And what do you think she wanted?"

"I am sure I don't know," said Mary, carelessly; "a yard of black crape, I suppose."

"She wanted to know," said Mr. Herbert, "if I could employ her to make up and trim those lace collars, caps, and under sleeves we sell at the store. I tell you, Mary, I could scarce keep the tears out of my eyes, she looked so sad. And then those poor little children, Mary! I thought of you, and how terrible it would be if you and our little Sue and Charley were left so destitute."

"Destitute?" replied Mary; "why her father is a man of property; her brother is in prosperous circumstances; and her cousin lives in one of the most fashionable squares in the city."

"Yes, wife, I know it; and that makes it all the harder for Mrs. Hall to get employment; because, people knowing this, take it for granted that her relatives help her, or *ought* to, and prefer to give employment to others whom they imagine need it more. This is natural, and perhaps I should have thought so too, had it been anybody but Harry Hall's wife; but all I could think of was, what Harry (poor fellow!) *would* have said, had he ever thought his little pet of a wife would have come begging to me for employment."

"What did you tell her?" said Mary.

"Why—you know the kind of work she wished, is done by forty hands, in a room directly over the store, under the superintendence of Betsy Norris; of course, they would *all* prefer doing the work at home, to coming down there to do it; but that is against our rules. I told her this, and also that if I made an exception in her favor, the forewoman would know it, because she had to prepare the work, and that would cause dissatisfaction among my hands. What do you think she said? she offered to come and sit down among those girls, and work *with* them. My God, Mary! Harry Hall's wife!"

"Of course that was out of the question, wife, for she could not bring her two children there, and she had no one to leave them with, and so she went away; and I looked after her, and those little bits of children, till they were out of sight, trying to devise some way to get her employment.

Cannot you think of anything, Mary? Are there no ladies you know, who would give her nice needlework?"

"I don't know anybody but Mrs. Slade," replied Mary, "who puts out work of any consequence, and she told me the other day that she never employed any of those persons who 'had seen better days;' that somehow she couldn't drive as good a bargain with them as she could with a common person, who was ignorant of the value of their labor."

"God help poor Mrs. Hall, then," exclaimed Herbert, "if *all* the sex are as heartless! *We* must contrive some way to help her, Mary—help her to *employment*, I mean, for I know her well enough to be sure that she would accept of assistance in no other way."

CHAPTER XLI

"*IS THIS THE HOUSE?*" said one of two ladies, pausing before Ruth's lodgings.

"I suppose so," replied the other lady; "they said it was No. 50— street, but it can't be, either; Ruth Hall couldn't live in such a place as this. Just look at that red-faced Irish girl leaning out the front window on her elbows, and see those vulgar red bar-room curtains; I declare, Mary, if Ruth Hall has got down hill so far as this, *I* can't keep up her acquaintance; just see how they stare at us here! if you choose to call you may—faugh! just smell that odor of cabbage issuing from the first entry. Come, come, Mary, take your hand off the knocker; I wouldn't be seen in that vulgar house for a kingdom."

"It seems *heartless*, though," said the other lady, blushing slightly, as she gathered up her six flounces in her delicately gloved-hand; "do you remember the afternoon we rode out to their pretty country-seat, and had that delicious supper of strawberries and cream, under those old trees? and do you remember how handsome and picturesque her husband looked in that broad Panama hat, raking up the hay when the thunder-shower came up? and how happy Ruth looked, and her children? 'Tis a dreadful change for her, I declare; if it were me, I believe I should cut my throat."

"That is probably just what her relatives would like to have her do," replied Mary, laughing; "they are as much mortified at her being here, as you and I are to be seen in such a quarter of the city."

"Why don't they provide for her, then," said the other lady, "at least till she can turn round? that youngest child is only a baby yet."

"Oh, that's *their* affair," answered Mary, "don't bother about it. Hyacinth has just married a rich, fashionable wife, and of course he cannot lose caste by associating with Ruth now; you cannot blame him."

"Well, that don't prevent him from *helping* her, does it?"

"Good gracious, Gertrude, do stop! if there's anything I hate, it is an argument. It is clearly none of our business to take her up, if her own people don't do it. Come, go to La Temps' with me, and get an ice. What a love of a collar you have on; it is handsomer than mine, which I gave fifty dollars for, but what is fifty dollars, when one fancies a thing? If I didn't make my husband's money fly, his second wife would; so I will save her ladyship that trouble;" and with an arch toss of her plumed head, the speaker and her companion entered the famous saloon of La Temps, where might be seen any sunny day, between the hours of twelve and three, the disgusting spectacle of scores of ladies devouring, *ad infinitum*, brandy-drops, Roman punch, Charlotte Russe, pies, cakes, and ices; and sipping "parfait amour," till their flushed cheeks and emancipated tongues prepared them to listen and reply to any amount of questionable nonsense from their attendant roué cavaliers.

CHAPTER XLII

"SOME FOLKS' PRIDE runs in queer streaks," said Betty, as she turned a beefsteak on the gridiron; "if I lived in such a grand house as this, and had so many fine clothes, I wouldn't let my poor cousin stand every Monday in my kitchen, bending over the wash-tub, and rubbing out her clothes and her children's, with my servants, till the blood started from her knuckles."

"Do you know what dis chil' would do, if she were Missis Ruth

Hall?" asked Gatty. "Well, she'd jess go right up on dat shed fronting de street, wid 'em, and hang 'em right out straight before all de grand neighbors, and shame Missis Millet; dat's what *dis* chil' would do."

"Poor Mrs. Ruth, she knows too much for that," replied Betty; "she shoulders that great big basket of damp clothes and climbs up one, two, three, four flights of stairs to hang them to dry in the garret. Did you see her sit down on the stairs last Monday, looking so pale about the mouth, and holding on to her side, as if she never would move again?"

"Yes, yes," said Gatty, "and here now, jess look at de fust peaches of de season, sent in for dessert; de Lor' he only knows what dey cost, but niggers musn't see noffing, not dey, if dey wants to keep dere place. But white folks *is* stony-hearted, Betty."

"Turn that steak over," said Betty; "now get the pepper; work and talk too, that's *my* motto. Yes, Gatty, I remember when Mrs. Ruth's husband used to ride up to the door of a fine morning, and toss me a large bouquet for Mrs. Millet, which Mrs. Ruth had tied up for her, or hand me a box of big strawberries, or a basket of plums, or pears, and how all our folks here would go out there and stay as long as they liked, and use the horses, and pick the fruit, and the like of that."

"Whar's her brudder, Massa Hyacinth? Wonder if *he* knows how tings is gwyin on?" asked Gatty.

"*He* knows fast enough, only he *don't* know," replied Betty, with a sly wink. "I was setting the table the other day, when Mrs. Millet read a letter from him to her husband. It seems he's got a fine place in the country, where he lives with his new bride. Poor thing, I hope he won't break her heart, as he did his first wife's. Well, he told how beautiful his place was, and how much money he had laid out on his garden, and hot-house, and things, and invited Mrs. Millet to come and see him; and then he said, 'he 'sposed Mrs. Ruth was getting on; he didn't know anything about her."

"Know about de debbel!" exclaimed Gatty, throwing down the pepper castor; "wonder whose fault dat is, Betty? 'Spose all dese folks of ours, up stairs, will go to de bressed place? When I heard Massa Millet have prayers dis morning, I jess wanted to ask him dat. You 'member what our minister, Mr. Snowball, said las' Sunday, 'bout de parabola of Dives and Lazarus, hey?"

"Parable," said Betty contemptuously. "Gatty, you are as ignorant as a hippopotamus. Come, see that steak now, done to a crisp; won't you catch it when you take it into breakfast. It is lucky I can cook and talk too."

CHAPTER XLIII

"SOMETHING FOR YOU, ma'am," said the maid-of-all-work to Ruth, omitting the ceremony of a premonitory knock, as she opened the door. "A bunch of flowers! handsome enough for Queen Victory; and a basket of apples all done up in green le'aves. It takes widders to get presents," said the girl, stowing away her tongue in her left cheek, as she partially closed the door.

"Oh, how pretty!" exclaimed little Nettie, to whom those flowers were as fair as Eve's first view of Paradise. "Give me *one* posy, mamma, only *one*;" and the little chubby hands were outstretched for a tempting rosebud.

"But, Nettie, dear, they are not for me," said Ruth; "there must be some mistake."

"Not a bit, ma'am," said the girl, thrusting her head into the half-open door; "the boy said they were 'for Mrs. Ruth Hall,' as plain as the nose on my face; and that's plain enough, for I reckon I should have got married long ago, if it hadn't been for my big nose. He was a country boy like, with a ploughman's frock on, and was as spotted in the face as a tiger-lily."

"Oh! I know," replied Ruth, with a ray of her old sunshiny smile flitting over her face; "it was Johnny Galt; he comes into market every day with vegetables. Don't you remember him, Katy? He used to drive our old Brindle to pasture, and milk her every night. You know dear papa gave him a suit of clothes on the Fourth of July, and a new hat, and leave to go to Plymouth to see his mother? Don't you remember, Katy, he used to catch butterflies for you in the meadow, and pick you nosegays of buttercups, and let you ride the pony to water, and show you where the little minnies lived in the brook? Have you forgotten the white chicken he brought you in his hat, which cried 'peep—peep,' and the cunning little speckled eggs he found for you in the woods, and the bright scarlet partridge berries he strung for a necklace for your throat, and the glossy green-oak-leaf-wreath he made for your hat?"

"Tell more—tell more," said Katy, with eyes brimming with joy; "smile more, mamma."

Aye, "Smile more, mamma." Earth has its bright spots; there must have been sunshine to make a shadow. All hearts are not calloused by selfishness; from the lips of the honest little donor goeth up each night and morning a prayer, sincere and earnest, for "the widow and the fatherless." The noisome, flaunting weeds of earth have not wholly choked the modest flower of gratitude. "Smile more, mamma!"

HOW CHEAP A THING is happiness! Golconda's mines were dross to that simple bunch of flowers! They lit the widow's gloomy room with a celestial brightness. Upon the dingy carpet Ruth placed the little vase, and dimpled limbs hovered about their brilliant petals; poising themselves daintily as the epicurean butterfly who circles, in dreamy delight, over the rose's heart, longing, yet delaying to sip its sweets.

A simple bunch of flowers, yet oh, the tale they told with their fragrant breath! "Smile, mamma!" for those gleeful children's sake; send back to the source that starting tear, ere like a lowering cloud it o'ercasts the sunshine of those beaming faces.

CHAPTER XLIV

"*MY DEAR,*" said Mrs. Millet, as the servant withdrew with the dessert, "Walter has an invitation to the Hon. David Greene's to-night."

No response from Mr. Millet, "the wooden man," one of whose pleasant peculiarities it was never to answer a question till the next day after it was addressed to him.

Mrs. Millet, quite broken in to this little conjugal eccentricity, proceeded; "It will be a good thing for John, Mr. Millet; I am anxious that all his acquaintances should be of the right sort. Hyacinth has often told me how much it made or marred a boy's fortune, the set he associated with. Herbert Greene has the air of a thorough-bred man already. You see now, Mr. Millet, the importance of Hyacinth's advice to us about five years ago, to move into a more fashionable neighborhood; to be sure rents are rather high here, but I am very sure young Snyder would never have thought of offering himself to Leila had not we lived at the court-end of the town. Hyacinth considers it a great catch in point of family, and I have no doubt Snyder is a nice fellow. I wish before you go, Mr. Millet, you would leave the money to buy Leila a velvet jacket; it will not cost more than forty dollars (lace, trimmings, and all); it will be very becoming to Leila. What, going? oh, I forgot to tell you, that Ruth's father was here this morning, bothering me just as I was dressing my hair for dinner. It seems that he is getting tired of furnishing the allowance he promised to give Ruth, and says that it is *our* turn now to do something. He is a great deal better off than we are, and so I told him; and also, that we were obliged to live in a certain style for the dear children's sake; beside, are we *not* doing something for her? I allow Ruth to do her washing in our kitchen every week, provided she finds her own soap. Stop a minute, Mr. Millet; *do* leave the forty dollars for Leila's jacket before you go. Cicchi, the artist, wants her to sit for a Madonna,—quite a pretty tribute to Leila's beauty; he only charges three hundred dollars; his study is No. 1, Clive street."

"S-t-u-d-i-o," said Mr. Millet, (slowly and oracularly, who, being on several school committees, thought it his duty to make an extra exertion, when the king's English was misapplied;) "s-t-u-d-i-o, Mrs. Millet;" and buttoning the eighth button of his overcoat, he moved slowly out the front door, and down the street to his counting-room, getting over the ground with about as much flexibility and grace of motion as the wooden horses on the stage.

CHAPTER XLV

"*COME HERE,* Katy," said Ruth, "do you think you could go *alone* to your grandfather Ellet's for once? My board bill is due to-day, and my head is so giddy with this pain, that I can hardly lift it from the pillow. Don't you think you can go without me, dear? Mrs. Skiddy is very particular about being paid the moment she sends in her bill."

"I'll try, mamma," replied little Katy, unwilling to disoblige her mother.

"Then bring your bonnet, dear, and let me tie it; be very, very careful crossing the streets, and don't loiter on the way. I have been hoping every moment to be better, but I cannot go."

"Never mind, mother," said Katy, struggling bravely with her reluctance, as she kissed her mother's cheek, and smiled a good-bye; but when she gained the crowded street, the smile faded away from the little face, her steps were slow, and her eyes downcast; for Katy, child as she was, knew that her grandfather was never glad to see them now, and his strange, cold tone when he spoke to her, always made her shiver; so little Katy threaded her way along, with a troubled, anxious, care-worn look, never glancing in at the shopkeepers' tempting windows, and quite forgetting Johnny Galt's pretty bunch of flowers, till she stood trembling with her hand on the latch of her grandfather's counting-room door.

"That *you!*" said her grandfather gruffly, from under his bent brows; "come for money *again?* Do you think your grandfather is made of money? people have to *earn* it, did you know that? I worked hard to earn mine. Have you done any thing to earn this?"

"No, Sir," said Katy, with a culprit look, twisting the corner of her apron, and struggling to keep from crying.

"Why don't your mother go to work and earn something?" asked Mr. Ellet.

"She cannot get any work to do," replied Katy; "she tries very hard, grandpa."

"Well, tell her to *keep on* trying, and you must grow up quick, and earn something too; money don't grow on trees, or bushes, did you know that? What's the reason your mother didn't come after it herself, hey?"

"She is sick," said Katy.

"Seems to me she's always sick. Well, there's a dollar," said her grandfather, looking at the bill affectionately, as he parted with it; "if you keep on coming here at this rate, you will get all my money away. Do you think it is right to come and get all my money away, hey? Remember now, you and your mother must earn some, *somehow*, d'ye hear?"

"Yes, Sir," said Katy meekly, as she closed the door.

There was a great noise and bustle in the street, and Katy was jostled hither and thither by the hurrying foot passengers; but she did not heed it, she was so busy thinking of what her grandfather had said, and wondering if she could not sell matches, or shavings, or sweep the crossings, or earn some pennies somehow, that she need never go to her grandfather again. Just then a little girl her own age, came skipping and smiling along, holding her father's hand. Katy looked at her and thought of *her* father, and then she began to cry.

"What is the matter, my dear?" said a gentleman, lifting a handful of Katy's shining curls from her face; "why do you cry, my dear?"

"I want *my* papa," sobbed Katy.

"Where is he, dear? tell me, and I will take you to him, shall I?"

"If you please, Sir," said Katy, innocently, "he has gone to heaven."

"God help you," said the gentleman, with moistened eyes, "where had you been when I met you?"

"Please, Sir—I—I—I had rather not tell," replied Katy, with a crimson blush.

"Very odd, this," muttered the gentleman; "what is your name, dear?"

"Katy, Sir."

"Katy what?" asked the gentleman. "Katy-did, I think! for your voice is as sweet as a bird's."

"Katy Hall, Sir."

"Hall? Hall?" repeated the gentleman, thoughtfully; "was your father's name Harry?"

"Yes," said Katy.

"Was he tall and handsome, with black hair and whiskers?"

"Oh, *so* handsome," replied Katy, with sparkling eyes.

"Did he live at a place called 'The Glen,' just out of the city?"

"Yes," said Katy.

"My child, my poor child," said the gentleman, taking her up in his arms and pushing back her hair from her face; "yes, here is papa's brow, and his clear, blue eyes, Katy. I used to know your dear papa."

"Yes?" said Katy, with a bright, glad smile.

"I used to go to his counting-house to talk to him on business, and I learned to love him very much, too. I never saw your mamma, though I often heard him speak of her. In a few hours, dear, I am going to sail off on the great ocean, else I would go home with you and see your mamma. Where do you live, Katy?"

"In——court," said the child. The gentleman colored and started, then putting his hand in his pocket and drawing out something that looked like paper, slipped it into little Katy's bag, saying, with delicate tact, "Tell your mamma, my dear, that is something I owed your dear papa; mind you carry it home safely; now give me a good-bye kiss, and may God forever bless you, my darling."

Little Katy stood shading her eyes with her hand till the gentleman was out of sight; it was so nice to see somebody who "loved papa;" and then she wondered why her grandfather never spoke so to her about him; and then she wished the kind gentleman were her grandpapa; and then she wondered what it was he had put in the bag for mamma; and then she recollected that her mamma told her "not to loiter;" and then she quickened her tardy little feet.

CHAPTER XLVI

KATY had been gone now a long while. Ruth began to grow anxious. She lifted her head from the pillow, took off the wet bandage from her aching forehead, and taking little Nettie upon her lap, sat down at the small window to watch for Katy. The prospect was not one to call up cheerful fancies. Opposite was one of those large brick tenements, let out by rapacious landlords, a room at a time at griping rents, to poor emigrants, and others, who were barely able to prolong their lease of life from day to day. At one window sat a tailor, with his legs crossed, and a torn straw hat perched awry upon his head, cutting and making coarse garments for the small clothing-store in the vicinity, whose Jewish owner reaped all the profits. At another, a pale-faced woman, with a handkerchief bound round her aching face, bent over a steaming wash-tub, while a little girl of ten, staggering under the weight of a basket of damp clothes, was stringing them on lines across the room to dry. At the next window sat a decrepit old woman, feebly trying to soothe in her palsied arms the wailings of a poor sick child. And there, too, sat a young girl, from dawn till dark, scarcely lifting that pallid face and weary eyes—stitching and thinking, thinking and stitching. God help her!

Still, tier above tier the windows rose, full of pale, anxious, care-worn faces—never a laugh, never a song—but instead, ribald curses, and the cries of neglected, half-fed children. From window to window, outside, were strung on lines articles of clothing, pails, baskets, pillows, feather-beds, and torn coverlets; while up and down the door-steps, in and out, passed ever a ragged procession of bare-footed women and children, to the small grocery opposite, for "a pint of milk," a "loaf of bread," a few onions, or potatoes, a cabbage, some herrings, a sixpence worth of poor tea, a pound of musty flour, a few candles, or a peck of coal—for all of which, the poor creatures paid twice as much as if they had the means to buy by the quantity.

The only window which Ruth did not shudder to look at, was the upper one of all, inhabited by a large but thrifty German family, whose love of flowers had taken root even in that sterile soil, and whose little pot of thriving foreign shrubs, outside the window sill, showed with what tenacity the heart will cling to early associations.

Further on, at one block's remove, was a more pretentious-looking house, the blinds of which were almost always closed, save when the colored servants threw them open once a day, to give the rooms an airing. Then Ruth saw damask chairs, satin curtains, pictures, vases, books, and pianos; it was odd that people who could afford such things should live in such a neighborhood. Ruth looked and wondered. Throngs of visitors went there—carriages rolled up to the door, and rolled away; gray-haired men, business men, substantial-looking family men, and foppish-looking young men; while half-grown boys loitered about the premises, looking mysteriously into the door when it opened, or into the window when a curtain was raised, or a blind flew apart.

Now and then a woman appeared at the windows. Sometimes the face was young and fair, sometimes it was wan and haggard; but, oh God! never without the stain that the bitterest tear may fail to wash away, save in the eyes of Him whose voice of mercy whispered, "Go, and sin no more."

Ruth's tears fell fast. She knew now how it could be, when every door of hope seemed shut, by those who make long prayers and wrap themselves in morality as with a garment, and cry with closed purses and averted faces, "Be ye warmed, and filled." She knew now how, when the heart, craving sympathy, craving companionship, doubting both earth and heaven, may wreck its all in one despairing moment on that dark sea, if it lose sight of Bethlehem's guiding-star. And then, she thought, "if he who saveth a soul from death shall hide a multitude of sins," oh! where, in the great reckoning-day, shall *he* be found who, 'mid the gloom of so dark a night, pilots such struggling bark on wrecking rocks?

"DEAR CHILD, I am so glad you are home," said Ruth, as Katy opened the door; "I began to fear something had happened to you. Did you see your grandfather?"

"Oh, mother!" exclaimed Katy, "please never send me to my grandpa again; he said we 'should get away all the money he had,' and he looked so dreadful when he said it, that it made my knees tremble. Is it stealing, mamma, for us to take grandpa's money away?"

"No," replied Ruth, looking a hue more pallid, if possible, than before. "No, no, Katy, don't cry; you shall never go there again for money. But, where is your bag? Why! what's this, Katy. Grandpa has made a mistake. You must run right back as quick as ever you can with this money, or I'm afraid he will be angry."

"Oh, grandpa didn't give me that," said Katy; "a gentleman gave me that."

"A gentleman?" said Ruth. "Why it is *money*, Katy. How came you to take money from a gentleman? Who was he?"

"Money!" exclaimed Katy. "Money!" clapping her hands. "Oh! I'm so glad. He didn't say it was money; he said it was something he owed papa;" and little Katy picked up a card from the floor, on which was pencilled, "For the children of Harry Hall, from their father's friend."

"Hush," whispered Katy to Nettie, "mamma is praying."

CHAPTER XLVII

"*WELL, I NEVER!*" said Biddy, bursting into Ruth's room in her usual thunder-clap way, and seating herself on the edge of a chair, as she polished her face with the skirt of her dress. "As sure as my name is Biddy, I don't know whether to laugh or to cry. Well, I've been expecting it. Folks that have ears can't help hearing when folks quarrel."

"What are you talking about?" said Ruth. "Who has quarreled? It is nothing that concerns me."

"Don't it though?" replied Biddy. "I'm thinking it *will* concern ye to pack up bag and baggage, and be off out of the house; for that's what we are all coming to, and all for Mrs. Skiddy. You see it's just here, ma'am. Masther has been threatnin' for a long time to go to Californy, where the gould is as plenty as blackberries. Well, misthress tould him, if ever he said the like o' that again, he'd rue it; and you know, ma'am, it's she that has a temper. Well, yesterday I heard high words again; and sure enough, after dinner to-day, she went off, taking Sammy and Johnny, and laving the bit nursing baby on his hands, and the boarders and all. And it's Biddy McFlanigan who'll be off, ma'am, and not be made a pack-horse of, to tend that teething child, and be here, and there, and everywhere in a minute. And so I come to bid you good-bye."

"But, Biddy—"

"Don't be afther keeping me, ma'am; Pat has shouldhered me trunk, and ye see I can't be staying when things is as they is."

THE INCESSANT CRIES of Mrs. Skiddy's bereaved baby soon bore ample testimony to the truth of Biddy's narration, appealing to Ruth's motherly sympathies so vehemently, that she left her room and went down to offer her assistance.

There sat Mr. John Skiddy, the forlorn widower, the ambitious Californian, in the middle of the kitchen, in his absconded wife's rocking-chair, trotting a seven months' baby on the sharp apex of his knee, alternately singing, whistling, and wiping the perspiration from his forehead, while the little Skiddy threw up its arms in the most frantic way, and held its breath with rage, at the awkward attempts of its dry nurse to restore peace to the family.

"Let me sweeten a little cream and water and feed that child for you, Mr. Skiddy," said Ruth. "I think he is hungry."

"Oh, thank you, Mrs. Hall," said Skiddy, with a man's determined aversion to owning "checkmated." "I am getting along famously with the little darling. Papa *will* feed him, so he *will*," said Skiddy; and, turning the maddened baby flat on his back, he poured down a whole tea-spoonful of the liquid at once; the natural consequence of which was a milky *jet d'eau* on his face, neckcloth, and vest, from the irritated baby, who resented the insult with all his mother's spirit.

Ruth adroitly looked out the window, while Mr. Skiddy wiped his face and sopped his neckcloth, after which she busied herself in picking up the ladles, spoons, forks, dredging-boxes, mortars, pestles, and other culinary implements, with which the floor was strewn, in the vain attempt to propitiate the distracted infant.

"I think I *will* spare the little dear to you a few minutes," said Skiddy, with a ghastly attempt at a smile, "while I run over to the bakery to get a loaf for tea. Mrs. Skiddy has probably been unexpectedly detained, and Biddy is so afraid of her labor in her absence, that she has taken French leave. I shall be back soon," said Skiddy, turning away in disgust from the looking-glass, as he caught sight of his limpsey dickey and collapsed shirt-bosom.

Ruth took the poor worried baby tenderly, laid it on its stomach across her lap, then loosening its frock strings, began rubbing its little fat shoulders with her velvet palm. There was a maternal magnetism in that touch; baby knew it! he stopped crying and winked his swollen eyelids with the most luxurious satisfaction, as much as to say, there, now, that's something like!

Gently Ruth drew first one, then the other, of the magnetized baby's chubby arms from its frock sleeves, substituting a comfortable loose nightdress for the tight and heated frock; then she carefully drew off its shoe, admiring the while the beauty of the little blue veined, dimpled foot, while Katy, hush as any mouse, looked on delightedly from her little cricket on the hearth, and Nettie, less philosophical, was more than half inclined to cry at what she considered an infringement of her rights.

Mr. Skiddy's reflections as he walked to the bakery were of a motley character. Upon the whole, he inclined to the opinion that it was "not good for man to be alone," especially with a nursing baby. The premeditated and unmixed malice of Mrs. Skiddy in leaving the baby, instead of Sammy or Johnny, was beyond question. Still, he could not believe that her desire for revenge would outweigh all her maternal feelings. She would return by-and-bye; but where could she have gone? People cannot travel with an empty purse; but, perhaps even now, at some tantalizing point of contiguity, she was laughing at the success of her nefarious scheme; and Mr. Skiddy's face reddened at the thought, and his arms instinctively took an a-kimbo attitude.

But then, perhaps, she *never meant* to come back. What was he to do with that baby? A wet-nurse would cost him six dollars a week; and, as to bringing up little Tommy by hand, city milk would soon finish him. And, to do Mr. Skiddy justice, though no Socrates, he was a good father to his children.

And now it was nearly dark. Was he doomed to sit up all night, tired as he was, with Tommy in one hand, and a spoon and pewter porringer in the other? Or, worse still, walk the floor in white array, till his joints, candle, and patience gave out? Then, there were the boarders to be seen to! He never realized before how *many* irons Mrs. Skiddy had daily in the fire. There was Mr. Thompson, and Mr. Johnson, on the first floor, (and his face grew hot as he thought of it,) had seen him in the kitchen looking so Miss-Nancy-like, as he superintended pots, kettles, and stews. *Stews?* there was not a dry thread on him that minute, although a cold north wind was blowing. Never mind, he was not such a fool as to tell of his little troubles; so he entered the bakery and bought an extra pie, and a loaf of plum-cake, for tea, to hoodwink the boarders into the belief that Mrs. Skiddy's presence was not at all necessary to a well-provided table.

Tea went off quite swimmingly, with Mr. John Skiddy at the urn. The baby, thanks to Ruth's maternal management, lay sweetly sleeping in his little wicker cradle, dreaming of a distant land flowing with milk and honey, and *looking* as if he was destined to a protracted nap; although it was very perceptible that Mr. Skiddy looked anxious when a door was shut hard, or a knife or fork dropped on the table; and he had several times been seen to close his teeth tightly over his lip, when a heavy cart rumbled mercilessly past.

Tea being over, the boarders dispersed their various ways; Ruth notifying Mr. Skiddy of her willingness to take the child whenever it became unmanageable. Then Mr. Skiddy, very gingerly, and with a cat-like tread, put away the tea-things, muttering an imprecation at the lid of the tea-pot, as he went, for falling off. Then, drawing the evening paper from his pocket, and unfurling it, (with one eye on the cradle,) he put up his weary legs and commenced reading the news.

Hark! a muffled noise from the cradle! Mr. Skiddy started, and applied his toe vigorously to the rocker—it was no use. He whistled—it didn't suit. He sang—it was a decided failure. Little Skiddy had caught sight of the pretty bright candle, and it was his present intention to scream till he was taken up to investigate it.

Miserable Skiddy! He recollected, now, alas! too late, that Mrs. Skiddy always carefully screened the light from Tommy's eyes while sleeping. He began to be conscious of a growing respect for Mrs. Skiddy, and a growing aversion to *her* baby. Yes; in that moment of vexation, with that unread evening paper before him, he actually called it *her* baby.

How the victimized man worried through the long evening and night—how he tried to propitiate the little tempest with the castor, the salt-cellar, its mother's work-box, and last, but not least, a silver cup he had received for his valor from the Atlantic Fire Company—how the baby, all-of-a-twist, like Dickens' young hero kept asking for "more"—how he laid it on its back, and laid it on its side, and laid it on its stomach, and propped it up on on end in a house made of pillows, and placed the candle at the foot of the bed, in the vain hope that that luminary might be graciously deemed by the infant tyrant a substitute for his individual exertions—and how, regardless of all these philanthropic efforts, little Skiddy stretched out his arms imploringly, and rooted suggestively at his father's breast, in a way to move a heart of stone—and how Mr. Skiddy said several words not to be found in the catechism—and how the daylight found him as pale as a potato sprout in a cellar, with all sorts of diagonal lines tattoed over his face by enraged little fingernails—and how the little horn, that for years had curled up so gracefully toward his nose, was missing from the corner of his moustache—are they not all written in the ambitious Californian's repentant memory?

CHAPTER XLVIII

"HOW SWEETLY they sleep," said Ruth, shading the small lamp with her hand, and gazing at Katy and Nettie; "God grant *their* names be not written, widow;" and smoothing back the damp tresses from the brow of each little sleeper, she sat down to the table, and drawing from it a piece of fine work, commenced sewing. "Only fifty-cents for all this ruffling and hemming," said Ruth, as she picked up the wick of her dim lamp; "only fifty cents! and I have labored diligently too, every spare moment, for a fortnight; this will never do," and she glanced at the little bed; "*they* must be clothed, and fed, and educated. Educated?" an idea struck Ruth; "why could not she teach school? But who would be responsible for the rent of her room? There was fuel to be furnished, and benches; what capital had *she* to start with? There was Mrs. Millet, to be sure, and her father, who, though they were always saying, "get something to do," would never assist her when she tried to do anything; how easy for them to help her to obtain a few scholars, or be responsible for her rent, till she could make a little headway. Ruth resolved, at least, to mention her project to Mrs. Millet, who could then, if she felt inclined, have an opportunity to offer her assistance in this way.

The following Monday, when her washing was finished, Ruth wiped the suds from her parboiled fingers on the kitchen roller, and ascending the stairs, knocked at the door of her cousin's chamber. Mrs. Millet was just putting the finishing touches to the sleeves of a rich silk dress of Leila's, which the mantua-maker had just returned.

"How d' ye do, Ruth," said she, in a tone which implied—what on earth do you want now?

"Very well, I thank you," said Ruth, with that sudden sinking at the heart, which even the *intonation* of a voice may sometimes give; "I can only stay a few minutes; I stopped to ask you, if you thought there was any probability of success, should I attempt to get a private school?"

"There is nothing to prevent your trying," replied Mrs. Millet, carelessly; "other widows have supported themselves; there was Mrs. Snow." Ruth sighed, for she knew that Mrs. Snow's relatives had given her letters of introduction to influential families, and helped her in various ways till she could get her head above water. "Yes," continued Mrs. Millet, laying her daughter's silk dress on the bed, and stepping back a pace or two, with her head on one side, to mark the effect of the satin bow she had been arranging; "yes—other widows support themselves, though, I am sure, I don't know how they do it—I suppose there must be a way—Leila! is that bow right? seems to me the dress needs a yard or two more lace; ten dollars will not make much difference; it will be such an improvement."

"Of course not," said Leila, "it will be a very great improvement; and by the way, Ruth, don't you want to sell me that coral pin you used to wear? it would look very pretty with this green dress."

"It was *Harry's* gift," said Ruth.

"Yes," replied Leila; "but I thought you'd be very glad to part with it for *money*."

A flush passed over Ruth's face. "Not *glad*, Leila," she replied, "for everything that once belonged to Harry is precious, though I might feel necessitated to part with it, in my present circumstances."

"Well, then," said Mrs. Millet, touching her daughter's elbow, "you'd better have it, Leila."

"Harry gave ten dollars for it," said Ruth.

"Yes, *originally*, I dare say," replied Mrs. Millet, "but nobody expects to get much for second-hand things. Leila will give you a dollar and a quarter for it, and she would like it soon, because when this north-east storm blows over, she wants to make a few calls on Snyder's relatives, in this very becoming silk dress;" and Mrs. Millet patted Leila on the shoulder.

"Good-bye," said Ruth.

"Don't forget the brooch," said Leila.

"I wish Ruth would go off into the country, or somewhere," remarked Leila, as Ruth closed the door. "I have been expecting every day that Snyder would hear of her offering to make caps in that work-shop; he is so fastidious about such things, being connected with the Tidmarshes, and that set, you know."

"Yes," said Leila's elder brother John, a half-fledged young M.D., whose collegiate and medical education enabled him one morning to astound the family breakfast-party with the astute information, "that vinegar was an acid." "Yes, I wish she would take herself off into the country, too. I had as lief see a new doctor's sign put up next door, as to see her face of a Monday, over that wash-tub, in our kitchen. I wonder if she thinks salt an improvement in soap-suds, for the last time I saw her there she was dropping in the tears on her clothes, as she scrubbed, at a showering rate; another thing, mother, I wish you would give her a lesson or two, about those children of hers. The other day I met her Katy in the street with the shabbiest old bonnet on, and the toes of her shoes all rubbed white; and she had the impertinence to call me "*cousin* John," in the hearing of young Gerald, who has just returned from abroad, and who dined with Lord Malden, in Paris. I could have wrung the little wretch's neck."

"It *was* provoking, John. I'll speak to her about it," said Mrs. Millet, "when she brings the coral pin."

CHAPTER XLIX

RUTH, after a sleepless night of reflection upon her new project, started in the morning in quest of pupils. She had no permission to refer either to her father, or to Mrs. Millet; and such being the case, the very fact of her requesting this favor of any one less nearly related, would be, of itself, sufficient to cast suspicion upon her. Some of the ladies upon whom she called were "out," some "engaged," some "indisposed," and all indifferent; besides, people are not apt to entrust their children with a person of whom they know nothing; Ruth keenly felt this disadvantage.

One lady on whom she called, "never sent her children where the teacher's own children were taught;" another preferred foreign teachers, "it was something to say that Alfred and Alfrida were 'finished' at Signor Vicchi's establishment;" another, after putting Ruth through the Catechism as to her private history, and torturing her with the most minute inquiries as to her past, present, and future, coolly informed her that "she had no children to send."

After hours of fruitless searching, Ruth, foot-sore and heart-sore, returned to her lodgings. That day at dinner, some one of the boarders spoke of a young girl, who had been taken to the Hospital in a consumption, contracted by teaching a Primary School in ——— street.

The situation was vacant; perhaps she could get it; certainly her education *ought* to qualify her to satisfy any "School Committee." Ruth inquired who they were; one was her cousin, Mr. Millet, the wooden man; one was Mr. Develin, the literary bookseller; the two others were strangers. Mr. Millet and Mr. Develin! and both aware how earnestly she longed for employment! Ruth looked at her children; yes, for their sake she would even go to the wooden man, and Mr. Develin, and ask if it were not possible for her to obtain the vacant Primary School.

CHAPTER L

MR. MILLET sat in his counting room, with his pen behind his ear, examining his ledger. "Do?" said he concisely, by way of salutation, as Ruth entered.

"I understand there is a vacancy in the 5th Ward Primary School," said Ruth; "can you tell me, as you are one of the Committee for that district, if there is any prospect of my obtaining it, and how I shall manage to do so."

"A-p-p-l-y," said Mr. Millet.

"When is the examination of applicants to take place?" asked Ruth.

"T-u-e-s-d-a-y," replied the statue.

"At what place?" asked Ruth.

"C-i-t-y–H-a-l-l," responded the wooden man, making an entry in his ledger.

Ruth's heroic resolutions to ask him to use his influence in her behalf, vanished into thin air, at this icy reserve; and, passing out into the street, she bent her slow steps in the direction of Mr. Develin's. On entering the door, she espied that gentleman through the glass door of his counting-room, sitting in his leathern arm-chair, with his hands folded, in an attitude of repose and meditation.

"Can I speak to you a moment?" said Ruth, lifting the latch of the door.

"Well—yes—certainly, Mrs. Hall," replied Mr. Develin, seizing a package of letters; "it is an uncommon busy time with me, but yes, certainly, if you have anything *particular* to say."

Ruth mentioned in as few words as possible, the Primary School, and her hopes of obtaining it, Mr. Develin, meanwhile, opening the letters and perusing their contents. When she had finished, he said, taking his hat to go out:

"I don't know but you'll stand as good a chance, Mrs. Hall, as anybody else; you can apply. But you must excuse me, for I have an invoice of books to look over, immediately."

Poor Ruth! And this was human nature, which, for so many sunny years of prosperity, had turned to her only its *bright* side! She was not to be discouraged, however, and sent in her application.

CHAPTER LI

EXAMINATION DAY CAME, and Ruth bent her determined steps to the City Hall. The apartment designated was already crowded with waiting applicants, who regarded, with jealous eye, each addition to their number as so much dimunition of their own individual chance for success.

Ruth's cheeks grew hot, as their scrutinizing and unfriendly glances were bent on her, and that feeling of utter desolation came over her, which was always so overwhelming whenever she presented herself as a suppliant for public favor. In truth, it was but a poor preparation for the inquisitorial torture before her.

The applicants were called out, one by one, in alphabetical order; Ruth inwardly blessing the early nativity of the letter H, for these anticipatory-shower-bath meditations were worse to her than the shock of a volley of chilling interrogations.

"Letter H."

Ruth rose with a flutter at her heart, and entered a huge, barren-looking room, at the further end of which sat, in august state, the dread committee. *Very* respectable were the gentlemen of whom that committee was composed; *respectable* was written all over them, from the crowns of their scholastic heads to the very tips of their polished boots; and correct and methodical as a revised dictionary they sat, with folded hands and spectacle-bestridden noses.

Ruth seated herself in the victim's chair, before this august body, facing a flood of light from a large bay-window, that nearly extinguished her eyes.

"What is your age?" asked the elder of the inquisitors.

Scratch went the extorted secret on the nib of the reporter's pen!

"Where was you educated?"

"Was Colburn, or Emerson, your teacher's standard for Arithmetic?"

"Did you cipher on a slate, or black-board?"

"Did you learn the multiplication table, skipping, or in order?"

"Was you taught Astronomy, or Philosophy, first?"

"Are you accustomed to a quill, or a steel-pen? lines, or blank-paper, in writing?"

"Did you use Smith's, or Jones' Writing-Book?"

"Did you learn Geography by Maps, or Globes?"

"Globes?" asked Mr. Squizzle, repeating Ruth's answer; "possible?"

"They use Globes at the celebrated Jerrold Institute," remarked Mr. Fizzle.

"Impossible!" retorted Mr. Squizzle, growing plethoric in the face; "Globes, sir, are exploded; no institution of any note uses Globes, sir. I know it."

"And I know you labor under a mistake," said Fizzle, elevating his chin, and folding his arms pugnaciously over his striped vest. "I am acquainted with one of the teachers in that highly-respectable school."

"And I, sir," said Squizzle, "am well acquainted with the Principal, who is a man of too much science, sir, to use globes, sir, to teach geography, sir."

At this, Mr. Fizzle settled down behind his dickey with a quenched air; and the very important question being laid on the shelf, Mr. Squizzle, handing Ruth a copy of "Pollock's Course of Time," requested her to read a marked passage, indicated by a perforation of his penknife. Poor Ruth stood about as fair a chance of proving her ability to read poetry, as would Fanny Kemble to take up a play, hap-hazard, at one of her dramatic readings, without a previous opportunity to gather up the author's connecting thread. Our heroine, however, went through the motions. This farce concluded, Ruth was dismissed into the apartment in waiting, to make room for the other applicants, each of whom returned with red faces, moist foreheads, and a "Carry-me-back-to-Old-Virginia" air.

An hour's added suspense, and the four owners of the four pair of inquisitorial spectacles marched, in procession, into the room in waiting, and wheeling "face about," with military precision, thumped on the table, and ejaculated:

"Attention!"

Instantaneously, five-and-twenty pair of eyes, black, blue, brown, and gray, were riveted; and each owner being supplied with pen, ink, and paper, was allowed ten minutes (with the four pair of spectacles levelled full at her) to express her thoughts on the following subject: "Was Christopher Columbus standing up, or sitting down, when he discovered America?"

The four watches of the committee men being drawn out, pencils began to scratch; and the terminus of the allotted minutes, in the middle of a sentence, was the place for each inspired improvisatrice to stop.

These hasty effusions being endorsed by appending each writer's signature, new paper was furnished, and "A-t-t-e-n-t-i-o-n!" was again ejaculated by a short, pursy individual, who seemed to be struggling to get out of his coat by climbing over his shirt collar. Little armies of figures were then rattled off from the end of this gentleman's tongue, with "Peter Piper Pipkin" velocity, which the anxious pen-women in waiting were expected to arrest in flying, and have the "sum total of the hull," as one of the erudite committee observed, already added up, when the illustrious arithmetician stopped to take wind.

This being the finale, the ladies were sapiently informed that, as only *one* school mistress was needed, only *one* out of the large number of applicants could be elected, and that "the Committee would now sit on them."

At this gratifying intelligence, the ladies, favored by a plentiful shower of rain, betook themselves to their respective homes; four-and-twenty, God help them! to dream of a reprieve from starvation, which, notwithstanding the six-hours' purgatory they had passed through, was destined to elude their eager grasp.

The votes were cast. Ruth was *not* elected. She had been educated, (whether fortunately or unfortunately, let the sequel of my story decide,) at a school where "Webster" was used instead of "Worcester." The greatest gun on the Committee was a Worcesterite. Mr. Millet and Mr. Develin always followed in the wake of *great* guns. Mr. Millet and Mr. Develin voted *against* Ruth.

CHAPTER LII

IT WAS FOUR O'CLOCK in the afternoon, and very tranquil and quiet at the Skiddy's. A tidy, rosy-cheeked young woman sat rocking the deserted little Tommy to sleep, to the tune of "I've been roaming." The hearth was neatly swept, the tin and pewter vessels hung, brightly polished, from their respective shelves. The Maltese cat lay winking in the middle of the floor, watching the play of a stray sunbeam, which had found its way over the shed and into the small window. Ruth and her children were quiet, as usual, in their gloomy back chamber. Mr. Skiddy, a few blocks off, sat perched on a high stool, in the counting-room of Messrs. Fogg & Co.

Noiselessly the front-door opened, and the veritable Mrs. Skiddy, followed by Johnny and Sammy, crept through the front entry and entered, unannouned, into the kitchen. The rosy-cheeked young woman looked at Mrs. Skiddy, Mrs. Skiddy looked at her, and Tommy looked at both of them. Mrs. Skiddy then boxed the rosy-cheeked young woman's ears, and snatching the bewildered baby from her grasp, ejected her, with lightning velocity, through the street-door, and turned the key. It was all the work of an instant. Sammy and Johnny were used to domestic whirlwinds, so they were not surprised into any little remarks or exclamations, but the cat, less philosophical, laid back her ears, and made for the ash-hole; while Mrs. Skiddy, seating herself in the rocking-chair, unhooked her traveling dress and reinstated the delighted Tommy into all his little infantile privileges.

Mr. Skiddy had now been a whole week a widower; time enough for a man in that condition to grow philosophical. In fact, Skiddy was content. He had tasted the sweets of liberty, and he liked them. The baby, poor little soul, tired of remonstrance, had given out from sheer weariness, and took resignedly as a little Christian to his pewter porringer. Yes, Skiddy liked it; he could be an hour behind his time without dodging, on his return, a rattling storm of abuse and crockery; he could spend an evening out, without drawing a map of his travels before starting. On the afternoon in question he felt particularly felicitous: first, because he had dined off fried liver and potatoes, a dish which he particularly affected, and which, on that very account, he could seldom get in his own domicil; secondly, he was engaged to go that very evening with his old love, Nancy Spriggins, to see the "Panorama of Niagara;" and he had left orders with Betty to have tea half an hour earlier in consequence, and to be sure and iron and air his killing plaid vest by seven o'clock.

As the afternoon waned, Skiddy grew restless; he made wrong entries in the ledger; dipped his pen into the sand-box instead of the inkstand, and several times said "Yes, dear," to his employer, Mr. Fogg, of Fogg Square.

Six o'clock came at last, and the emancipated Skiddy, turning his back on business, walked towards home, in peace with himself, and in love with Nancy Spriggins. On the way he stopped to purchase a bouquet of roses and geraniums with which to regale that damsel's olfactories during the evening's entertainment.

Striding through the front entry, like a man who felt himself to be master of his own house, Skiddy hastened to the kitchen to expedite tea. If he was not prepared for Mrs. Skiddy's departure, still less was he prepared for her return, especially with that tell-tale bouquet in his hand. But, like all other hen-pecked husbands, on the back of the scape-goat *Cunning*, he fled away from the uplifted lash.

"My *dear* Matilda," exclaimed Skiddy, "my own wife, how *could* you be so cruel? Every day since your departure, hoping to find you here on my return from the store, I have purchased a bouquet like this to present you. My dear wife, let by-gones *be* by-gones; my love for you is imperishable."

"V-e-r-y good, Mr. Skiddy," said his wife, accepting Nancy Spriggins's bouquet, with a queenly nod; "and now let us have no more talk of *California*, if you please, Mr. Skiddy."

"Certainly not, my darling; I was a brute, a beast, a wretch, a Hottentot, a cannibal, a vampire—to distress you so. Dear little Tommy! how pleasant it seems to see him in your arms again."

"Yes," replied Mrs. Skiddy, "I was not five minutes in sending that red-faced German girl spinning through the front-door; I hope you have something decent for us to eat, Skiddy. Johnny and Sammy are pretty sharp-set; why don't you come and speak to your father, boys!"

The young gentlemen thus summoned, slowly came forward, looking altogether undecided whether it was best to notice their father or not. A ginger-cake, however, and a slice of buttered bread, plentifully powdered with sugar, wonderfully assisted them in coming to a decision. As to Nancy Spriggins, poor soul, she pulled off her gloves, and pulled them on, that evening, and looked at her watch, and looked up street and down street, and declared, as "the clock told the hour for retiring," that man was a ———, a ———, in short, that woman was born to trouble, as the sparks are—to fly away.

MRS. SKIDDY resumed her household duties with as much coolness as if there had been no interregnum, and received the boarders at tea that night, just as if she had parted with them that day at dinner. Skiddy was apparently as devoted as ever; the uninitiated boarders opened their eyes in bewildered wonder; and *triumph* sat inscribed on the arch of Mrs. Skiddy's imposing Roman nose.

The domestic horizon still continued cloudless at the next morning's breakfast. After the boarders had left the table, the market prices of beef, veal, pork, cutlets, chops, and steaks, were discussed as usual, the bill of fare for the day was drawn up by Mrs. Skiddy, and her obedient spouse departed to execute her market orders.

CHAPTER LIII

"*WELL,* I hope you have been comfortable in my absence, Mrs. Hall," said Mrs. Skiddy, after despatching her husband to market, as she seated herself in the chair nearest the door; "ha! ha! John and I may call it quits now. He is a very good fellow—John; except these little tantrums he gets into once in a while; the only way is, to put a stop to it at once, and let him see who is master. John never will set a river on fire; there's no sort of use in his trying to take the reins—the man wasn't born for it. I'm too sharp for him, that's a fact. Ha! ha! poor Johnny! I *must* tell you what a trick I played him about two years after our marriage."

"You must know he had to go away on business for Fogg & Co., to collect bills, or something of that sort. Well, he made a great fuss about it, as husbands who like to go away from home always do; and said he should 'pine for the sight of me, and never know a happy hour till he saw me again,' and all that; and finally declared he would not go, without I would let him take my Daguerreotype. Of course, I knew that was all humbug; but I consented. The likeness was pronounced 'good,' and placed *by me* in his travelling trunk, when I packed his clothes. Well, he was gone a month, and when he came back, he told me (great fool) what a comfort my Daguerreotype was to him, and how he had looked at it twenty times a day, and kissed it as many more; whereupon I went to his trunk, and opening it, took out the case and showed it to him—*without the plate*, which I had taken care to slip out of the frame just before he started, and which he had never found out! That's a specimen of John Skiddy!—and John Skiddy is a fair specimen of the rest of his sex, let me tell you, Mrs. Hall. Well, of course he looked sheepish enough; and now, whenever I want to take the nonsense out of him, all I have to do is to point to that Daguerreotype case, which I keep lying on the mantel on purpose. When a woman is married,

Mrs. Hall, she must make up her mind either to manage, or to be managed; *I* prefer to manage," said the amiable Mrs. Skiddy; "and I flatter myself John understands it by this time. But, dear me, I can't stand here prating to you all day. I must look round and see what mischief has been done in my absence, by that lazy-looking red-faced German girl," and Mrs. Skiddy laughed heartily, as she related how she had sent her spinning through the front door the night before.

Half the forenoon was occupied by Mrs. Skiddy in counting up spoons, forks, towels, and baby's pinafores, to see if they had sustained loss or damage during her absence.

"Very odd dinner don't come," said she, consulting the kitchen clock; "it is high time that beef was on, roasting."

It *was* odd—and odder still that Skiddy had not appeared to tell her *why* the dinner didn't come. Mrs. Skiddy wasted no time in words about it. No; she seized her bonnet, and went immediately to Fogg & Co., to get some tidings of him; they were apparently quite as much at a loss as herself to account for Skiddy's nonappearance. She was just departing, when one of the subclerks, whom the unfortunate Skiddy had once snubbed, whispered a word in her ear, the effect of which was instantaneous. Did she let the grass grow under her feet till she tracked Skiddy to "the wharf," and boarded the "Sea-Gull," bound for California, and brought the crest-fallen man triumphantly back to his domicil, amid convulsions of laughter from the amused captain and his crew? No.

"There, now," said his amiable spouse, untying her bonnet," there's *another* flash in the pan, Skiddy. Anybody who thinks to circumvent Matilda Maria Skiddy, must get up early in the morning, and find themselves too late at that. Now hold this child," dumping the doomed baby into his lap, "while I comb my hair. Goodness knows you weren't worth bringing back; but when I set out to have my own way, Mr. Skiddy, Mount Vesuvius shan't stop me."

Skiddy tended the baby without a remonstrance; he perfectly understood, that for a probationary time he should be put "on the limits," the street-door being the boundary line. He heaved no sigh when his coat and hat, with the rest of his wearing apparel, were locked up, and the key buried in the depths of his wife's pocket. He played with Tommy, and made card-houses for Sammy and Johnny, wound several tangled skeins of silk for "Maria Matilda," mended a broken button on the closet door, replaced a missing knob on one of the bureau drawers, and appeared to be in as resigned and proper a frame of mind as such a perfidious wretch could be expected to be in.

Two or three weeks passed in this state of incarceration, during which the errand-boy of Fogg & Co. had been repeatedly informed by Mrs. Skiddy, that the doctor hoped Mr. Skiddy would soon be sufficiently convalescent to attend to business. As to Skiddy, he continued at intervals to shed crocodile tears over his past shortcomings, or rather his short-*goings!* In consequence of this apparently submissive frame of mind, he, one fine morning, received total absolution from Mrs. Skiddy, and leave to go to the store; which Skiddy peremptorily declined, desiring, as he said, to test the sincerity of his repentance by a still longer period of probation.

"Don't be a fool, Skiddy," said Maria Matilda, pointing to the Daguerreotype case, and then crowding his beaver down over his eyes; "don't be a fool. Make a B line for the store, now, and tell Fogg you've had an attack of *room-a-tism;*" and Maria Matilda laughed at her wretched pun.

Skiddy obeyed. No Uriah Heep could have out-done him in "'umbleness," as he crept up the long street, until a friendly corner hid him from the lynx eyes of Maria Matilda. Then "Richard was himself again"! Drawing a long breath, our flying Mercury whizzed past the mile-stones, and, before sun-down of the same day, was under full sail for California.

JUST ONE HALF HOUR our Napoleon in petticoats spent in reflection, after being satisfied that Skiddy was really "on the deep blue sea." In one day she had cleared her house of *boarders*, and reserving one room for herself and children, filled all the other apartments with *lodgers*; who paid her good prices, and taking their meals down town, made her no trouble beyond the care of their respective rooms.

About a year after a letter came from Skiddy. He was "disgusted" with ill-luck at gold-digging, and ill-luck everywhere else; he had been "burnt out," and "robbed," and everything else but murdered; and "'umbly" requested his dear Maria Matilda to send him the "passage-money to return home."

Mrs. Skiddy's picture should have been taken at that moment! My pen fails! Drawing from her pocket a purse well filled with her own honest earnings, she chinked its contents at some phantom shape discernible to her eyes alone; while through her set teeth hissed out, like ten thousand serpents, the word

"N—e—v—e—r!"

CHAPTER LIV

"*WHAT IS IT* on the gate? Spell it, mother," said Katy, looking wistfully through the iron fence at the terraced banks, smoothly-rolled gravel walks, plats of flowers, and grape-trellised arbors; "what is it on the gate, mother?"

"'Insane Hospital,' dear; a place for crazy people."

"Want to walk round, ma'am?" asked the gate-keeper, as Katy poked her little head in; "can, if you like." Little Katy's eyes pleaded eloquently; flowers were to her another name for happiness, and Ruth passed in.

"I should like to live here, mamma," said Katy.

Ruth shuddered, and pointed to a pale face pressed close against the grated window. Fair rose the building in its architectural proportions; the well-kept lawn was beautiful to the eye; but, alas! there was helpless age, whose only disease was too long a lease of life for greedy heirs. There, too, was the fragile wife, to whom *love* was breath—being!—forgotten by the world and him in whose service her bloom had withered, insane—only in that her love had outlived his patience.

"Poor creatures!" exclaimed Ruth, as they peered out from one window after another. "Have you had many deaths here?" asked she of the gate-keeper.

"Some, ma'am. There is one corpse in the house now; a married lady, Mrs. Leon."

"Good heavens!" exclaimed Ruth, "my friend Mary."

"Died yesterday, ma'am; her husband left her here for her health, while he went to Europe."

"Can I see the Superintendent," asked Ruth; "I must speak to him."

Ruth followed the gate-keeper up the ample steps into a wide hall, and from thence into a small parlor; after waiting what seemed to her an age of time, Mr. Tibbetts, the Superintendent, entered. He was a tall, handsome man, between forty and fifty, with a very imposing air and address.

"I am pained to learn," said Ruth, "that a friend of mine, Mrs. Leon, lies dead here; can I see the body?"

"Are you a relative of that lady?" asked Mr. Tibbetts, with a keen glance at Ruth.

"No," replied Ruth, "but she was very dear to me. The last time I saw her, not many months since, she was in tolerable health. Has she been long with you, Sir?"

"About two months," replied Mr. Tibbetts; "she was hopelessly crazy, refused food entirely, so that we were obliged to force it. Her husband, who is an intimate friend of mine, left her under my care, and went to the Continent. A very fine man, Mr. Leon."

Ruth did not feel inclined to respond to this remark, but repeated her request to see Mary.

"It is against the rules of our establishment to permit this to any but relatives," said Mr. Tibbetts.

"I should esteem it a great favor if you would break through your rules in my case," replied Ruth; "it will be a great consolation to me to have seen her once more;" and her voice faltered.

The appeal was made so gently, yet so firmly, that Mr. Tibbetts reluctantly yielded.

The matron of the establishment, Mrs. Bunce, (whose advent was heralded by the clinking of a huge bunch of keys at her waist,) soon after came in. Mrs. Bunce was gaunt, sallow and bony, with restless, yellowish, glaring black eyes, very much resembling those of a cat in the dark; her motions were quick, brisk, and angular; her voice loud, harsh, and wiry. Ruth felt an instantaneous aversion to her; which was not lessened by Mrs. Bunce asking, as they passed through the parlor-door:

"Fond of looking at corpses, ma'am? I've seen a great many in my day; I've laid out more'n twenty people, first and last, with my own hands.

Relation of Mrs. Leon's, perhaps?" said she, curiously peering under Ruth's bonnet. "Ah, only a friend?"

"This way, if you please, ma'am;" and on they went, through one corridor, then another, the massive doors swinging heavily to on their hinges, and fastening behind them as they closed.

"Hark!" said Ruth, with a quick, terrified look, "what's that?"

"Oh, nothing," replied the matron, "only a crazy woman in that room yonder, screaming for her child. Her husband ran away from her and carried off her child with him, to spite her, and now she fancies every footstep she hears is his. Visitors always thinks she screams awful. She can't harm you, ma'am," said the matron, mistaking the cause of Ruth's shudder, "for she is chained. She went to law about the child, and the law, you see, as it generally is, was on the man's side; and it just upset her. She's a sight of trouble to manage. If she was to catch sight of your little girl out there in the garden, she'd spring at her through them bars like a panther; but we don't have to whip her *very* often."

"Down here," said the matron, taking the shuddering Ruth by the hand, and descending a flight of stone steps, into a dark passage-way. "Tired arn't you?"

"Wait a bit, please," said Ruth, leaning against the stone wall, for her limbs were trembling so violently that she could scarcely bear her weight.

"*Now*," said she, (after a pause,) with a firmer voice and step.

"This way," said Mrs. Bunce, advancing towards a rough deal box which stood on a table in a niche of the cellar, and setting a small lamp upon it; "she didn't look no better than that, ma'am, for a long while before she died."

Ruth gave one hurried glance at the corpse, and buried her face in her hands. Well might she fail to recognize in that emaciated form, those sunken eyes and hollow cheeks, the beautiful Mary Leon. Well might she shudder, as the gibbering screams of the maniacs over head echoed through the stillness of that cold, gloomy vault.

"Were you with her at the last?" asked Ruth of the matron, wiping away her tears.

"No," replied she; "the afternoon she died she said, 'I want to be alone,' and, not thinking her near her end, I took my work and sat just outside the door. I looked in once, about half an hour after, but she lay quietly asleep, with her cheek in her hand,—so. By-and-bye I thought I would speak to her, so I went in, and saw her lying just as she did when I looked at her before. I spoke to her, but she did not answer me; she was dead, ma'am."

O, HOW MOURNFULLY sounded in Ruth's ears those plaintive words, "I want to be alone." Poor Mary! aye, better even in death "alone," than gazed at by careless, hireling eyes, since he who should have closed those drooping lids, had wearied of their faded light.

"Did she speak of no one?" asked Ruth; "mention no one?"

"No—yes; I recollect now that she said something about calling Ruth; I didn't pay any attention, for they don't know what they are saying, you know. She scribbled something, too, on a bit of paper; I found it under her pillow, when I laid her out. I shouldn't wonder if it was in my pocket now; I haven't thought of it since. Ah! here it is," said Mrs. Bunce, as she handed the slip of paper to Ruth.

It ran thus:—"I am not crazy, Ruth, no, no—but I shall be; the air of this place stifles me; I grow weaker—weaker. I cannot die here; for the love of heaven, dear Ruth, come and take me away."

"*ONLY THREE MOURNERS,*—a woman and two little girls," exclaimed a by-stander, as Ruth followed Mary Leon to her long home.

CHAPTER LV

THE SUDDEN CHANGE in Mrs. Skiddy's matrimonial prospects, necessitated Ruth to seek other quarters. With a view to still more rigid economy, she hired a room without board, in the lower part of the city.

Mrs. Waters, her new landlady, was one of that description of females, whose vision is bounded by a mop, scrubbing-brush, and dust-pan; who repudiate rainy washing days; whose hearth, Jowler, on the stormiest night, would never venture near without a special permit, and whose husband and children speak under their breath on baking and cleaning days. Mrs. Waters styled herself a female physician. She kept a sort of witch's cauldron constantly boiling over the fire, in which seethed all sorts of "mints" and "yarbs," and from which issued what she called a "potecary odor." Mrs. Waters, when not engaged in stirring this cauldron, or in her various housekeeping duties, alternated her leisure in reading medical books, attending medical lectures, and fondling a pet skull, which lay on the kitchen-dresser.

Various little boxes of brown-bread-looking pills ornamented the upper shelf, beside a row of little dropsical chunky junk bottles, whose labels would have puzzled the most erudite M.D. who ever received a diploma. Mrs. Waters felicitated herself on knowing how the outer and inner man of every son of Adam was put together, and considered the times decidedly "out of joint;" inasmuch that she, Mrs. Waters, had not been called upon by her country to fill some medical professorship.

In person Mrs. Waters was barber-pole-ish and ramrod-y, and her taste in dress running mostly to stringy fabrics, assisted the bolster-y impression she created; her hands and wrists bore a strong resemblance to the yellow claws of defunct chickens, which children play "scare" with about Thanksgiving time; her feet were of turtle flatness, and her eyes—if you ever provoked a cat up to the bristling and scratching point, you may possibly form an idea of them.

Mrs. Waters condescended to allow Ruth to keep the quart of milk and loaf of bread, (which was to serve for her bill of fare for every day's three meals,) on a swing shelf in a corner of the cellar. As Ruth's room was at the top of the house, it was somewhat of a journey to travel up and down, and the weather was too warm to keep it up stairs; to her dismay she soon found that the cellar-floor was generally more or less flooded with water, and the sudden change from the heated air of her attic to the dampness of the cellar, brought on a racking cough, which soon told upon her health. Upon the first symptom of it, Mrs. Waters seized a box of pills and hurried to her room, assuring her that it was "a sure-cure, and only three shillings a box."

"Thank you," said Ruth; "but it is my rule never to take medicine unless—"

"Oh, oh," said Mrs. Waters, bridling up; "I see—unless it is ordered by a physician, you were going to say; perhaps you don't know that *I* am a physician—none the worse for being a female. I have investigated things; I have dissected several cats, and sent in an analysis of them to the Medical Journal; it has never been published, owing, probably, to the editor being out of town. If you will take six of these pills every other night," said the doctress, laying the box on the table, "it will cure your cough; it is only three shillings. I will take the money now, or charge it in your bill."

"Three shillings!" Ruth was aghast; she might as well have asked her three dollars. If there was anything Ruth was afraid of, it was Mrs. Waters' style of woman; a loaded cannon, or a regiment of dragoons, would have had few terrors in comparison. But the music must be faced; so, hoping to avoid treading on her landlady's professional toes, Ruth said, "I think I'll try first what dieting will do, Mrs. Waters."

The door instantly banged to with a crash, as the owner and vender of the pills passed out. The next day Mrs. Waters drew off a little superfluous feminine bile, by announcing to Ruth, with a malignity worthy of her sex, "that she forgot to mention when she let her lodgings, that she should expect her to scour the stairs she traveled over, at least once a week."

CHAPTER LVI

IT WAS A SULTRY MORNING in July. Ruth had risen early, for her cough seemed more troublesome in a reclining posture. "I wonder what that noise can be?" said she to herself; whir—whir—whir, it went, all day long in the attic overhead. She knew that Mrs. Waters had one other lodger beside herself, an elderly gentleman by the name of Bond, who cooked his own food, and whom she often met on the stairs, coming up with a pitcher of water, or a few eggs in a paper bag, or a pie that he had bought of Mr. Flake, at the little black grocery-shop at the corner. On these occasions he always stepped aside, and with a deferential bow waited for Ruth to pass. He was a thin, spare man, slightly bent; his hair and whiskers curiously striped like a zebra, one lock being jet black, while the neighboring one was as distinct a white. His dress was plain, but very neat and tidy. He never seemed to have any business out-doors, as he stayed in his room all day, never leaving it at all till dark, when he paced up and down, with his hands behind him, before the house. "Whir—whir—whir." It was early sunrise; but Ruth had heard that odd noise for two hours at least. What *could* it mean? Just than a carrier passed on the other side of the street with the morning papers, and slipped one under the crack of the house door opposite.

A thought! why could not Ruth write for the papers? How very odd it had never occurred to her before? Yes, write for the papers—why not? She remembered that while at boarding-school, an editor of a paper in the same town used often to come in and take down her compositions in short-hand as she read them aloud, and transfer them to the columns of his paper. She certainly *ought* to write better now than she did when an inexperienced girl. She would begin that very night; but where to make a beginning? who would publish her articles? how much would they pay her? to whom should she apply first? There was her brother Hyacinth, now the prosperous editor of the Irving Magazine; oh, if he would only employ her? Ruth was quite sure she could write as well as some of his correspondents, whom he had praised with no niggardly pen. She would prepare samples to send immediately, announcing her intention, and offering them for his acceptance. This means of support would be so congenial, so absorbing. At the needle one's mind could still be brooding over sorrowful thoughts.

Ruth counted the days and hours impatiently, as she waited for an answer. Hyacinth surely would not refuse *her* when in almost every number of his magazine he was announcing some new contributor; or, if *he* could not employ her *himself*, he surely would be brotherly enough to point out to her some one of the many avenues so accessible to a man of extensive newspaperial and literary acquaintance. She would so gladly support herself, so cheerfully toil day and night, if need be, could she only win an independence; and Ruth recalled with a sigh Katy's last visit to her father, and then she rose and walked the floor in her impatience; and then, her restless spirit urging her on to her fate, she went again to the post office to see if there were no letter. How long the clerk made her wait! Yes, there *was* a letter for her, and in her brother's hand-writing too. Oh, how long since she had seen it!

Ruth heeded neither the jostling of office-boys, porters, or draymen, as she held out her eager hand for the letter. Thrusting it hastily in her pocket, she hurried in breathless haste back to her lodgings. The contents were as follows:

> "I have looked over the pieces you sent me, Ruth. It is very evident that writing never can be *your* forte; you have no talent that way. You may possibly be employed by some inferior newspapers, but be assured your articles never will be heard of out of your own little provincial city. For myself I have plenty of contributors, nor do I know of any of my literary acquaintances who would employ you. I would advise you, therefore, to seek some *unobtrusive* employment. Your brother,
>
> "HYACINTH ELLET."

A bitter smile struggled with the hot tear that fell upon Ruth's cheek. "I have tried the unobtrusive employment," said Ruth; "the wages are six cents a day, Hyacinth;" and again the bitter smile disfigured her gentle lip.

"No talent!"

"At another tribunal than his will I appeal."

"Never be heard of out of my own little provincial city!" The cold, contemptuous tone stung her.

"But they shall be heard of;" and Ruth leaped to her feet. "Sooner than he dreams of, too. I *can* do it, I *feel* it, I *will* do it," and she closed her lips firmly; "but there will be a desperate struggle first," and she clasped her hands over her heart as if it had already commenced; "there will be scant meals, and sleepless nights, and weary days, and a throbbing brow, and an aching heart; there will be the chilling tone, the rude repulse; there will be ten backward steps to one forward. *Pride* must sleep! but—" and Ruth glanced at her children—"it shall be *done*. They shall be proud of their mother. *Hyacinth shall yet be proud to claim his sister.*"

"What is it, mamma?" asked Katy, looking wonderingly at the strange expression of her mother's face.

"What is it, my darling?" and Ruth caught up the child with convulsive energy; "what is it? only that when you are a woman you shall remember this day, my little pet;" and as she kissed Katy's upturned brow a bright spot burned on her cheek, and her eye glowed like a star.

CHAPTER LVII

"*DOCTOR?*" said Mrs. Hall, "put down that book, will you? I want to talk to you a bit; there you've sat these three hours, without stirring, except to brush the flies off your nose, and my tongue actually aches keeping still."

"Sh-sh-sh," said the doctor, running his forefinger along to guide his purblind eyes safely to the end of the paragraph. "Sh-sh. 'It—is es-ti-ma-ted by Captain Smith—that—there—are—up'ards—of—ten—hundred—human—critters—in—the—Nor-West—sett-le-ment.' Well—Mis. Hall—well—" said the doctor, laying a faded ribbon mark between the leaves of the book, and pushing his spectacles back on his forehead, "what's to pay now? what do you want of me?"

"I've a great mind as ever I had to eat," said the old lady, pettishly, "to knit twice round the heel of this stocking, before I answer you; what do you think I care about Captain Smith? Travelers always lie; it is a part of their trade, and if they don't it's neither here nor there to me. I wish that book was in the Red Sea."

"I thought you didn't want it *read*," retorted the irritating old doctor.

"Now I suppose you call that funny," said the old lady. "I call it simply ridiculous for a man of your years to play on words in such a frivolous manner. What I was going to say was this, *i.e.* if I can get a chance to say it, if *you* have given up all idea of getting Harry's children, *I* haven't, and now is the time to apply for Katy again; for, according to all accounts, Ruth is getting along poorly enough."

"How did you hear?" asked the doctor.

"Why, my milliner, Miss Tiffkins, has a nephew who tends in a little grocery-shop near where Ruth boards, and he says that she buys a smaller loaf every time she comes to the store, and that the milkman told him that she only took a pint of milk a day of him now; then Katy has not been well, and what she did for doctors and medicines is best known to herself; she's so independent that she never would complain if she had to eat paving stones. The best way to get the child will be to ask her here on a visit, and say we want to cure her up a little with country air. You understand? that will throw dust in Ruth's eyes, and then we will take our own time about letting her go back you know. Miss Tiffkins says her nephew says that people who come into the grocery-shop are very curious to know who Ruth is; and old Mr. Flake, who keeps it, says that it wouldn't hurt her any, if she is a lady, to stop and talk a little, like the rest of his customers; he says, too, that her children are as close-mouthed as their mother, for when he just asked Katy what business her father used to do, and what supported them now he was dead, and if they lived all the time on bread and milk, and a few such little questions, Katy answered, 'Mamma does not allow me to talk to strangers,' and went out of the shop, with her loaf of bread, as dignified as a little duchess."

"Like mother, like child," said the doctor; "proud and poor, proud and poor; that tells the whole story. Well, shall I write to Ruth, Mis. Hall, about Katy?"

"No," said the old lady, "let me manage that; you will upset the whole business if you do. I've a plan in my head, and to-morrow, after breakfast, I'll take the old chaise, and go in after Katy."

In pursuance of this plan, the old lady, on the following day, climbed up into an old-fashioned chaise, and turned the steady old horse's nose in the direction of the city; jerking at the reins, and clucking and gee-ing him up, after the usual awkward fashion of sexegenarian female drivers. Using Miss Tiffkins's land-mark, the little black grocery-shop, for a guide-board, she soon discovered Ruth's abode; and so well did she play her part in commiserating Ruth's misfortunes, and Katy's sickly appearance, that the widow's kind heart was immediately tortured with the most unnecessary self-reproaches, which prepared the way for an acceptance of her invitation for Katy "for a week or two;" great promises, meanwhile, being held out to the child of "a little pony to ride," and various other tempting lures of the same kind. Still little Katy hesitated, clinging tightly to her mother's dress, and looking, with her clear, searching eyes, into her grandmother's face, in a way that would have embarrassed a less artful manœuverer. The old lady understood the glance, and put it on file, to be attended to at her leisure; it being no part of her present errand to play the unamiable. Little Katy, finally won over, consented to make the visit, and the old chaise was again set in motion for home.

CHAPTER LVIII

"HOW D'YE DO, RUTH?? asked Mr. Ellet, the next morning, as he ran against Ruth in the street; "glad you have taken my advice, and done a sensible thing at last."

"I don't know what you mean," answered Ruth.

"Why, the doctor told me yesterday that you had given Katy up to them, to bring up; you would have done better if you had sent off Nettie too."

"I have not 'given Katy up,'" said Ruth, starting and blushing deeply; "and they could not have understood it so; she has only gone on a visit of a fortnight, to recruit a little."

"Pooh—pooh!" replied Mr. Ellet. "The thing is quietly over with; now don't make a fuss. The old folks expect to keep her. They wrote to me about it, and I approved of it. It's the best thing all round; and, as I just said, it would have been better still if Nettie had gone, too. Now don't make a fool of yourself; you can go once in awhile, I suppose, to see the child."

"*How* can I go?" asked Ruth, looking her father calmly in the face; "it costs fifty cents every trip, by railroad, and you know I have not the money."

"That's for you to decide," answered the father coldly; "I can't be bothered about such trifles. It is the way you always do, Ruth, whenever I see you; but it is time I was at my office. Don't make a fool of yourself, now; mind what I tell you, and let well alone."

"Father," said Ruth; "father—"

"Can't stop—can't stop," said Mr. Ellet, moving rapidly down street, to get out of his daughter's way.

"Can it be possible," thought Ruth, looking after him, "that he could connive at such duplicity? Was the old lady's sympathy a mere stratagem to work upon my feelings? How unnecessarily I reproached myself with my supposed injustice to her? Can *good* people do such things? Is religion only a fable? No, no; 'let God be true, and every man a liar.'"

CHAPTER LIX

"*IS THIS* 'The Daily Type' office?" asked Ruth of a printer's boy, who was rushing down five steps at a time, with an empty pail in his hand.

"All you have to do is to ask, mem. You've got a tongue in your head, haven't ye? women folks generally has," said the little ruffian.

Ruth, obeying this civil invitation, knocked gently at the office door. A whir of machinery, and a bad odor of damp paper and cigar smoke, issued through the half-open crack.

"I shall have to walk in," said Ruth, "they never will hear my feeble knock amid all this racket and bustle;" and pushing the door ajar, she found herself in the midst of a group of smokers, who, in slippered feet, and with heels higher than their heads, were whiffing and laughing, amid the pauses of conversation, most uproariously. Ruth's face crimsoned as heels and cigars remained, in *status quo*, and her glance was met by a rude stare.

"I called to see if you would like a new contributor to your paper," said Ruth; "if so, I will leave a few samples of my articles for your inspection."

"What do you say, Bill?" said the person addressed; "drawer full as usual, I suppose, isn't it? more chaff than wheat, too, I'll swear; don't want any, ma'am; come now, Jo, let's hear the rest of that story; shut the door, ma'am, if you please."

"*ARE YOU THE EDITOR* of the 'Parental Guide'?" said Ruth, to a thin, cadaverous-looking gentleman, in a white neck-cloth, and green spectacles, whose editorial sanctum was not far from the office she had just left.

"I am."

"Do you employ contributors for your paper?"

"Sometimes."

"Shall I leave you this MS. for your inspection, sir?"

"Just as you please."

"Have you a copy of your paper here, sir, from which I could judge what style of articles you prefer?"

At this, the gentleman addressed raised his eyes for the first time, wheeled his editorial arm-chair round, facing Ruth, and peering over his green spectacles, remarked:

"Our paper, madam, is most em-phat-i-cal-ly a paper devoted to the interests of religion; no frivolous jests, no love-sick ditties, no fashionable sentimentalism, finds a place in its columns. This is a serious world, madam, and it ill becomes those who are born to die, to go dancing through it. Josephus remarks that the Saviour of the world was never known to smile. *I* seldom smile. Are you a religious woman, madam?"

"I endeavor to become so," answered Ruth.

"V-e-r-y good; what sect?"

"Presbyterian."

At this the white neck-clothed gentleman moved back his chair: "Wrong, madam, all wrong; I was educated by the best of fathers, but he was *not* a Presbyterian; his son is not a Presbyterian; his son's paper sets its face like a flint against that heresy; no, madam, we shall have no occasion for your contributions; a hope built on a Presbyterian foundation, is built on the sand. Good morning, madam."

DID RUTH DESPAIR? No! but the weary little feet which for so many hours had kept pace with hers, needed a reprieve. Little Nettie must go home, and Ruth must read the office signs as she went along, to prepare for new attempts on the morrow.

To-morrow? Would a brighter morrow *ever* come? Ruth thought of her children, and said again with a strong heart—*it will;* and taking little Nettie upon her lap she divided with her their frugal supper—a scanty bowl of bread and milk.

Ruth could not but acknowledge to herself that she had thus far met with but poor encouragement, but she knew that to climb, she must begin at the lowest round of the ladder. It were useless to apply to a long-established leading paper for employment, unless endorsed by some influential name. Her brother had coolly, almost contemptuously, set her aside; and yet in the very last number of his Magazine, which accident threw in her way, he pleaded for public favor for a young actress, whom he said had been driven by fortune from the sheltered privacy of home, to earn her subsistence upon the stage, and whose earnest, strong-souled nature, he thought, should meet with a better welcome than mere curiosity. "Oh, why not one word for me?" thought Ruth; "and how can I ask of strangers a favor which a brother's heart has so coldly refused?"

It was very disagreeable applying to the small papers, many of the editors of which, accustomed to dealing with hoydenish contributors, were incapable of comprehending that their manner towards Ruth had been marked by any want of that respectful courtesy due to a dignified woman. From all such contact Ruth shrank sensitively; their free-and-easy tone fell upon her ear so painfully, as often to bring the tears to her eyes. Oh, if Harry—but she must not think of him.

THE NEXT DAY Ruth wandered about the business streets, looking into office-entries, reading signs, and trying to gather from their "know-nothing" hieroglyphics, some light to illumine her darkened pathway. Day after day chronicled only repeated failures, and now, notwithstanding she had reduced their already meagre fare, her purse was nearly empty.

CHAPTER LX

IT WAS A WARM, sultry Sabbath morning; not a breath of air played over the heated roofs of the great, swarming city. Ruth sat in her little, close attic, leaning her head upon her hand, weary, languid and dejected. Life seemed to her scarce worth the pains to keep its little flame flickering. A dull pain was in her temples, a heavy weight upon her heart. Other Sabbaths, *happy* Sabbaths, came up to her remembrance; earth looked so dark to her now, heaven so distant, God's ways so inscrutable.

Hark to the Sabbath-bell!

Ruth took little Nettie by the hand, and led her slowly to church. Other families, *unbroken* families, passed her on their way; families whose sunny thresholds the destroying angel had never crossed. Oh why the joy to them, the pain to her? Sadly she entered the church, and took her accustomed seat amid the worshippers. The man of God opened the holy book. Sweet and clear fell upon Ruth's troubled ear these blessed words: "There remaineth, therefore, a rest for the people of God."

The bliss, the joy of heaven was pictured; life,—mysterious, crooked, unfathomable life, made clear to the eye of faith; sorrow, pain, suffering, ignominy even, made sweet for His sake, who suffered all for us.

Ruth weeps! weeps that her faith was for an instant o'erclouded; weeps that she shrank from breasting the foaming waves at the bidding of Him who said, "It is I, be not afraid." And she, who came there fluttering with a broken wing, went away singing, soaring.

Oh man of God! pressed down with many cares, anxious and troubled, sowing but not reaping, fearing to bring in no sheaves for the harvest, be of good courage. The arrow shot at a venture may to thine eye fall aimless; but in the Book of Life shalt thou read many an answer to the wrestling prayer, heard in thy closet by God alone.

CHAPTER LXI

"*FINE DAY,* Mr. Ellet," said a country clergyman to Ruth's father, as he sat comfortably ensconced in his counting-room. "I don't see but you look as young as you did when I saw you five years ago. Life has gone smoothly with you; you have been remarkably prospered in business, Mr. Ellet."

"Yes, yes," said the old gentleman, who was inordinately fond of talking of himself; "yes, yes, I may say that, though I came into Massachusetts a-foot, with a loaf of bread and a sixpence, and now,—well, not to boast, I own this house, and the land attached, beside my countryseat, and have a nice little sum stowed away in the bank for a rainy day; yes, Providence has smiled on my enterprise; my affairs are, as you say, in a *very* prosperous condition. I hope religion flourishes in your church, brother Clark."

"Dead—dead—dead, as the valley of dry bones," replied Mr. Clark with a groan. "I have been trying to 'get up a revival;' but Satan reigns—Satan reigns, and the right arm of the church seems paralysed. Sometimes I think the stumbling-block is the avaricious and money-grabbing spirit of its professors."

"Very likely," answered Mr. Ellet; "there is a great deal too much of that in the church. I alluded to it myself, in my remarks at the last church-meeting. I called it the accursed thing, the Achan in the camp, the Jonah which was to hazard the Lord's Bethel, and I humbly hope my remarks were blessed. I understand from the last Monthly Concert, brother Clark, that there are good accounts from the Sandwich Islands; twenty heathen admitted to the church in one day; good news that."

"Yes," groaned brother Clark, to whose blurred vision the Sun of Righteousness was always clouded; "yes, but think how many more are still, and always will be, worshipping idols; think how long it takes a missionary to acquire a knowledge of the language; and think how many, just as they become perfected in it, die of the climate, or are killed by the natives, leaving their helpless young families to burden the 'American Board.' Very sad, brother Ellet; sometimes, when I think of all this outlay of money and human lives, and so little accomplished, I—" (here a succession of protracted sneezes prevented Mr. Clark from finishing the sentence.)

"Yes," replied Mr. Ellet, coming to the rescue; "but if only *one* heathen had been saved, there would be joy forever in heaven. He who saveth a soul from death, you know, hideth a multitude of sins. I think I spoke a word in season, the other day, which has resulted in one admission, at least, to our church."

"It is to be hoped the new member will prove steadfast," said the well-meaning but hypochondriac brother Clark, with another groan. "Many a hopeful convert goes back to the world, and the last state of that soul is worse than the first. Dreadful, dreadful. I am heartsick, brother Ellet."

"Come," said Ruth's father, tapping him on the shoulder; "dinner is ready, will you sit down with us? First salmon of the season, green peas, boiled fowl, oysters, &c.; your country parishioners don't feed you that way, I suppose."

"N—o," said brother Clark, "no; there is no verse in the whole Bible truer, or more dishonored in the observance, than this, 'The laborer is worthy of his hire.' I'll stay to dinner, brother Ellet. You have, I bless God, a warm heart and a liberal one; your praise is in all the churches."

A self-satisfied smile played round the lips of Ruth's father, at this tribute to his superior sanctity; and seating himself at the well-spread table, he uttered an unusually lengthy grace.

"SOME MORE SUPPER, please, Mamma," vainly pleaded little Nettie.

CHAPTER LXII

RUTH had found employment. Ruth's MSS. had been accepted at the office of "The Standard." Yes, an article of hers was to be published in the very next issue. The remuneration was not what Ruth had hoped, but it was at least a *beginning*, a stepping-stone. What a pity that Mr. Lescom's (the editor's) rule was, not to pay a contributor, even after a piece was accepted, until it was printed—and Ruth so short of funds. Could she hold out to work so hard, and fare so rigidly? for often there was only a crust left at night; but, God be thanked, she should now *earn* that crust! It was a pity that oil was so dear, too, because most of her writing must be done at night, when Nettie's little prattling voice was hushed, and her innumerable little wants forgotten in sleep. Yes, it *was* a pity that good oil was so dear, for the cheaper kind crusted so soon on the wick, and Ruth's eyes, from excessive weeping, had become quite tender, and often very painful. Then it would be so mortifying should a mistake occur in one of her articles. She must write very legibly, for type-setters were sometimes sad bunglers, making people accountable for words that would set Worcester's or Webster's hair on end; but, poor things, *they* worked hard too—they had *their* sorrows, thinking, long into the still night, as they scattered the types, more of their dependent wives and children, than of the orthography of a word, or the rhetoric of a sentence.

Scratch—scratch—scratch, went Ruth's pen; the dim lamp flickering in the night breeze, while the deep breathing of the little sleepers was the watchword, *On!* to her throbbing brow and weary fingers. One o'clock—two o'clock—three o'clock—the lamp burns low in the socket. Ruth lays down her pen, and pushing back the hair from her forehead, leans faint and exhausted against the window-sill, that the cool night-air may fan her heated temples. How impressive the stillness! Ruth can almost hear her own heart beat. She looks upward, and the watchful stars seem to her like the eyes of gentle friends. No, God would *not* forsake her! A sweet peace steals into her troubled heart, and the overtasked lids droop heavily over the weary eyes.

Ruth sleeps.

DAYLIGHT! Morning *so* soon? All night Ruth has leaned with her head on the window-sill, and now she wakes unrefreshed from the constrained posture; but she has no time to heed *that*, for little Nettie lies moaning in her bed with pain; she lifts the little creature in her lap, rocks her gently, and kisses her cheek; but still little Nettie moans. Ruth goes to the drawer and looks in her small purse (Harry's gift); it is empty! then she clasps her hands and looks again at little Nettie. Must Nettie die for want of care? Oh, if Mr. Lescom would *only* advance her the money for the contributions he had accepted, but he said so decidedly that "it was a rule he *never* departed from;" and there were yet five long days before the next paper would be out. Five days! what might not happen to Nettie in five days? There was her cousin, Mrs. Millet, but she had muffled her furniture in linen wrappers, and gone to the springs with her family, for the summer months; there was her father, but had he not said "Remember, if you *will* burden yourself with your children, you must not look to me for help." Kissing little Nettie's cheek she lays her gently on the bed, whispering in a husky voice, "only a few moments, Nettie; mamma will be back soon." She closes the door upon the sick child, and stands with her hand upon her bewildered brow, thinking.

"*I BEG YOUR PARDON,* madam; the entry is so very dark I did not see you," said Mr. Bond; "you are as early a riser as myself."

"My child is sick," answered Ruth, tremulously; "I was just going out for medicine."

"If you approve of Homœopathy," said Mr. Bond, "and will trust me to prescribe, there will be no necessity for your putting yourself to that trouble; I always treat myself homœopathically in sickness, and happen to have a small supply of those medicines by me."

Ruth's natural independence revolted at the idea of receiving a favor from a stranger.

"Perhaps you disapprove of Homœopathy," said Mr. Bond, mistaking the cause of her momentary hesitation; "it works like a charm with children; but if you prefer not to try it, allow me to go out and procure you whatever you desire in the way of medicine; you will not then be obliged to leave your child."

Here was another dilemma—what *should* Ruth do? Why, clearly accept his first offer; there was an air of goodness and sincerity about him, which, added to his years, seemed to invite her confidence.

Mr. Bond stepped in, looked at Nettie, and felt her pulse. "Ah, little one, we will soon have you better," said he, as he left the room to obtain his little package of medicines.

"Thank you," said Ruth, with a grateful smile, as he administered to Nettie some infinitesimal pills.

"Not in the least," said Mr. Bond. "I learned two years since to doctor myself in this way, and I have often had the pleasure of relieving others in emergencies like this, from my little Homœopathic stores. You will find that your little girl will soon fall into a sweet sleep, and awake much relieved; if you are careful with her, she will, I think, need nothing more in the way of medicine, or if she should, my advice is quite at your service;" and, taking his pitcher of water in his hand, he bowed respectfully, and wished Ruth good morning.

Who was he? what was he? Whir—whir—there was the noise again! That he was a man of refined and courteous manners, was very certain. Ruth felt glad he was so much her senior; he seemed so like what Ruth had sometimes dreamed a kind father might be, that it lessened the weight of the obligation. Already little Nettie had ceased moaning; her little lids began to droop, and her skin, which had been hot and feverish, became moist and cool. "May God reward him, whoever he may be," said Ruth. "Surely it *is* blessed to *trust!*"

CHAPTER LXIII

IT WAS FOUR O'CLOCK of a hot August afternoon. The sun had crept round to the front piazza of the doctor's cottage. No friendly trees warded off his burning rays, for the doctor "liked a prospect;" *i.e.* he liked to sit at the window and count the different trains which whizzed past in the course of the day; the number of wagons, and gigs, and carriages, that rolled lazily up the hill; to see the village engine, the "Cataract," drawn out on the green for its weekly ablutions, and to count the bundles of shingles that it took to roof over Squire Ruggles' new barn. No drooping vines, therefore, or creepers, intruded between him and this pleasant "prospect." The doctor was an utilitarian; he could see "no use" in such things, save to rot timber and harbor vermin. So a wondrous glare of white paint, (carefully renewed every spring,) blinded the traveler whose misfortune it was to pass the road by the doctor's house. As I said, it was now four o'clock. The twelve o'clock dinner was long since over. The Irish girl had rinsed out her dish-towels, hung them out the back door to dry, and gone down to the village store to buy some new ribbons advertised as selling at an "immense sacrifice" by the disinterested village shopkeeper.

LET US PEEP into the doctor's sitting room; the air of this room is close and stifled, for the windows must be tightly closed, lest some audacious fly should make his mark on the old lady's immaculate walls. A centre table stands in the middle of the floor, with a copy of "The Religious Pilot," last year's Almanac, A Directory, and "The remarkable Escape of Eliza Cook, who was partially scalped by the Indians." On one side of the room hangs a piece of framed needle-work, by the virgin fingers of the old lady, representing an unhappy female, weeping over a very high and very perpendicular tombstone, which is hieroglyphiced over with untranslateable characters in red worsted, while a few herbs, not mentioned by botanists, are struggling for existence at its base. A friendly willow-tree, of a most extraordinary shade of blue green, droops in sympathy over the afflicted female, while a nondescript looking bird, resembling a dropsical bull-frog, suspends his song and one leg, in the foreground. It was principally to preserve this chef-d'œuvre of art, that the windows were hermetically sealed to the entrance of vagrant flies.

The old doctor, with his spectacles awry and his hands drooping listlessly at his side, snored from the depths of his arm-chair, while opposite him the old lady, peering out from behind a very stiffly-starched cap border, was "seaming," "widening," and "narrowing," with a precision and perseverance most painful to witness. Outside, the bee hummed, the robin twittered, the shining leaves of the village trees danced and whispered to the shifting clouds; the free, glad breeze swept the tall meadow-grass, and the village children, as free and fetterless, danced and shouted at their sports; but there sat little Katy, with her hands crossed in her lap, as she *had* sat for many an hour, listening to the never-ceasing click of her grandmother's needles, and the sonorous breathings of the doctor's rubicund nose. Sometimes she moved uneasily in her chair, but the old lady's uplifted finger would immediately remind her that "little girls must be seen and not heard." It was a great thing for Katy when a mouse scratched on the wainscot, or her grandmother's ball rolled out of her lap, giving her a chance to stretch her little cramped limbs. And now the village bell began to toll, with a low, booming, funereal sound, sending a cold shudder through the child's nervous and excited frame. What if *her* mother should die way off in the city? What if she should *always* live in this terrible way at her grandmother's? with nobody to love her, or kiss her, or pat her little head kindly, and say, "Katy, dear;" and again the bell boomed out its mournful sound, and little Katy, unable longer to bear the torturing thoughts it called up, sobbed aloud.

It was all in vain, that the frowning old lady held up her warning finger; the flood-gates were opened, and Katy could not have stopped her tears had her life depended on it.

Hark! a knock at the door! a strange footstep!

"Mother!" shrieked the child hysterically, "mother!" and flew into Ruth's sheltering arms.

"*WHAT shall* we do, doctor?" asked the old lady, the day after Ruth's visit. "I trusted to her not being able to get the money to come out here, and her father, I knew, wouldn't give it to her, and now here she has walked the whole distance, with Nettie in her arms, except a lift a wagoner or two gave her on the road; and I verily believe she would have done it, had it been twice the distance it is. I never shall be able to bring up that child according to my notions, while *she* is round. I'd forbid her the house, (she deserves it,) only that it won't sound well if she tells of it. And to think of that ungrateful little thing's flying into her mother's arms as if she was in the last extremity, after all we have done for her. I don't suppose Ruth would have left her with us, as it is, if she had the bread to put in her mouth. She might as well give her up, though, first as last, for she never will be able to support her."

"She's fit for nothing but a parlor ornament," said the doctor, "never was. No more business talent in Ruth Ellet, than there is in that chany image of yours on the mantle-tree, Mis. Hall. That tells the whole story."

CHAPTER LXIV

"I HAVE good news for you," said Mr. Lescom to Ruth, at her next weekly visit; "your very first articles are copied, I see, into many of my exchanges, even into the ———, which seldom contains anything but politics. A good sign for you Mrs. Hall; a good test of your popularity."

Ruth's eyes sparkled, and her whole face glowed.

"Ladies *like* to be praised," said Mr. Lescom, good-humoredly, with a mischievous smile.

"Oh, it is not that—not that, sir," said Ruth, with a sudden moistening of the eye, "it is because it will be bread for my children."

Mr. Lescom checked his mirthful mood, and said, "Well, here is something good for me, too; a letter from Missouri, in which the writer says, that if "Floy" (a pretty *nom-de-plume* that of yours, Mrs. Hall) is to be a contributor for the coming year, I may put him down as a subscriber, as well as S. Jones, E. May, and J. Noyes, all of the same place. That's good news for *me*, you see," said Mr. Lescom, with one of his pleasant, beaming smiles.

"Yes," replied Ruth, abstractedly. She was wondering if her articles were to be the means of swelling Mr. Lescom's subscription list, whether *she* ought not to profit by it as well as himself, and whether she should not ask him to increase her pay. She pulled her gloves off and on, and finally mustered courage to clothe her thought in words.

"Now that's just *like* a woman," replied Mr. Lescom, turning it off with a joke; "give them the least foot-hold, and they will want the whole territory. Had I not shown you that letter, you would have been quite contented with your present pay. Ah! I see it won't do to talk so unprofessionally to you; and you needn't expect," said he, smiling, "that I shall ever speak of letters containing new subscribers on your account. I could easily get you the offer of a handsome salary by publishing such things. No—no, I have been foolish enough to lose two or three valuable contributors in that way; I have learned better than that, 'Floy';" and taking out his purse, he paid Ruth the usual sum for her articles.

Ruth bowed courteously, and put the money in her purse; but she sighed as she went down the office stairs. Mr. Lescom's view of the case was a business one, undoubtedly; and the same view that almost any other business man would have taken, viz.: to retain her at her present low rate of compensation, till he was necessitated to raise it by a higher bid from a rival quarter. And so she must plod wearily on till that time came, and poor Katy must still be an exile; for she had not enough to feed her, her landlady having raised the rent of her room two shillings, and Ruth being unable to find cheaper accommodations. It *was* hard, but what could be done? Ruth believed she had exhausted all the offices she knew of. Oh! there was one, "The Pilgrim;" she had not tried there. She would call at the office on her way home.

The editor of "The Pilgrim" talked largely. He had, now, plenty of contributors; he didn't know about employing a new one. Had she ever written? and *what* had she written? Ruth showed him her article in the last number of "The Standard."

"Oh—hum—hum!" said Mr. Tibbetts, changing his tone; "so you are 'Floy,' are you?" (casting his eyes on her.) "What pay do they give you over there?"

Ruth was a novice in business-matters, but she had strong common sense, and that common sense said, he has no right to ask you that question; don't you tell him; so she replied with dignity, "My bargain, sir, with Mr. Lescom was a private one, I believe."

"Hum," said the foiled Mr. Tibbetts; adding in an under-tone to his partner, "sharp that!"

"Well, if I conclude to engage you," said Mr. Tibbetts, "I should prefer you would write for me over a different signature than the one by which your pieces are indicated at The Standard office, or you can write exclusively for my paper."

"With regard to your first proposal," said Ruth, "if I have gained any reputation by my first efforts, it appears to me that I should be foolish to throw it away by the adoption of another signature; and with regard to the last, I have no objection to writing exclusively for you, if you will make it worth my while."

"Sharp again," whispered Tibbetts to his partner.

The two editors then withdrawing into a further corner of the office, a whispered consultation followed, during which Ruth heard the words, "Can't afford it, Tom; hang it! we are head over ears in debt now to that paper man; good articles though—deuced good—must have her if we dispense with some of our other contributors. We had better begin low though, as to terms, for she'll go up now like a rocket, and when she finds out her value we shall have to increase her pay, you know."

(Thank you, gentlemen, thought Ruth, when the cards change hands, I'll take care to return the compliment.)

In pursuance of Mr. Tibbetts's shrewd resolution, he made known his "exclusive" terms to Ruth, which were no advance upon her present rate of pay at The Standard. This offer being declined, they made her another, in which, since she would not consent to do otherwise, they agreed she should write over her old signature, "Floy," furnishing them with two articles a week.

Ruth accepted the terms, poor as they were, because she could at present do no better, and because every pebble serves to swell the current.

MONTHS PASSED AWAY, while Ruth hoped and toiled, "Floy's" fame as a writer increasing much faster than her remuneration. There was rent-room to pay, little shoes and stockings to buy, oil, paper, pens, and ink to find; and now autumn had come, she could not write with stiffened fingers, and wood and coal were ruinously high, so that even with this new addition to her labor, Ruth seemed to retrograde pecuniarily, instead of advancing; and Katy still away! She must work harder—harder. Good, brave little Katy; she, too, was bearing and hoping on—mamma had promised, if she would stay there, patiently, she would certainly take her away just as soon as she had earned money enough; and mamma *never* broke her promise—*never;* and Katy prayed to God every night, with childish trust, to help her mother to earn money, that she might soon go home again.

And so, while Ruth scribbled away in her garret, the public were busying themselves in conjecturing who "Floy" might be. Letters poured in upon Mr. Lescom, with inquiries, even bribing him with the offer to procure a certain number of subscribers, if he would divulge her real name; to all of which the old man, true to his promise to Ruth, to keep her secret inviolate, turned a deaf ear. All sorts of rumors became rife about "Floy," some maintaining her to be a man, because she had the courage to call things by their right names, and the independence to express herself boldly on subjects which to the timid and clique-serving, were tabooed. Some said she was a disappointed old maid; some said she was a designing widow; some said she was a moon-struck girl; and all said she was a nondescript. Some tried to imitate her, and failing in this, abused and maligned her; the outwardly strait-laced and inwardly corrupt, puckered up their mouths and "blushed for her;" the hypocritical denounced the sacrilegious fingers which had dared to touch the Ark; the fashionist voted her a vulgar, plebeian thing; and the earnest and sorrowing, to whose burdened hearts she had given voice, cried God speed her. And still "Floy" scribbled on, thinking only of bread for her children, laughing and crying behind her mask,—laughing all the more when her heart was heaviest; but of this her readers knew little and would have cared less. Still her little bark breasted the billows, now rising high on the topmost wave, now merged in the shadows, but still steering with straining sides, and a heart of oak, for the nearing port of Independence.

Ruth's brother, Hyacinth, saw "Floy's" articles floating through his exchanges with marked dissatisfaction and uneasiness. That she should have succeeded in any degree without his assistance, was a puzzle, and the premonitory symptoms of her popularity, which his weekly exchanges furnished, in the shape of commendatory notices, were gall and wormwood to him. *Something* must be done, and that immediately. Seizing his pen, he despatched a letter to Mrs. Millet, which he requested her to read to Ruth, alluding very contemptuously to Ruth's articles, and begging her to use her influence with Ruth to desist from scribbling, and seek some other employment. *What* employment, he did not condescend to state; in fact, it was a matter of entire indifference to him, provided she did not cross his track. Ruth listened to the contents of the letter, with the old bitter smile, and went on writing.

CHAPTER LXV

A DULL, drizzling rain spattered perseveringly against Ruth's windows, making her little dark room tenfold gloomier and darker than ever. Little Nettie had exhausted her slender stock of toys, and creeping up to her mother's side, laid her head wearily in her lap.

"Wait just a moment, Nettie, till mamma finishes this page," said Ruth, dipping her pen again in the old stone inkstand.

The child crept back again to the window, and watched the little pools of water in the streets, as the rain-drops dimpled them, and saw, for the hundredth time, the grocer's boy carrying home a brown-paper parcel for some customers, and eating something from it as he went along; and listened to the milkman, who thumped so loudly on the back gates, and seemed always in such a tearing hurry; and saw the baker open the lid of his boxes, and let the steam escape from the smoking hot cakes and pies. Nettie wished she could have some of them, but she had long since learned *only to wish;* and then she saw the two little sisters who went by to school every morning, and who were now cuddling, laughingly together, under a great big umbrella, which the naughty wind was trying to turn inside out, and to get away from them; and then Nettie thought of Katy, and wished she had Katy to play with her, when mamma wrote such a long, long time;

and then little Nettie drew such a heavy sigh, that Ruth dashed down her pen, and taking her in her arms and kissing her, told her about,

> "Mistress McShuttle,
> Who lived in a coal-scuttle,
> Along with her dog and her cat,
> What she did there, I can't tell,
> But I know very well,
> That none of the party were fat."

And then she narrated the exciting adventures of "The Wise Men of Gotham," who went to sea in that rudderless bowl, and suffered shipwreck and "total *lass* of life," as the newsboys (God bless their rough-and-ready faces) call it; and then little Nettie's snowy lids drooped over her violet eyes, and she was far away in the land of dreams, where there are no little hungry girls, or tired, scribbling mammas.

Ruth laid the child gently on her little bed, and resumed her pen; but the spell was broken, and "careful and troubled about many things" she laid it down again, and her thoughts ran riot.

Pushing aside her papers, she discovered two unopened letters which Mr. Lescom had handed her, and which she had in the hurry of finishing her next article, quite forgotten. Breaking the seal of the first, she read as follows:

> "To 'Floy.'
>
> "I am a rough old man, Miss, and not used to writing or talking to ladies. I don't know who you are, and I don't ask; but I take 'The Standard,' and I like your pieces. I have a family of bouncing girls and boys; and when we've all done work, we get round the fire of an evening, while one of us reads your pieces aloud. It may not make much difference to you what an old man thinks, but I tell you those pieces have got the real stuff in 'em, and so I told my son John the other night; and *he* says, and *I* say, and neighbor Smith, who comes in to hear 'em, says, that you ought to make a book of them, so that your readers may keep them. You can put me down for three copies, to begin with; and if every subscriber to 'The Standard' feels as I do, you might make a plum by the operation. Suppose, now, you think of it?

"N.B.—John says, maybe you'll be offended at my writing to you, but I say you've got too much common sense.

Yours to command,

"JOHN STOKES."

"Well, well," said Ruth, laughing, "that's a thought that never entered this busy head of mine, John Stokes. *I* publish a book? Why, John, are you aware that those articles were written for bread and butter, not fame; and tossed to the printer before the ink was dry, or I had time for a second reading? And yet, perhaps, there is more freshness about them than there would have been, had I leisure to have pruned and polished them—who knows? I'll put your suggestion on file, friend Stokes, to be turned over at my leisure. It strikes me, though, that it will keep awhile. Thank you, honest John. It is just such readers as you whom I like to secure. Well, what have we here?" and Ruth broke the seal of the second letter. It was in a delicate, beautiful, female hand; just such a one as you, dear Reader, might trace, whose sweet, soft eyes, and long, drooping tresses, are now bending over this page. It said:

"DEAR 'FLOY':

"For you *are* 'dear' to me, dear as a sister on whose loving breast I have leaned, though I never saw your face. I know not whether you are young and fair, or old and wrinkled, but I know that your heart is fresh, and guileless, and warm as childhood's; and that every week your printed words come to me, in my sick chamber, like the ministrations of some gentle friend, sometimes stirring to its very depths the fountain of tears, sometimes, by odd and quaint conceits, provoking the mirthful smile. But 'Floy,' I love you best in your serious moods; for as earth recedes, and eternity draws near, it is the real and tangible, my soul yearns after. And sure I am, 'Floy,' that I am not mistaken in thinking that we both lean on the same Rock of Ages; both discern, through the mists and clouds of time, the Sun of Righteousness. I shall never see you, 'Floy,' on earth;—mysterious voices, audible only to the dying ear, are calling me away; and yet, before I go, I would send you this token of my love, for all the sweet and soul-strengthening words you have unconsciously sent to my sick chamber, to wing the weary, waiting hours. We shall *meet*, 'Floy'; but it will be where 'tears are wiped away.'

"God bless you, my unknown sister.

"Mary R. ———."

Ruth's head bowed low upon the table, and her lips moved; but He to whom the secrets of all hearts are known, alone heard that grateful prayer.

CHAPTER LXVI

THAT FIRST miserable day at school! Who that has known it—even with a mother's kiss burning on the cheek, a big orange bumping in the new satchel, and a promise of apple-dumplings for dinner, can review it without a shudder? Torturing—even when you can run home and "tell mother" all your little griefs; when every member of the home circle votes it "*a shame*" that Johnny Oakes laughed because you did not take your alphabet the natural way, instead of receiving it by inoculation, (just as he forgets that *he* did;) torturing—when Bill Smith, and Tom Simms, with whom you have "swapped alleys," and played "hockey," are there with their familiar faces, to take off the chill of the new school-room; torturing—to the sensitive child, even when the teacher is a sunny-faced young girl, instead of a prim old ogre. Poor little Katy! her book was before her; but the lines blurred into one indistinct haze, and her throat seemed filling to suffocation with long-suppressed sobs. The teacher, if he thought anything about it, thought she had the tooth-ache, or ear-ache, or head-ache; and Katy kept her own secret, for she had read his face correctly, and with a child's quick instinct, stifled down her throbbing little heart.

To the doctor, and "Mis. Hall," with their anti-progressive notions, a school was a school. The committee had passed judgment on it, and I would like to know who would be insane enough to question the decision of a School Committee? What did the committee care, that the consumptive teacher, for his own personal convenience, madly excluded all ventilation, and heated the little sheet-iron stove hotter than Shadrack's furnace, till little heads snapped, and cheeks crimsoned, and croup stood ready at the threshold to seize the first little bare throat that presented its perspiring surface to the keen frosty air? What did *they* care that the desks were so constructed, as to crook spines, and turn in toes, and round shoulders? What did they care that the funnel smoked week after week, till the curse of "weak eyes" was entailed on their victims for a lifetime? They had other irons in the fire, to which this was a cipher. For instance: the village pump was out of repair, and town-meeting after town-meeting had been called, to see who *shouldn't* make its handle fly. North Gotham said it was the business of East Gotham; East Gotham said the pump might rot before they'd bear the expense; not that the East Gothamites cared for expense—no; they scorned the insinuation, but they'd have North Gotham to know that East Gotham wasn't to be put upon. Jeremiah Stubbs, a staunch North Gothamite, stopped buying molasses and calico at "Ezekial Tibbs's East Gotham Finding Store;" and Ezekial Tibbs forbade, under penalty of losing his custom, the carpenter who was repairing his pig-sty, from buying nails any more of Jeremiah Stubbs, of North Gotham; matches were broken up; "own cousins" ceased to know one another, and the old women had a millennial time of it over their bohea, discussing and settling matters; no marvel that such a trifle as a child's school should be overlooked. Meantime there stood the pump, with its impotent handle, high and dry; "a gone sucker," as Mr. Tibbs facetiously expressed it.

"You can't go to school to-day, Katy, it is washing-day," said old Mrs. Hall; "go get that stool, now sit down on it, at my feet, and let me cut off those foolish dangling curls."

"Mamma likes them," said the child.

"I know it," replied the old lady, with a malicious smile, as she gathered a cluster of them in one hand and seized the scissors with the other.

"*Papa* liked them," said Katy, shrinking back.

"No, he didn't," replied the old lady; "or, if he did, 'twas only to please your foolish mother; any way they are coming off; if I don't like them, that's enough; you are always to live with me now, Katy; it makes no difference what your mother thinks or says about anything, so you needn't quote *her*; I'm going to try to make a good girl of you, *i.e.* if she will let you alone; you are full of faults, just as she is, and I shall have to take a great deal of pains with you. You ought to love me very much for it, better than anybody else in the world—don't you?"

(No response from Katy.)

"I say, Katy, you ought to love me better than anybody else in the world," repeated the old lady, tossing a handful of the severed ringlets down on the carpet. "Do you, Katy?"

"No, ma'am," answered the truthful child.

"That tells the whole story," said the doctor, as he started up and boxed Katy's ears; "now go up and stay in your room till I send for you, for being disrespectful to your grandmother."

"Like mother—like child," said the old lady, as Katy half shorn, moved like a culprit out of the room; then gathering up in her apron the shining curls, she looked on with a malicious smile, while they crisped and blackened in the glowing Lehigh fire.

But miserable as were the week-days—Sunday, after all, was the dreadful day for Katy; the long—long—long Sunday, when every book in the house was put under lock and key; when even religious newspapers, tracts, and memoirs, were tabooed; when the old people, who fancied they could not go to church, sat from sunrise to sunset in their best clothes, with their hands folded, looking speechlessly into the fire; when there was no dinner; when the Irish girl and the cat, equally lawless and heretical, went to see their friends; when not a sound was heard in the house, save the ticking of the old claw-footed-clock, that stood in the entry; when Katy crept up to her little room, and crouching in a corner, wondered if God *was* good—why he let her papa *die*, and why he did not help her mamma, who tried so hard to earn money to bring her home.

The last bright golden beam of the Sabbath sun had slowly faded away. One by one the stars came gliding out. He who held them all in their places, listening ever to the ceaseless music of their motion, yet bent a pitying ear to the stifled sob of a troubled child. Softly—sweetly—fell the gentle dew of slumber on weary eyelids, while angels came to minister. Tears glittered still on Katy's long lashes, but the little lips parted with a smile, murmuring "Papa." Sleep on—dream on—little Katy. He who noteth the sparrow's fall, hath given his angels charge to keep thee.

CHAPTER LXVII

IN ONE of the thousand business offices, in one of the thousand crowded streets of a neighboring city, sat Mr. John Walter, with his legs crossed, his right finger pressed against the right lobe of his organ of causality, his right elbow resting on his right knee, and the fingers of his left hand beating a sort of tattoo on a fresh copy of The Standard, which lay upon the table by his side. His attitude was one of profound meditation.

"Who *can* she be?" exclaimed Mr. Walter, in a tone of blended interest and vexation; "who can she be?" Mr. Walter raised his head, uncrossed his legs, took up The Standard, and re-read 'Floy's' last article slowly; often pausing to analyze the sentences, as though he would extort from them some hidden meaning, to serve as a clue to the identity of the author. After he had perused the article thus searchingly, he laid down The Standard, and again exclaimed, "Who *can* she be? she is a genius certainly, whoever she is," continued he, soliloquizingly; "a bitter life experience she has had too; she did not draw upon her imagination for this article. Like the very first production of her pen that I read, it is a wail from her inmost soul; so are many of her pieces. A few dozen of them taken consecutively, would form a whole history of wrong, and suffering, and bitter sorrow. What a singular being she must be, if I have formed a correct opinion of her; what powers of endurance! What an elastic, strong, brave, loving, fiery, yet soft and winning nature! A bundle of contradictions! and how famously she has got on too! it is only a little more than a year since her first piece was published, and now her articles flood the whole country; I seldom take up an exchange, which does not contain one or more of them. That first piece of hers was a stroke of genius—a real gem, although not very smoothly polished; ever since I read it, I have been trying to find out the author's name, and have watched her career with eager interest; *her* career, I say, for I suppose 'Floy' to be a woman, notwithstanding the rumors to the contrary. At any rate, my wife says so, and women have an instinct about such things. I wish I knew whether she gets well paid for her writings. Probably not. Inexperienced writers seldom get more than a mere pittance. There are so many ready to write (poor fools!) for the honor and glory of the thing, and there are so many ready to take advantage of this fact, and withhold from needy talent the moral right to a deserved remuneration. Thank heaven, I have never practiced this. The 'Household Messenger' does not yield me a very large income, but what it does yield is fairly earned. Why, bless me!" exclaimed Mr. Walter, suddenly starting up, and as suddenly sitting down again; "why has not this idea occurred to me before? yes, why not engage 'Floy' to write for the Household Messenger? How I wish I were rich, that I might give her such a price as she really deserves. Let me see; she now writes for The Standard, and The Pilgrim, four pieces a week for each; eight pieces in all; that is too much work for her to begin with; she cannot do herself justice; she ought not to write, at the outside, more than two pieces a week; then she could polish them up, and strengthen them, and render them as nearly perfect in execution as they are in conception. One piece a week would be as much as I should wish; could I possibly afford to pay her as much, or more for that one piece, as she now gets for eight? Her name is a tower of strength, but its influence would be frittered away, were she to write for more than one paper. If I could secure her pen all to myself, the advertising that such a connection would give The Messenger would be worth something. Ah me, were my purse only commensurate with my feelings. If I only knew who 'Floy' is, and could have an interview with her, I might perhaps arrange matters so as to benefit us both; and I *will* know," exclaimed Mr. Walter, jumping up and pacing the room rapidly; "I'll know before I'm a month older;" and the matter was settled; for when John Walter paced the floor rapidly, and said "I will," Fate folded her hands.

CHAPTER LXVIII

"*A LETTER* for 'Floy!'" said Mr. Lescom, smiling. "Another lover, I suppose. Ah! when you get to be my age," continued the old man, stroking his silver hair, "you will treat their communications with more attention." As he finished his remark, he held the letter up playfully for a moment, and then tossed it into Ruth's lap.

Ruth thrust it unread into her apron pocket. She was thinking of her book, and many other things of far more interest to her than lovers, if lover the writer were. After correcting the proof of her articles for the next week's paper, and looking over a few exchanges, she asked for and received the wages due her for the last articles published, and went home.

Ruth was wearied out; her walk home tired her more than usual. Climbing to her room, she sat down without removing her bonnet, and leaning her head upon her hand, tried to look hopefully into the future. She was soon disturbed by Nettie, who exploring her mother's pockets, and finding the letter, exclaimed, pointing to the three cent stamp, "May I have this pretty picture, mamma?"

Ruth drew forth the letter, opened the envelope, cut out the stamp for Nettie, who soon suspended it around her doll's neck for a medal, and then read the epistle, which ran as follows:

"To 'Floy':

"Madam,—I have long wished to communicate with you, long wished to know who you are. Since the appearance of your first article, I have watched your course with deep interest, and have witnessed your success with the most unfeigned pleasure. My reasons for wishing to make your acquaintance at this particular juncture, are partly business and partly friendly reasons. As you will see by a copy of the Household Messenger, which I herewith send you, I am its Editor. I know something about the prices paid contributors for the periodical press, and have often wondered whether you were receiving anything like such a remuneration as your genius and practical newspaperial talent entitle you to. I have also often wished to write you on the subject, and tell you what I think is your market-value—to speak in business phrase—as a writer; so that in case you are *not* receiving a just compensation, as things go, you might know it, and act accordingly. In meditating upon the subject, it has occurred to me that I might benefit you and myself at the same time, and in a perfectly legitimate manner, by engaging you to write solely for my paper. I have made a calculation as to what I can afford to give you, or rather what I *will* give you, for writing one article a week for me, the article to be on any subject, and of any length you please.

Such an arrangement would of course give you time to take more pains with your writing, and also afford you such leisure for relaxation, as every writer needs.

"Now what I wish you to do is this: I want you first to inform me what you get for writing for The Standard, and The Pilgrim, and if I find that I can afford to give you more, I will make you an offer. If I cannot give you more, I will not trouble you further on that subject; as I seek your benefit more than my own. In case you should accept any offer which I should find it proper to make, it would be necessary for you to tell me your *real* name; as I should wish for a written contract, in order to prevent any possibility of a misunderstanding.

"In conclusion, I beg that you will permit me to say, that whether or not arrangements are made for you to write for me, I shall be most happy to serve you in any way in my power. I have some experience in literary matters, which I will gladly place at your disposal. In short, madam, I feel a warm, brotherly interest in your welfare, as well as a high admiration for your genius, and it will afford me much pleasure to aid you, whenever my services can be made profitable.

"Very truly yours, JOHN WALTER."

Ruth sat with the letter in her hand. The time *had* been when not a doubt would have arisen in her mind as to the sincerity of the writer; but, alas! adversity is so rough a teacher! ever laying the cold finger of caution on the warm heart of trust! Ruth sighed, and tossed the letter on the table, half ashamed of herself for her cowardice, and wishing that she *could* have faith in the writer. Then she picked up the letter again. She examined the hand-writing; it was bold and manly. She thought it would be treating it too shabbily to throw it aside among the love-sick trash she was in the habit of receiving. She would read it again. The tone was respectful; *that won her*. The "Household Messenger"—"John Walter?"—she certainly had heard those names before. The letter stated that a copy of the paper had been sent her, but she had not yet received it. She recollected now that she had seen the "Household Messenger" among the exchanges at "The Standard" office, and remembered that she always liked its appearance, and admired its editorials; they were fearless and honest, and always on the side of the weak, and on the side of truth. Ruth also had an indistinct remembrance of having heard Mr. Walter spoken of by somebody, at some time, as a most energetic young man, who had wrung success from an unwilling world, and fought his way, single-handed, from obscurity to an honorable position in society, against, what would have been to many, overwhelming odds. "Hence the reason," thought Ruth, "his heart so readily vibrates to the chord of sorrow which I have struck. His experienced heart has detected in my writings the flutterings and desolation of his own." Ruth wanted to believe in Mr. Walter. She glanced at his letter again with increased interest and attention. It seemed so frank and kind; but then it was bold and exacting, too. The writer wished to know how much she received from the "Pilgrim," and "Standard," and what was her real name. Would it be prudent to entrust so much to an entire stranger? and the very first time he asked, too? Even granting he was actuated by the best of motives, would he not think if she told him all, without requiring some further guaranty on his part, that her confidence was too easily won? Would he not think her too indiscreet to be entrusted with his confidence? Would he not be apt to believe that she had not even sufficient discretion on which to base a business arrangement? And then, if his letter *had been* dictated by idle curiosity only, how unfortunate such an *exposé* of her affairs might be. No—she—could—not—do—it! But then, if Mr. Walter *were* honest, if he *really* felt such a brotherly interest in her, how sweet it would be to have him for a brother; a—*real*, *warm-hearted*, *brotherly brother*, such as she had never known. Ruth took up her pen to write to Mr. Walter, but as quickly laid it down. "Oh—I—cannot!" she said; "no, not to a stranger!" Then, again she seized her pen, and with a quick flush, and a warm tear, said, half pettishly, half mournfully, "Away with these ungenerous doubts! Am I never again to put faith in human nature?"

Ruth answered Mr. Walter's letter. She answered it frankly and unreservedly. She stated what wages she was then receiving. She told him her name. As she went on, she felt a peace to which she had long been a stranger. She often paused to wipe the tears—tears of happiness—from her eyes. It was so sweet to believe in *somebody* once more. She wrote a long letter—a sweet, sisterly letter—pouring out her long pent-up feelings, as though Mr. Walter had indeed been her brother, who, having been away ever since before Harry's death, had just returned, and consequently, had known nothing about her cruel sufferings. After she had sealed and superscribed the letter, she became excessively frightened at what she had done, and thought she never could send it to Mr. Walter; but another perusal of his letter reassured her. She rose to go to the post-office, and then became conscious that she had not removed her bonnet and shawl, but had sat all this while in walking costume! "Well," said she, laughing, "this *is* rather blue-stocking-y; however, it is all the better, as I am now ready for my walk." Ruth carried her letter to the post-office; dropping it into the letter-box with more hopeful feelings than Noah probably experienced when he sent forth the dove from the ark for the third time.

CHAPTER LXIX

MR. WALTER sat in his office, looking over the morning mail. "I wonder is this from 'Floy'?" he said, as he examined a compact little package. "It bears the right post-mark, and the handwriting is a lady's. A splendid hand it is, too. There's character in that hand; I hope 'tis 'Floy's.'"

Mr. Walter broke the seal, and glancing at a few sentences, turned to the signature. "Yes, it is 'Floy'! now for a revelation." He then commenced perusing the letter with the most intense interest. After reading the first page his eye began to flash, and his lip to quiver. "Poor girl—poor girl—heartless creatures—too bad—too bad," and other exclamations rather too warm for publication; finishing the letter and refolding it, he paced the room with a short, quick step, indicative of deep interest, and determined purpose. "It is too bad," he exclaimed; "shameful! the whole of it; and how hard she has worked! and what a pitiful sum those fellows pay her! it is contemptible. She has about made The Standard; it never was heard of to any extent before she commenced writing for it. It is perfectly outrageous; she shall not write for them another day, if I can help it! I will make her an offer at once. She will accept it; and then those Jews will be brought to their senses. Ha! ha! I know them! They will want to get her back; they will write to me about it, or at least Lescom will. That will give me a chance at him; and if I don't tell him a few truths in plain English, my name is not

John Walter." Then seating himself at his desk, Mr. Walter wrote the following letter to 'Floy':

> "DEAR SISTER RUTH,—If you will permit me to be so brotherly. I have received, read, and digested your letter; how it has affected me I will not now tell you. I wish to say, however, that on reading that portion of it which relates to the compensation you are now receiving, my indignation exhausted the dictionary! Why, you poor, dear little genius! what you write for those two papers is worth, to the proprietors, ten times what they pay you. But I will not bore you with compliments; I wish to engage you to write for the Household Messenger, and here is my offer: you to write one article a week, length, matter and manner, to your own fancy; I to pay you ———, the engagement to continue one year, during which time you are not to write for any other periodical, without my consent. My reason for placing a limitation to our engagement is, that you may be able to take advantage at that time of better offers, which you will undoubtedly have.
>
> "I enclose duplicates of a contract, which, if the terms suit, you will please sign and return one copy *by the next mail;* the other copy you will keep. Unless you accept my offer by return of mail it will be withdrawn. You may think this exacting; I will explain it in my next to your satisfaction. Most truly your friend,
>
> "JOHN WALTER."

This letter being despatched, thanks to the post-office department, arrived promptly at its destination the next morning.

Ruth sat with Mr. Walter's letter in her hand, thinking. "'If you do not accept my offer by return of mail, it will be withdrawn.' How exacting! 'the explanation of this to be given in my next letter,' ah, Mr. John Walter, I shall not have to wait till then," soliloquized Ruth; "I can jump at your reason; you think I shall mention it to Mr. Lescom, and that then he will interfere, and offer something by way of an equivalent to tempt me to reject it; that's it, Mr. John Walter! This bumping round the world has at least sharpened my wits!" and Ruth sat beating a tattoo with the toe of her slipper on the carpet, and looking very profound and wise. Then she took up the contract and examined it; it was brief, plain and easily understood, *even by a woman*, as the men say. "It is a good offer," said Ruth, "he is in earnest, so am I; it's a bargain." Ruth signed the document.

CHAPTER LXX

"GOOD AFTERNOON, 'Floy,'" said Mr. Lescom to Ruth, as she entered the Standard office, the day after she had signed the contract with Mr. Walter. "I was just thinking of you, and wishing for an opportunity to have a little private chat. Your articles are not as long as they used to be; you must be more liberal."

"I was not aware," replied Ruth, "that my articles had grown any shorter. However, with me, an article is an article, some of my shorter pieces being the most valuable I have written. If you would like more matter, Mr. Lescom, I wonder you have not offered me more pay."

"There it is," said Mr. Lescom, smiling; "women are never satisfied. The more they get, the more grasping they become. I have always paid you more than you could get anywhere else."

"Perhaps so," replied Ruth. "I believe I have never troubled you with complaints; but I *have* looked at my children sometimes, and thought that I must try somehow to get more; and I have sometimes thought that if my articles, as you have told me, were constantly bringing you new subscribers, friendship, if not justice, would induce you to raise my salary."

"*Friendship* has nothing to do with business," replied Mr. Lescom; "a bargain is a bargain. The law of supply and demand regulates prices in all cases. In literature, at present, the supply greatly exceeds the demand, consequently the prices are low. Of course, I have to regulate my arrangements according to my own interests, and not according to the interests of others. You, of course, must regulate your arrangements according to *your* interests; and if anybody else will give you more than I do, you are at liberty to take it. As I said before, *business* is one thing—*friendship* is another. Each is good in its way, but they are quite distinct."

As Mr. Lescom finished this business-like and logical speech, he looked smilingly at Ruth, with an air which might be called one of tyrannical benevolence; as if he would say, "Well, now, I'd like to know what you can find to say to that?"

"I am glad," replied Ruth, "that you think so, for I have already acted in accordance with your sentiments. I have had, and accepted, an offer of a better salary than you pay me. My object in calling this afternoon was to inform you of this; and to say, that I shall not be able to write any more for 'The Standard.'"

Mr. Lescom looked astonished, and gazed at Ruth without speaking, probably because he did not know exactly what to say. He had argued Ruth's case so well, while he supposed he was arguing his own, that nothing more could be said. Mr. Lescom, in reality, valued Ruth's services more than those of all his other contributors combined, and the loss of them was a bitter thing to him. And then, what would his subscribers say? The reason of Ruth's leaving might become known; it would not sound well to have it said that she quit writing for him because he did not, or could not, or would not pay her as much as others. Just then it occurred to him that engaging to write for another journal, did not necessarily preclude the possibility of her continuing to write for "The Standard." Catching eagerly at the idea, he said:

"Well, 'Floy,' I am really glad that you have been so fortunate. Of course I wish you to make as much as you can, and should be glad, did my circumstances admit, to give you a salary equal to what you can command elsewhere; but as I cannot give you more than I have been paying, I am glad somebody else will. Still, I see no reason why you should stop writing for 'The Standard.' Your articles will just be as valuable to me, as though you had made no new engagement."

"I am sorry to disappoint you, Mr. Lescom," replied Ruth, "but I cannot meet your wishes in this respect, as the contract I have signed will not permit me to write for any paper but 'The Household Messenger.'"

At this announcement Mr. Lescom's veil of good nature was rent in twain. "'The Household Messenger!' Ah! it's John Walter then, who has found you out? I don't wish to boast, but I must say, that I think you have made but a poor exchange. The whole thing is very unfortunate for you. I was just making arrangements to club with two other editors, and to offer you a handsome yearly salary for writing exclusively for our three papers;

but of course that arrangement is all knocked in the head now. It seems to me that you might have made an exception in favor of 'The Standard.' I have no doubt that Mr. Walter would have consented to let you write for it, as it was the first paper for which you ever wrote. He would probably do so now if you would ask him. He is an editor, and would understand the matter at once. He would see that I had more than ordinary claims upon you. What do you say to writing him on the subject?"

"I have no objection to doing so," replied Ruth, "if you think it will avail anything, though if I succeed in getting Mr. Walter's permission to write for *you*, I suppose Mr. Tibbetts, of The Pilgrim, will wish me to do the same for him, when he returns. I called at the Pilgrim office this morning, and his partner, Mr. Elder, said that he was out of town, and would not be home for several days, and that he would be greatly incensed when he heard I was going to leave, as I was getting very popular with his subscribers. Mr. Elder was very sorry himself, but he treated me courteously. By the way, Mr. Lescom, I think you had better write to Mr. Walter, as well as myself; you understand such matters, and can probably write more to the point than I can."

"Very well," said Mr. Lescom, "I will write to him at once, and you had better write now by the same mail, and have the letters both enclosed in one envelope."

Ruth took a seat at the editorial table, and wrote to Mr. Walter. The letters were sent at once to the Post-office, so as to catch the afternoon mail, and Ruth took her leave, promising to call on the morning of the second day after, to see Mr. Walter's reply, which, judging by his usual promptness, would arrive by that time.

CHAPTER LXXI

"*AH!* another letter from 'Floy,'" said Mr. Walter, as he seated himself in his office; "now I shall hear how Lescom and Tibbetts & Co., feel about losing her. 'Floy' had probably told them by the time she wrote, and they have probably told her that she owes her reputation to them, called her ungrateful, and all that sort of thing; let us see what she says."

After reading 'Floy's' letter, Mr. Walter laid it down and began muttering out his thoughts after his usual fashion. "Just as I expected; Lescom has worked on 'Floy's' kind heart till she really feels a sort of necessity not to leave him so abruptly, and requests me as a personal favor to grant his request, at least for a time; no, no, 'Floy'—not unless he will pay you five times as much as he pays you now, and allow you, besides, to write much, or little, as you please; but where is Lescom's communication? Ruth says he wrote by the same mail—ah, here it is:

"Mr. Walter:

Sir,—Mrs. Hall, 'Floy,' informs me that you have engaged her to write exclusively for the Household Messenger, and that you will not consent to her writing for any other publication. Perhaps you are not aware that *I* was the first to introduce 'Floy' to the public, and that I have made her reputation what it is. This being the case, you will not think it strange that I feel as if I had some claim on her, so long as I pay her as much as she can get elsewhere. I need not say to you that The Standard is in a very flourishing condition; its circulation having nearly doubled during the past year, and that my resources are such as to enable me to outbid all competitors for 'Floy's' services, if I choose to take such a course; but I trust you will at once perceive that The Standard should be made an exception to your contract, and permit 'Floy' still to write for it.

"Respectfully yours, F. Lescom."

"Well, upon my word," exclaimed Mr. Walter, when he had finished Mr. Lescom's letter; "if this is not the coolest piece of egotism and impudence that I ever saw; but it is no use wasting vitality about it. I will just answer the letter, and let things take their course; I have the weather-gage of him now, and I'll keep it; he shall have my reply to digest the first thing in the morning; I'll write to 'Floy' first, though."

On the designated Thursday, Ruth, according to her promise, called at the Standard office; something had occurred to detain Mr. Lescom, so she sat down and opened Mr. Walter's letter, which lay on the table waiting for her, and read as follows:

"Dear Ruth:

"I have just finished reading yours and Lescom's letters. Yours has touched me deeply. It was just like you, but you know little of the selfishness and humbuggery of some newspaper publishers; you seem really to think that you ought to write for Mr. Lescom, if he so much desires it. This is very good of you, and very amiable, but (forgive my want of gallantry) very foolish. You can now understand, if you did not before, why I desired you to sign the contract by return mail. I was afraid if you went to Mr. Lescom, or Mr. Tibbetts of The Pilgrim, *before signing it,* that they would impose upon your good womanly heart, and thereby gain an unfair advantage over you. I wished to surprise you into signing the contract, that I might have a fair and righteous advantage over them. And now, 'Floy,' please to leave the whole matter to me. I shall not consent to your writing for any paper, unless the proprietors will give you the full value of your articles—what they are really worth to them. If things turn out as I confidently expect they will, from your present popularity, you will soon be in a state of comparative independence. On the next page you will find a copy of my answer to Mr. Lescom's letter. Please keep me informed of the happenings at your end of the route.

"Yours most truly, John Walter."

Ruth then read Mr. Walter's letter to Mr. Lescom, as follows:

"F. Lescom, Esq.

"Sir,—Your letter in regard to 'Floy,' &c., is at hand. You say, that perhaps I am not aware that *you* were the first to introduce 'Floy' to the public, and that *you* have made her reputation. It is fortunate for *you* that she made The Standard the channel of her first communications to the public. I know this very well, but I am not aware, nor do I believe, that *you* have made her reputation; neither do I think that you believe this yourself. The truth is simply this; 'Floy' is a genius; her writings, wherever published, would have attracted attention, and stamped the writer as a person of extraordinary talent; hence her fame and success, the fruits of which *you* have principally reaped. As to 'Floy's' being under any obligations to you, I repudiate the idea entirely; the 'obligation' is all on the other side. *She* has made 'The Standard,' instead of you making *her* reputation. Her genius has borne its name to England, Scotland, Ireland,—wherever the English language is spoken,—and raised it from an obscure provincial paper to a widely-known journal. You say that you are wealthy, and can pay as much as anybody for 'Floy's' services; I wonder this has never occurred to you before, especially as she has informed you frequently how necessitous were her circumstances. You also inform me that the circulation of The Standard has nearly doubled the past year. This I can readily believe, since it is something more than a year since 'Floy' commenced writing for it. In reply to your declaration, 'that in case you are driven to compete for 'Floy's' services, you can outbid all competitors,' I have only to say that my contract with her is for one year; on its expiration, 'Floy' will be at liberty to decide for herself; you will then have an opportunity to compete for her pen, and enjoy the privilege of exhibiting your enterprise and liberality.

"Your ob't servant, JOHN WALTER."

Ruth waited some time after reading these letters, for Mr. Lescom to come in; but, finding he was still unexpectedly detained, she took a handful of letters, which the clerk had just received by mail for her, and bent her steps homeward.

CHAPTER LXXII

THE FIRST LETTER Ruth opened on her return, was a request from a Professor of some College for her autograph for himself and some friends; the second, an offer of marriage from a Southerner, who confessed to one hundred negroes, "but hoped that the strength and ardor of the attachment with which the perusal of her articles had inspired him, would be deemed sufficient atonement for this in her Northern eyes. The frozen North," he said, "had no claim on such a nature as hers; the sunny South, the land of magnolias and orange blossoms, the land of love, *should* be her chosen home. Would she not smile on him? She should have a box at the opera, a carriage, and servants in livery, and the whole heart and soul of Victor Le Pont."

The next was more interesting. It was an offer to "Floy" from a publishing house, to collect her newspaper articles into a volume. They offered to give her so much on a copy, or $800 for the copyright. An answer was requested immediately. In the same mail came another letter of the same kind from a distant State, also offering to publish a volume of her articles.

"Well, well," soliloquized Ruth, "business is accumulating. I don't see but I shall have to make a book in spite of myself; and yet those articles were written under such disadvantages, would it be *wise* in me to publish so soon? But Katy? and $800 copyright money?" Ruth glanced round her miserable, dark room, and at the little stereotyped bowl of bread and milk that stood waiting on the table for her supper and Nettie's; $800 *copyright money!* it *was* a temptation; but supposing her book should prove a hit? and bring double, treble, fourfold that sum, to go into her publisher's pockets instead of hers? how provoking! Ruth straightened up, and putting on a very resolute air, said, "No, gentlemen, I will *not* sell you my copyright; these autograph letters, and all the other letters of friendship, love, and business, I am constantly receiving from strangers, are so many proofs that I have won the public ear. No, I will not sell my copyright; I will rather deny myself a while longer, and accept the per-centage;" and so she sat down and wrote her publishers; but then caution whispered, what if her book should *not* sell? "Oh, pshaw," said Ruth, "it *shall!*" and she brought her little fist down on the table till the old stone inkstand seemed to rattle out "*it shall!*"

"Ah, here is another letter, which I have overlooked," said Ruth.

"To the distinguished and popular writer, 'Floy':

"Madam,—I trust you will excuse the liberty I take in writing you, when you get through with my letter. I am thus confident of your leniency, because it seems to me that my case is not only a plain, but an interesting one. To come to the point, without any circumlocutory delay, I am a young man with aspirations far above my station in life. This declaration is perfectly true in some senses, but not in every sense. My parents and my ancestors are and were highly respectable people. My name, as you will see when you come to my signature, is Reginald Danby. The Danby family, Madam, was founded by Sir Reginald Danby, who was knighted for certain gallant exploits on the field of Hastings, in the year 1066, by William the Conqueror. Sir Reginald afterward married a Saxon dame, named Edith, the daughter of a powerful land-owner; hence the Danby family. All this is of very little consequence, and I only mention it in a sort of incidental way, to show you that my declaration in regard to the respectability of my family is true, and fortified by unimpeachable historical evidence; and I will here remark, that you will always find any assertion of mine as well sustained, by copious and irrefragable proof.

"The respectability of our family being thus settled I come back to an explanation of what I mean by my 'having aspirations above my station in life.' It is this: I am poor. My family, though once wealthy, is now impoverished. The way this state of things came about, was substantially as follows: My grandfather, who was a strong-minded, thrifty gentleman, married into a poetical family. His wife was the most poetical member of said family; much of her poetry is still extant; it never was published, because in those days publishers were not as enterprising as they are now. We value these manuscripts very highly; still I should be willing to send you some of them for perusal, in case you will return them and pay the postage both ways, my limited means not permitting me to share that pleasure with you. As I have intimated, my grandmother reveled in poetry. She doated on Shakspeare, and about three months before my father's birth, she went to a theatre to witness the performance of 'The Midsummer Night's Dream.' She was enchanted! and, with characteristic decision, resolved to commit the entire play to memory. This resolution she executed with characteristic pertinacity, notwithstanding frequent and annoying interruptions, from various causes entirely beyond her control. She finished committing this immortal poem to memory, the very night my father was born. Time rolled on; my father, as he grew up, exhibited great flightiness of character, and instability of purpose, the result, undoubtedly, of his mother's committing 'The Midsummer Night's Dream' to memory under the circumstances which I have detailed. My father, owing to this unfortunate development of character, proved inadequate to the management of his estate, or, indeed, of any business whatever, and hence our present pecuniary embarrassments. Before quitting this painful branch of my subject, it will doubtless gratify you to have me state, that, inasmuch as my father married a woman of phlegmatic temperament, and entirely unpoetical mind, the balance of character has been happily restored to our family, so there is no fear for me. I am thus particular in my statements, because I have a high regard for truth, and for veracity, for accuracy in the *minutest* things; a phase of character which may be accounted for from the fact, that I have just gone through a severe and protracted course of mathematics. These preliminaries being thus fairly before you, I now come to the immediate topic of my letter, viz.: I wish to go through College; I have not the means. I wish you to help me. You are probably rich; I hope you are with all my heart. You must be able to command a high salary, and a great deal of influence. I don't ask you to lend me the money out of hand. What I propose is this: I will furnish you the subject for a splendid and thrilling story, founded on facts in the history of our family; the Danby family. In this book, my grandmother's poetry would probably read to advantage; if so, it would be a great saving, as her writings are voluminous. Your book would be sure to have a large sale, and the profits would pay my expenses at College, and perhaps leave a large surplus. This surplus should be yours, and I would also agree to pay back the sum used by me from my first earnings after graduation. I have thought over this matter a great deal, and the foregoing strikes me as the only way in which this thing can be done. If you can devise a better plan, I will of course gladly adopt it. I am not at all opinionated, but am always glad to listen to anything reasonable. Please let me hear from you as soon as possible, and believe me truly your friend and admirer,

"Reginald Danby."

CHAPTER LXXIII

MR. TIBBETTS, the editor of "The Pilgrim," having returned from the country, Ruth went to the Pilgrim office to get copies of several of her articles, which she had taken no pains to keep, never dreaming of re-publishing them in book form.

Mr. Tibbetts was sitting at his editorial desk, looking over a pile of manuscript. Ruth made known her errand, and also the fact of her being about to publish her book. He handed her a chair, and drawing another in front of her, said very stiffly, "My partner, Mr. Elder, Mrs. Hall, has astonished me by the information that you have very suddenly decided to withdraw from us, who first patronized you, and to write for the 'Household Messenger.'"

"Yes," replied Ruth, "I considered it my duty to avail myself of that increase of salary. My circumstances have been exceedingly straitened. I have two little ones dependent on my exertions, and *their* future, as well as my own, to look to. You have often told me that you already paid me all you could afford, so it was useless to ask you for more; beside, the contract I have accepted, obliged me to decline or accept it by return of mail, without communicating its contents."

"Ah! I see—I see," said Mr. Tibbetts, growing very red in the face, and pushing back his chair; "it is always the way young writers treat those who have made their reputation."

"Perhaps *your* making my reputation, may be a question open to debate," answered Ruth, stung by his tone; "I feel this morning, however, disinclined to discuss the question; so, if you please, we will waive it. You have always told me that you were constantly beset by the most talented contributors for patronage, so that of course you will nót find it difficult to supply my place, when I leave you."

"But you shall *not* leave," said Mr. Tibbetts, turning very pale about the mouth, and closing his lips firmly.

"*Shall not!*" repeated Ruth, rising, and standing erect before him. "*Shall* not, Mr. Tibbetts? I have yet to learn that I am not free to go, if I choose."

"Well, you are *not*," said Mr. Tibbetts; "that is a little mistake of yours, as I will soon convince you. Discontinue writing for 'The Pilgrim,' and I will immediately get out a cheap edition of your articles, and spoil the sale of your book;" and he folded his arms, and faced Ruth as if he would say, "Now writhe if you like; I have you."

Ruth smiled derisively, then answered in a tone so low that it was scarcely audible, "Mr. Tibbetts, you have mistaken your auditor. I am not to be frightened, or threatened, or *insulted*," said she, turning toward the door. "Even had I not myself the spirit to defy you, as I now do, for I will never touch pen to paper again for 'The Pilgrim,' you could not accomplish your threat; for think you my publishers will tamely fold their arms, and see *their* rights infringed? No, sir, you have mistaken both them and me;" and Ruth moved toward the door.

"Stay!" exclaimed Mr. Tibbetts, placing his hand on the latch; "when you see a paragraph in print that will sting your proud soul to the quick, know that John Tibbetts has more ways than one of humbling so imperious a dame."

"That will be hardly consistent," replied Ruth, in the same calm tone, "with the thousand-and-one commendatory notices of 'Floy'—the boasts you have made of the almost exclusive right to the *valuable services of so bright a literary star*."

"Of course you will not see such a paragraph in *my* paper," replied Mr. Tibbetts. "I am aware, most logical of women, that I stand committed before the public *there;* but I have many an editorial friend, scattered over the country, who would loan me *their* columns for this purpose."

"As you please," said Ruth. "It were a *manly* act; but your threat does not move *me*."

"I'll have my revenge!" exclaimed Tibbetts, as the last fold of Ruth's dress fluttered out the door.

CHAPTER LXXIV

THOSE OF MY READERS who are well acquainted with journalism, know that some of our newspapers, nominally edited by the persons whose names appear as responsible in that capacity, *seldom*, perhaps *never* contain an article from their pen, the whole paper being "made up" by some obscure individual, with more brains than pennies, whose brilliant paragraphs, metaphysical essays, and racy book reviews, are attributed (and tacitly fathered) by the comfortably-fed gentlemen who keep these, their factotums, in some garret, just one degree above starving point. In the city, where board is expensive, and single gentlemen are "taken in and done for," under many a sloping attic roof are born thoughts which should win for their originators fame and independence.

Mr. Horace Gates, a gentlemanly, slender, scholar-like-looking person, held this nondescript, and unrecognized relation to the Irving Magazine; the nominal editor, Ruth's brother Hyacinth, furnishing but one article a week, to deduct from the immense amount of labor necessary to their weekly issue.

"Heigho," said Mr. Gates, dashing down his pen; "four columns yet to make up; I am getting tired of this drudgery. My friend Seaten told me that he was dining at a restaurant the other day, when my employer, Mr. Hyacinth Ellet, came in, and that a gentleman took occasion to say to Mr. E., how much he admired *his* article in the last Irving Magazine, on 'City Life.' *His* article! it took me one of the hottest days this season, in this furnace of a garret, with the beaded drops standing on my suffering forehead, to write that article, which, by the way, has been copied far and wide. His article! and the best of the joke is (Seaten says) the cool way in which Ellet thanked him, and pocketed all the credit of it! But what's this? here's a note from the very gentleman himself:

"Mr. Gates:

"Sir,—I have noticed that you have several times scissorized from the exchanges, articles over the signature of 'Floy,' and inserted

> them in our paper. It is my wish that all articles bearing that signature should be excluded from our paper, and that no allusion be made to her, in any way or shape, in the columns of the Irving Magazine. As you are in our business confidence, I may say, that the writer is a sister of mine, and that it would annoy and mortify me exceedingly to have the fact known; and it is my express wish that you should not, hereafter, in any way, aid in circulating her articles.
>
> "Yours, &c., HYACINTH ELLET."

"What does that mean?" said Gates; "*his* sister? why don't he want her to write? I have cut out every article of hers as fast as they appeared; confounded good they are, too, and I call myself a judge; they are better, at any rate, than half our paper is filled with. This is all very odd—it stimulates my curiosity amazingly—*his* sister? married or unmarried, maid, wife, or widow? She can't be poor when he's so well off; (gave $100 for a vase which struck his fancy yesterday, at Martini's.) I don't understand it. 'Annoy and mortify him exceedingly;' what *can* he mean? I must get at the bottom of that; she is becoming very popular, at any rate; her pieces are traveling all over the country—and here is one, to my mind, as good as anything *he* ever wrote. Ha! ha! perhaps that's the very idea now—perhaps he wants to be the only genius in the family. Let him! if he can; if she don't win an enviable name, and in a very short time too, I shall be mistaken. I wish I knew something about her. Hyacinth is a heartless dog—pays me principally in fine speeches; and because I am not in a position just now to speak my mind about it. I suppose he takes me for the pliant tool I appear. By Jupiter! it makes my blood boil; but let me get another and better offer, Mr. Ellet, and see how long I will write articles for you to father, in this confounded hot garret. '*His* sister!' I will inquire into that. I'll bet a box of cigars she writes for daily bread—Heaven help her, if she does, poor thing!—it's hard enough, as I know, for a *man* to be jostled and snubbed round in printing-offices. Well, well, it's no use wondering, I must go to work; what a pile of books here is to be reviewed! wonder who reads all the books? Here is Uncle Sam's Log House. Mr. Ellet writes me that I must simply announce the book without comment, for fear of offending southern subscribers. The word 'slave' I know has been tabooed in our columns this long while, for the same reason. Here are poems by

Lina Lintney—weak as diluted water, but the authoress once paid Mr. Ellet a compliment in a newspaper article, and here is her 'reward of merit,' (in a memorandum attached to the book, and just sent down by Mr. Ellet;) 'give this volume a first-rate notice.' Bah! what's the use of criticism when a man's opinion can be bought and sold that way? it is an imposition on the public. There is 'The Barolds' too; I am to 'give that a capital notice,' because the authoress introduced Mr. Ellet into fashionable society when a young man. The grammar in that book would give Lindley Murray convulsions, and the construction of the sentences drive Blair to a mad-house. Well, a great deal the dear public know what a book is, by the reviews of it in this paper. Heaven forgive me the lies I tell this way on compulsion.

"The humbuggery of this establishment is only equalled by the gullability of the dear public. Once a month, now, I am ordered to puff every 'influential paper in the Union,' to ward off attacks on the Irving Magazine, and the bait takes, too, by Jove. That little 'Tea-Table Tri-Mountain Mercury,' has not muttered or peeped about Hyacinth's 'toadyism when abroad,' since Mr. Ellet gave me orders to praise 'the typographical and literary excellence of that widely-circulated paper.' Then, there is the editor of 'The Bugbear," a cut-and-thrust-bludgeon-pen-and-ink-desperado, who makes the mincing, aristocratic Hyacinth quake in his patent-leather boots. I have orders to toss him a sugar-plum occasionally, to keep his plebeian mouth shut; something after the French maxim, 'always to praise a person for what they *are not;*'—for instance, 'our very *gentlemanly* neighbor and contemporary, the discriminating and refined editor of The Bugbear, whose very readable and spicy paper,' &c., &c. Then, there is the *religious* press. Hyacinth, having rather a damaged reputation, is anxious to enlist them on his side, particularly the editor of 'The Religious Platform.' I am to copy at least one of his editorials once a fortnight, or in some way call attention to his paper. Then, if Hyacinth chooses to puff actresses, and call Mme. ——— a 'splendid personation of womanhood,' and praise her equivocal writings in his paper, which lies on many a family table to be read by innocent young girls, he knows the caustic pen of that religious editor will never be dipped in ink to reprove him. That is the way it is done. Mutual admiration-society—bah! I wish *I* had a paper. Wouldn't I call things by their right names? Would I know any sex in books? Would I praise a book because a woman wrote it? Would I abuse it for the same reason? Would I say, as one of our most able editors said not long since to his reviewer, 'cut it up root and branch; what right have these women to set themselves up for authors, and reap literary laurels?' Would I unfairly insert all the adverse notices of a book, and never copy one in its praise? Would I pass over the wholesale swindling of some aristocratic scoundrel, and trumpet in my police report, with heartless comments, the name of some poor, tempted, starving wretch, far less deserving of censure, in God's eye, than myself? Would I have my tongue or my pen tied in any way by policy, or interest, or clique-ism? No—sir! The world never will see a paper till mine is started. Would I write long descriptions of the wardrobe of foreign *prima donnas*, who bring their cracked voices, and reputations to our American market, and 'occupy suites of rooms lined with satin, and damask, and velvet,' and goodness knows what, and give their reception-soirees, at which they '*affably notice*' our toadying first citizens? By Jupiter! why *shouldn't* they be 'affable'? Don't they come over here for our money and patronage? Who cares how many 'bracelets' Signora ——— had on, or whose 'arm she leaned gracefully upon,' or whether her 'hair was braided or curled'? If, because a lord or a duke once 'honored her' by insulting her with infamous proposals, some few brainless Americans choose to deify her as a goddess, in the name of George Washington and common sense, let it not be taken as a national exponent. There are some few Americans left, who prefer ipecac in homœopathic doses."

CHAPTER LXXV

"HARK! Nettie. Go to the door, dear," said Ruth, "some one knocked."

"It is a strange gentleman, mamma," whispered Nettie, "and he wants to see you."

Ruth bowed as the stranger entered. She could not recollect that she had ever seen him before, but he looked very knowing, and, what was very provoking, seemed to enjoy her embarrassment hugely. He regarded

Nettie, too, with a very scrutinizing look, and seemed to devour everything with the first glance of his keen, searching eye. He even seemed to listen to the whir—whir—whir of the odd strange lodger in the garret overhead.

"I don't recollect you," said Ruth, hesitating, and blushing slightly; "you have the advantage of me, sir?"

"And yet you and I have been writing to each other, for a week or more," replied the gentleman, with a good-humored smile; "you have even signed a contract, entitling me to your pen-and-ink services."

"Mr. Walter?" said Ruth, holding out her hand.

"Yes," replied Mr. Walter, "I had business this way, and I could not come here without finding you out."

"Oh, thank you," said Ruth, "I was just wishing that I had some head wiser than mine, to help me decide on a business matter which came up two or three days ago. Somehow I don't feel the least reluctance to bore you with it, or a doubt that your advice will not be just the thing; but I shall not stop to dissect the philosophy of that feeling, lest in grasping at the shadow, I should lose the substance," said she, smiling.

While Ruth was talking, Mr. Walter's keen eye glanced about the room, noting its general comfortless appearance, and the little bowl of bread and milk that stood waiting for their supper. Ruth observed this, and blushed deeply. When she looked again at Mr. Walter, his eyes were glistening with tears.

"Come here, my darling," said he to Nettie, trying to hide his emotion.

"I don't know you," answered Nettie.

"But you will, my dear, because I am your mamma's friend."

"Are you Katy's friend?" asked Nettie.

"Katy?" repeated Mr. Walter.

"Yes, my *sister* Katy; she can't live here, because we don't have supper enough; pretty soon mamma will earn more supper, won't you mamma? Shan't you be glad when Katy comes home, and we all have enough to eat?" said the child to Mr. Walter.

Mr. Walter pressed his lips to the child's forehead with a low "Yes, my darling;" and then placed his watch chain and seals at her disposal, fearing Ruth might be painfully affected by her artless prattle.

Ruth then produced the different publishers' offers she had received for her book, and handed them to Mr. Walter.

"Well," said he, with a gratified smile, "I am not at all surprised; but what are you going to reply?"

"Here is my answer," said Ruth, "*i.e.* provided your judgment endorses it. I am a novice in such matters, you know, but I cannot help thinking, Mr. Walter, that my book will be a success. You will see that I have acted upon that impression, and refused to sell my copyright."

"You don't approve it?" said she, looking a little confused, as Mr. Walter bent his keen eyes on her, without replying.

"But I do though," said he; "I was only thinking how excellent a substitute strong common-sense may be for experience. Your answer is brief, concise, sagacious, and business-like; I endorse it unhesitatingly. It is just what I should have advised you to write. You are correct in thinking that your book will be popular, and wise in keeping the copyright in your own hands. In how incredibly short a time you have gained a literary reputation, Floy."

"Yes," answered Ruth, smiling, "it is all like a dream to me;" and then the smile faded away, and she shuddered involuntarily as the recollection of all her struggles and sufferings came vividly up to her remembrance.

Swiftly the hours fled away as Mr. Walter, with a brother's freedom, questioned Ruth as to her past life and drew from her the details of her eventful history.

"Thank God, the morning dawneth," said he in a subdued tone, as he pressed Ruth's hand, and bade her a parting good-night.

Ruth closed the door upon Mr. Walter's retreating figure, and sat down to peruse the following letters, which had been sent her to Mr. Walter's care, at the Household Messenger office.

"Mrs. or Miss 'Floy:'

"Permit me to address you on a subject which lies near my heart, which is, in fact, a subject of pecuniary importance to the person now addressing you. My story is to me a painful one; it would doubtless interest you; were it written and published, it would be a thrilling tale.

"Some months since I had a lover whom I adored, and who said he adored me. But as Shakspeare has said, 'The course of true love never did run smooth;' ours soon became an up-hill affair, my lover proved false, ceased his visits, and sat on the other side of the meetinghouse. On my writing to him and desiring an explanation, he insultingly replied, that I was not what his fancy had painted me. Was that *my* fault? false, fickle, ungenerous man! But I was not thus to be deceived and shuffled off. No; I employed the best counsel in the State and commenced an action for damages, determined to get some balm for my wounded feelings; but owing to the premature death of my principal witness, I lost the case and the costs were heavy. The excitement and worry of the trial brought on a fever, and I found myself on my recovery, five hundred dollars in debt; I intend to pay every cent of this, but how am I to pay it? My salary for teaching school is small and it will take me many years. I want you, therefore, to assist me by writing out my story and giving me the book. I will furnish all the facts, and the story, written out by your magic pen, would be a certain success. A publisher in this city has agreed to publish it for me if you will write it. I could then triumph over the villain who so basely deceived me.

"Please send me an early answer, as the publisher referred to is in a great hurry.

"Very respectfully yours,

"SARAH JARMESIN."

"Well," said Ruth, laughing, "my bump of invention will be entirely useless, if my kind friends keep on furnishing me with subjects at this rate. Here is letter No. 2."

"DEAR 'FLOY':

"My dog Fido is dead. He was a splendid Newfoundland, black and shaggy; father gave $10 for him when he was a pup. We all loved him dearly. He was a prime dog, could swim like a fish. The other morning we found him lying motionless on the door-step. Somebody had poisoned poor Fido. I cried all that day, and didn't play marbles for a whole week. He is buried in the garden, and I want you to write an epithalamium about him. My brother John, who is looking over my shoulder, is laughing like everything; he says 'tis an epitaph, not an epithalamium that I want, just as if *I* didn't know what I want? John is just home from college, and thinks he knows everything. It is my dog, and I'll fix his tombstone just as I like. Fellows in round jackets are not always fools. Send it along quick, please, 'Floy'; the stone-cutter is at work now. What a funny way they cut marble, don't they? (with sand and water.) Johnny Weld and I go there every recess, to see how they get on with the tombstone. Don't stick in any Latin or Greek, now, in your epithalamium. Our John cannot call for a glass of water without lugging in one or the other of them; I'm sick as death of it. I wonder if I shall be such a fool when I go to college. You ought to be glad you are a woman, and don't have to go. Don't forget Fido, now. Remember, he was six years old, black, shaggy, with a white spot on his forehead, and rather a short-ish tail—a prime dog, I tell *you*.

BILLY SANDS."

"It is a harrowing case, Billy," said Ruth, "but I shall have to let Fido pass; now for letter No. 3."

"DEAR MADAM:

"I address a stranger, and yet *not* a stranger, for I have read your heart in your many writings. In them I see sympathy for the poor, the sorrowing, and the dependent; I see a tender love for helpless childhood. Dear 'Floy,' I am an orphan, and that most wretched of all beings, a loving, but unloved wife. The hour so dreaded by all maternity draws near to me. It has been revealed to me in dreams that I shall not survive it. 'Floy,' will you be a mother to my babe? I cannot tell you why I put this trust in one whom I have only known through her writings, but something assures me it will be safe with you; that you only can fill my place in the little heart that this moment is pulsating beneath my own. Oh, do not refuse me. There are none in the wide world to dispute the claim I would thus transfer to you. Its father—but of him I will not speak; the wine-cup is my rival. Write me speedily. I shall die content if your arms receive my babe.

"Yours affectionately, MARY ANDREWS."

"Poor Mary! that letter must be answered," said Ruth, with a sigh;—"ah, here is one more letter."

"MISS, or MRS., or MADAM FLOY:

"I suppose by this time you have become so inflated that the honest truth would be rather unpalatable to you; nevertheless, I am going to send you a few plain words. The rest of the world flatters you—I shall do no such thing. You have written tolerably, all things considered, but you violate all established rules of composition, and are as lawless and erratic as a comet. You may startle and dazzle, but you are fit only to throw people out of their orbits. Now and then, there's a gleam of something like reason in your writings, but for the most part they are unmitigated trash—false in sentiment—unrhetorical in expression; in short, were you my daughter, which I thank a good Providence you are not, I should box your ears, and keep you on a bread and water diet till you improved. That you *can* do better, if you will, I am very sure, and that is why I take the pains to find fault, and tell you what none of your fawning friends will.

"You are not a genius—no, madam, not by many removes; Shakspeare was a genius—Milton was a genius—the author of 'History of the Dark Ages,' which has reached its fifteenth edition, was a genius—(you may not know you have now the honor of being addressed by him;) no, madam, you are not a genius, nor have I yet seen a just criticism of your writings; they are all either over-praised, or over-abused; you have a certain sort of talent, and that talent, I grant you, is peculiar; but a genius—no, no, Mrs., or Miss, or Madam Floy—you don't approach genius, though I am not without a hope that, if you are not spoiled by injudicious, sycophantic admirers, you may yet produce something creditable; although I candidly confess, that it is my opinion, that the *female* mind is incapable of producing anything which may be strictly termed *literature*.

"Your honest friend, WILLIAM STEARNS.

'Prof. of Greek, Hebrew, and Mathematics, in Hopetown College, and author of 'History of the Dark Ages.'"

"Oh vanity! thy name is William Stearns," said Ruth.

CHAPTER LXXVI

"*HAVE YOU EVER* submitted your head to a phrenological examination? asked Mr. Walter, as he made a call on Ruth, the next morning.

"No," said Ruth; "I believe that much more is to be told by the expression of people's faces than by the bumps upon their heads."

"And you a woman of sense!" replied Mr. Walter. "Will you have your head examined to please me? I should like to know what Prof. Finman would say of you, before I leave town."

"Well! yes! I don't mind going," said Ruth, "provided the Professor does not know his subject, and I see that there's fair play," said she, laughing; "but I warn you, beforehand, that I have not the slightest faith in the science."

Ruth tied on her bonnet, and was soon demurely seated in the Professor's office, with her hair about her shoulders. Mr. Walter sat at a table near, prepared to take notes in short-hand.

"You have an unusually even head, madam," said the Professor. "Most of the faculties are fully developed. There are not necessarily any extremes in your character, and when you manifest them, they are more the result of circumstances than the natural tendency of the mind. You are of a family where there was more than ordinary unity in the connubial relations; certainly in the marriage, if not in the after-life of your parents.

"Your physiology indicates a predominance of the nervous temperament; this gives unusual activity of mind, and furnishes the capacity for a great amount of enjoyment or suffering. Few enjoy or suffer with such intensity as you do. Your happiness or misery depends very much on surrounding influences and circumstances.

"You have, next, a predominance of the vital temperament, which gives great warmth and ardor to your mind, and enables you to enjoy physical comfort and the luxuries of life in a high degree. Your muscular system is rather defective; there not being enough to furnish real strength and stamina of constitution. Although you may live to be aged, you will not be able to put forth such vigorous efforts as you could do, were the motive or muscular temperament developed in a higher degree. You may think I am mistaken on this point, but I am not. You have an immense power of will, are energetic and forcible in overcoming obstacles, would display more than ordinary fortitude in going through trials and difficulties, and possess a tenacity of purpose and perseverance in action, which enable you to do whatever you are determined upon doing; but these are *mental* characteristics not *physical*, and your mind often tires out your body, and leaves you in a state of muscular prostration.

"Your phrenology indicates an unusual degree of respect and regard for whatever you value as superior. You never trifle with superiority. I do not mean conventional superiority or bombastic assumption, but what you really believe to be good and noble. As a child, you were very obedient, unless your sense of justice (which is very strong) was violated. In such a case, it was somewhat difficult for you to yield either ready or implicit obedience. You are religiously disposed. You are also characterized by a strong belief in Divine influences, providences, and special interpositions from on high. You are more than ordinarily spiritual in the tone of your mind. You see, or think you see, the hand of Providence in things as they transpire. You are also very conscientious, and this, combined with your firmness, which is quite strong, and supported by your faith in Providence, gives you a striking degree of what is called moral courage. When you believe you are right, there is no moving you; and your friends probably think that you are sometimes very obstinate; but let them convince your intellect and satisfy your conscience, and you will be quite tractable, more especially as you are characterized by unusual sympathy and tenderness of feeling. You too easily catch the spirit of others,—of those you love and are interested in, and feel as they feel, and enjoy or suffer as they do. You have very strong hope with reference to immortality and future happiness. When a young girl, you were remarkably abounding in your spiritual anticipations of what you were going to be as a woman.

"You possess an extraordinary degree of perseverance, but have not a marked degree of prompt decision. After you have *decided*, you act energetically, and are more sure to finish what you commence, than you are ready to begin a new enterprise. You are decidedly cautious, anxious, mindful of results, and desire to avoid difficulty and danger. You take all necessary care, and provide well for the future. Your cautiousness is, in fact, too active.

"You place a very high value on your character; are particularly sensitive to reproach; cannot tolerate scolding, or being found fault with. You can be quite reserved, dignified, and even haughty. You are usually kind and affable, but are capable of strong feelings of resentment. You make few enemies by your manner of speaking and acting. You are uniform in the manifestation of your affections. You do not form attachments readily, or frequently; on the contrary, you are quite particular in the choice of your friends, and are very devoted to those to whom you become attached. You manifested these same traits when a child, in the selection of playmates.

"Your love is a mental love—a regard for the mind, rather than the person of the individual. You appreciate the masculine mind as such, rather than the physical form. You have a high regard for chivalry, manliness, and intellectuality in man, but you also demand goodness, and religious devotion. It would give you pain to hear a friend speak lightly of what you consider sacred things; and I hardly think you would ever love a man whom you *knew* to be irreligious. Your maternal feelings are very strong. You are much interested in children. You sympathize with and understand them perfectly. You are, yourself, quite youthful in the tone of your mind; much younger than many not half your age. This, taken in connection with your sympathy with, and appreciation of, the character of children, enables you to entertain them, and win them to your wishes; but, at times, you are too anxious about their welfare. You are strongly attached to place, and are intensely patriotic. You believe in Plymouth Rock and Bunker Hill. You are not content without a home of your own; and yet, in a home of your own, you would not be happy without pleasant surroundings and associations, scenery, and such things as would facilitate improvement and enjoyment.

"You are very fond of poetry and beauty, wherever you see it,—of oratory, sculpture, painting, scenery, flowers, and beautiful sentiments. You must have everything nice; you cannot tolerate anything coarse or gross. The world is hardly finished nice enough for you. You are too exacting in this respect. The fact is, you are made of finer clay than most of us. You are particular with reference to your food, and not easily suited. You must have that which is clean and nice, or none. Whatever you do, such as embroidery, drawing, painting, needlework, or any artistic performance, is very nicely done. Your constructiveness is very large. You can plan well; can lay out work for others to advantage; can cut out things, and invent new and tasteful fashions. Your appreciation of colors is very nice; you can arrange and blend them harmoniously, in dress, in decoration of rooms, &c. You could make a slim wardrobe, and a small stock of furniture, go a great way, and get up a better looking parlor with a few hundred dollars, than some could with as many thousands.

"You exhibit a predominance of the reflective intellect over the perceptive, and are characterized for thought, judgment, and the power to comprehend ideas, more than for your knowledge of things, facts, circumstances or conditions of things. You remember and understand what you read, better than what you see and hear; still, you are more than ordinarily observant. In passing along the street, you would see much more than people in general, and would be able to describe very accurately the style, execution and quality of whatever you saw. You have a pliable mind. You love acting, and would excel as an actress. You have great powers of sarcasm. You enjoy fun highly, but it must be of the right kind. You will tolerate nothing low. You are precise in the use of language, and are a good verbal critic. You ought to be a good conversationist, and a forcible and spicy writer. In depicting character and describing scenes, you would be apt to display many of the characteristics which Dickens exhibits. Your aptness in setting-forth, your keen sense of the ludicrous, your great powers of amplification, and the intensity of your feelings, would enable you to produce a finely wrought out, and exquisitely colored picture. You have also an active sense of music; are almost passionately fond of that kind which is agreeable to you.

"You have more than ordinary fortitude, but are lacking in the influences of combativeness. Your temper comes to a crisis too soon; you cannot keep angry long enough to scold. You dislike contention. You read the minds of others almost instantaneously; and at once form a favorable or unfavorable impression of a person. You are secretive, and disposed to conceal your feelings; are anxious to avoid unnecessary exposure of your faults, and know how to appear to the best advantage. You have a good faculty of entertaining others, but can be with persons a long time without their becoming acquainted with you.

"You dream things true; truth comes to you in dreams, forewarnings, admonitions, &c.

"You are liable to be a very happy, or very unhappy, woman. The worst feature of your whole character, or tone of mind, arises from the influence of your education. Too much attention was paid to your mind, and not enough to your body. You were brought forward too early, and made a woman of too soon. Ideas too big for you were put into your mind, and it was not occupied enough about the ordinary affairs of life. This renders your mind too morbid and sensitive, and unfits you for encountering the disagreeable phases of life. You can endure disagreeable things with martyr-like firmness, but not with martyr-like resignation. They prey both on your mind and body, and wear heavily upon your spirit. You feel as though some one must go forward and clear the way for you to enjoy yourself; and if by any reverse of fortune, you have ever been thrown on your own resources, and forced to take care of yourself, you had to learn some lessons, which should have been taught you before you were sixteen years old. But in the general tone of your mind, in elevation of thought, feeling, sympathy, sentiment, and religious devotion, you rank far above most of us, above many who are, perhaps, better prepared to discharge the ordinary duties of life. In conclusion, I will remark, that very much might be said with reference to the operations of your mind, for we seldom find the faculties so fully developed, or the powers so versatile as in your case."

"Well," said Mr. Walter, with a triumphant air, as they left the Professor's office, "well, 'Floy,' what do you think?"

"I think we have received our $2 worth in flattery," replied Ruth, laughing.

"There is not a whit of exaggeration in it," said Mr. Walter. "The Professor has hit you off to the life."

"Well, I suppose it would be wasting breath to discuss the point with you," said Ruth, "so I will merely remark that I was highly amused when he said I should make a good actress. I have so often been told that."

"True; Comedy would be your forte, though. How is it that when looking about for employment, you never contemplated the stage?"

"Well, you know, Mr. Walter, that we May-Flower descendents hold the theatre in abhorrence. For myself, however, I can speak from observation, being determined not to take that doctrine on hearsay; I have witnessed many theatrical performances, and they only served to confirm my prejudices against the institution. I never should dream of such a means of support. Your Professor made one great mistake; for instance," said Ruth, "he thinks my physique is feeble. Do you know that I can walk longer and faster than any six women in the United States?"

"Yes," replied Mr. Walter, "I know all about that; I have known you, under a strong impetus, do six days' work in one, and I have known you after it prostrated with a nervous headache which defied every attempt at mitigation. He is right, Ruth, your mind often tires your body completely out."

"Another thing, your Professor says I do not like to be found fault with; now this is not quite true. I do not object, for instance, to *fair* criticism. I quarrel with no one who denies to my writings literary merit; they have a right to hold such an opinion, a right to express it. But to have one's book reviewed on hearsay, by persons who never looked between the covers, or to have isolated paragraphs circulated, with words italicized, so that gross constructions might be forced upon the reader, which the author never could dream of; then to have paragraphs taken up in that state, credited to you, and commented upon by horrified moralists,—that is what I call unfair play, Mr. Walter. When my sense of justice is thus wounded, I do feel keenly, and I have sometimes thought if such persons knew the suffering that such thoughtlessness, to baptize it by the most charitable name, may cause a woman, who must either weep in silence over such injustice, or do violence to her womanly nature by a public contention for her rights, such outrages would be much less frequent. It seems to me," said she earnestly, "were I a man, it would be so sweet to use my powers to defend the defenceless. It would seem to me so impossible to use that power to echo the faintest rumor adverse to a woman, or to keep cowardly silence in the shrugging, sneering, slanderer's presence, when a bold word of mine for the cause of right, might close his dastard lips."

"Bravo, Ruth, you speak like an oracle. Your sentiments are excellent, but I hope you are not so unsophisticated as to expect ever to see them put in universal practice. Editors are but men, and in the editorial profession, as in all other professions, may be found very shabby specimens of humanity. A petty, mean-spirited fellow, is seldom improved by being made an editor of; on the contrary, his pettiness, and meanness, are generally intensified. It is a pity that such unscrupulous fellows should be able to bring discredit on so intelligent and honorable a class of the community. However," said Mr. Walter, "we all are more or less responsible, for if the better class of editors refrained from copying abusive paragraphs, their circulation would be confined to a kennel class whose opinion is a matter of very little consequence."

"By the way, Ruth," said Mr. Walter, after walking on in silence a few rods, "how is it, in these days of female preachers, that you never contemplated the pulpit or lecture-room?"

"As for the lecture-room," replied Ruth, "I had as great a horror of that, as far as I myself am concerned, as the profession of an actress; but not long since I heard the eloquent Miss Lucy Stone one evening, when it really did appear to me that those Bloomers of hers had a mission! Still, I never could put them on. And as to the pulpit, I have too much reverence for that to think of putting my profane foot in it. It is part of my creed that a congregation can no more repay a conscientious, God-fearing, devoted minister, than—"

"*You* can help 'expressing your *real* sentiments,'" said Mr. Walter, laughing.

"As you please," replied Ruth; "but people who live in glass houses should not throw stones. But here we are at home; don't you hear the 'whir—whir'?"

CHAPTER LXXVII

AND NOW our heroine had become a regular business woman. She did not even hear the whir—whir of the odd lodger in the attic. The little room was littered with newspapers, envelopes, letters opened and unopened, answered and waiting to be answered. One minute she might be seen sitting, pen in hand, trying, with knit brows, to decipher some horrible cabalistic printer's mark on the margin of her proof; then writing an article for Mr. Walter, then scribbling a business letter to her publishers, stopping occasionally to administer a sedative to Nettie, in the shape of a timely quotation from Mother Goose, or to heal a fracture in a doll's leg or arm. Now she was washing a little soiled face, or smoothing little rumpled ringlets, replacing a missing shoe-string or pinafore button, then wading through the streets while Boreas contested stoutly for her umbrella, with parcels and letters to the post-office, (for Ruth must be her own servant,) regardless of gutters or thermometers, regardless of jostling or crowding. What cared she for all these, when Katy would soon be back—poor little patient, suffering Katy? Ruth felt as if wings were growing from her shoulders. She never was weary, or sleepy, or hungry. She had not the slightest idea, till long after, what an incredible amount of labor she accomplished, or how her *mother's heart* was goading her on.

"Pressing business that Mis. Hall must have," said her landlady, with a sneer, as Ruth stood her dripping umbrella in the kitchen sink. "Pressing business, running round to offices and the like of that, in such a storm as this. You wouldn't catch *me* doing it if I was a widder. I hope I'd have more regard for appearances. I don't understand all this flying in and out, one minute up in her room, the next in the street, forty times a day, and letters by the wholesale. It will take me to inquire into it. It may be all right, hope it is; but of course I like to know what is going on in my house. This Mis. Hall is so terrible close-mouthed, I don't like it. I've thought a dozen times I'd like to ask her right straight out who and what she is, and done with it; but I have not forgotten that little matter about the pills, and when I see her, there's something about her, she's civil enough too, that seems to say, 'don't you cross that chalk-mark, Sally Waters.' I never had lodgers afore like her and that old Bond, up in the garret. They are as much alike as two peas. *She* goes scratch—scratch—scratch; *he* goes whir—whir—whir. They haint spoke a word to one another since that child was sick. It's enough to drive anybody mad, to have such a mystery in the house. I can't make head nor tail on't. John, now, he don't care a rush-light about it; no more he wouldn't, if the top of the house was to blow off; but there's nothing plagues *me* like it, and yet I aint a bit curous nuther. Well, neither she nor Bond make me any trouble, there's that in it; if they did I wouldn't stand it. And as long as they both pay their bills so reg'lar, I shan't make a fuss; I *should* like to know though what Mis. Hall is about all the time."

PUBLICATION DAY came at last. There was *the* book. Ruth's book! Oh, how few of its readers, if it were fortunate enough to find readers, would know how much of her own heart's history was there laid bare. Yes, there was the book. She could recall the circumstances under which each separate article was written. Little shoeless feet were covered with the proceeds of this; a little medicine, or a warmer shawl was bought with that. This was written, faint and fasting, late into the long night; that composed while walking wearily to or from the offices where she was employed. One was written with little Nettie sleeping in her lap; another still, a mirthful, merry piece, as an escape-valve for a wretched heartache. Each had its own little history. Each would serve, in after-days, for a land-mark to some thorny path of by-gone trouble. Oh, if the sun of prosperity, after all, should gild these rugged paths! Some virtues—many faults—the book had—but God speed it, for little Katy's sake!

"*LET ME SEE,* please," said little Nettie, attracted by the gilt covers, as she reached out her hand for the book.

"Did you make those pretty pictures, mamma?"

"No, my dear—a gentleman, an artist, made those for me—*I* make pictures with a-b-c's."

"Show me one of your pictures, mamma," said Nettie.

Ruth took the child upon her lap, and read her the story of Gertrude. Nettie listened with her clear eyes fixed upon her mother's face.

"Don't make her die—oh, please don't make her die, mamma," exclaimed the sensitive child, laying her little hand over her mother's mouth.

Ruth smiled, and improvised a favorable termination to her story, more suitable to her tender-hearted audience.

"That is nice," said Nettie, kissing her mother; "when I get to be a woman shall I write books, mamma?"

"God forbid," murmured Ruth, kissing the child's changeful cheek; "God forbid," murmured she, musingly, as she turned over the leaves of her book; "no happy woman ever writes. From Harry's grave sprang 'Floy.'"

CHAPTER LXXVIII

"YOU HAVE A noble place here," said a gentleman to Ruth's brother, Hyacinth, as he seated himself on the piazza, and his eye lingered first upon the velvet lawn, (with its little clumps of trees) sloping down to the river, then upon the feathery willows now dipping their light green branches playfully into the water, then tossing them gleefully up to the sunlight; "a noble place," said he, as he marked the hazy outline of the cliffs on the opposite side, and the blue river which laved their base, flecked with many a snowy sail; "it were treason not to be poetical here; I should catch the infection myself, matter-of-fact as I am."

"Do you see that steamer yonder, floating down the river, Lewis?" said Hyacinth. "Do you know her? No? well she is named 'Floy,' after my sister, by one of her literary admirers."

"The ———! *your* sister? '*Floy*'—your *sister!* why, everybody is going mad to know who she is."

"Exactly," replied Hyacinth, running his white fingers through his curls; "'Floy' is my sister."

"Why the deuce didn't you tell a fellow before? I have wasted more pens, ink, and breath, trying to find her out, than I can stop to tell you about now, and here you have kept as mum as a mouse all the time. What did you do it for?"

"Oh, well," said Hyacinth, coloring a little, "'Floy' had an odd fancy for being *incog.*, and I, being in her confidence, you know, was on honor to keep her secret."

"But she *still wishes it kept*," said Lewis; "so her publishers, whom I have vainly pumped, tell me. So, as far as that goes, I don't see why you could not have told me before just as well as now."

Hyacinth very suddenly became aware of "an odd craft in the river," and was apparently intensely absorbed looking at it through his spy-glass.

"Hyacinth! I say, Hyacinth!" said the pertinacious Lewis, "I believe, after all, you are humbugging me. How *can* she be your sister? Here's a paragraph in ——— Sentinel, saying—" and Lewis drew the paper from his pocket, unfolded it, and put on his glasses with distressing deliberation:

"'We understand that "Floy," the new literary star, was in very destitute circumstances when she first solicited the patronage of the public; often wandering from one editorial office to another in search of employment, while wanting the commonest necessaries of life.' There, now, how can that be if she is 'your sister'? and you an editor, too, always patronizing some new contributor with a flourish of trumpets? Pooh, man! you are hoaxing;" and Lewis jogged him again by the elbow.

"Beg your pardon, my dear boy," said Hyacinth, blandly, "But 'pon my honor, I haven't heard a word you were saying, I was so intent upon making out that craft down the river. I'm a little afraid of that fog coming up, Lewis; suppose we join Mrs. Ellet in the drawing-room."

"Odd—very odd," soliloquized Lewis. "I'll try him again.—

"Did you read the panegyric on 'Floy' in 'The Inquisitor' of this morning?" said Lewis. "That paper, you know, is decidedly the highest literary authority in the country. It pronounces 'Floy's' book to be an 'unquestionable work of genius.'"

"Yes," replied Hyacinth, "I saw it. It is a great thing, Lewis, for a young writer to be *literarily connected;*" and Hyacinth pulled up his shirt-collar.

"But I understood you just now that nobody knew she *was* your sister, when she first published the pieces that are now collected in that book," said Lewis, with his characteristic pertinacity.

"There's that craft again," said Hyacinth; "can't you make her out, Lewis?"

"No—by Jove," replied Lewis, sarcastically; "I can't make anything out. I never was so be-fogged in my life;" and he bent a penetrating glance on the masked face before him. "It is past my finding out, at least just now; but I've a Yankee tongue in my head, so I don't despair, with time and perseverance;" and Lewis followed Hyacinth into the house.

"Confounded disagreeable fellow," soliloquized Hyacinth, as he handed him over to a knot of ladies in the drawing-room; "very awkward that paragraph; I wish I had the fellow who wrote it, at pistol-shot distance just now; well, if I am badgered on the subject of 'Floy's' poverty, I shall start a paragraph saying, that the story is only a publisher's trick to make her book sell; by Jove, they don't corner me; I have got out of worse scrapes than that before now, by the help of my wits and the lawyers, but I don't think a paper of any influence would attack me on that point; I have taken care to secure all the more prominent ones, long ago, by judicious puffs of their editors in the Irving Magazine. The only one I fear is ———, and I will lay an anchor to windward there this very week, by praising the editor's last stupid editorial. What an unmitigated donkey that fellow is."

CHAPTER LXXIX

"*HOW ARE YOU,* Walter," said Mr. Lewis, extending his hand; "fine day; how goes the world with you? They say *you* are a man who dares to 'hew to the line, let the chips fly in whose face they will.' Now, I want you to tell me if 'Floy' is *really* a sister of Hyacinth Ellet, the editor of 'The Irving Magazine.' I cannot believe it, though he boasted of it to me the other day, I hear such accounts of her struggles and her poverty. I cannot see into it."

"It is very easily understood," said Mr. Walter, with a dark frown on his face; "Mr. Hyacinth Ellet has always had one hobby, namely—social position. For that he would sacrifice the dearest friend or nearest relative he had on earth. His sister was once in affluent circumstances, beloved and admired by all who knew her. Hyacinth, at that time, was very friendly, of course; her husband's wine and horses, and his name on change, were things which the extravagant Hyacinth knew how to appreciate.

"Hall ('Floy's' husband) was a generous-hearted, impulsive fellow, too noble himself to see through the specious, flimsy veil which covered so corrupt a heart as Hyacinth's. Had he been less trusting, less generous to him, 'Floy' might not have been left so destitute at his death. When that event occurred, Hyacinth's regard for his sister evaporated in a lachrymose obituary notice of Hall in the Irving Magazine. The very day after his death, Hyacinth married Julia Grey, or rather married her fortune. His sister, after seeking in vain to get employment, driven to despair, at last resorted to her pen, and applied to Hyacinth, then the prosperous editor of the Irving Magazine, either to give her employment as a writer, or show her some way to obtain it. At that time Hyacinth was constantly boasting of the helping hand he had extended to young writers in their extremity, (whom, by the way, he paid in compliments after securing their articles,) and whom, he was constantly asserting, had been raised by him from obscurity to fame."

"Well," said Lewis, bending eagerly forward; "well, he helped his sister, of course?"

"He did no such thing, sir," said Mr. Walter, bringing his hand down on the table; "he did no such thing, sir; but he wrote her a cool, contemptuous, insulting letter, denying her all claim to talent, (she had sent him some specimen articles,) and advising her to seek some unobtrusive employment, (*what* employment he did not trouble himself to name,) and then ignored her existence; and this, too, when he was squandering money on 'distressed' actresses, etc."

"Well?" said Mr. Lewis, inquiringly.

"Well, sir, she struggled on bravely and single-handed, with the skeleton Starvation standing by her hearth-stone—she who had never known a wish ungratified during her married life, whose husband's pride in her was only equalled by his love. She has sunk fainting to the floor with hunger, that her children might not go supperless to bed. And now, when the battle is fought and the victory won, *he* comes in for a share of the spoils. It is 'my sister "Floy,"' and 'tis *his* 'literary reputation which was the stepping-stone to her celebrity as a writer.'

"To show you how much 'his reputation has helped her,' I will just state that, not long since, I was dining at a restaurant near two young men, who were discussing 'Floy.' One says, 'Have you read her book?' 'No,' said the other, with a sneer, 'nor do I want to; it is enough for me that Hyacinth Ellet claims her as a sister; *that* is enough to damn any woman.' Then," continued Mr. Walter, "there was an English paper, the editor of which, disgusted with Hyacinth's toadyisms, fopperies, and impudence while abroad, took occasion to cut up her book (as he acknowledged) because the writer was said to be Ellet's sister. That is the way *his* reputation has helped her."

"No wonder she is at sword's-point with him," remarked Mr. Lewis.

"She is not at sword's-point with him," replied Mr. Walter. "She simply chooses to retain the position her family assigned her when she was poor and obscure. They would not notice her then; she will not accept their notice now."

"Where was the old man, her father, all this time?" said Mr. Lewis, "was he alive and in good circumstances?"

"Certainly," said Mr. Walter; "and once in awhile he threw her a dollar, just as one would throw a bone to a hungry dog, with a 'begone!'"

"By Jove!" exclaimed Mr. Lewis, as he passed out, "what a heartless set."

CHAPTER LXXX

RUTH RETURNED from her daily walk to the Post Office, one morning, with a bundle of letters, among which was one from Mr. Walter. Its contents were as follows:

> "Dear Sister Ruth:
>
> "I wonder if you are enjoying your triumph half as much as I? But how should you, since you do not know of it? Your publishers inform me that orders are pouring in for your book faster than they can supply them. What do you think of that? 'Floy,' you have made a decided hit; how lucky that you had the foresight to hold on to your copyright. $800 will not be a circumstance to the little fortune you are going to make. Your success is glorious; but I don't believe you are half as proud of it as I am.
>
> "And now, I know of what you are thinking as well as if I were by your side. 'Tis of the little exile, 'tis of Katy. You would fly directly to bring her home. Can I be of any service to you in doing this? Business takes me your way day after to-morrow. Can you curb your impatience to see her till then? If so, I will accompany you. Please write me immediately.
>
> "Yours truly, John Walter."
>
> "P. S.—I send you a batch of letters, which came by this morning's mail, directed to 'Floy,' office of the Household Messenger."

Ruth tossed the "batch of letters" down unopened, and sprang to her feet; she tossed up Nettie; she kissed the astonished child till she was half strangled; she laughed, she cried, and then she sat down with her forehead in both her hands, for a prolonged reverie.

What *good* news about the book! How could she wait two days before she brought back Katy! And yet it would be a happy thing, that Mr. Walter, whose name was synonymous with good tidings, should be associated with her in the return of the child. Yes, she would wait. And when Katy *was* secured, what then? Why, she would leave forever a city fraught with such painful associations; she would make her a new home. Home? Her heart leaped!—comforts for Nettie and Katy,—clothes—food,—earned by her own hands!—Tears trickled through Ruth's fingers, and her heart went out in a murmured prayer to the "God of the widow and fatherless."

"May I play house with these?" said Nettie, touching Ruth's elbow, and pointing to the unopened letters.

"No, little puss," said Ruth, "not yet. Wait a bit till I have glanced at them;" and she broke the seal of one.

It was an offer of marriage from a widower. He had read an article of hers on "Step-Mothers," and was "very sure that a woman with *such* views could not fail to make a good mother for his children." He was thirty-five—good-looking, (every man who had written her a love-letter *was!*) good disposition—warm-hearted—would love her just as well as if he had never bent an adoring knee to Mrs. Dorrance No. 1—was not at all set in his ways—in fact preferred she should, in everything, save him the trouble of *choice;* would live in any part of the Union she desired, provided she would only consent to *the union*. These last two words Mr. Dorrance had italicised, as indicating, probably, that he considered it a pun fit even for the critical eye of an authoress.

"Oh, pshaw!" said Ruth, throwing the letter to Nettie, "make anything you like of it, pussy; it is of no value to me." The next letter ran as follows:

"Madam:

"I have the honor to be guardian to a young Southern lady (an orphan) of large fortune, who has just completed her education. She has taken a suite of apartments, and given me orders to furnish them without regard to expense, according to her fancy. I have directions to procure busts of Mrs. Hemans, Miss Landon, and several other distinguished female writers, among whom Miss Le Roy includes 'Floy,' (I have not the pleasure, madam, of knowing your true name,) with whose writings she has become familiar, and who is as great a favorite with her as she is with the multitude who have paid tribute to her genius.

"Please send me a line, (my address as below,) allowing me to inform my ward how her favorite wish can be best carried out.

"Yours truly, THOMAS PEARCE.

Ruth glanced around her little dark room and smiled. "I would rather, instead, that an artist would take a sketch of my room, now," said she; "that little black stove, where I have so often tried in vain to thaw my frozen fingers—that rickety old bed—the old deal table, with its yellow bowl of milk—that home-made carpet—those time-worn chairs—and then you, my little bright fairy, in the foreground;" and she pushed back the soft, glossy curls from Nettie's fair brow.

"No, no," said Ruth, "better reserve the niche destined for 'Floy' for some writer to whom ambition is not the hollow thing it is to me.

"Well, what have we here? Another letter?" Ruth broke the seal of letter No. 3, and read:

"DEAR MADAM:

"I am a poor devil, and worse editor; nevertheless, I have started a paper. If you will but allow me to put your name on it as Assistant Editress, I am sure it will go like a locomotive. If, in addition to this little favor, you could also advance me the sum of one hundred dollars, it would be an immense relief to your admirer,

"JOHN K. STAPLES.

"P. S.—Be sure you direct to John *K.* Staples, as there is another John Staples in this place, who is a great rascal.

J. K. S."

"Well!" exclaimed Ruth, "I did not believe I should ever be astonished again, but then—I had not heard from Mr. Staples. But here is another letter. Let us see what the contents of No. 4 are."

Letter No. 4 ran as follows:

"DEAR 'FLOY':

"I am a better son, a better brother, a better husband, and a better father, than I was before I commenced reading your articles. May God bless you for the words you have spoken (though unintentionally) so directly to me. May you be rewarded by Him to whom the secrets of all hearts are known.

"Your grateful friend, M. J. D."

"This will repay many a weary hour," said Ruth, as her tears fell upon the page.

CHAPTER LXXXI

THE RAIN had poured down without mitigation for seven consecutive days; the roads were in a very plaster-y state; dissevered branches of trees lay scattered upon the ground; tubs and hogsheads, which careful housewives had placed under dripping spouts, were full to overflowing; the soaked hides of the cattle looked sleek as their owners' pomatum'd heads of a Sunday; the old hen stood poised on one leg at the barn-door, till even her patience had given out; the farmers had mended all the old hoe and rake handles, read the Almanac through and through, and worn all the newspapers and village topics threadbare, when the welcome sun at last broke through the clouds, and every little and big puddle in the road hastened joyfully to reflect his beams.

Old Doctor Hall started down cellar for his "eleven o'clock mug of cider;" to his dismay he found his slippered pedestals immersed in water, which had risen above the last step of the cellar-stairs.

"A pretty piece of work this rain has made, Mis. Hall," said the doctor, stamping his wet feet and blowing his nose, as he returned from his visit to the lower regions; "the water has overflowed the cellar, and got most up to those hams that you set such store by. You'd better tell Bridget to climb over the heads of those barrels, and get the hams out before they are clean sp'iled."

Before the last words had fairly left the doctor's mouth the old lady's cap-strings were seen flying towards the kitchen.

"I shan't do it, for anybody," exclaimed the new help, as she placed her red arms a-kimbo. "I'm not going to risk my neck going over those tittlish barrels in that dark cellar, for all the hams that was ever cured."

"You can carry a lamp with you," suggested the old lady.

"I shan't do it, I tell you," said the vixen; "help is skerse out here in the country, and I can get a new place before sundown, if I like."

"Katy!" screamed the old lady, with a shrill voice, "Katy!"

Katy started from her corner and came out into the entry, in obedience to the summons.

"Come here, Katy; Bridget is as contrary as a mule, and won't go into the cellar to get those hams. I cannot go in after 'em, nor the doctor either, so you must go in and bring them out yourself. Climb up on those barrel heads, and then feel your way along to the further corner; go right down the cellar-stairs now, quick."

"Oh, I cannot! I *dare* not!" said Katy, trembling and shrinking back, as the old lady pushed her along toward the cellar-door.

"I'm *so* afraid," said the child, peeping down the cellar-stairs, with distended eyes, "oh, *don't* make me go down in that dark place, grandma."

"Dark, pooh!" said the old lady; "what are you afraid of? rats? There are not more than half-a-dozen in the whole cellar."

"Can't Bridget go?" asked Katy; "oh, I'm *so* afraid."

"Bridget *won't*, so there's an end of that, and I'm not going to lose a new girl I've just got, for your obstinacy; so go right down this minute, rats or no rats."

"Oh, I can't! if you kill me I can't," said Katy, with white lips, and clinging to the side of the cellar-door.

"But I say you shall," said the old lady, unclinching Katy's hands; "don't you belong to me, I'd like to know? and can't I do with you as I like?"

"No!" said Ruth, receiving the fainting form of her frightened child; "no!"

"Doctor! doctor!" said the old lady, trembling with rage; "are you master in this house or not?"

"Yes—when *you* are out of it," growled the doctor; "what's to pay now?"

"Why, matter enough. Here's Ruth," said the old lady, not noticing the doctor's taunt; "Ruth interfering between me and Katy. If you will order her out of the house, I will be obliged to you. I've put up with enough of this meddling, and it is the last time she shall cross this threshold."

"You never spoke a truer word," said Ruth, "and my child shall cross it for the last time with me."

"Humph!" said the doctor, "and you no better than a beggar! The law says if the mother can't support her children, the grand-parents shall do it."

"The mother *can*—the mother *will*," said Ruth. "I have already earned enough for their support."

"Well, if you have, which I doubt, I hope *you earned it honestly*," said the old lady.

Ruth's heightened color was the only reply to this taunt. Tying her handkerchief over Katy's bare head, and wrapping the trembling child in a shawl she had provided, she bore her to a carriage, where Mr. Walter and his brother-in-law, (Mr. Grey,) with little Nettie, awaited them; the door was quickly closed, and the carriage whirled off. The two gentlemen alternately wiped their eyes, and looked out the window as Katy, trembling, crying, and laughing, clung first to her mother, and then to little Nettie, casting anxious, frightened glances toward the prison she had left, as the carriage receded.

Weeping seemed to be infectious. Ruth cried and laughed, and Mr. Grey and Mr. Walter seemed both to have lost the power of speech. Little Nettie was the first to break the spell by offering to lend Katy her bonnet.

"We will do better than that," said Ruth, smiling through her tears; "we will get one for Katy when we stop. See here, Katy;" and Ruth tossed a purse full of money into Katy's lap. "You know, mother said she would come for you as soon as she earned the money."

"Yes, and I *knew* you would, mother; but—it was so very—" and the child's lips began to quiver again.

"She is so excited, poor thing," said Ruth, drawing her to her bosom;

"don't talk about it now, Katy; lean your head on me and take a nice nap;" and the weary child nestled up to her mother, while Nettie put one finger on her lip, with a sagacious look at Mr. Walter, as much as to say, "*I* will keep still if *you* will."

"She does not resemble you as much as Nettie does," said Mr. Grey to Ruth, in a whisper.

"She is like her father," said Ruth; the "resemblance is quite startling when she is sleeping; the same breadth of forehead, the same straight nose, and full lips.

"Yes, it has often been a great solace to me," said Ruth, after a pause, "to sit at Katy's bedside, and aid memory by gazing at features which recalled so vividly the loved and lost;" and she kissed the little nestler.

"Nettie," said Mr. Walter, "is Ruth 2d, in face, form and feature."

"I wish the resemblance ended there," whispered Ruth, with a sigh. "These rose-tinted dawns too often foreshadow the storm-cloud."

CHAPTER LXXXII

AN HOUR after the conversation narrated in the last chapter, the driver stopped at a fine-looking hotel.

"This is the place, then, where you are going to stay for a few weeks, before you leave this part of the country for ———," said Mr. Walter; "allow me to speak for a dinner for us all; such a day as this does not dawn on us often in this world;" and he glanced affectionately at little Katy.

The party was soon seated round a plentifully-furnished table. Nettie stopped at every other mouthful to look into Katy's eyes, or to kiss her, while little Katy gazed about bewilderingly, and grasped her mother's hand tightly whenever her ear caught the sound of a strange voice or footstep.

"Will you have some soup, little puss?" said Mr. Walter, after they were seated at the table, pulling one of Nettie's long curls.

"Ask my mother," replied the child, with a quizzical look; "she's the *soup*-erintendent."

Mr. Walter threw up his hands, and a general shout followed this precocious sally.

"Come, come," said Mr. Walter, when he had done laughing; "you have begun too early, little puss; come here and let me feel your head. I must take a phrenological look at you. Bless me! what an affectionate little creature you must be," said he, passing his hand over her head; "stick a pin there now, while I examine the rest of your bumps."

"You must not stick a pin in my head," said Nettie; "I don't like that way of expressing an o-*pin*-ion."

"No further examination is necessary," said the extinguished Mr. Walter; "I have done with *you*, Miss Nettie. What do you mean?" whispered he to Ruth, "by having such a child as that? Are we going to have another genius in the family?"

"I don't know about that," said Ruth, laughing; "she often says such things when she gets excited and hilarious, but I never encourage it by notice, and you must not; my physician told me not to teach her anything, and by all means not to let her see the inside of a school-room at present."

"Well, well," said Mr. Walter, "Miss Nettie and I must have a tilt at punning some day. You had better engage, Ruth, to furnish the Knickerbocker with smart repartees for his 'Children's Table,' from your own fireside."

"*Prenez garde*," whispered Ruth, "don't spoil her. Such a child needs careful training; she is high-spirited, warm-hearted, and sensitive;" and Ruth sighed.

"I interpret your thoughts," said Mr. Walter; "but we must have no backward glances to-day. Those children will never suffer what you have suffered; few women ever did. Ruth, for the thousandth time I tell you, you are a brave woman!"

"—Upon my word," said Mr. Walter, suddenly, blushing and thrusting his hand in his pocket, "I have committed the sin so common to all *man*-kind; carried letters for you round in my pocket all this time, without delivering them: here they are. I never saw a woman have so many letters as you do, 'Floy;' you'll need a private secretary before long."

Ruth broke the seal of one, saying, "You'll excuse me a few moments," and read:

"To 'Floy':

"Dear Madam,—We have established a very successful Infant School in our neighborhood, numbering about fifty pupils. Our first anniversary occurs next month. It is our intention to gather together the parents and children, and have a sort of jubilee; hymns will be sung, and short pieces spoken. We should be very much obliged to you if you would write us a little dialogue to be repeated by two little girls, of the age of six; something sweet and simple, such as you know how to write. We make no apology for thus intruding on your time, because we know your heart is with the children.

"Yours respectfully, John Dean.
"Secretary of the Leftbow Infant School."

"Patience, gentlemen, while I read No. 2," said Ruth. No. 2 ran as follows:

"Dear 'Floy':

"Old Guardy has sent me up to this academy. I hate academies. I hate Guardy's. I hate everything but snipe shooting and boating. Just now I am in a horrid fix. Every fellow in this academy has to write a composition once a week. I cannot do it. I never could. My talents don't lie in that way. I don't know where they do lie. What I want of you is to write those compositions for me. You can do it just as easy as water runs down hill. You could scratch one off while I am nibbing my pen. Old Phillips will think they are uncommon smart for me; but never mind, I shall keep dark, and you are such a good soul I know you can't refuse. My cigars have been out two whole days; so you may know that I have no funds, else I would send you a present.

"Yours truly, Hal. Hunnewell."

After glancing over this letter Ruth broke into a merry laugh, and saying, "This is too good to keep," read it aloud for the amusement of the company, who unanimously voted Hal. Hunnewell a composition every week, for his precocious impudence.

"Come, now," said Mr. Walter, as Ruth took up No. 3, "if you have another of the same sort, let us hear it, unless it be of a confidential nature."

Ruth looked over the letter a moment, and then read:

"DEAR 'FLOY':

"Mamma has read me some of your stories. I like them very much. You say you love little children. Don't you think we've got a bran new baby! It came last night when I was asleep in my trundle-bed. It is a little pink baby. Mamma says it will grow white by-and-bye. It has got such funny little fingers; they look all wrinkled, just like our maid's when she has been at the wash-tub. Mother has to stay in bed with him to keep him warm, he's such a little cold, shaky thing. He hasn't a bit of hair, and he scowls like everything, but I guess he'll be pretty by-and-bye. Anyhow I love him. I asked mother if I might not write and tell you about him, and she laughed and said, I don't know who 'Floy' is, not where she lives; but Uncle Jack (he gives me lots of candy and dolls) said that I must send it to 'Floy's' publishers! I don't know what a publisher is, and so I told Uncle Jack; and he laughed and said he would lose *his* guess if I didn't have something to do with them one of these days. I don't know what that meant either, and when I asked him, he said 'go away, Puss.' I think it is very nice to have an Uncle Jack at Christmas and New Year's, but other times they only plague little children. I wish I could see you. How do you look? I guess you look like mamma; mamma has got blue eyes, and soft brown hair, and her mouth looks very pleasant when she smiles. Mamma's voice is as sweet as a robin's, so papa says. Papa is a great big man, so big that nobody could ever hurt me, or mamma. Papa wants to see you too. Won't you write me a letter, a little letter all to myself? I've got a box made of rosewood, with a lock and key on it, where I'd hide it from Uncle Jack, (that would tease him!) Uncle Jack wants to see you too, but I hope you never will let him, for he's such a terrible tease, he'd plague you dreadfully. I guess our baby would send his love to you if he only knew you. Please write me soon, and send it to Kitty Mills, care of Uncle Jack Mills, and please seal it up all tight, so he cannot peep into it.

"P.S.—I want you to write a book of stories for little girls, and don't make them end bad, because it makes me cry; nor put any ghosts in them, because it scares me; or have any 'moral' down at the bottom, because Uncle Jack always asks me if I skipped it. Write something funny, won't you? I like funny things, and fairy stories. Oh, I like fairy stories so *much!* Wasn't it nice about the mice and the pumpkin, in Cinderella? Make them all end well, won't you?

"Your affectionate little KITTY."

"I suppose you do not feel any curiosity to know what the papers say about your book," said Mr. Walter, as Ruth refolded her letters. "I have quite a stock of notices in my pocket, which I have saved up. You seem to have taken the public heart by storm. You could not desire better notices; and the best of it is, they are spontaneous—neither begged nor in a measure demanded, by a personal call upon the editors."

"What on earth do you mean?" asked Ruth.

"Look at 'the spirit of '76' flashing from her eyes," said Mr. Grey, laughing, as he pointed at Ruth.

"I mean this," said Mr. Walter, "that not long since I expressed my surprise to an able critic and reviewer, that he could praise a certain book, which he must have known was entirely deficient in merit of any kind. His answer was: 'The authoress of that book made a call on me at my office, deprecated in the strongest terms any adverse criticism in the paper with which I am connected; said that other papers would take their tone from mine, that it was her first book, and that her pen was her only means of support, &c., &c. What can a man do under such circumstances?' said my informant."

"How *could* she?" said Ruth. "Of what ultimate advantage could it be? It might have procured the sale of a few copies at first, but a book, like water, will find its level. But what astonishes me most of all is, that any able reviewer should be willing to risk his reputation as a critic by such promiscuous puffery. How are the people to know when he speaks his *real* sentiments? It strikes me," said Ruth, laughing, "that such a critic should have some cabalistic mark by which the initiated may understand when he speaks truthfully. It is such a pity!" continued Ruth thoughtfully; "it so neutralizes criticism. It is such a pity, too, that an authoress could be found so devoid of self-respect as to do such a thing. It is such an injury to those women who would disdain so to fetter criticism; who would launch their book like a gallant ship, prepared for adverse gales, not sneaking near the shore or lowering their flag for fear of a stray shot."

"Do you know, Ruth," said Mr. Walter, "when I hear you talk, I no longer wonder at Hyacinth's lack of independence and common sense; his share must, by some unaccountable mistake, have been given to you in addition to your own. But where are the children?"

They looked around; Katy and Nettie, taking advantage of this prolonged discussion, had slid from the table, in company with a plate of nuts and raisins, and were holding an animated conversation in a further corner.

"Why! what a great, big mark on your arm, Katy," exclaimed Nettie; "how *did* it come?"

"Hush!" replied Katy; "grandma did it. She talked very bad about mamma to grandpa, and I started to go up into my little room, because, you know, I *couldn't* bear to hear it; and she called to me, and said, 'Katy, what are you leaving the room for?' and you know, Nettie, mamma teaches us always to tell the truth, so I said, 'because I cannot bear to stay and hear you say what is not true about my mamma.' And then grandma threw down her knitting, seized me by the arm, and set me down, oh, *so* hard, on a chair; and said, 'but you *shall* hear it.' Then, oh, Nettie, I *could not* hear it, so I put my fingers in both ears; and then she beat me, and left that place on my arm, and held both my hands while she made me listen."

During this recital, Nettie's eyes glowed like living coals. When Katy concluded, she clenched her little fists, and said:

"Katy, why didn't you strike her?"

Katy shook her head, and said in a low tone, "Oh, Nettie, she would have killed me! When she got angry she looked just like that picture of Satan we saw once in the shop window."

"Katy, I *must* do something to her," said Nettie, closing her teeth together, and planting her tiny foot firmly upon the floor; "she *shan't* talk so about mamma. Oh, if I was only a big woman!"

"I suppose we must *forgive* her," said Katy thoughtfully.

"*I* won't," said the impulsive little Nettie, "never—never—never."

"Then you cannot say your prayers," said the wise little Katy; "'forgive us, as we forgive those who have trespassed against us.'"

"What a pity!" exclaimed the orthodox Nettie; "don't you wish that hadn't been put in? What *shall* we do, Katy?"

"Nettie," said her mother, who had approached unnoticed, "what did you mean when you said just now, that you wished you were a big woman?"

Nettie hung her head for a minute, and twisted the corner of her apron irresolutely; at last she replied with a sudden effort, "you won't love me, mamma, but I will tell you; I wanted to cut grandma's head off."

Little Katy laughed outright, as the idea of this Lilliputian combatant presented itself. Ruth looked serious. "That is not right, Nettie," said she; "your grandmother is an unhappy, miserable old woman. She has punished herself worse than anybody else could punish her. She is more miserable than ever now, because I have earned money to support you and Katy. She *might* have made us all love her, and help to make her old age cheerful; but now, unless she repents, she will live miserably, and die forsaken, for nobody can love her with such a temper. This is a dreadful old age, Nettie!"

"I *think* I'll forgive her," said Nettie, jumping into her mother's lap; "but I hope I shan't ever hear her say anything against you, mother. I'm glad I wasn't Katy. Didn't you ever wish, Katy, that she might fall down stairs and break her neck, or catch a fever, or something?"

"Oh, mother, what a funny girl Nettie is!" said Katy, laughing till the tears came; "I had almost forgotten her queer ways! Oh, how grandmother *would* have boxed your ears, Nettie!"

The incorrigible Nettie cut one of her pirouettes across the room, and snapped her fingers by way of answer to this assertion.

WHILE RUTH and her children were conversing, the two gentlemen were quite as absorbed in another corner of the apartment.

"It astonishes me," said Mr. Grey to Mr. Walter, "that 'Floy' should be so little elated by her wonderful success."

"It will cease to do so when you know her better," said Mr. Walter; "the map of life has been spread out before her; she has stood singing on its breezy heights—she has lain weeping in its gloomy valleys. Flowers have strewn her pathway—and thorns have pierced her tender feet. The clusters of the promised land have moistened her laughing lip—the Dead Sea apple has mocked her wasted fingers. Rainbows have spanned her sky like a glory, and storms have beat pitilessly on her defenceless head. Eyes have beamed upon her smiling welcome. When wounded and smitten, she fainted by the way, the priest and the Levite have passed by on the other side. 'Floy' knows every phase of the human heart; she knows that she was none the less worthy because poor and unrecognized; she knows how much of the homage now paid her is due to the *showy setting* of the gem; therefore, she takes all these things at their true valuation. Then, my friend," and Mr. Walter's voice became tremulous, "amid all these 'well done' plaudits, *the loved voice is silent*. The laurel crown indeed is won, but the feet at which she fain would cast it have finished their toilsome earth-march."

"*IT IS TIME* we gentlemen were going; let us talk business now," said Mr. Walter, as Ruth returned from her conversation with the children. "How long did you propose remaining here, Ruth?"

"For a month or so," she replied. "I have several matters I wish to arrange before bidding adieu to this part of the country. I shall try to get through as soon as possible, for I long to be settled in a permanent and comfortable home."

"I shall return this way in a month or six weeks," said Mr. Walter, "and if you are ready at that time, I shall be most happy to escort you and your children to your new residence."

"Thank you," said Ruth. "Good-bye, good-bye," shouted both the children, as the two gentlemen left the room.

CHAPTER LXXXIII

"*I DON'T KNOW* about holding you *both* in my lap at once," said Ruth smiling, as Nettie climbed up after Katy.

"Do, please," said Nettie, "and now let us have a nice talk; tell us where we are going to live, mamma, and if we can have a kitty or a rabbit, or some live thing to play with, and if we are going to school, and if you are going to leave off writing now, and play with Katy and me, and go to walk with us, and ride with us. Shan't we have some rides? What is the matter, mamma?" said the little chatterbox, noticing a tear in her mother's eye.

"I was thinking, dear, how happy we are."

"Isn't that funny?" said Nettie to Katy, "that mamma should cry when she is happy? I never heard of such a thing. *I* don't cry when I'm happy. Didn't we have a good dinner, Katy? Oh, I like this house. It was such an old dark room we used to live in, and there was nothing pretty to look at, and mamma kept on writing, and I had nothing to play with, except a little mouse, who used to peep out of his hole, when it came dark, for some supper. I liked him, he was so cunning, but I couldn't give him any supper, because—" here the little chatterbox glanced at her mother, and then placing her mouth to Katy's ear, whispered, with a look the gravity of which was irresistible, "because mamma couldn't support a mouse."

Ruth laughed heartily as she overheard the remark, and Nettie thought her mother more of a puzzle than ever that she should keep laughing and crying so in the wrong place.

"What have you there, Nettie?" asked Katy.

"Something," said Nettie, looking very wise, as she hid her chubby hands under her pinafore. "It is a secret. Mamma and I know," said she with a very important air, "don't we, mamma? Would you tell Katy, mother, if you were me?"

"Certainly," said Ruth; "you know it would not be pleasant to keep such a great secret from Katy."

Nettie looked very searchingly into her mother's eyes, but she saw nothing there but sincerity.

"Won't you *ever* tell, Katy ever? it is a terrible secret."

"No," replied Katy, laughing.

"Not even to Mr. Walter?" asked Nettie, who had learned to consider Mr. Walter as their best friend, and the impersonation of all that was manly and chivalrous.

Katy shook her head negatively.

"Well, then," said Nettie, hanging her head with a pretty shame, "*I'm in love!*"

Katy burst into an uncontrollable fit of laughter, rocking herself to and fro, and ejaculating, "Oh! mamma! oh! did you ever? Oh, how funny!"

"Funny?" said Nettie, with the greatest naîvete, "it wasn't funny at all; it was very nice. I'll tell you all how it happened, Katy. You see I used to get so tired when you were away, when I had nobody to play with, and mamma kept up such a thinking. So mamma said I might go to a little free school opposite, half-a-day, when I felt like it, and perhaps that would amuse me. Mamma told the teacher not to trouble herself about teaching me much. Well, I sat on a little low bench, and right opposite me, across the room, was such a *pretty* little boy! his name was Neddy. He had on a blue jacket, with twelve bright buttons on it; I counted them; and little plaid pants and drab gaiters; and his cheeks were so rosy, and his hair so curly, and his eyes so bright, oh, Katy!" and Nettie clasped her little hands together in a paroxysm of admiration. "Well, Katy, he kept smiling at me, and in recess he used to give me half his apple, and once, when nobody was looking,—*would* you tell her mamma?" said Nettie, doubtfully, as she ran up to her mother. "Won't you tell, now, Katy, certainly?" again asked Nettie.

"No," promised Katy.

"Not even to Mr. Walter?"

"No."

"Well, once, when the teacher wasn't looking, Katy, he took a piece of chalk and wrote 'Nettie' on the palm of his hand, and held it up to me and then kissed it;" and Nettie hid her glowing face on Katy's neck, whispering, "wasn't it beautiful, Katy?"

"Yes," replied Katy, trying to keep from laughing.

"Well," said Nettie, "I felt most ashamed to tell mamma, I don't know why, though. I believe I was afraid that she would call it 'silly,' or something; and I felt just as if I should cry if she did. But, Katy, she did not think it silly a bit. She said it was beautiful to be loved, and that it made everything on earth look brighter; and that she was glad little Neddy loved me, and that I might love him just as much as ever I liked—just the same as if he were a little girl. Wasn't *that* nice?" asked Nettie. "I always mean to tell mamma everything; don't you, Katy?"

"But you have not told Katy, yet, what you have hidden under your apron, there," said Ruth.

"Sure enough," said Nettie, producing a little picture. "Well, Neddy whispered to me one day in recess, that he had drawn a pretty picture on purpose for me, and that he was going to have a lottery; I don't know what a lottery is; but he cut a great many slips of paper, some long and some short, and the one who got the longest was to have the picture. Then he put a little tiny mark on the end of the longest, so that I should know it; and then I got the picture, you know."

"Why did he take all that trouble?" asked the practical Katy. "Why didn't he give it to you right out, if he wanted to?"

"Because—because," said Nettie, twirling her thumbs, and blushing with a little feminine shame at her boy-lover's want of independence, "he said—he—was—afraid—the—boys—would—laugh at him if they found it out."

"Well, then, I wouldn't have taken it, if I had been you," said the phlegmatic Katy.

"But, you know, I *loved* him so," said Nettie naîvely.

CHAPTER LXXXIV

DAYS AND WEEKS flew by. Katy and Nettie were never weary of comparing notes, and relating experiences. Nettie thought gloomy attics, scant fare and cross landladies, the climax of misery; and Katy considered a score of mile-stones, with Nettie and a loving mother at one end, and herself and a cross grandmother at the other, infinitely worse.

"Why, you can't tell anything about it," said Katy. "Grandma took away a little kitty because I loved it, and burned up a story-book mamma brought me, and tore up a letter which mamma printed in big capitals on a piece of paper for me to read when I was lonesome; and she wouldn't let me feed the little snow-birds when they came shivering round the door; and she made me eat turnips when they made me sick; and she said I must not run when I went to school, for fear it would wear my shoes out; and she put me to bed *so* early; and I used to lie and count the stars (I liked the seven little stars all cuddled up together best); and sometimes I looked at the moon and thought I saw faces and mountains in it, and I wondered if it was shining into mamma's window; and then I thought of you all snug in mamma's bed; and then I cried and cried, and got up and looked out into the road, and wondered if I could not run away in the night, when grandmother was asleep. Oh, Nettie, she was a *dreadful* grandmother! She tried to make me stop loving mother. She told me that she loved you better than she did me; and then I wanted to die. I thought of it every night. I knew it was not true, but it kept troubling me. And then she said that very likely mamma would go off somewhere without letting me know anything about it, and never see me again. And she always said such things just as I was going to bed; and then you know I could not get to sleep till almost morning, and when I did, I dreamed such dreadful dreams."

"Your poor little thing!" exclaimed Nettie, with patronizing sympathy, to her elder sister, and laying her cheek against hers, "you poor little thing! Well, mamma and I had a horrid time, too. You can't imagine! The wind blew into the cracks of the room *so* cold; and the stove smoked; and I was afraid to eat when we *had* any supper, for fear mamma would not have enough. She always said 'I am not hungry, dear,' but I think she did it to make me eat more. And one night mamma had no money to buy candles, and she wrote by moonlight; and I often heard her cry when she thought I was asleep; and I was so afraid of mamma's landladies, they screamed so loud, and scowled at me so; and the grocer's boy made faces at me when I went in for a loaf of bread, and said 'Oh, ain't we a fine lady, ain't we?' And the wheel was off my old tin cart—and—oh—dear—Katy—" and Nettie's little voice grew fainter and fainter, and the little chatterbox and her listener both fell asleep.

Ruth, as she listened in the shadow of the further corner, thanked God that they who had had so brief an acquaintance with life's joys, so early an introduction to life's cares, were again blithe, free, and joyous, as childhood ever should be. How sweet to have it in her power to hedge them in with comforts, to surround them with pleasures, to make up to them for every tear of sorrow they had shed,—to repay them for the mute glance of sympathy—the silent caress—given, they scarce knew why, (but, oh, how touching! how priceless!) when her own heart was breaking.

And there they lay, in their pretty little bed, sleeping cheek to cheek, with arms thrown around each other. Nettie—courageous, impulsive, independent, irrepressible, but loving, generous, sensitive, and noble-hearted. Katy—with veins through which the life-blood flowed more evenly, thoughtful, discriminating, diffident, reserved, (so proud of those magnetic qualities in her little sister, in which she was lacking, as to do injustice to her own solid but less showy traits;) needing ever the kind word of encouragement, and judicious praise, to stimulate into life the dormant seeds of self-reliance. Ruth kissed them both, and left their future with Him who doeth all things well.

TWELVE O'CLOCK at night! Ruth lies dreaming by the side of her children.

She dreams that she roves with them through lovely gardens, odorous with sweets; she plucks for their parched lips the luscious fruits; she garlands them with flowers, and smiles in her sleep, as their beaming eyes sparkle, and the rosy flush of happiness mantles their cheeks. But look! there are three of them! Another has joined the band—a little shadowy form, with lambent eyes, and the smile of a seraph. Blessed little trio. Follows another! He has the same shadowy outline—the same sweet, holy, yet familiar eyes. Ruth's face grows radiant. The broken links are gathered up; the family circle is complete!

With the sudden revulsion of dream-land, the scene changes. She dreams that the cry of "fire! fire!" resounds through the streets; bells ring—dogs howl—watchmen spring their rattles—boys shout—men whoop, and halloo, as they drag the engine over the stony pavements. "Fire! fire!" through street after street, she dreams the watch-word flies! Windows are thrown up, and many a night-capped head is thrust hastily out, and as hastily withdrawn, when satisfied of the distant danger. Still, on rush the crowd; the heavens are one broad glare, and still the wreathed smoke curls over the distant houses. From the doors and windows of the doomed building, the forked flame, fanned by the fury of the wind, darts out its thousand fiery tongues. Women with dishevelled locks, and snow-white vestments, rush franticly out, bearing, in their tightened clasp, the sick, maimed, and helpless; while the noble firemen, heedless of risk and danger, plunge fearlessly into the heated air of the burning building.

NOW RUTH moves uneasily on her pillow; she becomes conscious of a stifling, choking sensation; she slowly opens her eyes. God in heaven! it is not all a dream! With a wild shriek she springs from the bed, and snatching from it her bewildered children, flies to the stairway. It has fallen in! She rushes to the window, her long hair floating out on the night-breeze.

A smothered groan from the crowd below. "They are lost!" The showering cinders, and falling rafters, have shut out the dreadful tableau! No—the smoke clears away! That portion of the building still remains, and Ruth and her children are clinging to it with the energy of despair. Who shall save them? for it were death to mount that tottering wall. Men hold their breath, and women shriek in terror. See! a ladder is raised; a gallant fireman scales it. Katy and Nettie are dropped into the outstretched arms of the crowd below; the strong, brave arm of Johnny Galt is thrown around Ruth, and in an instant she lies fainting in the arms of a by-stander.

THE BUTCHERING, ambitious conqueror, impudently issues his bulletins of killed and wounded, quenching the sunlight in many a happy home. The world shouts bravo! bravo! Telegraph wires and printing-presses are put in requisition to do him honor. Men unharness the steeds from his triumphal car, and draw him in triumph through the flower-garlanded streets. Woman—gentle woman, tosses the slaughtering hero wreaths and chaplets; but who turned twice to look at brave Johnny Galt, as, with pallid face, and smoky, discolored garments, he crawled to his obscure home, and stretched his weary limbs on his miserable couch? And yet the clinging grasp of rescued helplessness was still warm about his neck, the thrilling cry, "save us!" yet rang in the ears of the heedless crowd. God bless our gallant, noble, but *unhonored* firemen.

CHAPTER LXXXV

"*STRANGE* we do not hear from John," said Mrs. Millet to her wooden husband, as he sat leisurely sipping his last cup of tea, and chewing the cud of his reflections; "I want to hear how he gets on; whether he is likely to get any practice, and if his office is located to suit him. I hope Hyacinth will speak a good word for him; it is very hard for a young man in a strange place to get employment. I really pity John; it must be so disagreeable to put up with the initiatory humiliations of a young physician without fortune in a great city."

"Can't he go round and ask people to give him work, just like cousin Ruth?" asked a sharp little Millet, who was playing marbles in the corner.

"It is time you were in bed, Willy," said his disconcerted mother, as she pointed to the door; "go tell Nancy to put you to bed.

"As I was saying, Mr. Millet, it is very hard for poor John—he is so sensitive. I hope he has a nice boarding-house among refined people, and a pleasant room with everything comfortable and convenient about it; he is so fastidious, so easily disgusted with disagreeable surroundings. I hope he will not get low-spirited. If he gets practice I hope he will not have to *walk* to see his patients; he ought to have a nice chaise, and a fine horse, and some trusty little boy to sit in the chaise and hold the reins, while he makes his calls. I hope he has curtains to his sleeping-room windows, and a nice carpet on the floor, and plenty of bed-clothes, and gas-light to read by, and a soft lounge to throw himself on when he is weary. Poor John—I wonder why we do not hear from him. Suppose you write to-day, Mr. Millet?"

Mr. Millet wiped his mouth on his napkin, stroked his chin, pushed back his cup two degrees, crossed his knife and fork transversely over his plate, moved back his chair two feet and a half, hemmed six consecutive times, and was then safely delivered of the following remark:

"My—over-coat."

The overcoat was brought in from its peg in the entry; the left pocket was disembowelled, and from it was ferreted out a letter from 'John,' (warranted to keep!) which had lain there unopened three days. Mrs. Millet made no remark;—that day had gone by;—she had ate, drank, and slept, with that petrifaction too long to be guilty of any such nonsense. She sat down with a resignation worthy of Socrates, and perused the following epistle:

"Dear Mother:

"Well, my sign hangs out my office-door, 'Doctor John Millet,' and here I sit day after day, waiting for patients—I should spell it *patience*. This is a great city, and there are plenty of accidents happening every hour in the twenty-four, but unluckily for me there are more than plenty of doctors to attend to them, as every other door has one of their signs swinging out. Hyacinth has been sick, and I ran up there the other day, thinking, as he is a public man, it might be some professional advantage to me to have my name mentioned in connection with his sickness; he has a splendid place, six or eight servants, and everything on a corresponding scale.

To think of Ruth's astonishing success! I was in hopes it might help me a little in the way of business, to say that she was my cousin; but she has cut me dead. How could *I* tell she was going to be so famous, when I requested her not to allow her children to call me 'cousin John' in the street? I tell you, mother, we all missed a figure in turning the cold shoulder to her; and how much money she has made! I might sit in my office a month, and not earn so much as she can by her pen in one forenoon. Yes—there's no denying it, we've all made a great mistake. Brother Tom writes me from college that at a party the other night, he happened to mention (incidentally, of course) that 'Floy' was his cousin, when some one near him remarked, 'I should think the less said about that, by 'Floy's' relatives, the better.' It frets Hyacinth to a frenzy to have her poverty alluded to. He told me that he had taken the most incredible pains to conciliate editors whom he despised, merely to prevent any allusion to it in their columns. I, myself, have sent several anonymous paragraphs to the papers for insertion, contradicting the current reports, and saying that ''Floy' lost her self-respect before she lost her friends.' I don't suppose that was quite right, but I must have an eye to my practice, you know, and it might injure me if the truth were known. I find it very difficult, too, to get any adverse paragraph in, she is getting to be such a favorite (*i.e.* anywhere where it will *tell;*) the little scurrilous papers, you know, have no influence.

"It is very expensive living here; I am quite out of pocket. If you can get anything from father, I wish you would. Hyacinth says I must marry a rich wife as he did, when I get cornered by duns. Perhaps I may, but your rich girls are invariably homely, and I have an eye for beauty. Still there's no knowing what gilded pill I may be tempted to swallow if I don't get into practice pretty soon. Hyacinth's wife makes too many allusions to 'her family' to suit me (or Hyacinth either if the truth must be told, but he hates a dun worse, so that squares it, I suppose). Love to Leila.

"Your affectionate son, JOHN MILLET."

CHAPTER LXXXVI

"*GOOD AFTERNOON,* Mrs. Hall," said one of the old lady's neighbors; "here is the book you lent me. I am much obliged to you for it. I like it better than any book I have read for a long while. You said truly that if I once began it, I should not lay it down till I had finished it."

"Yes," said the old lady, "I don't often read a book now-a-days; my eyes are not very strong, (blue eyes seldom are, I believe," said she, fearing lest her visitor should suspect old Time had been blurring them;) "but that book, now, just suits me; there is common-sense in it. Whoever wrote that book is a good writer, and I hope she will give us another just like it. 'Floy' is a queer name; I don't recollect ever hearing it before. I wonder who she is."

"So do I," said the visitor; "and what is more, I mean to find out. Oh, here comes Squire Dana's son; he knows everything. I'll ask *him*. Yes, there he comes into the gate; fine young man Mr. Dana. They *do* say he's making up to Sarah Jilson, the lawyer's daughter; good match, too."

"Good afternoon," said both the ladies in a breath; "glad to see you, Mr. Dana; folks well? That's right. We have just been saying that you could tell us who 'Floy,' the author of that charming book, 'Life Sketches,' really is."

"You are inclined to quiz me," said Mr. Dana. "I think it should be *you* who should give *me* that information."

"Us?" exclaimed both the old ladies; "us? we have not the slightest idea who she is; we only admire her book."

"Well, then, I have an unexpected pleasure to bestow," said Mr. Dana, rubbing his hands in great glee. "Allow me to inform you, Mrs. Hall, that 'Floy' is no more, nor less, than your daughter-in-law,—Ruth."

"*Im*possible!" screamed the old lady, growing very red in the face, and clearing her throat most vigorously.

"I assure you it is true. My informant is quite reliable. I am glad you admire your daughter-in-law's book, Mrs. Hall; I quite share the feeling with you."

"But I don't admire it," said the old lady, growing every moment more confused; "there are several things in it, now I think of them, which I consider highly immoral. I think I mentioned them to you, Mrs. Spear," said she, (trusting to that lady's defective memory,) "at the time I lent it to you."

"Oh no, you didn't," replied Mrs. Spear; "you said it was one of the best and most interesting books you ever read, else I should not have borrowed it. I am very particular what I put in my children's way."

"Well, I couldn't have been thinking of what I was saying," said the old lady; "the book is very silly, a great part of it, beside being very bold, for a woman, and as I said before, really immoral."

"It is highly recommended by the religious press," said Mr. Dana, infinitely amused at the old lady's sudden change of opinion.

"You can't tell," said the old lady; "I have no doubt she wrote those notices herself."

"She has made an ample fortune, at any rate," said the young man; "more than I ever expect to make, if I should scribble till dooms-day."

"Don't believe it," said the old lady, fidgeting in her chair; "or, if she has, it won't last long."

"In that case she has only to write another book," said the persistent Mr. Dana; "her books will always find a ready market."

"We shall see," said the old lady bridling; "it is my opinion she'll go out like the wick of a candle. People won't read a second edition of such trash. Ruth Hall 'Floy'? Humph! that accounts,—humph! Well, anyhow, if she *has* made money, she had her nose held to the grindstone pretty well first; that's one comfort. *She* 'Floy'? Humph! That accounts. Well, sometimes money is given for a curse; I've heern tell of such things.

"—Yes, yes, I've heern tell of such things," muttered the old lady, patting her foot, as her two visitors left. "Dreadful grand, Ruth—'Floy' feels now, I suppose. A sight of money she's made, has she? A great deal she knows how to invest it. Invest it! What's the use of talking about that? It will be invested on her back, in silk gowns, laces, frumpery, and such things. I haven't a silk gown in the world. The least she could do, would be to send me one, for the care of that child.

"—Yes, laces and feathers, feathers and laces. The children, too, all tricked out like little monkeys, with long ostrich legs, and short, bob-tailed skirts standing out like opery girls, and whole yards of ribbin streaming from their hair, I'll warrant. The Catechize clean driven out of Katy's head. Shouldn't be at all astonished if they went to dancing school, or any other immoral place.

"—Wonder where they'll live? In some grand hotel, of course; dinner at six o'clock, black servants, gold salt-cellars and finger-glasses; nothing short of that'll suit now; humph. Shouldn't be astonished any day to hear Ruth kept a carriage and servants in livery, or had been to Victory's Court in lappets and diamonds. She's just impudent enough to do it. She isn't afraid of anybody nor anything. Dare say she will marry some Count or Duke; she has no more principle.

"—Humph! I suppose she is crowing well over me. V-e-r-y w-e-l-l; the wheel may turn round again, who knows? In fact, I am sure of it. How glad I *should* be! Well, I must say, I didn't think she had so much perseverance. I expected she'd just sit down, after awhile, and fret herself to death, and be well out of the way.

"—'Floy'! humph. I suppose I shan't take up a newspaper now without getting a dose about her. I dare say that spiteful young Dana will call here again just to rile me up by praising her. What a fool I was to get taken in so about that book. But how should I know it was hers? I should as soon have thought of her turning out Mrs. Bonaparte, as an authoress. Authoress! Humph! Wonder how the heels of her stockings look? S'pose she wears silk ones now, and French shoes; she was always as proud as Lucifer of her foot.

"—Well, I must say, (as long as there's nobody here to hear me,) that she *beats all*. Humph! She'll collapse, though; there's no doubt of *that*. I've heard of balloons that alighted in mud-puddles."

CHAPTER LXXXVII

"*GOOD MORNING,* Mr. Ellet!" said Mr. Jones, making an attempt at a bow, which the stiffness of his shirt-collar rendered entirely abortive; "how d'ye do?"

"Oh, how are you, Mr. Jones? I was just looking over the Household Messenger here, reading my daughter 'Floy's' pieces, and thinking what a great thing it is for a child to have a good father. 'Floy' was carefully brought up and instructed, and this, you see, is the result. I have been reading several of her pieces to a clergyman, who was in here just now. I keep them on hand in my pocket-book, to exhibit as a proof of what early parental education and guidance may do in developing latent talent, and giving the mind a right direction."

"I was not aware 'Floy' *was* your daughter," replied Mr. Jones; "do you know what time she commenced writing? what was the title of her first article and what was her remuneration?"

"Sir?" said Mr. Ellet, wishing to gain a little time, and looking very confused.

"Perhaps I should not ask such questions," said the innocent Mr. Jones, mistaking the cause of Mr. Ellet's hesitation; "but I felt a little curiosity to know something of her early progress. What a strong desire you must have felt for her ultimate success; and how much your influence and sympathy must have assisted her. Do you know whether her remuneration at the commencement of her career as a writer, was above the ordinary average of pay?"

"Yes—no—really, Mr. Jones, I will not venture to say, lest I should make a mistake; my memory is apt to be so treacherous."

"She wrote merely for amusement, I suppose; there could be no *necessity* in *your* daughter's case," said the blundering Mr. Jones.

"Certainly not," replied Mr. Ellet.

"It is astonishing how she can write so feelingly about the poor," said Mr. Jones; "it is so seldom that an author succeeds in depicting truthfully those scenes for which he draws solely upon the imagination."

"My daughter, 'Floy,' has a very vivid imagination," replied Mr. Ellet, nervously. "Women generally have, I believe; they are said to excel our sex in word-painting."

"I don't know but it may be so," said Jones. "'Floy' certainly possesses it in an uncommon degree. It is difficult else to imagine, as I said before, how a person, who has always been surrounded with comfort and luxury, could describe so feelingly the other side of the picture. It is remarkable. Do you know how much she has realized by her writings?"

"There, again," said the disturbed Mr. Ellet, "my memory is at fault; I am not good at statistics."

"Some thousands, I suppose," replied Mr. Jones. "Well, how true it is, that 'to him who hath shall be given!' Now, here is your literary daughter, who has no need of money, realizes a fortune by her books, while many a destitute and talented writer starves on a crust."

"Yes," replied Mr. Ellet, "the ways of Providence are inscrutable."

CHAPTER LXXXVIII

"FEMALE LITERATURE seems to be all the rage now," remarked a gentleman, who was turning over the volumes in Mr. Develin's book store, No. 6 Literary Row. "Who are your most successful lady authors?"

"Miss Pyne," said Mr. Develin, "authoress of 'Shadows,' Miss Taft, authoress of 'Sunbeams,' and Miss Bitman, authoress of 'Fairyland.'"

"I have been told," said the gentleman, "that 'Life Sketches,' by 'Floy,' has had an immense sale—a larger one, in fact, than any of the others; is that so?"

"It has had a *tolerable* sale," answered Mr. Develin, coldly. "I might have published it, I suppose, had I applied; but I had a very indifferent opinion of the literary talent of the authoress. The little popularity it *has* had, is undoubtedly owing to the writer being a sister of Hyacinth Ellet, the Editor of 'The Irving Magazine.'"

"But *is* she his sister," said the gentleman; "there are many rumors afloat; one hardly knows what to believe."

"No doubt of it," said Mr. Develin; "in fact, I, myself, *know* it to be true. 'Floy' is his sister; and it is altogether owing to the transferring of her articles, by him, to the columns of his paper, and his liberal endorsement of them, that she has had any success."

"Indeed," said the gentleman; "why I was a subscriber both for 'The Standard,' when her first article appeared in it, and also for 'The Irving Magazine,' and I am very sure that nothing of hers was copied in the latter until she had acquired an enviable popularity all over the Union. No, sir," said Mr. Walter, (for it was he,) "I know a great deal more about 'Floy' and her writings than *you* can tell me, and some little about yourself. I have often heard of the version you give of this matter, and I came in to satisfy myself if it had been correctly reported to me. Now, allow me to set you right, sir," said he, with a stern look. "The Editor of 'The Irving Magazine' never recognized 'Floy' as his sister, till the universal popular voice had pronounced its verdict in her favor. Then, when the steam was up, and the locomotive whizzing past, he jumps on, and says, 'how fast *we* go!'"

"I think you are mistaken, sir," replied Mr. Develin, with a faint attempt to retain his position.

"I am not mistaken, sir; I know, personally, that in the commencement of her literary career, when one or two articles of hers were copied into his paper by an assistant in the office, he positively forbade her *nom de plume* being again mentioned, or another of her articles copied into the Irving Magazine. He is a miserable time-server, sir. Fashion is his God; he recognizes only the drawing-room side of human nature. Sorrow in satin he can sympathize with, but sorrow in rags is too plebeian for his exquisite organization.

"Good morning, Mr. Develin; good morning, sir. The next time I hear of your giving a version of this matter, I trust it will be a correct one," added he with a stern look.

"Well," exclaimed Mr. Walter, as he walked down street, "of all mean meanness of which a man can be guilty, the meanest, in my estimation, is to rob a woman of her justly-earned literary fame, and I wish, for the credit of human nature, it were confined to persons of as limited mental endowments and influence as the one I have just left."

CHAPTER LXXXIX

"*OH, HOW FRIGHTENED* I was!" exclaimed Nettie, as her mother applied some healing salve to a slight burn on her arm; "how frightened I was, at that fire!"

"You mean, how frightened you were *after* the fire," replied her mother, smiling; "you were so bewildered, waking up out of that sound sleep, that I fancy you did not understand much about the danger till after good Johnny Galt saved you."

"If I did not love Neddy so much, I should certainly give Johnny Galt my picture," said Nettie, with a sudden outburst of enthusiasm.

"I will see that Johnny Galt is rewarded," replied Ruth. "But this is the day Mr. Walter was to have come. I hope Johnny Galt will meet him at the Dépôt as he promised, else he will be so alarmed about our safety when he learns of the fire. Dear me! how the rain comes down, it looks as though it meant to persevere."

"Yes, and *pour-severe* too," said Nettie, with an arch look at her mother.

Katy and Ruth had not finished laughing at this sally, when Mr. Walter was announced.

His greeting was grave, for he trembled to think of the danger they had escaped. After mutual congratulations had been exchanged, a detailed account of their escape given, and Johnny Galt's heroism duly extolled, Mr. Walter said:

"Well, I am glad to find you so comfortably housed after the fire; but the sooner I take all of you under my charge, the better, I think. What do you say to starting for ——— to-morrow? Are you sufficiently recovered from your fright and fatigue?"

"Oh, yes," replied Ruth, laughing; "do we not look as good as new? Our wardrobe, to be sure, is in rather a slender condition; but that is much easier remedied than a slender purse, as I have good reason to know."

"Very well, then," said Mr. Walter; "it is understood that we go to-morrow. I have some business to look after in the morning; shall you object to waiting till after dinner?"

"Not at all," replied Ruth. "In my opinion, nothing can equal the forlornness of forsaking a warm bed, to start breakfastless on a journey, with one's eyes half open."

"'Floy,'" said Mr. Walter, taking a package from his pocket, "I have obeyed your directions, and here is something which you may well be proud of;" and he handed Ruth a paper. It ran thus:

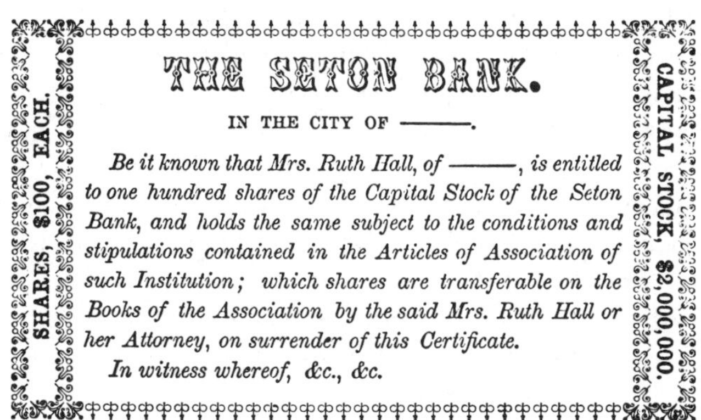

SHARES, $100, EACH.

THE SETON BANK.

IN THE CITY OF ———.

Be it known that Mrs. Ruth Hall, of ———, is entitled to one hundred shares of the Capital Stock of the Seton Bank, and holds the same subject to the conditions and stipulations contained in the Articles of Association of such Institution; which shares are transferable on the Books of the Association by the said Mrs. Ruth Hall or her Attorney, on surrender of this Certificate.

In witness whereof, &c., &c.

CAPITAL STOCK, $2,000,000.

"There," said Mr. Walter, laughing, "imagine yourself, if you can, in that dismal attic one year ago, a bank stock holder! Now confess that you are proud of yourself."

"We are proud of her," said the talkative Nettie; "if she is not proud of herself. Don't you think it is too bad, Mr. Walter, that mamma won't let Katy and me tell that 'Floy' is our mother? A little girl who lived at the hotel that was burnt up, said to Katy, that her uncle had just given her Life Sketches for a birth-day present, and told her that she must try and write as well as 'Floy' one of these days; and Katy looked at me, and I looked at Katy; and oh, isn't it *too bad*, Mr. Walter, that mamma won't let us tell, when we want to so much?"

"Well," said Mr. Walter, laughing, "I have only one little remark to make about that, namely, I have no doubt you two young ladies discovered some time before I did, that when your mamma says *No*, there is an end to all argument."

CHAPTER XC

THE MORNING of the next day was bright and fair. After dinner our travelling party entered the carriage in waiting, and proceeded on their way; the children chattering as usual, like little magpies, and Ruth and Mr. Walter occupied with their own solitary reflections.

One of the greatest luxuries of *true* friendship is the perfect freedom one feels, irrespective of the presence of another, to indulge in the mood of the moment—whether that mood be grave or gay, taciturn or loquacious, the unspeakable deliciousness of being reprieved from talking at a mark, hampered by no fear of incivility or discourtesy. Ruth had found this a great charm in the society of Mr. Walter, who seemed perfectly to understand and sympathize with her varied moods. On the present occasion she particularly felt its value—oppressed as she was by the rush of thoughts, retrospective and anticipatory—standing as it were on the threshold of a new epoch in her changing existence.

"Where are we going, mother?" asked Katy, as the carriage passed through a stone-gateway, and down a dim avenue of ancient trees.

"To dear papa's grave," replied Ruth, "before we leave this part of the country."

"Yes!" murmured Katy, in a low whisper.

IT WAS VERY BEAUTIFUL, that old avenue of pine trees, through which the setting sun was struggling faintly, now resting like a halo on some moss-grown grave-stone, now gilding some more ambitious monument of Mammon's raising. The winding cemetery paths, thronged by day with careless feet, were silent now. No lightsome laughter echoed through those leafy dells, grating upon the ear which almost listened for the loved voice. No strange eye, with curious gaze, followed the thoughtful group, speculating upon their heart's hidden history; but, now and then, a little loitering bird, tempted beyond its mate to lengthen its evening flight, flitted, with a brief gush of song, across their pathway. Hushed, holy, and unprofaned, was this Sabbath of the dead! Aching hearts here throbbed with pain no longer; weary feet were still; busy hands lay idly crossed over tired breasts; babes, who had poised one tiny foot on life's turbid ocean brink, then shrank back affrighted at its surging waves, here slept their peaceful sleep.

THE MOON HAD SILVERED the old chapel turrets, and the little nodding flowers glistened with dew-drops, but still Ruth lingered. Old memories were thronging, thick and fast, upon her;—past joys—past sorrows—past sufferings;—and yet the heart, which felt them all so keenly, would soon lie pulseless amid these mouldering thousands. There was a vacant place left by the side of Harry. Ruth's eye rested on it—then on her children—then on Mr. Walter.

"So help me God," reverently murmured the latter, interpreting the mute appeal.

AS THE CARRIAGE rolled from under the old stone gateway, a little bird, startled from out its leafy nest, trilled forth a song as sweet and clear as the lark's at heaven's own blessed gate.

"Accept the omen, dear Ruth," said Mr. Walter. "Life has much of harmony yet in store for you."

OTHER WRITINGS

Newspaper Articles

THE MODEL HUSBAND

As the following account of a "Model Husband" is from a lady in good position in society, we can but suppose her model husband is the true style of a husband, and what all good married men should be. In looking over our nearly forty years of married life, we find that our good wife has never exacted quite so much of us, but she merely waived her rights, I suppose.—Editor

[Original note preceding "The Model Husband," Fanny Fern's first article]

HIS POCKET-BOOK is never empty when his wife calls for money. He sits up in bed, at night, feeding Thomas Jefferson Smith with a pap spoon, while his wife takes a comfortable nap and dreams of the new shawl she means to buy at Warren's the next day. As "one good turn deserves another," he is allowed to hold Tommy *again* before breakfast, while Mrs. Smith curls her hair. He never makes any complaints about the soft molasses gingerbread that is rubbed into his hair, coat, and vest, during these happy, conjugal seasons. He always laces on his wife's boots, lest the exertion should make her too red in the face before going out to promenade Washington St. He never calls any woman "*pretty*," before Mrs. Smith. He never makes absurd objections to her receiving bouquets, or the last novel, from Captain this, or Lieutenant that. He don't set his teeth and stride down to the store like a victim every time his wife presents him with another little Smith. He gives the *female* Smiths French gaiter boots, parasols, and silk dresses without stint, and the boys, new jackets, pop guns, velocipedes and crackers, without any questions asked. He never breaks the seal of his wife's billet doux, or peeps over her shoulder while she is answering the same. He never holds the drippings of the umbrella over her new bonnet while his last new hat is innocent of a rain-drop. He never complains when he is late home to dinner, though the little Smiths have left him nothing but bones and crusts.

He never takes the newspaper and reads it, before Mrs. Smith has a chance to run over the advertisements, deaths, and marriages, etc. He always gets into bed *first*, cold nights, to *take off the chill* for his wife. He never leaves his trousers, drawers, shoes, etc., on the floor, when he goes to bed, for his wife to break her neck over, in the dark, if the baby wakes and needs a dose of Paregoric. If the children in the next room scream in the night, he don't expect *his wife* to take an air-bath to find out what is the matter. He has been known to wear Mrs. Smith's night-cap in bed, to make the baby think he is its mother.

When he carries the children up to be christened, he holds them right *end up*, and don't tumble their frocks. When the minister asks him the *name*—he says "*Lucy—Sir*," distinctly, that he need not mistake it for *Lucifer*. He goes home and trots the child, till the sermon is over, while his wife remains in church to receive the congratulations of the parish gossips.

If Mrs. Smith has company to dinner and there are not strawberries enough, and his wife looks at him with a sweet smile, and offers to help *him*, (at the same time *kicking him gently* with her slipper under the table) he always replies, "No, I thank you, dear, they don't agree with me."

Lastly, he approves of "Bloomers" and "pettiloons," for he says women *will* do as they like—he should as soon think of driving the nails into his own coffin, as trying to stop them—"cosy?"—it's *unpossible*![1]

Olive Branch
June 28, 1851

THOUGHTS ON DRESS

MR. EDITOR,—While the gentlemen are making such a parade and fuss about ladies' dress, Bloomerism, and the like, I who, for one, still reside in petticoats, beg leave to enquire, if a cravat or handkerchief, doubled and twisted round a gentleman's neck, this hot weather, tight enough too (ye railers at corsets) to stop the circulation, is a whit more reasonable than dresses lined with whalebone at the waist? I would also humbly submit to their consideration, whether a dickey, starched stiff enough to cut the flesh under the ears, is *altogether* comfortable?

These thoughts suggested themselves to me last Sunday, as such thoughts sometimes will, spite of pulpit, parson or preaching, and without previous preparation, as I witnessed the vain attempts of a young man in the pew before me, to get his head in a comfortable position to look over the top of his dickey and see the singers, without cutting his ears off! Then just as I began to attend to the sermon again, I heard the most extraordinary noise—such a *creaking*!—I grew quite nervous, trying to discover the cause. Finally, I saw a gentleman in the pew loosen one or two buttons of his waistcoat—still I was nonplussed—at last I had it! The vest was lined round the edges underneath with morocco, and as it was buttoned very tightly at the waist, to show off his figure to the best advantage, it made a noise much resembling that you hear from an old rusty chaise top that has been some time out of use.

Then I read the following paragraph in one of the newspapers the other day: "A gentleman informs us that out of one hundred young ladies he met in the street to-day, ninety-nine were sucking the handles of their parasols." Crusty old Benedict![1] Did you ever see a man that could live a minute (except he was in bed) without a cane? And did you ever see one, unless his head was white with age and he needed it for its legitimate use, that wasn't whipping his boots with it, or rubbing it against his lips? Take the mote out of your own eye, brother Benedict, before you meddle with the sisters.

Then the tight pantaloons that have been worn; if a lady dropped her handkerchief, she never dared to ask her cavalier to pick it up, because she knew it would never do for him to pretend to hear her, unless he carried a needle and thread in his pocket to repair damages.

Then the days of *straps*! how the buttons used to fly off! "*Peggotty*"[2] *didn't begin*! My brothers had their feet in my lap two-thirds of the time, sewing on those tormented buttons. I resolved then I never would be married, and shouldn't if the fashion had not changed.

I used to think the men were all such handsome figures, too, till I found out that the breasts of their coats are padded and stuffed like a turkey for roasting.

And now, one more and I have done. I noticed since warm weather came and white hats (felt and beaver) are worn, that every man I meet has *a crape* on. I examined the bills of mortality, made enquiries concerning the cholera and small pox, and made preparations to go into the country awhile—till I learned to-day, to my utter astonishment, that it is merely a whim of fashion, because it is considered becoming!! I'd like to see the breeze that would be raised if we wore a black ribbon on our bonnets for *fashion*!

Olive Branch
July 19, 1851

DEACONS' DAUGHTERS AND MINISTERS' SONS

"*DEACONS' DAUGHTERS* and ministers' sons" are a proverb and a bye-word all the world over.[1] As to "ministers' sons," clear the way when you see 'em coming! but with regard to deacons' daughters, 'tis a sore subject with me. *I'm a deacon's daughter myself*, and I don't like this twitting on facts. I'm sure I could tell you of a hundred girls wilder than ever *I* was. Besides, I'd like to know if my papa's mantle of gravity was expected to be capacious enough to cover us—*his nine daughters*—when he accepted the office of deacon. Does goodness come by *inheritance*? tell me *that*! and do we imbibe their Assembly's Catechism and the Ten Commandments with our mother's milk? Not a bit of it; the consequence is, I was born an untameable romp—and a romp I remained, and nobody would have thought of noticing it, either, if *Deacon* hadn't been prefixed to my papa's name.

"Unhitched the engine from the cars," did I? Mis-mated all the gentlemen's boots at the hotel, and stuck pins in the toes when they were put out to be brushed, and half of 'em were too late for the cars in consequence, and Sam the bootblack *swore terribly*. Well, *that* showed *his* parents didn't bring him up right—and as to being "late for the cars" men always *will* lie in bed till dinner time, if they can—*boots or no boots*. "Stole pies at boarding-school," hey? and then [“]threw the plate out the window to escape detection and cut a great gash in our minister's son's nose." Well—didn't I tell you when I began that *they* were always getting into scrapes? how did *I* know his nose was underneath? and when I tore that horrid rent in my new black silk, and my governess kept me at home of a holiday to darn it, and I stuck it together with a piece of *court-plaster*, and ran off to play, didn't I, instead of getting a patent for the invention, get a sound cuffing? and isn't that the way *genius* is *always* misapprehended? And when old Zekiel Smith went to sleep in church, with his queue hanging over into our pew, and I pinned it tight down by the ribbon, and half pulled his scalp off when he got up, how did *I* know it was *his own hair*? Had it belonged to a *wig* as I supposed, he wouldn't have *felt it*. Any way, I lost *my* dinner 'cause he made such a fuss about a trifle, and had to be locked up till tea-time, when I told a story and said I was "sorry" as I was bid.

Did I say I was "*untameable*"? Well, *that's a mistake*; there was *one thing* that would make me snap off as short as a pipe-stem in the midst of my tantrums; take all the color out of my face, and make me look as sober as the Deacon himself—and that was *the sight of our sexton*! Did you ever see a distorted carving of "Time with a scythe" on a country tomb-stone? Well that was *Joab* to the life! all bones, joints, sinews and eyes! with a cold, slimy sort of a look that said to me, as plain as looks *could* say, "you'd better believe you won't *always* carry on *that* way, my dear." You may be sure I never played any of my tricks on *him*. Didn't I hope he might catch the small-pox or be quietly removed in some way? Half laughing, half crying, didn't I exact a promise from my father that he never should touch *me*? And now let me tell you, between you and me confidentially, it wasn't that *dear father's* fault that I wasn't a good girl; I had "line upon line—precept upon precept" but—I was a "deacon's daughter," and that means in plain English that what good qualities I possessed nobody would see, and those that were bad, were ten times magnified—*because I was expected to be as good as my father*.

Olive Branch
August 9, 1851

AUNT HETTY ON MATRIMONY

"*NOW GIRLS,*" said Aunt Hetty, "put down your embroidery and worsted work; do something sensible, and stop building air-castles, and talking of lovers and honey-moons. It makes me sick; it is perfectly antimonial. Love is a farce; matrimony is a humbug; husbands are domestic Napoleons, Neroes, Alexanders,—sighing for other hearts to conquer, after they are sure of yours. The honey-moon is as short-lived as a lucifer-match;[1] after that you may wear your wedding-dress at the wash tub, and your night-cap to meeting, and your husband wouldn't know it. You may pick up your own pocket-handkerchief, help yourself to a chair, and split your gown across the back reaching over the table to get a piece of butter, while he is laying in his breakfast as if it was the last meal he should eat this side of Jordan. When he gets through he will aid your digestion,—while you are sipping your first cup of coffee,—by inquiring what you'll have for dinner; whether the cold lamb was all ate yesterday; if the charcoal is all out, and what you gave for the last green tea you bought. Then he gets up from the table, lights his cigar with the last evening's paper, that you have not had a chance to read; gives two or three whiffs of smoke,—which are sure to give you a headache for the forenoon,—and, just as his coat-tail is vanishing through the door, apologizes for not doing 'that errand' for you yesterday,—thinks it doubtful if he can to-day,—'so *pressed with business*.' Hear of him at eleven o'clock, taking an ice-cream with some ladies at a confectioner's, while you are at home new-lining his old coat-sleeves. Children by the ears all day, can't get out to take the air, feel as crazy as a fly in a drum; husband comes home at night, nods a 'How d'ye do, Fan,' boxes Charley's ears, stands little Fanny in the corner, sits down in the easiest chair in the warmest corner, puts his feet up over the grate, shutting out all the fire, while the baby's little pug nose grows blue with the cold; reads the newspaper all to himself, solaces his inner man with a hot cup of tea, and, just as you are laboring under the hallucination that he will ask you to take a mouthful of fresh air with him, he puts on his dressing-gown and slippers, and begins to reckon up the family expenses! after which he lies down on the sofa, and you keep time with your needle, while he sleeps till nine o'clock. Next morning, ask him to leave you a 'little money,'—he looks at you as if to be sure that you are in your right mind, draws a sigh long enough and strong enough to inflate a pair of bellows, and asks you 'what you want with it, and if a half a dollar won't do?'—Gracious king! as if those little shoes, and stockings, and petticoats could be had for half a dollar! Oh girls! set your affections on cats, poodles, parrots or lap dogs; but let matrimony alone. It's the hardest way on earth of getting a living—you never know when your work is done. Think of carrying eight or nine children through the measles, chicken pox, rash, mumps, and scarlet fever, some of 'em twice over; it makes my head ache to think of it. Oh, you may scrimp and save, and twist and turn, and dig and delve, and economise *and die*, and your husband will marry again, take what you have saved to dress his second wife with, and she'll take your portrait for a fireboard, and,—but, what's the use of talking? I'll warrant every one of you'll try it, the first chance you get! there's a sort of bewitchment about it, somehow. I wish one half the world warn't fools, and the other half idiots, I do. Oh, dear!"

Olive Branch
Dec. 6, 1851

FAMILY JARS

"Domestic peace can never be *preserved* in family jars."

MR. JEREMIAH STUBBS was rash enough to remark, one morning, to his wife Keziah, "that, after all, women had little or nothing to do; that he only wished she knew the responsibilities of a man of business." (Jeremiah kept a small shop, well stocked with maple sugar, suspicious looking doughnuts, ancient pies and decayed lemons.)—"Yes, Keziah, if you only knew the responsibilities of a *man of business*," said Jeremiah, fishing up the corner of his dickey from a questionable looking red neckerchief that protected his jugular.

"Well, let me know 'em, then," said his wife, tying on her bonnet. "Seeing is believing. We will change works for one day. You get breakfast, tend the baby, and wash and dress the other three children, and I'll go down and open shop."

Jeremiah didn't exactly look for this termination to the discussion; but he was a man, and of course never backed out; so he took a survey of the premises, wondering which end to begin, while Keziah went on her way rejoicing, took down the shutters like a master-workman, opened shop, made a fire, arranged the tempting wares above mentioned, with feminine ingenuity; putting the best side of everything uppermost, and wishing she had nothing else to do, from day to day, but stand behind the counter and sell them.

This accomplished, she went home to breakfast. There sat Jeremiah, in a chair, in the middle of the room, with one side of his beard shaved off, and the lather drying on the remainder, trotting a little blue-looking wretch, in a yellow flannel night-gown, who was rubbing some soft gingerbread into his bosom with his little fists, by way of amusement. The coffee had boiled over into the ashes, and Thomas Jefferson and Napoleon Buonaparte Stubbs were stirring up the miniature pond with Jeremiah's razor. James Madison was still between the sheets, vociferating loudly for "his breakfast."

Looking with a curious eye over the pile of scorched toast for a piece that was eatable, Keziah commenced her breakfast, referring her interesting young family to their paternal derivative for a supply of their numerous wants. At last he placed a cup of muddy coffee before him, congratulating himself that his labors were ended, when the baby, considering it an invasion of his rights, made a dive at it, and he sprang from his chair with the scalding contents dripping from his unwhisperables, and—a word that church-members don't use—hissing from between his teeth.

Calm as a summer morning, Keziah replaced her time-worn straw upon her head, telling Jerry that her children must be prepared for school at nine o'clock, the room must be swept and righted, the breakfast things washed, the potatoes boiled, and the mince-meat prepared for dinner by twelve. Her husband grinned a ghastly smile, and told her "that was easy done." No such thing. The comb could'nt be found; he had to wipe James Madison's presidential phiz-mahogany on the corner of the table-cloth. Napoleon Buonaparte's pinafore had been used to wipe the dishes; Thomas Jefferson had rejoiced twice in a pair of boxed ears, for devouring the contents of the sugar-bowl; and that little yellow flannel night-gown was clutching at his heels, every step he took over the floor.

"Miserable Jeremiah! did'nt you wish you were a woman?" Well, "time and tide wait for no man." Twelve o'clock came, and so did Keziah. Her husband would rather have seen the ——— hem! The bed was unmade, the children's hair stood up "seven ways of a Sunday," the cat was devouring the meat, the baby had the chopping knife, and Napoleon Buonaparte was playing ball with the potatoes.

Jeremiah's desire for immediate emancipation overcame his pride, and passing his arms *half way* around Keziah's waist, (it was so large that he always made a chalk mark where he left off embracing, that he might know where to begin again,) he told her she was an angel, and he was a poor miserable wretch, and was ready to acknowledge his mistake. Keziah very quietly withdrew from his arm, told him the bargain was made for the day, and she would change works at night; and treating herself to a piece of bread and butter, she departed. Jerry sat for a minute looking into the fire, then reaching down a huge parcel of maple-sugar, he put it on the floor, and seating all the young hopefuls round it, turned the key on them and the scene of his cares, mounted his beaver on his aching head, and rushed to ———'s for a *whiskey punch!* The room was nice and tidy, the fire was comfortable, the punch was *strong*, and Jeremiah was *weak*. He woke *about dark*, from troubled dreams of broomsticks and curtain lectures, and not having sufficient courage to encounter their fulfilment, has left Keziah to the glorious independence of a "*California widow*."[1]

True Flag
Jan. 10, 1852

HINTS TO YOUNG WIVES

SHOULDN'T I LIKE to make a bon-fire of all the "Hints to Young Wives," "Married Woman's Friend," etc., and throw in the authors after them? I have a little neighbor who believes all they tell her is gospel truth, and lives up to it. The minute she sees her husband coming up the street, she makes for the door, as if she hadn't another minute to live, stands in the entry with her teeth chattering in her head till he gets all his coats and mufflers, and overshoes, and what-do-you-call-'ems off, then chases round (like a cat in a fit) after the boot-jack; warms his slippers and puts 'em on, and dislocates her wrist carving at the table for fear it will tire him.

Poor little innocent fool! she imagines that's the way to preserve his affection. Preserve a fiddlestick! The consequence is, he's sick of the sight of her; snubs her when she asks him a question, and after he has eaten her good dinners takes himself off as soon as possible, bearing in mind the old proverb "that too much of a good thing is good for nothing." Now the truth is just this, and I wish all the women on earth had but one ear in common, so that I could put this little bit of gospel into it:—Just so long as a man isn't quite as sure as if he knew for certain, whether nothing on earth could ever disturb your affection for him, he is your humble servant, but the very second he finds out (or thinks he does) that he has possession of every inch of your heart, and no neutral territory—he will turn on his heel and march off whistling "Yankee Doodle!"

Now it's no use to take your pocket handkerchief and go snivelling round the house with a pink nose and red eyes; not a bit of it! If you have made the interesting discovery that you were married for a sort of upper servant or housekeeper, just *fill that place and no other*, keep your temper, keep all his strings and buttons and straps on; and then keep him at a distance as a housekeeper should—"them's my sentiments!" I have seen one or two men in my life who could bear to be loved (as a woman with a soul knows how), without being spoiled by it, or converted into a tyrant—but they are rare birds, and should be caught, stuffed and handed over to Barnum! Now as the ministers say, "I'll close with an interesting little incident that came under my observation."

Mr. Fern came home one day when I had such a crucifying headache that I couldn't have told whether I was married or single, and threw an old coat into my lap to mend. Well, I tied a wet bandage over my forehead, "left all flying," and sat down to it—he might as well have asked me to make a *new* one; however I new lined the sleeves, mended the button-holes, sewed on new buttons down the front, and all over the coat tails—when finally it occurred to me (I believe it was a suggestion of Satan,) that the *pocket* might need mending; so I turned it inside out, and *what do you think I found?* A *love-letter from him to my dress-maker*!! I dropped the coat, I dropped the work-basket, I dropped the buttons, I dropped the baby (it was a *female*, and I thought it just as well to put her out of future misery) and then I hopped up into a chair front of the looking-glass, and remarked to the young woman I saw there, "*F-a-n-n-y F-e-r-n! if you—are—ever—such—a—confounded fool again*"—*and I wasn't*.

Olive Branch
Feb. 14, 1852

INSIGNIFICANT LOVE

> "You, young, loving creature, who dream of your lover by night and by day—you fancy that he does the same of you? One hour, perhaps, your presence has captivated him, subdued him even to weakness; the next, he will be in the world, working his way as a man among men, forgetting, for the time being, your very existence. Possibly, if you saw him, his outer self, so hard and stern, so different from the self you know, would strike you with pain. Or else his inner and diviner self, higher than you dream of, would turn coldly from *your insignificant love*."

"*INSIGNIFICANT LOVE!!*" I like *that*, I do. More especially when out of ten couple you meet, *nine* of the wives are as far above their husbands, in point of mind, as the stars are above the earth. For the credit of the *men* I should be sorry to say how many of 'em would be *minus* coats, hats, pantaloons, cigars, &c., were it not for *their wives' earnings;* or how many smart speeches and talented sermons have been concocted by their better halves, (while *rocking the cradle,*) to be delivered to the public at the proper time, *parrot fashion,* by the *lords* (?!) of creation.

Wisdom will die with the *men,* there's no gainsaying *that!* Catch a regular, smart, talented, energetic woman, and it will puzzle you to find a man that will compare with her for go-aheadativeness. The more obstacles she encounters, the harder she struggles, and the more you try to put her down, *the more you won't do it.* Children are obliged to write under their crude drawings, "this is a dog," or, "this is a horse." If it were not for coats and pants, we should be obliged to label, "this is a man," in ninety-nine cases out of a hundred!

"Insignificant love!" Why does a man offer himself a dozen times to the *same* woman? Pity to take so much pains for such a *trifle!* "Insignificant love!" Who gets you on your feet again, when you fail in business, by advancing the nice little sum settled on herself by her anxious pa? Who cheers you up, when her nerves are all in a double twisted knot, and you come home with your face long as the moral law? Who wears her old bonnet *three winters,* while you smoke, and drive, and go to the opera, and the Lord knows where, beside? Who sits up till the small hours, *to help you find the way up your own staircase?* Who darns your old coat, next morning, just as if you were a man, instead of a *brute?* And who scratches any woman's eyes out, who dares insinuate that her husband is superior to you!

"Insignificant love!" I wish I knew the man who wrote that article! I'd appoint his *funeral tomorrow,* and it *should come off, too!!*

Olive Branch
April 10, 1852

MISTAKEN PHILANTHROPY

"Don't moralize to a man who is on his back;—help him up, set him firmly on his feet, and then give him advice and means."

THERE'S AN OLD-FASHIONED, verdant piece of wisdom, *altogether* unsuited for the enlightened age we live in; fished up, probably, from some musty old newspaper, edited by some eccentric man troubled with that inconvenient appendage called *a heart!* Don't pay any attention to it. If a poor wretch—male or female—comes to you for charity, whether allied to you by your own mother, or mother Eve, put on the most stoical, "get thee behind me," expression you can muster. Listen to him with the air of a man who "thanks God he is not as *other men* are." If the story carry conviction with it, and *truth* and *sorrow go hand in hand,* button your coat up tighter over your pocket-book, and give him a piece of—*good advice!* If you know anything about him, try to rake up some imprudence or mistake he may have made in the course of his life, and bring that up as a reason *why* you can't give him anything more substantial, and tell him that his present condition is probably a *salutary discipline* for those same peccadilloes! Ask him more questions than there are in the Assembly's Catechism, about his private history, and when you've *pumped* him high and dry, try to teach him—on an empty stomach—the "*duty of submission.*" If the tear of wounded sensibility begins to flood the eye, and a hopeless look of discouragement settles down upon the face, "wish him well," and *turn your back upon him* as quick as possible.

Should you at any time be seized with an unexpected *spasm of generosity,* and make up your mind to bestow some worn-out old garment, that will hardly hold together till the recipient gets it home, you've *bought him, body and soul;* of course, you are entitled to the gratitude of a *life-time!* If he ever presumes to think differently from you after that, he is an "ungrateful wretch," and "ought to suffer." As to the "golden rule," that was made in *old times;* everything is changed *now;* it is not suited to our meridian.

People shouldn't *get* poor; if they do, *you* don't want to be bothered with it. It is disagreeable; it hinders your digestion. You would rather see Dives than Lazarus;[1] and, it is my opinion, your taste will be gratified in that particular,—in the other world, if not in this!

Olive Branch
June 5, 1852

WOMAN'S WICKEDNESS

"Don't marry a woman *under twenty*. She hasn't *come to her wickedness* before then."—*Blackwood's Magazine*

WELL—! If I *knew* any bad words, I'm *awful* afraid I should *say* 'em!! I just wish I had hold of the perpetrator of that with a pair of tongs, I'd bottle him up in *sperrits*, and keep him for a terror to liars, as sure as his name is "Kit North."[1]

"Set a thief to catch a thief!" How came *you* to know when that crisis in a woman's life occurs? Answer me *that*! I'll tell you what *my* opinion is; and won't charge you any *fee* for it either! A woman "comes to her *wickedness*" *when she comes to her* HUSBAND!!—and if she knew anything *good before*, it all "goes by the board," *then*; it's no more use to her afterwards, than the fifth wheel of a coach! Don't you know, you wicked calumniator, that thunder don't sour milk more effectually than matrimony does women's tempers?

"*Come to their wickedness*, indeed! Snowflakes and soot! They'd never know the *meaning* of the *word* "wicked," if *your sex* were blotted out of existence! We should have a perfect little heaven upon earth—a regular terrestrial Paradise—no runaway matches, no cases of—c—onscience! no divorces, no deviltry of any kind. Women would keep *young* till the millennium; in fact, millennium would be merely a *nominal* jubilee! because it would have *already come*. The world would be an universal garden of pretty, rosy, laughing women; no masculine mildew to mar their beauty or bow their sweet heads, the blessed year round!

Now you'd better repent of your sins, Mr. What's-your-name; for as sure as preaching, you will go where you'll have *nothing to do* but *think of 'em*! and you won't find any *women there*, either; *for they all go to the other place*!

Olive Branch
June 5, 1852

A WHISPER TO ROMANTIC YOUNG LADIES

"A crust of bread, a pitcher of wine, a thatched roof, and love,— there's happiness for you."

GIRLS! that's a humbug! The very *thought* of it makes me groan. It's all moonshine. In fact, men and moonshine in my dictionary are synonymous.

Water and a crust! RATHER spare diet! May do for the honey-moon. Don't make much difference *then*, whether you eat shavings or sardines— but when you return to *substantials*, and your wedding dress is put away in a trunk for the benefit of posterity, if you can get your husband to *smile* on anything short of a "sirloin" or a roast turkey, you are a lucky woman.

Don't every married woman know that a man is as savage as a New Zealander when he's hungry? and when he comes home to an empty cupboard and meets a dozen little piping mouths, (necessary accompaniments of "cottages" and "love,") clamorous for supper, "*Love* will have the *sulks*," or my name isn't Fanny. Lovers have a trick of getting disenchanted, too, when they see their Aramintas[1] with dresses pinned up round the waist, hair powdered with sweeping, faces scowled up over the wash-tub, and soap-suds dripping from red elbows.

A Whisper to Romantic Young Ladies

We know these little accidents never happen in novels—where the heroine is always "dressed in white, with a rose-bud in her hair," and lives on blossoms and May dew! There are no wash-tubs or gridirons in *her* cottage; *her* children are born cherubim, with a seraphic contempt for dirt pies and molasses. *She* remains "a beauty" to the end of the chapter, and "steps out" just in time to anticipate her first gray hair, her husband drawing his last breath at the same time, as a dutiful husband *should*; and not falling into the unromantic error of outliving his grief, and marrying a second time!

But this humdrum life, girls, is another affair, with its washing and ironing and cleaning days, when children expect boxed ears, and visitors picked-up dinners. All the "romance" there is in it, you can put under a three-cent piece!

St. Paul says they who marry do well enough, but they who *don't* marry do WELL-ER! Sensible man that. Nevertheless, had *I* flourished in those times, I would have undertaken to change his sentiments; for those old-fashioned gentlemen were worth running after.

One half the women marry for fear they shall be old maids. Now I'd like to know why an old maid is to be snubbed, any more than an old bachelor? Old bachelors receive "the mitten,"[2] occasionally, and old maids have been known to *outlive several "offers."* They are both useful in their way—particularly old bachelors!

Now *I* intend to be an "old maid;" and I shall found a mutual accommodation society, and admit old bachelors honorary members. They shall wait on *us* evenings, and we'll hem their pocket handker*chers* and mend their gloves. No *boys under thirty* to be admitted. Irreproachable dickeys, immaculate shirt-bosoms and faultless boots *indispensable*. Gentlemen always to sit on the *opposite* side of the room—no refreshments but *ices*! *Instant expulsion* the consequence of the first attempt at love-making! No allusion to be made to Moore or Byron! The little "*bye-laws*" of the society *not* to be published! Moonlight evenings, the sisters are not at home! the moon being considered, from time immemorial, an unprincipled magnetiser!

True Flag
June 12, 1852

SUNSHINE AND YOUNG MOTHERS

> "FOLLY—For girls to expect to be happy without marriage. Every woman was made for a mother, consequently, babies are as necessary to their 'peace of mind,' as health. If you wish to look at melancholy and indigestion, look at an old maid. If you would take a peep at sunshine, look in the face of a young mother."

NOW I WON'T STAND THAT! I'm an old maid myself; and I'm neither melancholy nor indigestible! My "PIECE *of mind*" I'm going to give you, (in a minute!) and I never want to *touch* a baby except with a *pair of tongs!* "Young mothers and sunshine!" Worn to fiddling strings before they are twenty-five! When an old lover turns up he thinks he sees his grandmother, instead of the dear little Mary who used to make him feel as if he should crawl out of the toes of his boots! Yes! my mind is *quite* made up about *matrimony*; but as to the "*babies*," (sometimes I think, and then again I don't know!) but on *the whole I believe* I consider 'em a d———ecided humbug! It's a *one-sided* partnership, this marriage! the *wife casts up all the accounts!*

"Husband" gets up in the morning and pays his "*devours*" to the looking-glass; curls his fine head of hair; puts on an immaculate shirt bosom; ties an excruciating cravat; sprinkles his handkerchief with cologne; stows away a French roll, an egg, and a cup of coffee; gets into the omnibus, looks *slantendicular* at the pretty girls, and makes love between the pauses of business during the forenoon *generally*. Wife must "hermetically seal" the windows and exclude all the fresh air, (because the baby had the "snuffles" in the night;) and sits gasping down to the table more dead than alive, to finish her breakfast. Tommy turns a cup of hot coffee down his bosom; Juliana has torn off the string of her school-bonnet; James "wants his geography covered;" Eliza can't find her satchel; the butcher wants to know if she'd like a joint of mutton; the milkman would like his money; the ice man wants to speak to her "just a minute;" the baby swallows a bean; husband sends the boy home from the store to say *his partner* will dine with him; the cook leaves "all flying," to go to her "sister's dead baby's wake," and husband's thin coat must be ironed before noon. "*Sunshine and young mothers!!*" Where's my smelling-bottle?

Olive Branch
July 3, 1852

A PRACTICAL BLUE STOCKING

"*HAVE YOU CALLED* on your old friend, James Lee, since your return?" said Mr. Seldon to his nephew.

"No, sir; I understand he has the misfortune to have a blue stocking for a wife, and whenever I have thought of going there, a vision with inky fingers, frowzled hair, rumpled dress, and slip-shod heels has come between me and my old friend,—not to mention thoughts of a disorderly house, smoky puddings, and dirty-faced children. Defend *me* from a wife who spends her time dabbling in ink, and writing for the papers. I'll lay a wager James has n't a shirt with a button on it, or a pair of stockings that is not full of holes. Such a glorious fellow as he used to be, too!" said Harry, soliloquizingly, "so dependent upon somebody to love him. By Jove, it's a hard case."

"Harry, will you oblige me by calling there?" said Mr. Seldon with a peculiar smile.

"Well, yes, if you desire it; but these married men get so metamorphosed by their wives, that it's a chance if I recognize the melancholy remains of my old friend. A literary wife!" and he shrugged his shoulders contemptuously.

At one o'clock the next afternoon, Harry might have been seen ringing the bell of James Lee's door. He had a very ungracious look upon his face, as much as to say,—"My mind is made up for the worst, and I must bear it for Jemmy's sake."

The servant ushered him into a pretty little sitting-room, not expensively furnished, but neat and tasteful. At the further end of the room were some flowering plants, among which a sweet-voiced canary was singing. Harry glanced round the room; a little light-stand or Chinese table stood in the corner, with pen, ink, and papers scattered over it.

"I knew it," said Harry; "there's the sign! horror of horrors! an untidy, slatternly blue stocking! how I shall be disgusted with her! Jemmy's to be pitied."

He took up a book that lay upon the table, and a little manuscript copy of verses fell from between the leaves. He dropped the book as if he had been poisoned; then picking up the fallen manuscript with his thumb and forefinger, he replaced it with an impatient pshaw! Then he glanced round the room again,—no! there was not a particle of dust to be seen, even by his prejudiced eyes; the windows were transparently clean; the hearth-rug was longitudinally and mathematically laid down; the pictures hung "plumb" upon the wall; the curtains were fresh and gracefully looped; and, what was a greater marvel, there was a child's dress half finished in a dainty little work-basket, and a thimble of fairy dimensions in the immediate neighborhood thereof. Harry felt a perverse inclination to examine the stitches, but at the sound of approaching footsteps he braced himself up to undergo his mental shower-bath.

A little lady tripped lightly into the room, and stood smilingly before him; her glossy black hair was combed smoothly behind her ears, and knotted upon the back of a remarkably well-shaped head; her eyes were black and sparkling, and full of mirth; her dress fitted charmingly to a very charming little figure; her feet were unexceptionally small, and neatly gaitered; the snowy fingers of her little hand had not the slightest "soupçon" of ink upon them, as she extended them in token of welcome to her guest.

Harry felt very much like a culprit, and greatly inclined to drop on one knee, and make a clean breast of a confession, but his evil bachelor spirit whispered in his ear,—"Wait a bit, she's fixed up for company; cloven foot will peep out by and by!"

Well, they sat down! The lady knew enough,—he heard that before he came;—he only prayed that he might not be bored with her book-learning, or blue stockingism. It is hardly etiquette to report private conversations for the papers,—so I will only say that when James Lee came home, two hours after, he found his old friend Harry in the finest possible spirits, tête-à-tête with his "blue" wife. An invitation to dinner followed. Harry demurred; he had begun to look at the little lady through a very bewitching pair of spectacles, and he hated to be disenchanted—and a *blue stocking dinner*!

However, his objections, silent though they were, were over-ruled. There was no fault to be found with that table-cloth, or those snowy napkins; the glasses were clean, the silver bright as my lady's eyes; the meats cooked to a turn, the gravies and sauces perfect, and the dessert well got up and delicious. Mrs. Lee presided with ease and elegance; the custards and preserves were of her own manufacture, and the little prattler, who was introduced with them, fresh from her nursery bath, with moist ringlets, snowy robe, and dimpled shoulders, looked charmingly well cared for.

As soon as the two gentlemen were alone, Harry seized his friend's hand, saying, with a half smile, "James, I feel like an unmitigated scoundrel! I have heard your wife spoken of as a 'blue stocking,' and I came here prepared to pity you as the victim of an unshared heart, slatternly house, and indigestible cooking; but may I die an old bachelor if I don't wish that woman, who has just gone out, was *my wife*."

James Lee's eyes moistened with gratified pride. "You don't know *half*," said he. "Listen;—some four years since I became involved in business; at the same time my health failed me; my spirits were broken, and I was getting a discouraged man. Emma, unknown to me, made application as a writer to several papers and magazines. She soon became very popular; and not long after placed in my hands the sum of three hundred dollars, the product of her labor. During this time, no parental or household duty was neglected; and her cheerful and steady affection raised my drooping spirits, and gave me fresh courage to commence the world anew. She still continues to write, although, as you see, my head is above water. Thanks to *her* as my guardian angel, for she says, 'We must lay up something for a rainy day.' God bless her sunshiny face!"

The entrance of Emma put a stop to any further eulogy, and Harry took his leave in a very indescribable and penitential frame of mind, doing ample penance for his former unbelieving scruples, by being very uncomfortably in love with—a "Blue Stocking."

Olive Branch
Aug. 2, 1852

THOUGHTS BORN OF A CARESS

"O, WHAT A NICE PLACE to cry!" said a laughing little girl, as she nestled her head lovingly on her mother's breast.

The words were spoken playfully, and the little fairy was all unconscious how much *meaning* lay hid in them; but they brought the tears to my eyes, for I looked forward to the time when care and trial should throw their shadows over that laughing face,—when adversity should overpower,—when summer friends should fall off like autumn leaves before the rough blast of misfortune,—when the faithful breast she leaned upon should be no longer warm with love and life,—when, in all the wide earth, there should be for that little one "no nice place to cry."

God shield the motherless! A *father* may be left,—kind, affectionate, considerate, perhaps;—but a man's affections form but a small fraction of his existence. His thoughts are far away, even while his child clambers on his knee. The distant ship with its rich freight, the state of the money-market, the fluctuations of trade, the office, the shop, the bench; and he answers at random the little lisping immortal, and gives the child a toy, and passes on. The little, sensitive heart has borne its childish griefs through the day unshared. She don't understand the reason for anything, and nobody stops to tell her. Nurse "don't know," the cook is "busy," and so she wanders restlessly about, through poor mamma's empty room. Something is wanting. Ah, there is no "nice place to cry!"

Childhood passes; blooming maidenhood comes on; lovers woo; the mother's quick instinct, timely word of caution, and omnipresent watchfulness, are not there. She gives her heart, with all its yearning sympathies, into unworthy keeping. A fleeting honey-moon, then the dawning of a long day of misery; wearisome days of sickness; the feeble moan of the first-born; no mother's arm in which to place, with girlish pride, the little wailing stranger; lover and friend afar; no "*nice place to cry*!"

Thank God!—not unheard by Him, who "wipeth all tears away," goeth up that troubled heart-plaint from the despairing lips of the motherless!

Olive Branch
Aug. 21, 1852

THE TEAR OF A WIFE

> "The tear of a loving girl is like a dew-drop on a rose; but on the cheek of a wife, is a drop of poison to her husband."

IT IS "an ill wind that blows *nobody* any good." Papas will be happy to hear that twenty-five dollar pocket-handkerchiefs can be dispensed with *now*, in the bridal *trousseau*. Their "occupation's gone"! Matrimonial tears "are poison." There is no knowing what you will do, girls, with that escape-valve shut off; but that is no more to the point, than—whether you have anything to smile at or not; one thing is settled—*you mustn't cry*! Never mind back aches, and side aches, and head aches, and dropsical complaints, and smoky chimneys, and old coats, and young babies! *Smile*! *It flatters your husband*. He wants to be *considered* the source of your happiness, whether he was baptized *Nero* or *Moses*! Your mind *never* being supposed to be occupied with any other subject than himself, of course a tear is a tacit reproach. Besides, you miserable little whimperer, what have you to cry for? A-i-n-t y-o-u m-a-r-r-i-e-d? Isn't that the *summum bonum*—the height of feminine ambition? You *can't* get beyond *that*! It's the *jumping-off place*! You've arriv!—got to the end of your journey! Stage puts up *there*! You've nothing to do but retire on your laurels, and spend the rest of your life endeavoring to be thankful that you are Mrs. John Smith! "*Smile*!" *you simpleton*!

Olive Branch
Aug. 28, 1852

SOLILOQUY OF A HOUSEMAID

OH DEAR, DEAR! Wonder if my mistress knows I'm made of flesh and blood? I've been up stairs five times, in fifteen minutes, to hand her things about four feet from her rocking-chair! *Ain't I tired*? Wish I could be rich once, just to show ladies how to treat their servants! *Such* a rheumatiz as I've got in my shoulders, going up on that shed in the rain. It's "Sally do this," and "Sally do that," till I wish I hadn't been baptized at all; and I might as well go *farther* back while I'm about it, and say I don't know what I was born for! Didn't master say some AWFUL words about those eggs? Oh, I can't stand it—haven't heart enough left to swear by.

Now, instead of ordering me round like a dray-horse, if they'd look up *smiling like*, now and then, or ask me how my rheumatiz did; or even say good morning, Sally—or show some sort of interest in a fellow-cretur, I should know whether it was worth while to try to live or not. A soft word would ease the wheels of my treadmill amazingly, and wouldn't *kill them*, any how!

Look at my clothes; all at sixes and sevens; can't get time to sew on a string or button, except at night, and then I'm so sleepy I can't but tell whether I'm the candle or the candle's *me*! They call "Sunday a day of rest," too, I guess!—more company, more care, more confusion than any day in the week! If I own a soul, I haven't heard how to take care of it, for many a long day. Wonder if my master and mistress calculate to *pay* me for *that*, if I lose it? It's a question in *my* mind. Land of Goshen! I ain't sure I've got a mind!—there's that bell again!

True Flag
Sept. 11, 1852

BETTER NEVER TO HAVE LOVED

"Tis better to have loved and lost, than never to have loved at all."

OH NO; NO!—else you have never passed from the shield of a broad, true breast, where for long years you had been lovingly folded, to a widow's weeds, and the rude jostling, and curious gaze, of the heartless crowd!—never knew long, wretched days, that seemed to have no end—never turned, with a stifled sob, from the clasp of loving little arms, and the uplifted gaze of an eye upon whose counterpart you had watched the death-film gather,—never saw that sunny little face overshadowed with grief, when *other* children gleefully called "*Papa!*" nor ever heard the wail of a little one, who might never remember its father's face!—

No! no!—or you have never turned shudderingly away in the crowded street, from the outline of a form, or the cast of a face, or the tone of a voice, that brought the dead mockingly before you!—never lain upon a sick bed, among careless strangers, lacking comforts where luxury once abounded, and listening in vain for that footfall, whose lightest tread could charm your pain away!—never draped from your aching sight the pictured lineaments, that quickened busy and torturing memory, till your heart was breaking!—never waked from a dream of *Paradise*, to weep unavailing, bitter tears at *the sad reality!*—and never (alas!) bent your rebellious knee at God's altar, when your tongue was dumb to praise Him and your lips refused to kiss the Smiter's rod!

Oh no; no! Better *never* to have *loved!*—Ten fold more gloomy, is the murky day, whose sunny morning was ushered in with dazzling, golden brightness! Agonising is the death-struggle of the shipwrecked mariner who perishes *in sight* of shore and *home!* Harshly fall careless words, upon the ear trained to the music of a loving voice! Wearily stumble the tender feet unguarded by love's watchful eye! Oh no; no! better *never to have loved!*—He, whose first breath was drawn in a dungeon, never pines for green fields, and blue skies, and a freer air!—God pity the desolate, loving heart, the *only star* of whose sky has gone out in utter darkness!

Musical World and Times
Oct. 9, 1852

WHEN MEN ARE SICK

"Men have a proscriptive right to fret."

SHOULDN'T WONDER! Such a tempest in a thimble if they happen to prick a finger! All the servants sent flying down cellar to collect cobwebs from old wine bottles; *and* up garret to hunt over old bags for a scrap of linen, the right width, and length, and thickness; court-plaster bisected; strings unravelled; dozens of old gloves be-scissor'd to find the "cot" *elect*. Telegraphic despatch sent to the firm of "Fuss & Fidget," to say that Fidget has met with a *serious accident*—quite disabled from attending to business. Surtout pulled off; slippers and dressing-gown substituted; *Mrs. Fidget* "not at home" to visitors; big children sent up garret to play, baby and door-bell *muffled!*—blinds closed, straw strewn before the house; flags at "half mast," and the very mischief to play for four and twenty hours, till Mr. Fidget is convalescent!

Musical World and Times
Oct. 23, 1852

ALL ABOUT SATAN

"Satan finds some mischief still
For idle hands to do."

TO BE SURE HE DOES! I know all about him! There's no knowing what *would* happen, if the houses now-a-days were not filled up, one half with babies and the other half with old stockings! Then a man can tell pretty near, what his wife is about!—sure to find her, year in and year out, in that old calico wrapper, in that old ricketty rocking-chair, with the last new twins in her arms, when he wants a button sewed on his coat to go to the opera. *No other way, you see!*

Women are getting *altogether* too smart now-a-days; there *must* be a stop put to it! people are beginning to get alarmed! I don't suppose there has been such a universal crowing since the roosters in Noah's ark were let out, as there was among the editors when that *"Swisshelm" baby* [1] was born! It's none of *my* business, but it *did* seem to me *rather* a *circular singumstance* that she should be cut short in her editorial career that way! I suppose, however, that baby will grow out of her arms one of these days, spite of fate; and then, if there's no *providential interposition*, she may resume her pen again. Well, I hope it will be a *warning!* the fact is, *women* have no business to be crowding into the editorial chair. Supposing they *know* enough to fill it (which I *doubt!* hem!) they oughter "hide their light under a b"—aby!

I tell you, editors *won't stand* it, to have their masculine toes trod on that way. They'll have to sign a "quit claim" to their "dickeys" by and by! I wonder what the world's coming to! What do you suppose our fore*fathers* and *foremothers* would say, to see a woman sitting up in the editorial chair, as pert as a piper, with a pen stuck behind her little ears? phew! I hope *I* never shall see such a horrid sight!

Olive Branch
Oct. 23, 1852

LITTLE MARY'S STORY

"*MARY!*" said the younger of two little girls, as they nestled under a coarse coverlid, one cold night in December, "tell me about Thanksgiving-day before papa went to heaven. I'm cold and hungry, and I can't go to sleep;—I want something nice to think about."

"Hush!" said the elder child, "don't let dear mamma hear you; come nearer to me;"—and they laid their cheeks together.

"I fancy papa was rich. We lived in a very nice house. I know there were pretty pictures on the wall; and there were nice velvet chairs, and the carpet was thick and soft, like the green moss-patches in the wood;—and we had pretty gold-fish on the side-table, and Tony, my black nurse, used to feed them. And papa!—you can't remember papa, Letty,—he was tall and grand, like a prince, and when he smiled he made me think of angels. He brought me toys and sweetmeats, and carried me out to the stable, and set me on Romeo's live back, and laughed because I was afraid! And I used to watch to see him come up the street, and then run to the door to jump in his arms;—he was a *dear, kind* papa," said the child, in a faltering voice.

"*Don't* cry," said the little one; "please tell me some more."

"Well, Thanksgiving-day we were *so* happy; we sat around such a *large* table, with so many people,—aunts and uncles and cousins,—I can't think why they *never* come to see us *now*, Letty,—and Betty made such sweet pies, and we had a big—big turkey; and papa would have me sit next to him, and gave me the wishbone, and all the plums out of his pudding; and after dinner he would take me in his lap, and tell me 'Red Riding Hood,' and call me 'pet,' and 'bird,' and 'fairy.' O, Letty, I can't tell any more; I believe I'm going to cry."

"I'm very cold," said Letty. "Does papa know, up in heaven, that we are poor and hungry now?"

"Yes—no—I can't tell," answered Mary, wiping away her tears; unable to reconcile her ideas of heaven with such a thought. "Hush!—mamma will hear!"

Mamma *had* "heard." The coarse garment, upon which she had

toiled since sunrise, dropped from her hands, and tears were forcing themselves, thick and fast, through her closed eyelids. The simple recital found but too sad an echo in that widowed heart.

Musical World and Times
Nov. 20, 1852

OWLS KILL HUMMING-BIRDS

"We are not to suppose that the oak wants stability because its light and changeable leaves dance to the music of the breeze;—nor are we to conclude that a man wants solidity and strength of mind because he may exhibit an occasional playfulness and levity."

NO, INDEED! So, if you have the bump of mirthfulness developed, don't marry a tombstone. You come skipping into the parlor, with your heart as light as a feather, and your brain full of merry fancies. There he sits! stupid—solemn—and forbidding.

You go up and lay your hand on his arm; he's magnitized about as much as if an omnibus-driver had punched him in the ribs for his fare; and looks in your face with the same expression he'd wear if contemplating his ledger.

You turn away and take up a newspaper. There's a witty paragraph; your first impulse is to read it aloud to him. No use! He wouldn't see through it till the middle of next week. Well, as a sort of escape-valve to your *ennui*, you sit down to the piano and dash off a waltz; he interrupts you with a request for a dirge.

Your little child comes in,—Heaven bless her!—and utters some one of those innocent prettinesses which are always dropping like pearls from children's mouths. You look to see him catch her up and give her a smothering kiss. Not he! He's too *dignified*!

Altogether, he's about as genial as the north side of a meeting-house.

And so you go plodding through life with him to the dead-march of his own leaden thoughts. *You* revel in the sunbeams; *he* likes the shadows. You are on the hill-tops; he is in the plains. Had the world been made to his order, earth, sea, and sky would have been one universal pall—not a *green* thing in it except *himself*! No vine would "cling," no breeze "dally," no zeyphr "woo." Flowers and children, *women and squirrels*, would never have existed. The sun would have been quenched out for being too mercurial, and we should have crept through life by the light of the pale, cold moon!

No—no—make no such shipwreck of yourself. Marry a man who is not too ascetic to enjoy a good, merry laugh. *Owls kill humming-birds!*

True Flag
Dec. 11, 1852

A LITTLE BUNKER HILL

> "No person should be delicate about asking for what is properly his due. If he neglects doing so, he is deficient in that spirit of independence which he should observe in all his actions. Rights are rights, and, if not granted, should be demanded."

A LITTLE "Bunker Hill" atmosphere about that! It suits my republicanism; but I hope no female sister will be such a novice as to suppose it refers to any but *masculine* rights. In the first place, my dear woman, "female rights" is debatable ground; what you may call a "vexed question." In the next place (just put your ear down, a *little* nearer), granted we *had* "rights," the more we "demand," the *more we shan't get 'em.* I've been converted to that faith this some time. No sort of use to waste lungs and leather trotting to *Sigh*-racuse[1] about it. The instant the subject is mentioned, the lords of creation are up and dressed; guns and bayonets the order of the day; *no surrender* on every flag that floats! The only way left is to pursue the "Uriah Heep" policy; look *'umble*, and be almighty cunning. Bait 'em with submission, and then throw the noose over the will. Appear not to have any choice, and as true as gospel you'll get it. Ask *their* advice, and they'll be sure to follow *yours*. Look *one* way, and *pull another*! Make your reins of silk, *keep out of sight, and drive where you like*!

Olive Branch
Dec. 18, 1852

THE TIME TO CHOOSE

> Mrs. Chrissholm says:—"The best time to choose a wife is early in the morning. If a young lady is at all inclined to sulks and slatternness, it is just before breakfast. As a general thing, a woman don't get on her temper, till after 10 A.M."

MEN never look slovenly before breakfast—no indeed! Never run round vestless in their stocking-feet, with dressing-gown inside out; soiled handkerchief hanging by one corner out of the pocket; minus dickey; minus neck-tie; pantaloon straps flying at their heels; suspenders streaming from their waistband; chin shaved on one side, lathered on the other; last night's coat and pants on the floor, just where they hopped out of them; face snarled up in forty wrinkles, because the chamber fire won't burn; and because it snows; and because the office-boy hasn't been for the keys; and because the newspaper hasn't come; and because they smoked too many cigars *by one dozen*, the night before; and because they lost *that* bet, and can't pay the *Scot-t*; and because there's an omelet instead of a chicken-leg for breakfast; and because they are out of sorts and shaving-soap; and out of cigars and credit; and can't *any how* "get their temper on," till they get some money and a mint julep!

Any time "before 10 o'clock," is the time to "choose" a husband—*perhaps!*

True Flag
Jan. 1, 1853

PRAISE FROM A WOMAN

Miss Fanny Fiddlestick's Soliloquy, On Reading a

Complimentary Notice of Herself, By a Lady.

PRAISE FROM A WOMAN!' What did I ever do to *injure her*, I'd like to know? *There's something behind that!* If she had abused me now, I should have been as placid as an oyster. Here, pussy, come taste this cup of tea for me; I'll give you ten minutes to repent of all your feline flirtations, on that back shed, with *promiskus* Grimalkins; for ten to one you'll keel over in a fit as soon as you've swallowed it. I don't touch it till I know whether it's poisoned or not. There's more cats than Ferns in the world, and complimentary notices from a female woman look suspicious. I shall be up and dressed, now I tell you. There's a bundle just come in. When I open it *alone*, I guess you'll know it; I've heard of infernal machines before to-day. I don't touch it off without a minister and Marshal Tukey, I promise you. Praise from a woman! Oh, this Fanny isn't verdant, if she is a Fern! There's something behind it! When a woman pats you with one hand you may be morally certain she's going to scratch you with the other. Here;—hands off! clear the track of all petticoats! I'm going to the pistol gallery to take lessons in shooting. That complimentary notice is the *fore end of a runner* of something.

Olive Branch
Jan. 22, 1853

CHILDREN'S RIGHTS

MEN'S RIGHTS! Women's rights! I throw down the gauntlet for children's rights! Yes, little pets, Fanny Fern's about "takin' notes," and she'll "print 'em," too, if you don't get your dues. She has seen you seated by a pleasant window, in a railroad car, with your bright eyes dancing with delight, at the prospect of all the pretty things you were going to see, forcibly ejected by some overgrown Napoleon, who fancied your place, and thought, in his wisdom, that children had no taste for anything but sugar-candy. Fanny Fern knew better. She knew that the pretty trees and flowers, and bright blue sky, gave your little souls a thrill of delight, though you could not tell why; and she knew that great big man's soul was a great deal smaller than yours, to sit there and read a stupid political paper, when such a glowing landscape was before him, that he might have feasted his eyes upon. And she longed to wipe away the big tear that you didn't dare to let fall; and she understood how a little girl or boy, that didn't get a ride every day in the year, should not be quite able to swallow that great big lump in the throat, as he or she sat jammed down in a dark, crowded corner of the car, instead of sitting by that pleasant window.

Yes; and Fanny has seen you sometimes, when you've been muffled up to the tip of your little nose in woollen wrappers, in a close, crowded church, nodding your little drowsy heads, and keeping time to the sixth-lie and seventh-lie of some pompous theologian, whose preaching would have been high Dutch to you, had you been wide awake.

And she has seen you sitting, like little automatons, in a badly-ventilated school-room, with your nervous little toes at just such an angle, for hours; under the tuition of a Miss Nancy Nipper, who didn't care a rush-light whether your spine was as crooked as the letter S or not, if the Great Mogul Committee, who marched in once a month to make the "grand tour," voted her a "model school-marm."

Yes, and that ain't all. She has seen you sent off to bed, just at the witching hour of candle-light, when some entertaining guest was in the middle of a delightful story, that you, poor, miserable "little pitcher," was doomed never to hear the end of! Yes, and she has seen "the line and plummet" laid to you so rigidly, that you were driven to deceit and evasion; and then seen you punished for the very sin your tormentors helped you to commit. And she has seen your ears boxed just as hard for tearing a hole in your best pinafore, or breaking a China cup, as for telling as big a lie as Ananias and Sapphira did.[1]

And when, by patient labor, you had reared an edifice of tiny blocks,—fairer in its architectural proportions, to your infantile eye, than any palace in ancient Rome,—she has seen it ruthlessly kicked into a shattered ruin, by somebody in the house, whose dinner hadn't digested!

Never mind. I wish I was mother to the whole of you! Such glorious times as we'd have! Reading pretty books, that had no big words in 'em; going to school where you could sneeze without getting a rap on the head for not asking leave first; and going to church on the quiet, blessed Sabbath, where the minister—like our dear Saviour—sometimes remembered to "take little children in his arms, and bless them."

Then, if you asked me a question, I wouldn't pretend not to hear; or lazily tell you I "didn't know," or turn you off with some fabulous evasion, for your memory to chew for a cud till you were old enough to see how you had been fooled. And I'd never wear such a fashionable gown that you couldn't climb on my lap whenever the fit took you; or refuse to kiss you, for fear you'd ruffle my curls, or my collar, or my temper,—not a bit of it; and then you should pay me with your merry laugh, and your little confiding hand slid ever trustingly in mine.

O, I tell you, my little pets, Fanny is sick of din, and strife, and envy, and uncharitableness!—and she'd rather, by ten thousand, live in a little world full of fresh, guileless, loving little children, than in this great museum full of such dry, dusty, withered hearts.

Olive Branch
Jan. 29, 1853

SEWING MACHINES

THERE'S "nothing new under the sun;"—so I've read, somewhere; either in Ecclesiastes or Uncle Tom's Cabin; but at any rate, I was forcibly reminded of the profound wisdom of the remark, upon seeing a great flourish of trumpets in the papers about a "Sewing Machine," that had been *lately invented.*

Now if *I* know anything of history, that discovery dates back as far as the Garden of Eden. If *Mrs. Adam* wasn't *the first sewing machine, I'll give up guessing*. Didn't she go right to work making aprons, before she had done receiving her bridal calls from the beasts and beastesses? Certainly she did, and I honor her for it, too.

Well—do you suppose all her pretty little descendants who ply their "busy fingers in the upper lofts of tailors, and hatters, and vest-makers, and 'finding' establishments," are going to be superseded by that dumb old thing? Do you suppose their young and enterprising patrons prefer the creaking of a crazy machine to the music of their young voices? Not by a great deal!

It's something, I can tell you, for them to see their pretty faces light up, when they pay off their wages of a Saturday night (small fee enough! too often, God knows!) Pity that the *shilling heart* so often accompanies the *guinea means*.

Oh, launch out, gentlemen! Don't *always* look at things with a *business* eye. Those fragile forms are young, to toil so unremittingly. God made no distinction of *sex* when he said—"The laborer is worthy of his hire." Man's cupidity puts that interpretation upon it.

Those young operatives in your employ, pass, in their daily walks, forms youthful as their own, "clothed in purple and fine linen," who "*toil not, neither do they spin*." Oh, teach them not to look after their "satin and sheen," purchased at such a fearful cost, with a discouraged sigh!

For one, I can never pass such a "fallen angel" with a "stand aside" feeling. A neglected youth, an early orphanage, poverty, beauty, coarse fare, the weary day of toil lengthened into night,—a mere pittance its reward. Youth, health, young blood, and the practised wile of the ready tempter! *Oh, where's the marvel?*

Think of all this, when you poise that hardly earned dollar, on your business finger. What if it were your own delicate sister? Let a LITTLE heart creep into that shrewd bargain. 'Twill be an investment in the Bank of Heaven, that shall return to you four-fold.

True Flag
Jan. 29, 1853

"I CAN'T."

APOLLO!—what a face! Doleful as a hearse; folded hands; hollow chest; whining voice; the very picture of cowardly irresolution. Spring to your feet, hold up your head, set your teeth together, draw that fine form of yours up to the height that God made it; draw an immense long breath, and look about you. What do you see? Why, all creation taking care of number one;—pushing ahead like the car of Juggernaut,[1] over live victims. There it is; and you can't help it. Are you going to lie down and be crushed?

By all that is holy, no!—dash ahead! You've as good a right to mount the triumphal car as your neighbor. Snap your fingers at croakers. If you can't get *round* a stump, leap over it, high and dry. Have nerves of steel, a will of iron. Never mind sideaches, or heartaches, or headaches; dig away without stopping to breathe, or to notice envy or malice. Set your target in the clouds and aim at it. If your arrow falls short of the mark, what of that? Pick it up and go at it again. If you should *never* reach it, you'll shoot higher than if you only aimed at a bush. Don't whine, if your friends fall off. At the first stroke of good luck, by Mammon! they'll swarm around you like a hive of bees, till you are disgusted with human nature.

"*I can't*!" O, pshaw! I throw my glove in your face, if I *am* a woman! You are a disgrace to corduroys. What! a *man* lack courage? A *man* want independence? A *man* to be discouraged at obstacles? A man afraid to face anything on earth, save his Maker? Why! I have the most unmitigated contempt for you, you little pusillanimous pussy cat! There is nothing manly about you, except your whiskers.

True Flag
Mar. 12, 1853

LOOK ON THIS PICTURE, AND THEN ON THAT

"*FATHER IS COMING!*" and little, round faces grow long, and merry voices are hushed, and toys are hustled into the closet; and mamma glances nervously at the door; and baby is bribed with a lump of sugar to keep the peace; and father's business face relaxes not a muscle; and the little group huddle like timid sheep in a corner, and tea is despatched as silently as if speaking were prohibited by the statute book; and the children creep like culprits to bed, marvelling that baby dare crow so loud, now that "Father has come."

"*FATHER IS COMING!*" and bright eyes sparkle for joy, and tiny feet dance with glee, and eager faces press against the window-pane; and a bevy of rosy lips claim kisses at the door; and picture-books lie unrebuked on the table; and tops, and balls, and dolls, and kites are discussed; and little Susy lays her soft cheek against the paternal whiskers with the most fearless "abandon;" and Charley gets a love-pat for his "medal;" and mamma's face grows radiant; and the evening paper is read,—not silently, but aloud,—and tea, and toast, and time vanish with equal celerity, for jubilee has arrived, and "Father has come!"

Olive Branch
Apr. 2, 1853

DON'T DISTURB HIM!

> "If your husband looks grave, let him alone; don't disturb or annoy him."

OH, PSHAW! were I married, the soberer my husband looked, the more fun I'd rattle about his ears. *Don't disturb him!* I guess so! I'd salt his coffee—and pepper his tea—and sugar his beef-steak—and tread on his toes—and hide his newspaper—and sew up his pockets—and put pins in his slippers—and dip his cigars in water,—and I wouldn't stop for the Great Mogul, till I had shortened his long face to my liking. Certainly, he'd "get vexed;" there wouldn't be any fun in teasing him if he didn't; and that would give his melancholy blood a good, healthful start; and his eyes would snap and sparkle, and he'd say, "Fanny, WILL you be quiet or not?" and I should laugh, and pull his whiskers, and say decidedly, *"Not!"* and then I should tell him he hadn't the slightest idea how handsome he looked when he was vexed, and then he would pretend not to hear the compliment—but would pull up his dickey, and take a sly peep in the glass (for all that!) and then he'd begin to grow amiable, and get off his stilts, and be just as agreeable all the rest of the evening *as if he wasn't my husband;* and all because I didn't follow that stupid bit of advice "to let him alone." Just as if *I* didn't know! Just imagine ME, Fanny, sitting down on a cricket in the corner, with my forefinger in my mouth, looking out the sides of my eyes, and waiting till that man got ready to speak to me! You can see at once it would be—be—. Well, the amount of it is, *I shouldn't do it!*[1]

Olive Branch
Apr. 9, 1853

BORROWED LIGHT

> "Don't rely too much on the torches of others;—light one of your own."

DON'T YOU DO IT!—borrowed light is all the fashion. For instance, you wake up some morning, fully persuaded that your destiny lies undeveloped in an inkstand. Well, select some popular writer; read over his or her articles carefully; note their peculiarities and fine points, and then copy your model just as closely as possible. Borrow whole sentences, if you like, taking care to transpose the words a little. Baptize all your heroes and heroines at the same font;—be facetious, sentimental, pathetic, terse, or diffuse, just like your leader. It *may* astonish you somewhat to ascertain how articles which *read so easy* are, after all, so difficult of *imitation*; but, go on, only take the precaution, at every step, to sneer at your model, for the purpose of throwing dust in people's eyes.

Of course, nobody sees through it; nobody thinks of the ostrich who hides his *head* in the sand, imagining his *body* is not seen. Nobody laughs at your servility; nobody exclaims, "There's a counterfeit!" Nobody says, what an unintentional compliment you pay your leader.

In choosing your signature, bear in mind that nothing goes down, now-a-days, but *alliteration*. For instance, Delia Daisy, Fanny Foxglove, Harriet Honeysuckle, Lily Laburnum, Paulena Poppy, Minnie Mignonette, Julia Jonquil, Seraphina Sunflower, etc., etc.

If anybody has the impertinence to charge you with being a literary pirate, don't you stand it. Bristle up like a porcupine, and declare that it is a vile insinuation; that you are a full-rigged craft yourself, cruising round on your own hook, and scorning to sail under false colors. There's nothing like a little impudence!

That's the way it's done, my dear. Nobody but regular workers ever "light a torch of their own." It's an immensity of trouble to get it burning; and it is sure to draw round it every little buzzing, whizzing, stinging insect there is afloat. No, no!—make *somebody else* light the torch, and do you flutter round in its rays; only be careful not to venture so near the blaze as to singe *those flimsy wings* of yours.

True Flag
Apr. 9, 1853

HUNGRY HUSBANDS

> "The hand that can make a pie is a continual feast to the husband that marries its owner."

WELL, it is a humiliating reflection, that the straightest road to a man's heart is through his palate. He is never so amiable as when he has discussed a roast turkey. Then's your time, "Esther," for "half his kingdom," in the shape of a new bonnet, cap, shawl, or dress. He's too complacent to dispute the matter. Strike while the iron is hot; petition for a trip to Niagara, Saratoga, the Mammoth Cave, the White Mountains, or to London, Rome, or Paris. Should he demur about it, the next day cook him another turkey, and pack your trunk while he is eating it.

There's nothing on earth so savage—except a bear robbed of her cubs—as a hungry husband. It is as much as your life is worth to sneeze till dinner is on the table, and his knife and fork are in vigorous play. Tommy will get his ears boxed, the ottoman will be kicked into the corner, your work-box be turned bottom upwards, and the poker and tongs will beat a tattoo on that grate that will be a caution to dilatory cooks.

After the first six mouthfuls you may venture to say your soul is your own; his eyes will lose their ferocity, his brow its furrows, and he will very likely recollect to help you to a cold potato! Never mind—*eat it*. You might have to swallow a worse pill—for instance, should he offer to kiss you, for of course you couldn't love such a carnivorous animal!

Well, learn a lesson from it—keep him well fed and languid—live yourself on a low diet, and cultivate your thinking powers; and you'll be as spry as a cricket, and hop over all the objections and remonstrances that his dead-and-alive energies can muster. Yes, feed him well, and he will stay contentedly in his cage, like a gorged anaconda. If he was *my* husband, wouldn't I make him heaps of *pison* things! Bless me! I've made a mistake in the spelling; it should have been *pies-and-things!*

True Flag
Apr. 23, 1853

MR. PUNCH MISTAKEN

"A man will own that he is in the wrong—a woman, never; she is only *mistaken*."—*Punch*.

MR. PUNCH, did you ever see an enraged American female? She is the expressed essence of wild-cats. Perhaps you didn't know it, when you penned that incendiary paragraph; or, perhaps you thought that in crossing the "big pond," salt water might neutralize it; or, perhaps you flattered yourself we should not see it, over here; but here it is, in my clutches, in good strong English: I am not even "*mistaken*."

Now, if you will bring me a live specimen of the genus homo, who was ever known "to own that he was in the wrong," I will draw in my horns and claws, and sneak ingloriously back into my American shell. But you can't do it, Mr. Punch! You never saw that curiosity, either in John Bull's skin or Brother Jonathan's. 'Tis an animal which has never yet been discovered, much less captured.

A man own he was in the wrong! I guess so! You might tear him in pieces with red-hot pincers, and he would keep on singing out "I didn't do it; I didn't do it." No, Mr. Punch, a man never "owns up" when he is in the wrong; especially if the matter in question be one which he considers of no importance; for instance, the non-delivery of a letter, which may have been entombed in his pocket for six weeks.

No sir; he just settles himself down behind his dickey, folds his belligerent hands across his stubborn diaphragm, plants his antagonistic feet down on terra-firma as if there were a stratum of loadstone beneath him, and thunders out,

"Come one, come all; this rock shall fly
From its firm base, as soon as I."

Musical World and Times
May 7, 1853

"LITTLE BENNY"

SO THE simple head-stone said. Why did my eyes fill? I never saw the little creature. I never looked in his laughing eye, or heard his merry shout, or listened for his tripping tread; I never pillowed his little head, or bore his little form, or smoothed his silky locks, or laved his dimpled limbs, or fed his cherry lips with dainty bits, or kissed his rosy cheek as he lay sleeping.

I did not see his eye grow dim; or his little hand droop powerless; or the dew of agony gather on his pale forehead: I stood not with clasped hands and suspended breath, and watched the look that comes but once, flit over his cherub face. And yet, "little Benny," my tears are falling; for, *somewhere*, I know there's an empty crib, a vacant chair, useless robes and toys, a desolate hearth-stone and a weeping mother.

"*Little Benny.*"

It was all her full heart could utter; and it was enough. It tells the whole story.

Musical World and Times
May 14, 1853

MRS. STOWE'S UNCLE TOM

"Mrs. Stowe's *Uncle Tom* is too graphic ever to have been written by a *woman*."—*Exchange*.

"*TOO GRAPHIC* to be written by a woman?" D'ye hear that, Mrs. Stowe?[1] or has English thunder stopped your American ears? Oh, I can tell you, Mrs. "Tom Cabin," that you've got to pay "for the bridge that has carried you over." Do you suppose that you can quietly take the wind out of everybody's sails, the way you have, without having harpoons, and lampoons, and all sorts of *miss*—iles thrown after you? No indeed; every distanced scribbler is perfectly frantic; they stoutly protest your book shows no genius, which fact is unfortunately corroborated by the difficulty your publishers find in disposing of it; they are transported with rage in proportion as *you* are *translated*. Everybody whose cat ever ran through your great grandfather's entry "knows all about you," and how long it took you to cut your first "wisdom tooth." Then all the bitter sectarian enemies your wide awake brothers have evoked, and who are afraid to measure lances with them, huddle into a corner to revenge by "making mouths" at their sister!

Certainly; what right had you to get an "invitation to Scotland" free gratis? or to have "Apsley House" placed at your disposal, as soon as your orthodox toes touched English ground? or to have "a silver salver" presented to you? or to have lords and ladies, and dukes and duchesses paying homage to you? or in short to raise such a little young tornado to sweep through the four quarters of the globe? *You?* nothing but a woman—an *American* woman! and a *Beecher* at that! It is perfectly insufferable—one genius in a family is enough. There's your old patriarch father—God bless him!—there's material enough in him to make a dozen ordinary men, to say nothing of "Henry Ward" who's not so great an idiot as he might be! You see you had no "call," Mrs. Tom Cabin, to drop your babies and darning-needle to immortalize your name.

Well, I hope your feminine shoulders are broad enough and strong enough to bear all the abuse your presumption will call down upon you. All the men in your family, your husband included, belong to "the cloth," and consequently can't practice pistol shooting; there's where your enemies have you, you little simpleton! that's the only objection I have to Mr. Fern's "taking orders," for I've quite a penchant for ministers.

I trust you are convinced by this time that "Uncle Tom's Cabin" is a "flash in the pan." I'm sorry you have lost so much money by it, but it will go to show you, that women should have their ambition bounded by a gridiron, and a darning needle. If you had not meddled with your husband's *divine* inkstand for such a *dark* purpose, nobody would have said you was "40 years old and looked like an Irish woman;" and between you and me and the vestry door, I don't believe they've done with you yet; for I see that every steamer tosses fresh laurels on your orthodox head, from foreign shores, and foreign powers. Poor *unfortunate* Mrs. Tom Cabin! Ain't you to be pitied.

Olive Branch
May 28, 1853

THE CHARITY ORPHANS

"*PLEASANT SIGHT,* is it not?" said my friend glancing complacently at a long procession of little charity children, who were passing, two and two—two and two—with closely cropped heads, little close-fitting sun-bonnets and dark dresses; "pleasant sight, is it not, Fanny?" Yes—no—*no*, said I, courageously, it gives me the heart-ache. "Oh, I see as you do, that their clothes are clean and whole, and that they are drilled like a little regiment of soldiers, (heads up,) but I long to see them step out of those prim ranks, and shout and scamper. I long to stuff their little pockets full of anything—everything, that other little pets have. I want to get them round me, and tell them some comical stories to take the care-worn look out of their anxious little faces. I want to see them twist their little heads round when they hear a noise, instead of keeping them straight forward as if they were "on duty." I want to know if anybody tucks them up comfortably when they go to bed, and gives them a good-night kiss. I want to know if they get a beaming smile, and a kind word in the morning. I want to know who soothes them when they are in pain; and if they *dare say so*, when they feel lonely, and have the heart-ache. I want to see the tear roll freely down the cheek, (instead of being wiped slyly away,) when they see happy little ones trip gaily past, hand in hand, with a kind father, or mother. I want to know if "Thanksgiving" and "Christmas" and "New Year's" and "*Home*" are anything but empty sounds in their orphan ears.

I know their present state is better than vicious poverty, and so I try to say with my friend, "it is a pleasant sight;" but the words die on my lip;

for full well I know it takes something more than food, shelter and clothing, to make a child happy. Its little heart, like a delicate vine, *will* throw out its tendrils for something to *lean on*—something to *cling to*; and so I can only say again, the sight of those charity orphans gives me the heart-ache.[1]

Olive Branch
June 4, 1853

WHO WOULD BE THE LAST MAN?

> "Fanny Fern says, 'If there were but one woman in the world, the men would have a terrible time.' Fanny is right; but we would ask her what kind of a time the *women* would have if there were but *one man* in existence?"—*NY Musical World and Times*.

WHAT KIND OF A TIME would they have? Why, of course no grass would grow under their slippers! The "Wars of the Roses," the battles of Waterloo and Bunker Hill would be a farce to it. Black eyes would be the rage, and both caps and characters would be torn to tatters. I imagine it would not be much of a millennium either to the moving cause of the disturbance. He would be as crazy as a fly in a drum, or as dizzy as a bee in a ten-acre lot of honeysuckles, uncertain where to alight. He'd roll his bewildered eyes from one exquisite organization to another, and frantically and diplomatically exclaim—"How happy could I be with either, were t'other dear charmer away!"

"What kind of a time would the women have, were there only one man in the world?"

Why, they'd resort to *arms* of course! What kind of a time would they have? What is that to *me?* They might "take their own time," every "Miss

Lucy" of 'em, for all *I* should care; and so might the said man himself; for with me, the limited supply would not increase the value of the article.

Olive Branch
June 11, 1853

APOLLO HYACINTH

"There is no better test of moral excellence, than the keenness of one's sense, and the depth of one's love, of all that is beautiful."
—*Donohue*.

I DON'T ENDORSE that sentiment. I am acquainted with Apollo Hyacinth.[1] I have read his prose, and I have read his poetry; and I have cried over both, till my heart was as soft as my head, and my eyes were as red as a rabbit's. I have listened to him in public, when he was, by turns, witty, sparkling, satirical, pathetic, till I could have added a codicil to my will, and left him all my worldly possessions; and possibly you have done the same. He has, perhaps, grasped you cordially by the hand, and, with a beaming smile, urged you, in his musical voice, to "call on him and Mrs. Hyacinth;" and you have called: but, did you ever find him "in?" You have invited him to visit you, and have received a "gratified acceptance," in his elegant chirography; but, *did he ever come?* He has borrowed money of you, in the most elegant manner possible; and, as he deposited it in his beautiful purse, he has assured you, in the choicest and most happily chosen language, that he "should never forget your kindness;" but, *did he ever pay?*

Should you die to-morrow, Apollo would write a poetical obituary notice of you, which would raise the price of pocket-handkerchiefs; but should your widow call on him in the course of a month, to solicit his patronage to open a school, she would be told "he was out of town," and that it was "quite uncertain when he would return."

Apollo has a large circle of relatives; but his "keenness of perception, and deep love, of the beautiful" are so great, that none of them *exactly* meet his views. His "moral excellence," however, does not prevent his making the most of them. He has a way of dodging them adroitly, when they call for a reciprocation, either in a business or a social way; or, if, at any time, there is a necessity for inviting them to his house, he does it when he is at his *country* residence, where their *greenness* will not be out of place.

Apollo never says an uncivil thing—never; he prides himself on that, as well as on his perfect knowledge of human nature; therefore, his sins are all sins of omission. His tastes are very exquisite, and his nature peculiarly sensitive; consequently, he cannot bear trouble. He will tell you, in his elegant way, that trouble "annoys" him, that it "bores" him; in short, that it unfits him for life—for business; so, should you hear that a friend or relative of his, even a brother or a sister, was in distress, or persecuted in any manner, you could not do Apollo a greater injury (in his estimation) than to inform him of the fact. It would so grate upon his sensitive spirit,—it would so "annoy" him; whereas, did he not hear of it until the friend, or brother, or sister, were relieved or buried, he could manage the matter with his usual urbanity and without the slightest draught upon his exquisitely sensitive nature, by simply writing a pathetic and elegant note, expressing the keenest regret at not having known "all about it" in time to have "flown to the assistance of his dear"—&c.

Apollo prefers friends who can stand grief and annoyance, as a rhinoceros can stand flies—friends who can bear their own troubles and all his—friends who will stand between him and everything disagreeable in life, and never ask anything in return. To such friends he clings with the most touching tenacity—as long as he can use them; but let their good name be assailed, let misfortune once overtake them, and his "moral excellence" compels him, at once, to ignore their existence, until they have been extricated from all their troubles, and it has become perfectly safe and *advantageous* for him to renew the acquaintance.

Apollo is keenly alive to the advantages of social position, (not having always enjoyed them;) and so, his Litany reads after this wise: From all questionable, unfashionable, unpresentable, and vulgar persons, Good Lord, deliver us!

Musical World and Times
June 18, 1853

DOLLARS AND DIMES

"Dollars and dimes, dollars and dimes,
An empty pocket is the worst of crimes."

YES; and don't you presume to show yourself anywhere, until you get it filled. "Not among good people?" No, my dear Simplicity, not among "good people." They will receive you with a galvanic ghost of a smile, scared up by an indistinct recollection of the "ten commandments," but it will be as short-lived as their stay with you. You are not welcome—that's the amount of it. They are all in a perspiration lest you should be delivered of a request for their assistance, before they can get rid of you. They are "very busy," and what's more, they always will be busy when you call, until you get to the top of fortune's ladder.

Climb, man! climb! Get to the top of the ladder, though adverse circumstances and false friends break every round in it! and see what a glorious and extensive prospect of human nature you'll get when you arrive at the summit! Your gloves will be worn out shaking hands with the very people who didn't recognize your existence two months ago. "You must come and make me a long visit;" "you must stop in at any time;" "*you'll* always be welcome;" it is such a *long* time since they had the pleasure of a visit from you, that they begin to fear you never intended to come; and they'll cap the climax by inquiring with an injured air, "if you are nearsighted, or why you have so often passed them in the street without speaking."

Of course, you will feel very much like laughing in their faces, and *so you can*. You can't do anything *wrong*, now that your "pocket is full." At the most, it will only be "an eccentricity." You can use anybody's neck for a footstool, bridle anybody's mouth with a silver bit, and have as many "golden opinions" as you like. You won't see a frown again between this and your tombstone!

Olive Branch
June 18, 1853

HAVE WE ANY MEN AMONG US?

WALKING ALONG the street the other day, my eye fell upon this placard,—

MEN WANTED

Well; they have been "wanted" for some time; but the article is not in the market, although there are plenty of spurious imitations. Time was, when a lady could decline writing for a newspaper without subjecting herself to paragraphic attacks from the editor, invading the sanctity of her private life. Time was, when she could decline writing without the editor's revenging himself, by asserting falsely that "he had often refused her offered contributions?" Time was, when if an editor heard a vague rumor affecting a lady's reputation, he did not endorse it by republication, and then meanly screen himself from responsibility by adding, "we presume, however, that this is only an *on dit!*" Time was, when a lady could be a successful authoress, without being obliged to give an account to the dear public of the manner in which she appropriated the proceeds of her honest labors. Time was, when whiskered braggadocios in railroad cars and steamboats did not assert, (in blissful ignorance that they were looking the lady authoress straight in the face!) that they were "on the most intimate terms of friendship with her!" Time was, when *milk-and-water husbands and relatives* did not force a defamed woman to unsex herself in the manner stated in the following paragraph:

> "MAN SHOT BY A YOUNG WOMAN,—One day last week, a young lady of good character, daughter of Col.———, having been calumniated by a young man, called upon him, armed with a revolver. The slanderer could not, or did not deny his allegations; whereupon she fired, inflicting a dangerous if not a fatal wound in his throat."

Yes; it is very true that there are "MEN wanted." Wonder how many 1854 will furnish?

Musical World and Times
Sept. 24, 1853

"WHO LOVES A RAINY DAY?"

THE BORED EDITOR; who, for one millennial day, in slippered feet, controls his arm chair, exchanges, stove, and inkstand; who has time to hunt up delinquent subscribers; time to decipher hieroglyphical manuscripts; time to make a bonfire of bad poetry; time to kick out lozenge boys and image venders; time to settle the long-standing quarrel between Nancy, the type-setter, and Bill, the foreman, and time to write complimentary letters to himself for publication in his own paper, and to get up a new humbug prospectus for the dear, confiding public.

Who loves a rainy day?

The little child of active limb, reprieved from bench, and book, and ferule; between whom and the wire-drawn phiz of grim propriety, those friendly drops have drawn a misty vail; who is now free to laugh, and jump, and shout, and ask the puzzling question—free to bask in the sunny smile of her, to whom no sorrow can be trivial that brings a cloud over that sunny face, or dims the brightness of that merry eye.

Who loves a rainy day?

The crazed clergyman, who can face a sheet of paper, uninterrupted by dyspeptic Deacon Jones, or fault-finding brother Grimes; or cautious Mr. Smith; or the afflicted Miss Zelia Zephyr, who, for several long years, has been "unable to find out the path of duty;" or the zealous old lady Bunce, who hopes her pastor will throw light on the precise locality fixed upon in the future state for idiots, and those heathen who have never seen a missionary.

Who loves a rainy day?

The disgusted clerk, who, lost in the pages of some care-beguiling volume, forgets the petticoat destiny which relentlessly forces him to unfurl endless yards of tinsel lace and ribbon, for lounging dames, with empty brains and purses, whose "chief end" it seems to be to put him through an endless catechism.

Who loves a rainy day?

The tidy little housewife, who, in neat little breakfast-cap and dressing-gown, overlooks the short-comings of careless cook and housemaid; explores cupboards, cellars, pantries, and closets; disembowels old bags, old boxes, old barrels, old kegs, old firkins; who, with her own dainty hand, prepares the favorite morsel for the dear, absent, toiling husband, or, by the cheerful nursery fire, sews on the missing string or button, or sings to soothing slumbers a pair of violet eyes, whose witching counterpart once stole her girlish heart away.

Who loves a rainy day?

I do! Let the rain fall; let the wind moan; let the leafless trees reach out their long attenuated fingers and tap against my casement: pile on the coal; wheel up the arm-chair; all hail loose ringlets and loose dressing-robe. Not a blessed son or daughter of Adam can get here to-day! Unlock the old writing desk; overlook the old letters. There is a bunch tied with a ribbon blue as the eyes of the writer. Matrimony quenched their brightness long time ago.

Irish *help* (?) and crying babies,
I grieve to say, are 'mong the may-be's!

And here is a package written by a despairing Cœlebs—[1]once intensely interested in the price of hemp and prussic acid; now the rotund and jolly owner of a princely house, a queenly wife, and six rollicksome responsibilities. Query: whether the faculty ever dissected a *man* who had died of a "broken heart?"

Here is another package. Let the fire purify them; never say you *know* your friend till his tombstone is over him.

What Solomon says "handwriting is an index of character!" Give him the cap and bells, and show him those bold penmarks. They were traced by no Di Vernon![2] Let me sketch the writer:—A blushing, smiling, timid, loving little fairy, as ever nestled near a true heart; with a step like the fall of a snowflake, and a voice like the murmur of a brook in June. Poor little Katie! she lays her cheek now to a little cradle sleeper's, and starts at the distant footstep, and trembles at the muttered curse, and reels under the brutal blow, and, woman-like—loves on!

And what have we here? A sixpence with a ribbon in it! Oh, those Saturday and Wednesday afternoons, with their hoarded store of nuts and candy—the broad, green meadow, with its fine old trees—the crazy old swing, and the fragrant tumble in the grass—the wreath of oak leaves, the bunch of wild violets, the fairy story book, the little blue jacket, the snowy shirt-collar, the curly, black head, with its soft, blue eyes. Oh, first love, sugar-candy, torn aprons, and kisses! where have ye flown?

What is this? only a pressed flower; but it tells me of a shadowy wood—of a rippling brook—of a bird's song—of a mossy seat—of whispered leaf-music—of dark, soul-lit eyes—of a voice sweet, and low, and thrilling—of a vow never broken till death chilled the lips that made it. Little need to look at the pictured face that lies beside me. It haunts me sleeping or waking. I shall see it again—life's trials passed.

Saturday Evening Post
Jan. 28, 1854

MRS. ADOLPHUS SMITH SPORTING THE "BLUE STOCKING"

WELL, I think I'll finish that story for the editor of the "Dutchman." Let me see; where did I leave off? The setting sun was just gilding with his last ray—"Ma, I want some bread and molasses"—(yes, dear,) gilding with his last ray the church spire—"Wife, where's my Sunday pants?" (*Under the bed, dear,*) the church spire of Inverness, when a—"There's nothing under the bed, dear, but your lace cap"—(Perhaps they are in the coal hod in the closet,) when a horseman was seen approaching—"Ma'am, the *pertators* is out; not one for dinner"—(Take some turnips,) approaching, covered with dust, and—"Wife! the baby has swallowed a button"—(*Reverse him*, dear—take him by the heels,) and waving in his hand a banner, on which was written—"Ma! I've torn my pantaloons"—liberty or death! The inhabitants rushed *en masse*—"Wife! WILL you leave off scribbling? (Don't be disagreeable, Smith, I'm just getting inspired,) to the public square, where De Begnis, who had been secretly—"Butcher wants to see you, ma'am"—secretly informed of the traitors'—"Forgot *which* you said, ma'am, sausages or mutton chop"—movements, gave orders to fire; not less than twenty—"My gracious! Smith, you haven't been *reversing* that child all this time; he's as black as your coat; and that boy of YOURS has torn up the first sheet of my manuscript. There! it's no use for a married woman to cultivate her intellect.—Smith, hand me those twins.[1]

Fern Leaves, Second Series
1854

A BROADWAY SHOP REVERIE

FORTY DOLLARS for a pocket-handkerchief! My dear woman! you need a straight-jacket, even though you may be the fortunate owner of a dropsical purse.

I won't allude to the legitimate use of a pocket-handkerchief; I won't speak of the sad hearts *that* "forty dollars," in the hands of some philanthropist, might lighten; I won't speak of the "crows' feet" that will be penciled on your fair face, when your laundress carelessly sticks the point of her remorseless smoothing iron through the flimsy fabric, or the constant espionage you must keep over your treasure, in omnibuses, or when promenading; but I *will* ask you how many of the lords of creation, for whose especial benefit you array yourself, will know whether that cobweb rag fluttering in your hand cost forty dollars, or forty cents?

Pout if you like, and toss your head, and say that you "don't dress to please the gentlemen." I don't hesitate to tell you (at this distance from your finger nails) that is a downright—mistake! and that the enormous sums most women expend for articles, the cost of which few, save shopkeepers and butterfly feminines, know, is both astounding and ridiculous.

True, you have the sublime gratification of flourishing your forty-dollar handkerchief, of sporting your twenty-dollar "Honiton collar,"[1] or of flaunting your thousand-dollar shawl, before the envious and admiring eyes of some weak sister, who has made the possible possession of the article in question a profound and lifetime study; you may pass, too, along the crowded *pavé*, laboring under the hallucination, that every passer-by appreciates your dry-goods value. *Not a bit of it!* Yonder is a group of gentlemen. You pass them in your promenade; they glance carelessly at your *tout-ensemble*, but their eyes rest admiringly on a figure close behind you. It will chagrin you to learn that this locomotive loadstone has on a seventy-five cent hat, of simple straw—a dress of lawn, one shilling per yard—a twenty-five cent collar, and a shawl of the most unpretending price and fabric.

All these items you take in at a glance, as you turn upon her your aristocratic eye of feminine criticism to extract, if possible, the talismanic secret of her magnetism. What is it? Let me tell you. Nature, willful dame, has an aristocracy of her own, and in one of her independent freaks has so daintily fashioned your rival's limbs, that the meanest garb could not *mar* a grace, nor the costliest fabric *add* one. Compassionating her slender purse, nature has also added an artistic eye, which accepts or rejects fabrics and colors with unerring taste; hence her apparel is always well chosen and harmonious, producing the *effect* of a rich toilet at the cost of "a mere song;" and as she sweeps majestically past, one understands why Dr. Johnson pronounced a woman to be "perfectly dressed when one could never remember what she wore."

Now, I grant you, it is very provoking to be eclipsed by a star *without a name*—moving out of the sphere of "upper-ten"-dom—a woman who never wore a "camel's hair shawl," or owned a diamond in her life; after the expense you have incurred, too, and the fees you have paid to Madame Pompadour and Stewart for the first choice of their Parisian fooleries. It is harrowing to the sensibilities. I appreciate the awkwardness of your position; still, my compassion jogs my invention vainly for a remedy—unless, indeed, you consent to crush such democratic presumption, by *labelling* the astounding price of the dry-goods upon your aristocratic back.[2]

Fern Leaves, Second Series
1854

TOM PAX'S CONJUGAL SOLILOQUY

MRS. PAX is an authoress. I knew it when I married her. I liked the idea. I had not tried it then. I had not a clear idea what it was to have one's wife belong to the public. I thought marriage was marriage, brains not excepted. I was mistaken. Mrs. Pax is very kind: I don't wish to say that she is not. Very obliging: I would not have you think the contrary; but when I put my arm round Mrs. Pax's waist, and say, "Mary, I love you," she smiles in an absent, moonlight-kind of a way, and says, "Yes, to-day is Wednesday, is it not? I must write an article for 'The Weekly Monopolizer' to-day." That dampens my ardor; but presently I say again, being naturally affectionate, "Mary, I love you;" she replies (still abstractedly), "Thank you, how do you think it will do to call my next article for 'The Weekly Monopolizer,' 'The Stray Waif?'"

Mrs. Pax sews on all my shirt-buttons with the greatest good humor: I would not have you think she does not; but with her thoughts still on "The Weekly Monopolizer," she sews them on the flaps, instead of the wristbands. This is inconvenient; still Mrs. Pax is kindness itself; I make no complaint.

I am very fond of walking. After dinner I say to Mrs. Pax, "Mary, let us take a walk." She says, "Yes, certainly, I must go down town to read the proof of my article for 'The Monopolizer.'" So, I go down town with Mrs. Pax. After tea I say, "Mary, let us go to the theater to-night;" she says, "I would be very happy to go, but the atmosphere is so bad there, the gas always escapes, and my head must be clear to-morrow, you know, for I have to write the last chapter of my forthcoming work, 'Prairie Life.'" So I stay at home with Mrs. Pax, and as I sit down by her on the sofa, and as nobody comes in, I think that this, after all, is better, (though I must say my wife looks well at the Opera, and I like to take her there). I put my arm around Mrs. Pax. It is a habit I have. In comes the servant; and brings a handful of letters for her by mail, directed to "Julia Jesamine!" (that's my wife's *nom-de-plume*). I remove my arm from her waist, because she says "they are probably business letters which require immediate notice." She sits down at the table, and breaks the seals. Four of them are from fellows who want "her autograph." *Mrs. Pax's* autograph! The fifth is from a gentleman who, delighted with her last book, which he says "mirrored his own soul" (how do you suppose Mrs. Pax found out how to "mirror *his* soul?") requests "permission to correspond with the charming authoress." "Charming!" my wife! "his soul!" Mrs. Pax! The sixth is from a gentleman who desires "the loan of five hundred dollars, as he has been unfortunate in business, and has heard that her works have been very remunerative." Five hundred dollars for John Smith, from my wife! The seventh letter is from a man at the West, offering her her own price to deliver a lecture before the Pigtown Young Men's Institute. *I like that!*

Mrs. Pax opens her writing desk; it is one I gave her; takes some delicate buff note-paper; I gave her that, too; dips her gold pen (my gift) into the inkstand, and writes—writes till eleven o'clock. Eleven! and I, her husband, Tom Pax, sit there and wait for her.

The next morning when I awake, I say, "Mary dear?" She says, "Hush! don't speak, I've just got a capital subject to write about for 'The Weekly Monopolizer.'" Not that I am *complaining* of Mrs. Pax, not at all; not that I don't like my wife to be an authoress; I do. To be sure I can't say that I knew *exactly* what it involved. I did not know, for instance, that the Press in speaking of her by her *nom-de-plume* would call her "Our Julia," but I would not have you think I object to her being literary. On the contrary, I am not sure that I do not rather like it; but I ask the Editor of "The Weekly Monopolizer," as a man—as a Christian—as a husband—if he thinks it right—if it is doing as he would be done by—to monopolize my wife's thoughts as early as five o'clock in the morning? I merely ask for information. I trust I have no resentful feelings toward the animal.

New York Ledger
Feb. 9, 1856

PEEPS FROM UNDER A PARASOL

PEOPLE DESCRIBE ME, without saying "by your leave;" a little thought has just occurred to me that two can play at that game! I don't go about with my eyes shut—no tailor can "take a measure" quicker than I, as I pass along.

There is Richard Grant White;[1] now don't he look like a greyhound on two legs? I never see him, but I feel like challenging him to his speed in running a race; (in which, by the way, he would be sure to come off second best).

There are Drs. Chapin, and Bethune;[2] whose well-to-do appearance in this world quite neutralizes their Sunday exhortations to "set one's affections on a better." There's Greeley[3]—but why describe the town pump? he has been handle-d enough, to keep him from Rust-ing. There's that Epicurean Rip-lie,[4] critic of the *New York Tribune*; if I have spelt his name wrong, it was because I was thinking of the unmitigated fibs he has told in his book reviews! There's Col. Fuller,[5] editor of the *New York Evening Mirror*, handsome, witty and saucy. There's Mr. Young, editor of the *Albion*,[6] who looks too much like a gentleman, to have abused in so wholesale a manner, the lady-writers of America. . . . There's Richard Storrs Willis,[7] or, Storrs Richard Willis, or, Willis Richard Storrs, (it is a way that family have to keep changing their names) editor of the *Musical World*; not a bad paper either; Richard has a fine profile, a trim, tight figure, always exceptionably arrayed; and has a gravity of mien most edifying to one who has eaten bread and molasses out of the same plate with him.

Behind that beard coming down the street in that night-gown overcoat, is Mr. Charles A. Dana,[8] of the *New York Tribune*, who is ready to say, "Now lettest thou thy servant depart in peace," when he shall have made the *New York Tribune* like unto the *London Times*. Charles should remember, that the motto of the *London Times* is *Fair Play*—not the *appearance* of fair play. There's Bayard Taylor—[9] "the Oriental Bayard." Now I don't suppose Bayard is to blame for being a *pretty* man, or for looking so nice and bandbox-y. But if some public benefactor *would* tumble his hair and shirt collar, and tie his cravat in a loose sailor knot; and if Bayard himself *would* open that little three-cent piece mouth of his a l-i-t-t-l-e wider when he lectures, it would take a load off my mind! I write this in full view of the Almighty *Tribune*, and also set up before him, certain "Leaves" for a target, by way of reprisal.

Then there is Henry Ward Beecher;[10] who is getting what people call "peart," on his increasing popularity, and who seems now-a-days more anxious to startle, and astonish, than to edify, and spiritualise: He—Henry Ward, says, the "eating is vulgar." It is just possible that it may be, but I have never thought so, except when I have seen the male and female members of the Beecher family, D. D.'s—and authoresses—munching oranges, apples, and peanuts, in the street.

Yes, Henry Ward is getting spoiled; ah! many a man who steers his bark safely on a stormy sea, rides into any port but Heaven, on the waves of popular favor. . . .

And there is Mr. James Parton,[11] author of the *Life of Horace Greeley*, whom I occasionally meet. Jim is five feet ten inches, and modest—wears his hair long, and don't believe in a devil—has written more good anonymous articles now floating unbaptized through newspaperdom, (on both sides of the water) than any other man, save himself, would suffer to go unclaimed. Jim believes in Carlyle and lager bier—can write a book better than he can tie a cravat; though since his late marriage I am pleased to observe a wonderful improvement in this respect. It is my belief, that Jim is destined by steady progress, to eclipse many a man who has shot up like a rocket, and who will fizzle out and come down like a stick. . . .

And here comes Barnum; poor Barnum! late so *riant* and rosy. Kick not the prostrate lion, ye crowing changelings; you may yet feel his paws in your faces; Mammon grant it! not for the love I bear to "woolly horses," but for the hate I bear to pharasaical summer friends. . . .

And here come Lester[12] and Laura Keene[13] (not together! Thespis forbid!) I *must* like Laura's energy and determination, and I *do* wonder at the weight of business those fair and fragile shoulders bear; I *must* honor any woman who snaps her finger at repeated discouragements to gain an honest livelihood; yes, long-visaged, saucer-eyed Pharasee, even though she be "an actress." I hear whispers *against* the pretty Laura. Of course—who that is successful—who that is attractive escapes them? When a man is defamed, a fist, a pistol, or the law rights him: a woman thus situated, if silent, is guilty; if rasped to a public vindication of her rights, is bold, revengeful and unwomanly. *So* "get thee behind me, defaming limb of Satan!" for the indomitable Laura shall, in *my* eyes, be worthy of honor, until proven otherwise.

And there's Jordan; a hero for a boarding-school Miss. If I might be allowed to name a fault, it is his excessive modesty.

And Lester—but his fine person needs no eulogium of mine; I *have* sometimes thought he himself was not unconscious of it! And Wallack,[14] with his lovely grandchild by the hand; (Autumn and Spring)—you will see no picture in the artist's studio more touching and sweet.

And here, by the rood, comes Fanny Fern! Fanny is a woman. For that she is not to blame, though since she first found it out, she has never ceased to deplore it. She might be prettier, she might be younger. She might be older, she might be uglier. She might be better, she might be worse. She has been both over-praised and over-abused, and those who have abused her worst, have imitated and copied her most.

One thing may be said in favor of Fanny: she was NOT, thank Providence, born in the beautiful, backbiting; sanctimonious, slandering; clean, contumelious; pharasaical, phiddle-de-dee; peck-measure city—of Boston!

Look?

Which? How? Where?

Why *there*; don't you see? there's Potiphar Curtis.

Potiphar Curtis![15] ye gods, what a name! Pity my ignorance, Reader, I had not then heard of the great "Howadji;" the only Potiphar I knew of being that much abused ancient who—but never mind him; suffice it to say, I had not heard of "Howadji;" and while I stood transfixed with his ridiculous cognomen, his coat tails, like his namesake's rival's, were disappearing in the distance. So I cannot describe him for you; but I give you my word, should I ever see him, to do him justice to the tips of his boots; which I understand are of immaculate polish. I have read his "Papers" though, and to speak in the style of the patronising critics who review lady-books, they are very well—*for a man.*

And speaking of books, here comes Walt Whitman, author of *Leaves of Grass*, which, by the way, I have not yet read. His shirt collar is turned off from his muscular throat, and his shoulders are thrown back as if even in that fine, ample chest of his, his lungs had not sufficient play-room. Mark his voice! rich—deep—and clear, as a clarion note. In the most crowded thoroughfare, one would turn instinctively on hearing it, to seek out its owner. Such a voice is a gift as rare as it is priceless. A fig for phrenology! Let me but hear the *voice* of a man or a woman and I will tell you the stuff its owners are made of. One of the first things I noticed in New York was the sharp, shrill, squeaking, unrefined, vixenish, *uneducated* voices of its women. How inevitably such disenchanting discord, breaks the spell of beauty!

Fair New Yorkers keep your mouths *shut*, if you would conquer.

By what magnetism has our mention of voices conjured up the form of Dr. LOWELL MASON?[16] And yet, there he is, as majestic as Old Hundred—as popular—and apparently as indestructible by *Time*. I would like to see a pupil of his who does not love him. I defy anyone to look at this noble, patriarchal chorister (as he leads the *Congregational Singing* on the Sabbath, in Dr. Alexander's church) with an unmoistened eye. How fitting his position—and oh! how befitting God's temple, the praises of "*all* the people." . . .

Ah—here is Dr. Skinner![17] no misnomer that: but what a logician—what an orator! Not an unmeaning sentence—not a superfluous word—not an unpolished period escapes him. In these days of superficial, botched, evangelical apprentice-work, it is a treat to welcome a master-workman. Thank Providence, *all* the talent is not on the side of Beelzebub!

Vinegar cruets and vestry-meetings! here come a group of Bostonians! Mark their puckered, spick-and-span self-complaisance! Mark that scornful gathering up of their skirts as they sidle away from the gorgeous Magdalen who, God pity and help her, *may* repent in her robes of unwomanly shame, but they in their "mint and anise," white-washed garments—*never*!

I close with a little quotation, not that it has anything to do with my subject, but that it is merely a poetical finish to my article. Some people have a weakness for poetry; I have; it is from the pen of the cant-hating HOOD.[18]

"A pride there is of rank—a pride of birth,
A pride of learning and a pride of purse,

A London pride—in short, there be on earth
A host of prides, some better and some worse.
But of all prides, since Lucifer's attaint,
The proudest swells a *self-elected saint*.
To picture that cold pride, so harsh and hard,
Fancy a peacock, in a poultry yard;
Behold him in conceited circles sail,
Strutting and dancing, and planted stiff
In all his pomp and pageantry, as if
He felt 'the eyes of Europe' on his tail!"[19]

New York Ledger
March 29,
Apr. 12, 19, 1856

"LEAVES OF GRASS"

WELL BAPTIZED: fresh, hardy, and grown for the masses.[1] Not more welcome is their natural type to the winter-bound, bed-ridden, and spring-emancipated invalid. "Leaves of Grass" thou art unspeakably delicious, after the forced, stiff, Parnassian exotics for which our admiration has been vainly challenged.

Walt Whitman, the effeminate world needed thee. The timidest soul whose wings ever drooped with discouragement, could not choose but rise on thy strong pinions.

"Undrape—you are not guilty to me, nor stale nor discarded;
I see through the broadcloth and gingham whether or no. . . .

O despairer, here is my neck,
You shall *not* go down! Hang your whole weight upon me."

Walt Whitman, the world needed a "Native American" of thorough, out-and-out breed—enamored of *women* not *ladies, men* not *gentlemen*;

something beside a mere Catholic-hating Know-Nothing;[2] it needed a man who dared speak out his strong, honest thoughts, in the face of pusillanimous, toadeying, republican aristocracy; dictionary-men, hypocrites, cliques and creeds; it needed a large-hearted, untainted, self-reliant, fearless son of the Stars and Stripes, who disdains to sell his birthright for a mess of pottage; who does

> "Not call one greater or one smaller,
> That which fills its period and place being equal to any;"

who will

> "Accept nothing which all cannot have their counterpart of
> on the same terms."

Fresh "Leaves of Grass"! not submitted by the self-reliant author to the fingering of any publisher's critic, to be arranged, re-arranged and disarranged to his circumscribed liking, till they hung limp, tame, spiritless, and scentless. No. It were a spectacle worth seeing, this glorious Native American, who, when the daily labor of chisel and plane was over, himself, with toil-hardened fingers, handled the types to print the pages which wise and good men have since delighted to endorse and to honor. Small critics, whose contracted vision could see no beauty, strength, or grace, in these "Leaves," have long ago repented that they so hastily wrote themselves down shallow by such a premature confession. Where an Emerson, and a Howitt[3] have commended, my woman's voice of praise may not avail; but happiness was born a twin, and so I would fain share with others the unmingled delight which these "Leaves" have given me.

I say unmingled; I am not unaware that the charge of coarseness and sensuality has been affixed to them.[4] My moral constitution may be hopelessly tainted—or too sound to be tainted, as the critic wills—but I confess that I extract no poison from these "Leaves"—to me they have brought only healing. Let him who can do so, shroud the eyes of the nursing babe lest it should see its mother's breast. Let him look carefully between the gilded covers of books, backed by high-sounding names, and endorsed by parson and priest, lying unrebuked upon his own family table; where the asp of sensuality lies coiled amid rhetorical flowers. Let him examine well the paper dropped weekly at his door, in which virtue and religion are rendered disgusting, save when they walk in satin slippers, or, clothed in purple and fine linen, kneel on a damask "*prie-dieu*."

Sensual! No—the moral assassin looks you not boldly in the eye by broad daylight; but Borgia-like takes you treacherously by the hand, while from the glittering ring on his finger he distils through your veins the subtle and deadly poison.

Sensual? The artist who would inflame, paints you not nude Nature, but stealing Virtue's veil, with artful artlessness now conceals, now exposes, the ripe and swelling proportions.

Sensual? Let him who would affix this stigma upon "Leaves of Grass," write upon his heart, in letters of fire, these noble words of its author:

"In woman I see the bearer of the great fruit, which is immortality
. . . the good thereof is not tasted by *roues*, and never can be. . . .
Who degrades or defiles the living human body is cursed,
Who degrades or defiles the body of the dead is not more cursed."

Were I an artist I would like no more suggestive subjects for my easel than Walt Whitman's pen has furnished.

"The little one sleeps in its cradle,
I lift the gauze and look a long time, and silently brush away
flies with my hand.
The farmer stops by the bars of a Sunday and looks at the
oats and rye. . . .
Earth of the slumbering and liquid trees!
Earth of departed Sunset!
Earth of the mountain's misty topt!
Earth of the vitreous pour of the full moon just tinged with blue!
Earth of shine and dark mottling the tide of the river!
Earth of the limpid grey of clouds brighter and clearer for my sake!
Far swooping elbowed earth! Rich apple-blossomed earth!
Smile, for your lover comes!"

I quote at random, the following passages which appeal to me:

"A morning glory at my window, satisfies me more than the
metaphysics of books. . . .

Logic and sermons never convince.
The damp of the night drives deeper into my soul."

Speaking of animals, he says:

"I stand and look at them sometimes half the day long.
They do not make me sick, discussing their duty to God. . . .
Whoever walks a furlong without sympathy, walks to his funeral dressed in his shroud. . . .
I hate him that oppresses me,
I will either destroy him, or he shall release me. . . .
I find letters from God dropped in the street, and every one is signed by God's name,
And I leave them where they are, for I know that others will punctually come forever and ever. . . .
—Under Niagara, *the cataract falling like a veil over my countenance*."

Of the grass he says:

"It seems to me *the beautiful uncut hair of graves*."

I close the extracts from these "Leaves," which it were easy to multiply, for one is more puzzled what to leave unculled, than what to gather, with the following sentiments; for which, and for all the good things included between the covers of his book, Mr. Whitman will please accept the cordial grasp of a woman's hand:

"The wife—and she is not one jot less than the husband,
The daughter—and she is just as good as the son,
The mother—and she is every bit as much as the father."

New York Ledger
May 10, 1856

MY OLD INK-STAND AND I;

Or, The First Article in the New House

WELL, old Ink-stand, what do you think of this? Haven't we got well through the woods, hey? A few scratches and bruises we have had, to be sure, but what of that? Didn't you whisper where we should come out, the first morning I dipped my pen in your sable depths, in the sky-parlor of that hyena-like Mrs. Griffin? With what an eagle glance she discovered that my bonnet-ribbon was undeniably guilty of two distinct washings, and, emboldened by my shilling de laine, and the shabby shoes of little Nell, inquired "if I intended taking in slop-work into *her* apartments?" How distinctly I was made to understand that Nell was not to speak above a whisper, or in any way infringe upon the rights of her uncombed, unwashed, unbaptized, uncomfortable little Griffins. Poor little Nell, who clung to my gown with childhood's instinctive appreciation of the hard face and wiry voice of our jailor. With what venom I overheard her inform Mr. Griffin that "they must look sharp for the rent of their sky-parlor, as its tenant lived on bread and milk, and wore her under-clothes rough-dry, because she could not afford to pay for ironing them!" Do you remember *that*, old Ink-stand? And do you remember the morning she informed me, as you and I were busily engaged in our first article, that I must "come and scrub the stairs which led up to my room;" and when I ventured humbly to mention, that this was not spoken of in our agreement, do you remember the Siddons-like air with which she thundered in our astonished ears—"Do it, or tramp!" And do you remember how you vowed "if I did tramp," you would stand by me, and help me out of the scrape? and haven't you *done* it, old Ink-stand? And don't you wish old Griffin, and all the little Griffins, and their likes, both big and little, here and elsewhere, could see this bran-new pretty house that you have helped me into, and the dainty little table upon which I have installed you, untempted by any new papier-mache modern marvel?

Turn my back on *you*, old Ink-stand! Not I. Throw you aside, for your shabby exterior, as we were thrown aside, when it was like drawing teeth to get a solitary shilling to buy you at a second-hand shop? Perish the thought!

Yes, old Ink-stand, Griffin, and all that crew, should see us now. Couldn't we take the wind out of their sails? Couldn't we come into their front door, instead of their "back gate?" Didn't they "*always know* that there was something in us?" We can forgive them, though, can't we? By the title deed, and insurance policy, of this bran-new pretty house, which their sneers have helped us into, and whose doors shall always be open to those who have cheered us on, we'll do it.

Dropped many a tear into you, have I? Well—who cares? You know, very well, that every rough word aimed at my quivering ears, was an extra dollar in my purse; every rude touch of my little Nell, strength and sinew to my unstrung nerves and flagging muscles. I say, old Ink-stand, look at Nell now! Does any landlady lay rough hands on those plump shoulders? Dare she sing and run, and jump and play to her heart's content? Didn't you yourself buy her that hoop and stick, and those dolls, and that globe of gold-fish? Don't you feed and clothe her, every day of her sunshiny life? Haven't you agreed to do it, long years to come? and won't you teach her, as you have me, to defy false friends, and ill-fortune? And won't you be to my little Nell a talisman, when my eyes grow dim, and hers brighten? Say, old Ink-stand?

New York Ledger
July 19, 1856

AWE-FUL THOUGHTS

"This had, from the very beginning of their acquaintance, induced in her that *awe*, which is the most delicious feeling a wife can have toward her husband."

Awe-ful Thoughts

"*AWE!*"—awe of a man whose whiskers you have trimmed, whose hair you have cut, whose cravats you have tied, whose shirts you have "put into the wash," whose boots and shoes you have kicked into the closet, whose dressing-gown you have worn while combing your hair; who has been down cellar with you at eleven o'clock at night to hunt for a chicken-bone; who has hooked your dresses, unlaced your boots, fastened your bracelets, and tied on your bonnet; who has stood before your looking-glass, with thumb and finger on his proboscis, scraping his chin; whom you have buttered, and sugared, and toasted, and tea-ed; whom you have seen asleep with his mouth wide open! Ri—diculous!

New York Ledger
November 1, 1856

TO GENTLEMEN

A Call to Be a Husband

YES, I did say that "it is not every man who has a call to be a husband;" and I am not going to back out of it.

Has that man a call to be a husband, who, having wasted his youth in excesses, looks around him at the eleventh hour for a "virtuous young girl" (such men have the effrontery to be *very* particular on this point), to nurse up his damaged constitution, and perpetuate it in their offspring?

Has that man a call to be a husband, who, believing that the more the immortal within us is developed in this world, the higher we shall rank with heavenly intelligences in the next, yet deprecates for a wife a woman of thought and intellect, lest a marriage with such should peril the seasoning of his favorite pudding, or lest she might presume in any of her opinions to be aught else than his echo?

Has that man a call to be a husband, who, when the rosy maiden he married is transformed by too early an introduction to the cares and trials of maternity, into a feeble, confirmed invalid, turns impatiently from the restless wife's sick-room, to sun himself in the perfidious smile of one whom he would blush to name in that wife's pure ears?

Has *he* any call to be a husband, who adds to his wife's manifold cares that of selecting and providing the household stores, and inquires of her, at that, how she spent the surplus shilling of yesterday's appropriation?

Has *he* any call to be a husband, who permits his own relatives, in his hearing, to speak disrespectfully or censoriously of his wife?

Has *he* any call to be a husband, who reads the newspaper from beginning to end, giving notice of his presence to the weary wife, who is patiently mending his old coat, only by an occasional "Jupiter!" which may mean, to the harrowed listener, that we have a President worth standing in a driving rain, at the tail of a three-mile procession, to vote for, or—the contrary? and who, after having extracted every particle of news the paper contains, coolly puts it in one of his many mysterious pockets, and goes to sleep in his chair?

Has *he* a call to be a husband, who carries a letter, intended for his wife, in his pocket for six weeks, and expects any thing short of "gun-powder tea" for his supper that night?

Has he a call to be a husband, who leaves his wife to blow out the lamp, and stub her precious little toes while she is navigating for the bed-post?

Has he a call to be a husband, who tells his wife "to walk on a couple of blocks and he will overtake her," and then joins in a hot political discussion with an opponent, after which, in a fit of absence of mind, he walks off home, leaving his wife transformed by his perfidy into "a pillar of salt?"

Has he any call to be a husband, who sits down on his wife's best bonnet, or puts her shawl over her shoulders upside down, or wrong side out at the Opera?

Has he any call to be a husband, who goes "unbeknown" to his wife, to some wretch of a barber, and parts, for twenty-five cents, with a beard which she has coaxed from its first infantile sprout, to luxuriant, full-grown, magnificent, unsurpassable hirsuteness, and then comes home to her horrified vision a pocket edition of Moses?

Has he any call to be a husband, who kisses his wife only on Saturday night, when he winds up the clock and pays the grocer, and who never notices, day by day, the neat dress, and shining bands of hair arranged to please his stupid milk-and-water-ship?

New York Ledger
Dec. 13, 1856

HAS A MOTHER A RIGHT TO HER CHILDREN?

MOST UNQUESTIONABLY, law or no law.[1] Let us begin at the beginning. Let us take into consideration the physical prostration of mind and body endured by mothers antecedent to the birth of their off-spring; their extreme nervousness and restlessness, without the ability for locomotion; the great nameless horror which hangs over those who, for the first time, are called upon to endure agonies that no man living would have fortitude to bear more than once, even at their shortest period of duration; and which, to those who have passed through it, is intensified by the vivid recollection (the only verse in the Bible which I call in question being this—"She remembereth no more her pains, for joy that a man-child is born into the world"). Granted that the mother's life is spared through this terrible ordeal, she rises from her sick-bed, after weeks of prostration, with the precious burden in her arms which she carried so long and so patiently beneath her heart. Oh, the continuous, tireless watching necessary to preserve the life and limbs of this fragile little thing! At a time, too, of all times, when the mother most needs relaxation and repose. It is known only to those who have passed through it. Its reward is with Him who seeth in secret.

I speak now only of *good* mothers; mothers who deserve the high and holy name. Mothers who in their unselfish devotion look not at their capacity to endure, but the duties allotted to them (would that husbands and fathers did not so often leave it to the tombstone to call their attention to the former). Mothers, whose fragile hands keep the domestic treadmill in as unerring motion as if no new care was superadded in the feeble wail of the new-born infant. Mothers whose work is literally *never* done; who sleep with one eye open, entrusting to no careless hireling the precious little life. Mothers who can scarce secure to themselves five mintues of the morning hours free from interruption, to ask God's help that a feeble, tried woman may hold evenly the scales of domestic justice amid the conflicting elements of human needs and human frailties. Now I ask you—shall any human law, for any conceivable reason, wrest the child of such a mother from her frenzied clasp?

Shall any human law give into a man's hand, though that man be the child's own father, the sole right to its direction and disposal? Has not she, who suffered, martyr-like, these crucifying pains—these wearisome days and sleepless nights, *earned* this her sweet reward?

Shall any virtuous woman, who is in the full possession of her mental faculties, how poor soever she may be, be *beggared* by robbing her of that which has been, and, thank God! will be the salvation of many a down-trodden wife?

New York Ledger
Apr. 4, 1857

PARENT AND CHILD

or, Which Shall Rule.

"*GIVE ME TWO CENTS,* I say, or I'll kick you!"

I turned to look at the threatener. It was a little fellow about as tall as my sun-shade, stamping defiance at a fine, matronly-looking woman, who must have been his mother, so like were her large black eyes to the gleaming orbs of the boy. "Give me two cents, I say, or I'll kick you," he repeated, tugging fiercely at her silk dress to find the pocket, while every feature in his handsome face was distorted with passion. Surely she will not do it, said I to myself, anxiously awaiting the issue, as I apparently examined some ribbons in a shop-window; surely she will not be so mad, so foolish, so untrue to herself, so untrue to her child, so belie the beautiful picture of healthy maternity, so God-impressed in that finely-developed form and animated face. Oh, if I might speak to her, and beg her not to do it, thought I, as she put her hand in her pocket, and the fierce look died away on the boy's face, and was succeeded by one of triumph; if I might tell her that she is fostering the noisome weeds that will surely choke the flowers—sowing the wind to reap the whirlwind.

"But the boy is so passionate; it is less trouble to grant his request than to deny him." Granting this were so; who gave you a right to weigh your own case in the balance with your child's soul? Who gave you a right to educate him for a convict's cell, or the gallows? But, thoughtless, weakly indulgent, cruel-kind mother, it is not easier, as you selfishly, short-sightedly reason, to grant his request than to deny it; not easier for him—not easier for you. The appetite for rule grows by what it feeds on. Is he less domineering now than he was yesterday? Will he be less so to-morrow than he is to-day? Certainly not.

"But I have not time to contest every inch of ground with him." Take time then—make time; neglect every thing else, but neglect not that. With every child comes this turning point: *Which shall be the victor—my mother or I?* and it must be met. She is no true mother who dodges or evades it. True—there will be a fierce struggle at first; but be firm as a rock; recede not one inch; there may be two, three, or even more, but the battle once won, as won it shall be if you are a faithful mother, it is won for this world—ay, perhaps for another.

"But I am not at liberty to control him thus; when parents do not pull together in the harness, the reins of government will slacken; when I would restrain and correct him, his father interferes; children are quick-witted, and my boy sees his advantage. What can I do, unsustained and single-handed?" True—true—God help the child then. Better for him had he never been born; better for you both, for so surely as the beard grows upon that little chin, so surely shall he bring your gray hairs with sorrow to the grave; and so surely shall he curse you for your very indulgence, before he is placed in the dishonored one your parental hands are digging for him.

These things need not be—ought not to be. Oh! if parents had but a firm hand to govern, and yet a ready ear for childish sympathy; if they would agree—whatever they might say in private—never to differ in presence of their children, as to their government; if the dissension-breeding "Joseph's coat" were banished from every hearthstone; if there were less weak indulgence and less asceticism; if the bow were neither entirely relaxed, nor strained so tightly that it broke; if there were less out-door dissipation, and more home-pleasures; if parents would not forget that they were once children, nor, on the other hand, forget that their children will be one day parents; if there were less form of godliness, and more godliness (for children are Argus-eyed; it is not what you preach, but what you practice), we should then have no beardless skeptics, no dissolute sons, no runaway marriages, no icy barriers between those rocked in the same cradle—nursed at the same breast.

New York Ledger
May 9, 1857

MALE CRITICISM ON LADIES' BOOKS

> "Courtship and marriage, servants and children, these are the great objects of a woman's thoughts, and they necessarily form the staple topics of their writings and their conversation. We have no right to expect anything else in a woman's book."—*N.Y. Times*

IS IT in feminine novels *only* that courtship, marriage, servants and children are the staple? Is not this true of all novels?—of Dickens, of Thackeray, of Bulwer and a host of others? Is it peculiar to feminine pens, most astute and liberal of critics? Would a novel be a novel if it did not treat of courtship and marriage? and if it could be so recognized, would it find readers? When I see such a narrow, snarling criticism as the above, I always say to myself, the writer is some unhappy man, who has come up without the refining influence of mother, or sister, or reputable female friends; who has divided his migratory life between boarding-houses, restaurants, and the outskirts of editorial sanctums; and who knows as much about reviewing a woman's book, as I do about navigating a ship, or engineering an omnibus from the South Ferry, through Broadway, to Union Park. I think I see him writing that paragraph in a fit of spleen—of *male* spleen—in his small boarding-house upper chamber, by the cheerful light of a solitary candle, flickering alternately on cobwebbed walls, dusty wash-stand, begrimed bowl and pitcher, refuse cigar stumps, boot-jacks, old hats, buttonless coats, muddy trousers, and all the wretched accompaniments of solitary, selfish male existence, not to speak of his own puckered, unkissable face; perhaps, in addition, his boots hurt, his cravat-bow persists in slipping under his ear for want of a pin, and a wife to pin it (poor wretch!) or he has been refused by some pretty girl, as he deserved to be (narrow-minded old vinegar-cruet!) or snubbed by some lady authoress; or, more trying than all to the male constitution, has had a weak cup of coffee for that morning's breakfast.

But seriously—we have had quite enough of this shallow criticism (?) on lady-books. Whether the book which called forth the remark above quoted, was a good book or a bad one, I know not: I should be inclined to think the *former* from the dispraise of such a pen. Whether ladies can write novels or not, is a question I do not intend to discuss; but that some of them have no difficulty in finding either publishers or readers is a matter of history; and that gentlemen often write over feminine signatures would seem also to argue that feminine literature is, after all, in good odor with the reading public. Granted that lady-novels are not all that they should be—is such shallow, unfair, wholesale, sneering criticism (?) the way to reform them? Would it not be better and more manly to point out a better way kindly, justly, *and above all, respectfully?* or—what would be a much harder task for such critics—write a better book!

New York Ledger
May 23, 1857

IN THE DUMPS

WHAT DOES ail me? I'm as blue as indigo. Last night I was as gay as a bob-o'-link—perhaps that is the reason. Good gracious, hear that wind howl! Now low—now high—till it fairly shrieks; it excites me like the pained cry of a human. There's my pretty California flower—blue as a baby's eyes; all shut up—no wonder—I wish my eyes were shut up, too. What *does* ail me? I think it is that dose of a Boston paper I have just been reading (for want of something better to do), whose book critic calls "Jane Eyre" an "*immoral* book." Donkey! It is vain to hope that *his* life has been as pure and self-sacrificing as that of "Charlotte Bronte." There's the breakfast-bell—and there's Tom with that autumn-leaf colored vest on, that I so hate. Why don't men wear pretty vests? Why can't they leave off those detestable stiff collars, stocks, and things, that make them all lòok like choked chickens, and which hide so many handsomely-turned throats, that a body never sees, unless a body is married, or unless a body happens to see a body's brothers while they are shaving. Talk of women's throats—you ought to see a whiskered throat I saw once——Gracious, how blue I am! Do you suppose it is the weather? I wish the sun would shine out and try me. See the inch-worms on that tree. That's because it is a pet of mine. Every thing I like goes just that way. If I have a nice easy dress that I can sneeze in, it is sure to wear out and leave me to the crucifying alternative of squeezing myself into one that is not broke into my figure. I hate new gowns—I hate new shoes—I hate new bonnets—I hate any thing new except new—spapers, and I was born reading them.

There's a lame boy—now why couldn't that boy have been straight? There's a rooster driving round a harem of hens; what do the foolish things run for? If they didn't run, he couldn't chase them—of course not. Now it's beginning to rain; every drop perforates my heart. I could cry tears enough to float a ship. Why *need* it rain?—patter—patter—skies as dull as lead—trees nestling up to each other in shivering sympathy; and that old cow—I hate cows—they always make a dive at me—I suppose it is because they are females; that old cow stands stock still, looking at that pump-handle just where, and as she did, when I went to bed last night. Do you suppose that a cow's tail ever gets tired lashing flies from her side; do you suppose her jaws ever ache with that eternal munching? If there is any place I like, it is a barn; I mean to go a journey this summer, not "to see Niagara"—but to see a barn. Oh, the visions I've had on haymows! oh, the tears I've shed there—oh, the golden sunlight that has streamed down on me through the chinks in the raftered roof—oh, the cheerful swallow-twitterings on the old cross-beams—oh, the cunning brown mice scampering over the floor—oh, the noble bay-horse with his flowing mane, and arching neck, and satin sides, and great *human* eyes. Strong as Achilles—gentle as a woman. Pshaw! women were never half so gentle to me. *He* never repulsed me when I laid my head against his neck for sympathy. *Brute* forsooth! I wish there were more such brutes. Poor Hunter—he's dead, of course, because I loved him;—the *trunk-maker* only knows what has become of his hide and my books. What of that? a hundred years hence and who'll care? I don't think I love any thing—or care for any thing to-day. I don't think I shall ever have any feeling again for any body or any thing. Why don't somebody turn that old rusty weather-cock, or play me a triumphant march, or bring me a dew-gemmed daisy?

There's a funeral—a *child's* funeral! Oh—what a wretch I am! Come here—you whom I love—you who love me; closer—closer—let me twine my arms about you, and God forgive me for shutting my eyes to his sunshine.

New York Ledger
July 4, 1857

MOTHER'S ROOM

MOTHER'S ROOM! How we look back to it in after years, when she who sanctified it is herself among the sanctified. How well we remember the ample cushioned chair, with its all-embracing arms, none the worse in our eyes for having rocked to sleep so many little forms now scattered far and wide, divided from us perhaps by barriers more impassable than the cold, blue sea. Mother's room—where the sun shone in so cheerily upon the flowering plants in the low, old-fashioned window seats, which seemed to bud and blossom at the least touch of her caressing fingers; on which no blight or mildew ever came, no more than on the love which outlived all our childish waywardness, all our childish folly. The cozy sofa upon which childish feet were never forbidden to climb; upon which curly heads could dream, unchidden, the fairy dreams of childhood. The closet which garnered tops, and dolls, and kites, and whips, and toys, and upon whose upper shelf was that infallible, old-fashioned panacea for infancy's aches and pains—brimstone and molasses! The basket, too, where was always the very string we wanted; the light-stand round which we gathered, and threaded needles (would we had threaded thousands more) for eyes dimmed in our service; and the cheerful face that smiled across it such loving thanks.

Mother's room! where our matronly feet returned when *we* were mothers; where we lifted our little ones to kiss the wrinkled face, beautiful with its halo of goodness; where we looked on well pleased to see the golden locks we worshipped, mingling lovingly with the silver hairs; where—as the fond grand-mamma produced in alarming profusion, cakes and candy for the little pets, we laughingly reminded her of *our* baby days, when she wisely told us such things were "unwholesome;" where *our* baby caps, yellow with time, ferreted from some odd bag or closet, were tried on our own babies' heads, and we sat, wondering where the months and years had flown between then and now;—and looking forward, half-sighing, to just such a picture, when we should play, what seemed to us now, with our smooth skins, round limbs, and glossy locks, such an impossible part.

Mother's room! where we watched beside her patient sick-bed through the long night, gazing hopelessly at the flickering taper, listening to the pain-extorted groan, which no human skill, no human love, could avert or relieve; waiting with her the dawning of that eternal day, seen through a mist of tears, bounded by no night.

Mother's room! where the mocking light strayed in through the half-opened shutters, upon her who, for the first time, was blind to our tears, and deaf to our cries; where busy memory could bring back to us no look, no word, no tone, no act of hers, not freighted with godlike love. Alas!—alas for us then, if turning the tables, she showed us this long debt of love unappreciated—unpaid!

New York Ledger
Aug. 15, 1857

FRESH LEAVES

By Fanny Fern

THIS LITTLE VOLUME has just been laid upon our table.[1] The publishers have done all they could for it, with regard to outward adorning. No doubt it will be welcomed by those who admire this lady's style of writing: we confess ourselves not to be of that number. We have never seen Fanny Fern, nor do we desire to do so. We imagine her, from her writings, to be a muscular, black-browed, grenadier-looking female, who would be more at home in a boxing gallery than in a parlor,—a vociferous, demonstrative, strong-minded horror,—a woman only by virtue of her dress. Bah! the very thought sickens us. We have read, or, rather, tried to read, her halloo-there effusions. When we take up a woman's book we expect to find gentleness, timidity, and that lovely reliance on the patronage of our sex which constitutes a woman's greatest charm. We do not wish to be startled by bold expressions, or disgusted with exhibitions of masculine weaknesses. We do not desire to see a woman wielding the scimitar blade of sarcasm. If she be, unfortunately, endowed with a gift so dangerous, let her—as she values the approbation of our sex—fold it in a napkin. Fanny's strong-minded nose would probably turn up at this inducement. Thank heaven! there are still women who *are* women—who know the place Heaven assigned them, and keep it—who do not waste floods of ink and paper, brow-beating men and stirring up silly women;—who do not teach children that a game of romps is of as much importance as Blair's

Philosophy;—who have not the presumption to advise clergymen as to their duties, or lecture doctors, and savans;—who live for something else than to astonish a gaping, idiotic crowd. Thank heaven! there are women writers who do not disturb our complacence or serenity; whose books lull one to sleep like a strain of gentle music; who excite no antagonism, or angry feeling. Woman never was intended for an irritant: she should be oil upon the troubled waters of manhood—soft and amalgamating, a necessary but unobtrusive ingredient;—never challenging attention—never throwing the gauntlet of defiance to a beard, but softly purring beside it lest it bristle and scratch.

The very fact that Fanny Fern has, in the language of her admirers, "elbowed her way through unheard of difficulties," shows that she is an antagonistic, pugilistic female. One must needs, forsooth, get out of her way, or be pushed one side, or trampled down. How much more womanly to have allowed herself to be doubled up by adversity, and quietly laid away on the shelf of fate, than to have rolled up her sleeves, and gone to fisticuffs with it. Such a woman may conquer, it is true, but her victory will cost her dear; it will neither be forgotten nor forgiven—let her put that in her apron pocket.

As to Fanny Fern's grammar, rhetoric, and punctuation, they are beneath criticism. It is all very well for her to say, those who wish commas, semi-colons and periods, must look for them in the printer's case, or that she who finds ideas must not be expected to find rhetoric or grammar; for our part, we should be gratified if we had even found any ideas!

We regret to be obliged to speak thus of a lady's book: it gives us great pleasure, when we can do so conscientiously, to pat lady writers on the head; but we owe a duty to the public which will not permit us to recommend to their favorable notice an aspirant who has been unwomanly enough so boldly to contest every inch of ground in order to reach them—an aspirant at once so high-stepping and so ignorant, so plausible, yet so pernicious. We have a conservative horror of this pop-gun, torpedo female; we predict for Fanny Fern's "Leaves" only a fleeting autumnal flutter.

New York Ledger
Oct. 10, 1857

A WORD ON THE OTHER SIDE

HEAVEN give our sex patience to read such trash as the following: "If irritation should occur, a woman must expect to hear from her husband a strength and vehemence of language far more than the occasion requires."

Now, with my arms a-kimbo, I ask, *why* a woman should "expect" it? Is it bcause her husband claims to be her intellectual superior? Is it because he is his wife's natural protector? Is it because an unblest marriage lot is more tolerable to her susceptible organization and monotonous life, than to his hardier nature relieved by out-door occupations? Is it because the thousand diversions which society winks at and excuses in his case, are stamped in hers as guilty and unhallowed? Is it because maternity has never gasped out in his hearing its sacred agony? Is it because no future wife is to mourn in that man's imitative boy his father's low standard of a husband's duty?

Oh, away with such one-sided moralizing; that the law provides no escape from a brutal husband, who is breaking his wife's heart, unless he also attempts breaking her head, should be, and, I thank God, is, by every magnanimous and honorable man—and, alas, they are all too few—a wife's strongest defence. I have no patience with those who would reduce woman to a mere machine, to be twitched this way and twitched that, and jarred, and unharmonized at the dogged will of a stupid brute. (This does not sound pretty, I know; but when a woman is irritated, men "must expect to hear a strength and vehemence of language far more than the occasion requires!") I have no patience with those who preach one code of morality for the wife, and another for the husband. If the marriage vow allows him to absent himself from his house under cover of darkness, scorning to give account of himself, it also allows it to her. There is no sex designated in the fifth commandment. "*Thou* shalt not," and "*thou*," and "*thou*!" There is no excuse that I have ever yet heard offered for a man's violation of it, that should not answer equally for his wife. What is right for him is just as right for her. It is right for neither. The weakness of their cause who plead for license in this sin, was never better shown than in a defence lately set up in this city, viz., that "without houses of infamy our wives and daughters would not be safe."

Oh, most shallow reasoner, *how safe* are our "wives and daughters" with them? Let our medical men, versed in the secrets of family histories, answer! Let weeping wives, who mourn over little graves, tell you!

But while women submit to have their wifely honor insulted, and their lives jeopardized by the legalized or un-legalized brutality of husbands, just so long they will have to suffer it, and I was going to say, just so long they *ought*. Let not those women who have too little self-respect to take their lives in their hands, and say to a dissolute husband, this you can never give, and this you shall not therefore take away—whine about "their lot." "But the children?" Aye—the children—shame that the law should come between them and a good mother! Still—better let her leave them, than remain to bring into the world their puny brothers and sisters. Does she shrink from the toil of self-support? What toil, let me ask, could be more hopeless, more endless, *more degrading* than that from which she turns away?

There are all phases of misery. A case has recently come under my notice, of a wife rendered feeble by the frequently recurring cares and pains of maternity, whose husband penuriously refuses to obtain medical advice or household help, when her tottering step and trembling hands tell more eloquently than words of mine could do, her total unfitness for family duties. And this when he has a good business—when, as a mere matter of policy, it were dollars in his short-sighted pocket to hoard well her strength, who, in the pitying language of Him who will most surely avenge her cause, "hath done what she could."

Now I ask *you*, and *you*, and *you*, if this woman should lay down her life on the altar of that man's selfishness? I ask you if he is not her murderer, as truly, but not as mercifully, as if our most righteous, woman-protecting law saw him place the glittering knife at her throat? I ask you if she has not as God-given a right to her life, as he has to his? I ask you if, through fear of the world, she should stay there to die? I ask you if that world could be sterner, its eye colder, its heart flintier, its voice harsher, than that from which she turns—all honor to her self-sacrificing nature—*sorrowing* away?

Perhaps you ask would I have a woman, for every trifling cause, "leave her husband and family?" Most emphatically, *No*. But there are aggravated cases for which the law provides no remedy—from which it affords no protection; and that hundreds of suffering women bear their chains because they have not courage to face a scandal-loving world, to whom it matters not a pin that their every nerve is quivering with suppressed agony, is no proof to the contrary of what I assert. What I say is this: in such cases, let a woman who *has the self-sustaining power* quietly take her fate in her own hands, and right herself. Of course she will be misjudged and abused. *It is for her to choose whether she can better bear this at hands from which she has a rightful claim for love and protection, or from a nine-days-wonder-loving public.* These are bold words; but they are needed words—words whose full import I have well considered, and from the responsibility of which I do not shrink.

New York Ledger
Oct. 24, 1857

WHERE HAVE I BEEN, AND WHAT HAVE I SEEN?

WELL—in the first place, I have been to see Miss Hosmer's[1] statue of "Beatrice Cenci," and I hope all who read this will go, too. Now, if you look for an artistic description of it, you must look somewhere else; there are plenty of walking dictionaries who will prate to you about the "pose" of the figure, etc., as they look through their cold, scientific spectacles. I shall simply say that to my eye it is so surpassingly lovely, I could almost weep that no breath of life will ever warm it into love. If there is a fault in those undulating limbs, and in that sweet, sad, child-like face, I thank the gods my eye was too dull to perceive it; and I thank the gods, too, that the young sculptress has had the courage to assert herself—to be what nature intended her to be—a genius—even at the risk of being called un-feminine, eccentric, and unwomanly. "Unwomanly?" because crotchet-stitching and worsted foolery could not satisfy her soul! Unwomanly? because she galloped over the country on horseback, in search of health and pleasure, instead of drawing on her primrose kids, and making a lay-figure of herself, to exhibit the fashions, by dawdling about the streets. Well, *let* her be unwomanly, then, I say; I wish there were more women bitten with the same complaint; let her be "eccentric," if nature made her so, so long as she outrages only the feelings of those conservative old ladies of both sexes, who would destroy individuality by running all our sex in the same mold of artificial nonentity—who are shocked if a woman calls things by their right names—who are such double-distilled fools, that they cannot see that a frank, natural, hearty, honest woman may be safely trusted, when your Miss Nancies [2] would be found kissing behind the door. Show me a cut-and-dried "proper" person of either sex, and I will show you one whose evil inclinations wait only upon opportunity. Show me a long face, and I'll invariably show you an arrant hypocrite. Show me a woman who rests the tips of her prudish fingers on a man's coat sleeve when she takes his arm, and I will show you a woman who will run away with him the first chance she gets, be he married or single.

"What have I seen?" I have seen the portrait of "Rosa Bonheur;" [3] with the short, dark hair pushed back, man-fashion, from an open, fine, spirited, and not unhandsome face; with the delicate white hand which I acknowledge feeling a most masculine inclination to "propose" for, resting upon the arm of—(dear Miss Nancies of both sexes, pray forgive me, I must say it)—resting on the arm of a tremendous great bull; which it was actually refreshing to see after the kidded dandies we had just left in Broadway. "And this is Rosa Bonheur," said I. Well, Miss Rosa, it is my opinion that you are sufficient unto yourself, and would consider a husband only in the light of an incumbrance. I am very sure that a woman who can paint such animals as yours, would have to wait till a race of men has sprung up, very different from those unchivalric wretches who stand in this warm gallery *with their hats on*, in the presence of so many ladies, not to mention your talented self. "Ah, my dear," said an old gentleman to whom I made this last remark, "the good old stock has nearly run out; you mustn't expect it, my dear." And so I don't—but if men only knew how to be gallant without being effeminate, how to be manly and yet to be tender, *wouldn't* we adore them? But, good gracious, they don't; and so I am glad that a new order of woman is arising like the Bonheurs and Hosmers, who are evidently sufficient unto themselves, both as it regards love and bread and butter; in the meantime, there are plenty of monosyllabic dolls left for those men who, being of small mental stature themselves, are desirous of finding a wife who will "look up to them."

New York Ledger
Dec. 19, 1857

THE CHILD WHOM NOBODY CAN DO ANYTHING WITH

I WONDER is it foreordained that there shall be one child in every family whom "nobody can do anything with?" Who tears around the paternal pasture with its heels in the air, looking at rules, as a colt does at fences, as good things to jump over. We all know that the poor thing must be "broken in," and all its graceful curvetings sobered down to a monotonous jog-trot; that it must be taught to bear heavy burdens, and to toil up many a steep ascent at the touch of the spur; but who that has climbed the weary height does not pass the halter round the neck of the pretty creature with a half-sigh, that its happy day of careless freedom should be soon ended?

How it bounds away from you, making you almost glad that your attempt was a failure; how lovingly your eye follows it, as it makes the swift breathless circle, and stops at a safe distance to nod you defiance. Something of all this every loving parent has felt, while trying to reduce to order the child whom "nobody can do anything with."

Geography, grammar and history seem to be put into one ear, only to go out at the other. The multiplication table might as well be written in Arabic, for any idea it conveys, or lodges, if conveyed, in the poor thing's head. Temperate, torrid, and frigid zones may all be of a temperature, for all she can remember, and her mother might have been present at the creation of the world, or at the birth of the Author of it, for aught she can chronologically be brought to see.

But look! she is tired of play, and has taken up her pencil to draw; she has had no instruction; but peep over her shoulder and follow her pencil; there is the true artist touch in that little sketch, though she does not know it—a freedom, a boldness which teaching may regulate, never impart. Now she is tired of drawing, and takes up a volume of poems, far beyond the comprehension, one would think, of a child of her years, and though she often miscalls a word, and knows little and cares less about commas and semi-colons, yet not the finest touch of humor or pathos escapes her, and the poet would be lucky, were he always sure of so appreciative a reader. She might tell you that France was bounded south by the Gulf of Mexico, but you yourself could not criticise Dickens or Thackeray with more discrimination.

Down goes the book, and she is on the tips of her toes pirouetting. She has never seen a dancing-school, nor need she; perfectly modeled machinery cannot but move harmoniously; she does not know, as she floats about, that she is an animated poem. Now she is tired of dancing, and she throws herself into an old arm-chair, in an attitude an artist might copy, and commences to sing; she is ignorant of quavers, crotchets and semi-breves, of tenors, baritones and sopranos, and yet you, who have heard them with rapturous encores, stop to listen to her simple melody.

Now she is down in the kitchen playing cook; she turns a beef-steak as if she had been brought up in a restaurant, and washes dishes for fun, as if it had been always sober earnest; singing, dancing and drawing the cook's portrait at intervals, and all equally well done.

Now send that child to any school in the land, where "Moral Science" is hammered remorselessly and uselessly into curly heads, and she would be pronounced an incorrigible dunce. Idiotically stupid parrot-girls would ride over her shrinking, sensitive shame-facedness, rough-shod. She would be kept after school, kept in during recess, and have a discouraging list of bad recitation marks as long as Long Island; get a crooked spine, grow ashamed of throwing snow-balls, have a chronic headache, and an incurable disgust of teachers and schools, as well she might.

She is like a wild rose, creeping here, climbing there, blossoming where you least expect it, on some rough stone wall or gnarled trunk, at its own free, graceful will. You may dig it up and transplant it into your formal garden if you like, but you would never know it more for the luxuriant wild-rose, this "child whom nobody can do anything with."

Some who read this may ask, and properly, is such a child never to know the restraint of rule? I would be the last to answer in the negative, nor (and here it seems to me the great agony of outraged childhood comes in) would I have parents or teachers stretch or dwarf children of all sorts, sizes and capacities, on the same narrow Procrustean bed of scholastic or parental rule. No farmer plants his celery and potatoes in the same spot, and expects it to bear good fruit. Some vegetables he shields from the rude touch, the rough wind, the blazing sun; he knows that each requires different and appropriate nurture, according to its capacities. Should they who have the care of the immortal be less wise?

"You have too much imagination, you should try to crush it out," was said many years ago to the writer, in her school-days, by one who should have known that "He who seeth the end from the beginning," bestows *no* faculty to be "crushed out;" that this very faculty it is which has placed the writer, at this moment, beyond the necessity of singing, like so many of her sex, the weary "Song of the Shirt."[1]

New York Ledger
Jan. 23, 1858

WHAT CAME OF A VIOLET

BEFORE ME lies a little violet, the forerunner of spring, with a sweet, faint, delicate perfume like a baby's breath. It should give me a joy, and yet my tears are dropping on its purple leaves.

Why? Has life been such a holyday to you, that your heart never grew sick at a perfume or a well-remembered song hummed beneath your window, or a form, or a face, which was, and yet was not, which mockingly touched a chord that for years you had carefully covered over, every vibration of which was torture unutterable? Have you never rushed franticly into a crowd—somewhere, anywhere to be rid of yourself? Did you never laugh and talk so incessantly and so gaily, that your listeners asked wonderingly and reproachfully, "Does she ever *think?*" Did you ever walk till your feet tottered beneath you, and still press on, as if urged by some invisible, irresistible power? Did you never listen to the tick—tick—of your watch, night after night, with dilated eyes that would not close, with limbs so weary that you could not change your posture, and lips so parched you could not even cry, God help me, and your brain one vast workshop, where memory was forging racks, and chains, and screws, and trying their strength on every quivering nerve? Did you never hail the first streak of dawn, as an angel whom you implored to lay a cool hand on your brow, and bring you peace or oblivion? and did you never see that day's sun set in clouds, like its predecessors, and the stars come forth one by one, with searching eyes, staring into the windows of your soul with a free, bold gaze, that irritated and maddened you?

You never did? Well, then, how can you understand why I shed tears over a violet? Ask your Maker that it may be a long day before sorrow brings you such knowledge, and if you have a child, and that child a girl, whose heritage is your intense nature, ask Him to take the cup of life from her lips ere she prays to have it done, ere the fair things of earth shrivel away before her eyes like a scroll.

Poor little violet, live out thy day. I needs must love thee; I know this was not the story nature told thee to tell me, and yet it will never be an old tale while warm hearts beat, and life's pain is more than life's pleasure.

Blessed is that woman whom a new bonnet or a new dress can satisfy, who can contemplate her diamond rings, and not know a wish ungratified, who leaves reflections to her mirror, and is never reminded of her heart save by her corset-lacings.

New York Ledger
May 8, 1858

A LAW MORE NICE THAN JUST

HERE I have been sitting twiddling the morning paper between my fingers this half hour, reflecting upon the following paragraph in it: "Emma Wilson was arrested yesterday for wearing man's apparel."[1] Now, why this should be an actionable offense is past my finding out, or where's the harm in it, I am as much at a loss to see. Think of the old maids (and weep) who have to stay at home evening after evening, when, if they provided themselves with a coat, pants and hat, they might go abroad, instead of sitting there with their noses flattened against the window-pane, looking vainly for "the Coming Man." Think of the married women who stay at home after their day's toil is done, waiting wearily for their thoughtless, truant husbands, when they might be taking the much needed independent walk in trousers, which custom forbids to petticoats. And this, I fancy, may be the secret of this famous law—who knows? It *wouldn't* be pleasant for some of them to be surprised by a touch on the shoulder from some dapper young fellow, whose familiar treble voice belied his corduroys. That's it, now. What a fool I was not to think of it—not to remember that men who make the laws, make them to meet all these little emergencies.

Everybody knows what an everlasting drizzle of rain we have had lately, but nobody but a woman, and a woman who lives on fresh air and out-door exercise, knows the thraldom of taking her daily walk through a three weeks' rain, with skirts to hold up, and umbrella to hold down, and puddles to skip over, and gutters to walk round, and all the time in a fright lest, in an unguarded moment, her calves should become visible to some one of those rainy-day philanthropists who are interested in the public study of female anatomy.

One evening, after a long rainy day of scribbling, when my nerves were in double-twisted knots, and I felt as if myriads of little ants were leisurely traveling over me, and all for want of the walk which is my daily salvation, I stood at the window, looking at the slanting, persistent rain, and took my resolve: "*I'll do it*," said I, audibly, planting my slipper upon the carpet. "Do what?" asked Mr. Fern, looking up from a big book. "Put on a suit of your clothes and take a tramp with you," was the answer. "You dare not," was the rejoinder; "you are a little coward, only saucy on paper." It was the work of a moment, with such a challenge, to fly up stairs and overhaul my philosopher's wardrobe. Of course we had fun. Tailors must be a stingy set, I remarked, to be so sparing of their cloth, as I struggled into a pair of their handiwork, undeterred by the vociferous laughter of the wretch who had solemnly vowed to "cherish me" through all my tribulations. "Upon my word, everything seems to be narrow where it ought to be broad, and the waist of this coat might be made for a hogshead; and, ugh! this shirt collar is cutting my ears off, and you have not a decent cravat in the whole lot, and your vests are frights, and what am I to do with my hair?" Still no reply from Mr. Fern, who lay on the floor, faintly ejaculating, between his fits of laughter, "Oh, my! by Jove!—oh! by Jupiter!"

Was that to hinder me? Of course not. Strings and pins, women's never-failing resort, soon brought broadcloth and kerseymere to terms. I parted my hair on one side, rolled it under, and then secured it with hair-pins; chose the best fitting coat, and cap-ping the climax with one of those soft, cosy hats, looked in the glass, where I beheld the very fac-simile of a certain musical gentleman, whose photograph hangs this minute in Brady's entry.[2]

Well, Mr. Fern seized his hat, and out we went together. "Fanny," said he, "you must not take my arm; you are a fellow." "True," said I. "I forgot; and you must not help me over puddles, as you did just now, and do, for mercy's sake, stop laughing. There, there goes your hat—I mean *my* hat; confound the wind! and down comes my hair; lucky 'tis dark, isn't it?" But oh, the delicious freedom of that walk; after we were well started! No skirts to hold up, or to draggle their wet folds against my ankles; no stifling vail flapping in my face, and blinding my eyes; no umbrella to turn inside out, but instead, the cool rain driving slap into my face, and the resurrectionized blood coursing through my veins, and tingling in my cheeks. To be sure, Mr. Fern occasionally loitered behind, and leaned up against the side of a house to enjoy a little private "guffaw," and I could now and then hear a gasping "Oh, Fanny! Oh, my!" but none of these things moved me, and if I don't have a nicely-fitting suit of my own to wear rainy evenings, it is because—well, there *are* difficulties in the way. Who's the best tailor?

Now, if any male or female Miss Nancy who reads this feels shocked, let 'em! Any woman who likes, may stay at home during a three weeks' rain, till her skin looks like parchment, and her eyes like those of a dead fish, or she may go out and get a consumption dragging round wet petticoats; I won't—I positively declare I won't. I shall begin *evenings* when *that* suit is made, and take private walking lessons with Mr. Fern, and they who choose may crook their backs at home for fashion, and then send for the doctor to straighten them; I prefer to patronize my shoe-maker and tailor. I've as good a right to preserve the healthy body God gave me, as if I were not a woman.

New York Ledger
July 10, 1858

A LAW MORE NICE THAN JUST

Number II

AFTER ALL, having tried it I affirm, that nothing reconciles a woman quicker to her feminity, than an experiment in male apparel, although I still maintain that she should not be forbidden by law to adopt it when necessity requires; at least, not till the practice is amended by which a female clerk, who performs her duty equally well with a male clerk, receives less salary, simply because she is a woman.

To have to jump on to the cars when in motion, and scramble yourself on to the platform as best you may without a helping hand; to be nudged roughly in the ribs by the conductor with, "your fare, sir?" to have your pretty little toes trod on, and no healing "beg your pardon," applied to the smart; to have all those nice-looking men who used to make you such crushing bows, and give you such insinuating smiles, pass you without the slightest interest in your coat tails, and perhaps push you against the wall or into the gutter, with a word tabooed by the clergy. In fine, to dispense with all those delicious little politenesses, (for men are great bears to each other,) to which one has been accustomed, and yet feel no inclination to take advantage of one's corduroys and secure an equivalent by making interest with the "fair sex," stale to you as a thrice-told tale. Isn't *that* a situation?

To be subject to the promptings of that unstifleable feminine desire for adornment, which is right and lovely within proper limits, and yet have no field for your operations. To have to conceal your silken hair, and yet be forbidden a becoming moustache, or whiskers, or beard—(all hail beards, I say!). To choke up your nice throat with a disguising cravat; to hide your bust (I trust no Miss Nancy is blushing) under a baggy vest. To have nobody ask you to ice cream, and yet be forbidden, by your horrible disgust of tobacco, to smoke. To have a gentleman ask you "the time sir?" when you are new to the geography of your watch-pocket. To accede to an invitation to test your "heft," by sitting down in one of those street-weighing chairs, and have one of the male bystanders, taking hold of your foot, remark, "Halloo, sir, you must not rest these upon the ground while you are being weighed;" and go grinning away in your coat-sleeve at your truly feminine faux pas.

And yet—and yet—to be able to step over the ferry-boat chain when you are in a distracted hurry, like any other fellow, without waiting for that tedious unhooking process, and quietly to enjoy your triumph over scores of impatient-waiting crushed petticoats behind you; to taste that nice lager beer "on draught;" to pick up contraband bits of science in a Medical Museum, forbidden to crinoline, and hold conversations with intelligent men, who supposing you to be a man, consequently talk sense to you. That is worth while.

Take it all in all, though, I thank the gods I am a woman. I had rather be loved than make love; though I could beat the makers of it, out and out, if I did not think it my duty to refrain out of regard to their feelings, and the final disappointment of the deluded women! But—oh, dear, I want to do such a quantity of "improper" things, that there is not the slightest real harm in doing. I want to see and know a thousand things which are forbidden to flounces—custom only can tell why—I can't. I want the free use of my ankles, for this summer at least, to take a journey; I want to climb and wade, and tramp about, without giving a thought to my clothes; without carrying about with me a long procession of trunks and boxes, which are the inevitable penalty of feminity as at present appareled. I hate a Bloomer, such as we have seen—words are weak to say how much; I hate myself as much in a man's dress; and yet I want to run my fingers through my cropped hair some fine morning without the bore of dressing it; put on some sort of loose blouse affair—it must be pretty, though—and a pair of Turkish trousers—*not* Bloomers—and a cap, or hat—and start; nary a trunk—"nary" a bandbox. Wouldn't that be fine? But propriety scowls and says, "ain't you ashamed of yourself, Fanny Fern?" *Yes, I am,* Miss Nancy. I *am* ashamed of myself, that I haven't the courage to carry out what would be so eminently convenient, and right, and proper under the circumstances. I am ashamed of myself that I sit like a fool on the piazza of some hotel every season, gazing at some distant mountain, which every pulse and muscle of my body, and every faculty of my soul, are urging me to climb, that I may "see the kingdoms of the earth and the glory of them." I *am* ashamed of myself that you, Miss Nancy, with your uplifted forefinger and your pursed-up mouth, should keep me out of a dress in which only I can hope to do such things. Can't I make a compromise with you, Miss Nancy? for I'm getting restless, as these lovely summer days pass on. I'd write you such long accounts of beautiful things, Miss Nancy—things which God made for female as well as male eyes to see; and I should come home so strong and healthy, Miss Nancy—a freckle or two, perhaps—but who cares? O-h-n-o-w, Miss Nancy, d-o—Pshaw! you cross old termagant! May Lucifer fly away wid ye.

New York Ledger
July 17, 1858

BLACKWELL'S ISLAND

PRIOR to visiting Blackwell's Island,[1] my ideas of that place were very forlorn and small-pox-y. It makes very little difference, to be sure, to a man, or a woman, shut up in a cell eight feet by four, how lovely are the out-door surroundings; how blue the river that plashes against the garden wall below, flecked with white sails, and alive with gay pleasure-seekers, whose merry laugh has no monotone of sadness, that the convict wears the badge of degradation; and yet, after all, one involuntarily says to one's self, so instinctively do we turn to the cheerful side, I am glad they are located on this lovely island. Do you shrug your shoulders, Sir Cynic, and number over the crimes they have committed? Are *your* crimes against society less, that they are written down only in God's book of remembrance? Are *you* less guilty that you have been politic enough to commit only those that a short-sighted, unequal human law sanctions? Shall I pity these poor wrecks of humanity less, because they are so recklessly self-wrecked? because they turn away from my pity? Before I come to this, I must know, as their Maker knows, what evil influences have encircled their cradles. How many times, when their stomachs have been empty, some full-fed, whining disciple, has presented them with a Bible or a Tract, saying, "Be ye warmed and filled." I must know how often, when their feet have tried to climb the narrow, up-hill path of right, the eyes that have watched, have watched only for their halting; never noting, as God notes, the steps that did *not* slip—never holding out the strong right hand of help when the devil with a full larder was tugging furiously at their skirts to pull them backward; but only saying "I told you so," when he, laughing at your pharisaical stupidity, succeeded.

I must go a great way back of those hard, defiant faces, where hate of their kind seems indelibly burnt in; back—back—to the soft blue sky of infancy, overclouded before the little one had strength to contend with the flashing lightning and pealing thunder of misfortune and poverty which stunned and blinded his moral perceptions. I cannot see that mournful procession of men, filing off into those dark cells, none too dark, none too narrow, alas! to admit troops of devils, without wishing that some white-winged angel might enter too; and when their shining eyeballs peer at my retreating figure through the gratings, my heart shrieks out in its pain—oh! believe that there is pity here—only pity; and I hate the bolts and bars, and I say this is *not* the way to make bad men good; or, at least if it be, these convicts should not, when discharged, be thrust out loose into the world with empty pockets, and a bad name, to earn a speedy "through-ticket" back again. I say, if this *be* the way, let humanity not stop here, but take one noble step forward, and when she knocks off the convict's fetters, and lands him on the opposite shore, let her not turn her back and leave him there as if her duty were done; but let her *there* erect a noble institution where he can find a *kind* welcome and *instant* employment; before temptation, joining hands with his necessities, plunge him again headlong into the gulf of sin.

And here seems to me to be the loose screw in these institutions; admirably managed as many of them are, according to the prevalent ideas on the subject. You may tell me that I am a woman, and know nothing about it; and I tell you that I *want* to know. I tell you, that I don't believe the way to restore a man's lost self-respect is to degrade him before his fellow-creatures; to brand him, and chain him, and poke him up to show his points, like a hyena in a menagerie. No wonder that he growls at you, and grows vicious; no wonder that he eats the food you thrust between the bars of his cage with gnashing teeth, and a vow to take it out of the world somehow, when he gets out; no wonder that he thinks the Bible you place in his cell a humbug, and God a myth. I would have you startle up his self-respect by placing him in a position to show that you trusted him; I would have you give him something to hold in charge, for which he is in honor responsible; appeal to his *better* feelings, or if they smoulder almost to extinction, fan them into a flame for him out of that remnant of God's image which the vilest can never wholly destroy. *Anything but shutting a man up with hell in his heart to make him good.* The devils may well chuckle at it. And above all, tear down that taunting inscription over the prison-hall door at Blackwell's Island—"The way of transgressors is hard"—and place instead of it, "Neither do I condemn thee; go and sin no more."

New York Ledger
Aug. 14, 1858

BLACKWELL'S ISLAND NO. 3

YOU CAN STEP ASIDE, Mrs. Grundy;[1] what I am about to write is not for your over-fastidious ear. *You*, who take by the hand the polished *roué*, and welcome him with a sweet smile into the parlor where sit your young, trusting daughters; you, who "have no business with his private life, so long as his manners are gentlemanly;" you who, while saying this, turn away with bitter, unwomanly words from his penitent, writhing victim. I ask no leave of *you* to speak of the wretched girls picked out of the gutters of New York streets, to inhabit those cells at Blackwell's Island. I speak not to *you* of what was tugging at my heartstrings as I saw them, that beautiful summer afternoon, file in, two by two, to their meals, followed by a man carrying a cowhide in his hand, by way of reminder; all this would not interest you; but when you tell me that these women are not to be named to ears polite, that our sons and our daughters should grow up ignorant of their existence, I stop my ears. As if they could, or did! As if they can take a step in the public streets without being jostled or addressed by them, or pained by their passing ribaldry; as if they could return from a party or concert at night, without meeting droves of them; as if they could, even in broad daylight, sit down to an ice-cream without having one for a *vis-à-vis*. As if they could ride in a car or omnibus, or cross in a ferry-boat, or go to a watering-place, without being unmistakably confronted by them. No, Mrs. Grundy; you know all this as well as I do. You would push them "anywhere out of the world," as unfit to live, as unfit to die; *they*, the weaker party, while their partners in sin, for whom you claim greater mental superiority, and who, by your own finding, should be much better able to learn and *to teach* the lesson of self-control—to them you extend perfect absolution. Most consistent Mrs. Grundy, get out of my way while I say what I was going to, without fear or favor of yours.

If I believed, as legislators, and others with whom I have talked on this subject, pretend to believe, they best know why, that God ever made one of those girls for the life they lead, for this in plain Saxon is what their talk amounts to, I should curse Him. If I could temporize as they do about it, as a "necessary evil," and "always has been, and always will be," and (then add this beautiful tribute to manhood) "that pure women would not be safe were it not so"—and all the other budget of excuses which this sin makes to cover its deformity—I would forswear my manhood.

You say their intellects are small, they are mere animals, naturally coarse and grovelling. Answer me this—are they, or are they not *immortal?* Decide the question whether *this* life is to be *all* to them. Decide before you shoulder the responsibility of such a girl's future. Granted she has only *this* life. God knows how much misery may be crowded into that. But you say, "Bless your soul, why do you talk to *me?* I have nothing to do with it; I am as virtuous as St. Paul." St. Paul was a bachelor, and of course is not my favorite apostle; but waiving that, I answer, you *have* something to do with it when you talk thus, and throw your influence on the wrong side. No matter how outwardly correct your past life may have been, if you *really believe* what you say, I would not give a fig for your virtue if temptation and opportunity favored; and if you talk so for talk's sake, and do not believe it, you had better "tarry at Jericho till your beard be grown."

But you say to me, "Oh, you don't know anything about it; men are differently constituted from women; woman's sphere is home." That don't suspend the laws of her being. That don't make it that she don't need sympathy and appreciation. That don't make it that she is never weary and needs amusement to restore her. Fudge. I believe in no difference that makes this distinction. Women lead, most of them, lives of unbroken monotony, and have much more need of exhilarating influences than men, whose life is out of doors in the breathing, active world. Don't tell me of shoemakers at their lasts, and tailors at their needles. Do either ever have to lay down their customers' coats and shoes fifty times a day, and wonder when the day is over why their work is *not* done, though they have struggled through fire and water to finish it? Do not both tailor and shoemaker have at least the variation of a walk to or from the shop to their meals? Do not their customers talk their beloved politics to them while they stitch, and do not their "confrères" run for a bottle of ale and crack merry jokes with them as their work progresses? Sirs! if monotony is to be avoided in man's life as injurious, if "variety" and exhilaration must always be the spice to his pursuits, how much more must it be necessary to a sensitively organized woman? If home is not sufficient (and I will persist that any *industrious*, *virtuous*, *unambitious* man, may have a home if he chooses); if home is not sufficient for him, why should it suffice for her? whose work is never done—who can have literally *no* such thing as system (and here's where a mother's discouragement comes in), while her babes are in their infancy; who often says to herself at night, though she would not for worlds part with one of them, "I can't tell what I have accomplished to-day, and yet I have not been idle a minute;" and day after day passes on in this way, and perhaps for weeks she does not pass the threshold for a breath of air, and yet men talk of "monotony!" and being "differently constituted," and needing amusement and exhilaration; and "business" is the broad mantle which it is not always safe for a wife to lift. I have no faith in putting women in a pound, that men may trample down the clover in a forty-acre lot. But enough for that transparent excuse.

The great Law-giver made no distinction of sex, as far as I can find out, when he promulgated the seventh commandment, nor should we. You tell me "society makes a difference;" more shame to it—more shame to the women who help to perpetuate it. You tell me that infidelity on the wife's part involves an unjust claim upon the husband and provider; and I ask you, on the other hand, if a good and virtuous wife has not a right to expect *healthy* children?

Let both be equally pure; let every man look upon every woman, whatsoever her rank or condition, as a sister whom his manhood is bound to protect, even, if need be, against herself, and let every woman turn the cold shoulder to any man of her acquaintance, how polished soever he may be, who would degrade her sex. Then this vexed question would be settled; there would be no such libels upon womanhood as I saw at Blackwell's Island, driven in droves to their cells. No more human traffic in those gilded palaces, which our children must not hear mentioned, forsooth! though their very fathers may help to support them, and which our tender-hearted legislators "can't see their way clear about." Then our beautiful rivers would no longer toss upon our island shores the "dead bodies of unfortunate young females."

New York Ledger
Aug. 28, 1858

THE "COMING" WOMAN

MEN OFTEN SAY, "When *I* marry, my wife must be this, that and the other," enumerating all physical, mental, and moral perfections. One cannot but smile to look at the men who say these things; smile to think of the equivalent they will bring for all the amiability, beauty, health, intellectuality, domesticity, and faithfulness they so modestly require; smile to think of the perforated hearts, damaged morals, broken-down constitutions, and irritable tempers, which the bright, pure, innocent girl is to receive with her wedding ring. If one half the girls knew the previous life of the men they marry, the list of old maids would be wonderfully increased.

Doubted? Well, if there is room for a doubt now, thank God the "coming" woman's Alpha and Omega will not be matrimony. *She* will not of necessity sour into a pink-nosed old maid, or throw herself at any rickety old shell of humanity, whose clothes are as much out of repair as his morals. No, the future man will have to "step lively;" *this* wife is not to be had for the whistling. He will have a long canter round the pasture for her, and then she will leap the fence and leave him limping on the ground. Thick-soled boots and skating are coming in, and "nerves," novels and sentiment (by consequence) are going out. The coming woman, as I see her, is not to throw aside her needle; neither is she to sit embroidering worsted dogs and cats, or singing doubtful love ditties, and rolling up her eyes to "the chaste moon."

Heaven forbid she should stamp round with a cigar in her mouth, elbowing her fellows, and puffing smoke in their faces; or stand on the free-love platform, *public or private—call it by what specious name you will*—wooing men who, low as they may have sunk in their own self-respect, would die before they would introduce her to the unsullied sister who shared their cradle.

Heaven forbid the coming woman should not have warm blood in her veins, quick to rush to her cheek, or tingle at her fingers' ends when her heart is astir. No, the coming woman shall be no cold, angular, flat-chested, narrow-shouldered, skimpy sharp-visaged Betsey, but she shall be a bright-eyed, full-chested, broad-shouldered, large-souled, intellectual being; able to walk, able to eat, able to fulfill her maternal destiny, and able—if it so please God—to go to her grave happy, self-poised and serene, though unwedded.

New York Ledger
Feb. 12, 1859

AMIABLE CREATURES

AMIABLE CREATURES are the majority of women—to each other; charitable—above all things *charitable!*[1] Always ready to acknowledge each other's beauty, or grace, or talent. Never sneer down a sister woman, or pay her a patronizing compliment with the finale of the inevitable—"*but.*" Never run the cool, impertinent eye of calculation over her dress, noting the cost of each article, and summing up the amount in a contemptuous toss, whether it amounts to fifty cents or five hundred dollars, more likely when it is the latter! Never say to a gentleman who praises a lady, what a pity she squints! Never say of an authoress, oh yes—she has talent, but *I* prefer the domestic virtues; as if a combination of the two were necessarily impossible, or as if the speaker had the personal knowledge which qualified her to pronounce on that individual case.

Well-bred, too, are women to sister woman.—Never discuss the color of her hair, or the style of its arrangement, her smile, her gait, so that she can hear every word of it. Never take it for granted that she is making a dead-set at a man, to whom she is only replying—"Very well, I thank you, sir." Never sit in church and stare her out of countenance, while mentally taking her measure, or nudge some one to look at her, while recapitulating within ear-shot all the contemptible gossip which weak-minded, empty-headed women are so fond of retailing.

Now just let a dear woman visit you. Don't you *know* that her eyes are peering into every corner and crevice of your house all the while she is "*dear*"-ing and "*sweet*"-ing you? Don't you know that her lynx eyes are on the carpet for possible spots, or mismatched roses? Don't she touch her fingers to the furniture for stray particles of dust? Don't she hold her tumblers up to the light, and examine microscopically the quality of your table-cloths and napkins, and improvise an errand into your kitchen to inspect your culinary arrangements, to the infinite disgust of Bridget? Don't she follow you like a spectre all over the house, till you are as nervous as a cat in a cupboard? Don't she sit down opposite you for dreary hours, with folded hands, and that horseleech—"now-talk-to-me" air—which quenches all your vitality—and sets you gaping, as inevitably as a minister's "*seventeenthly.*"

Ah, the children! How could I forget the little children? *I clasp the hand of universal woman on that;* Heaven knows I don't want to misrepresent them. And after all, do I ever allow anybody to abuse them but me? Never!

New York Ledger
March 12, 1859

A WHISPER TO MOTHERS

SOME MOTHERS seem unwilling to recognize a child's individuality. "She is such a strange child—so different from other children," a mother remarked in my hearing, with a sigh of discontent; as if all children should be made after one model; as if one of the greatest charms of life were not individuality; as if one of the dreariest, and weariest, and least improving, and most stagnating things in the world, were not a family or neighborhood which was only a mutual echo and re-echo.

"Different from other children!" Well—*let her be different;* you can't help it if you would—you ought not if you could. It is not your mission, or that of any parent, to crush out this or that faculty or bias which is God-implanted for wise purposes. You are only to modify and direct such by judicious counsel. A child who thinks for itself, prefers waiting upon itself, and is naturally self-sustained, is of course much more trouble than a heavy-headed child, who "stays put" wherever and however you choose to "dump" him down; but it is useless to ask which, with equally good training, will be the most efficient worker in the great life-field. Suppose he *does* question your opinions occasionally, don't be in a hurry to call it "impertinence;" don't be too lazy or too dignified to argue the matter with him; thank God rather, that his faculties are wide awake and active. Nor does it necessarily follow that such a child must be contumacious or disobedient. Such a nature, however, should be tenderly dealt with. Firm yet *gentle* words—never injustice or harsh usage. You may tell such a child to "hold its tongue" when it corners you in an argument, often, without any intentional disrespect, but you cannot prevent its thinking. It should not follow that a young person must, as a matter of course, though they mostly do, adopt the parental religious creed. Some parents I have known unwise enough to insist upon this. A forced faith for the wear and tear of life's trials, is but a broken reed to lean upon. On these subjects talk yourself; let your child talk, and then let him, like yourself, be free to think and choose, when this is done.

Out of twenty violets in a garden, you shall not find any two alike, but this does not displease you. One is a royal purple, another a light lilac; one flecked with little bright golden spots, another shaded off with different tints of the same violet color, with a delicacy no artist could improve. You plant them, and let them all grow and develop according to their nature, now and then plucking off a dead leaf, now loosening the earth about the roots, or watering or giving it shade or sunshine, as the case may be, but you don't try to erase the delicate tints upon its leaves and substitute others which you fancy are better. No human fingers could recreate what you would mar—you know that; so you bend over it lovingly, and let it nod to the breeze, and bend pliantly to the shower, or lift its sweet face, when the sun shines out, and through all its various changes you do not sigh for monotony. So, when I see a family of children, I like the mother's blue eyes reproduced, and the father's black eyes. I like the waving, sunny locks, and the light brown, and the raven; I like the peach-blossom skin, and the gipsy olive, round the same hearthstone, all rocked in the same cradle. Each is beautiful of its kind; the variety pleases me. Just so I like diversity in regard to temperament and mental faculties. Each have their merits; Heaven forbid they should be rolled and swathed up like mental mummies, bolt upright, rigid, and fearfully repeated; no collision of mind to strike out new ideas, no progress, no improvement. Surely this is not the age for that.

New York Ledger
Apr. 16, 1859

ALL ABOUT LOVERS

NOTHING LIKE the old-fashioned long "engagements," say we. Then you have a chance to find out something about a young man before marriage. Now-a-days matrimony follows so close upon the heels of "an offer," that it is no wonder our young people have a deal of sad thinking to do afterward. There are a thousand little things in daily intercourse of any duration, which are constantly resolving themselves into tests of character; slight they may be, but very significant. Some forlorn old lady must have an escort home of a cold evening; she walks slow, and tells the same story many times: see how your lover comports himself under this. He is asked to read aloud to the home circle, some book which he has already perused in private, or some one in which he is not at all interested: watch him then. Notice, also, if he invariably takes the most comfortable chair in the room, "never thinking" to offer it to a person who may enter till he or she is already seated. Invite him to carve for you at table. Give him a letter to drop in the post-office, and find out if it ever leaves that grave—his pocket. Open and read his favorite newspaper before *he* gets a chance to do so. Mislay his cigar-case. Lose his cane. Sit *accidentally* on his new beaver. Praise another man's coat or cravat. Differ from him in a favorite opinion. Put a spoonful of gravy on his meat instead of his potatoes. Ah, you may laugh! But just try him in these ways, and see how he will wear; for it is not the great things of this life over which we mortals stumble. A rock we walk around; a mountain we cross: *it is the unobserved, unexpected, unlooked-for little sticks and pebbles which cause us to halt on life's journey*.

New York Ledger
July 30, 1859

INDEPENDENCE

"*FOURTH OF JULY*." Well—I don't feel patriotic. Perhaps I might if they would stop that deafening racket. Washington was very well, if he *couldn't* spell, and I'm glad we are all free; but as a woman—I shouldn't know it, didn't some orator tell me. Can I go out of an evening without a hat at my side? Can I go out with one on my head without danger of a station-house? Can I clap my hands at some public speaker when I am nearly bursting with delight? Can I signify the contrary when my hair stands on end with vexation? Can I stand up in the cars "like a gentleman" without being immediately invited "to sit down"? Can I get into an omnibus without having my sixpence taken from my hand and given to the driver? Can I cross Broadway without having a policeman tackled to my helpless elbow?

Can I go to see anything *pleasant*, like an execution or a dissection? Can I drive that splendid "Lantern,"[1] distancing—like his owner—all competitors? Can I have the nomination for "Governor of Vermont," like our other contributor, John G. Saxe? Can I be a Senator, that I may hurry up that millennial International Copyright Law?[2] Can I *even* be President? Bah—you know I can't. "*Free*!" Humph!

New York Ledger
July 30, 1859

HOUSE-FURNISHING BY PROXY

THE IDEA of giving an upholsterer an unlimited order to furnish a house for you à-la-mode, and then cooly walking into it as you would into a great, glaring hotel! As if the *charm* of having money were not that you could gratify your own independent, personal tastes and fancies; that your eye could rest on these forms, colors, and contrasts, that you yourself particularly liked to see, instead of having a duplicate of Fitz-Fool's house round the corner crammed down your throat.

No pleasant associations with this, that, or the other thing, that you and your husband strolled into a store, at your leisure, to purchase for sheer love of its beauty, or admiration of its convenience. How, when sent home, it seemed in a sort hallowed to you for that reason: how you talked about it, and admired it, and then laughed at each other for being so foolish, and then went and did the very same thing a day or two after, and kept on doing it, till your house was full of things, every one of which had its own little, pleasant home-story for you every time you should look at it; which you did—not on state occasions, or on "receptions," (those mean, modern shifts to save gas, parlor furniture, and dry-goods,) but *all the time*, and because you *bought them to make home bright*; to be *used*, not to be locked up or tied in bags for the delectation of "company."

Now you may see whole blocks of houses of the Fitz-Fool stamp in New York; too fine for daylight, or even for use. Gloomy looking piles of brown stone, with closed blinds, enclosing pale children, piled away up in fourth-story, back nurseries, with stacks of brick chimneys for a prospect, and a cross nurse to teach them how *not* to enjoy themselves. Now, if fashion obliged me to keep an upholstery shop like these people, I'd have *my house* somewhere else. I'd have my children there too, where we need not be exiled from the parlor, or any other room in it, on account of its superb fixings. In short, I would either go without all this vulgar upholstery, or, buying it, I would be sublimely indifferent to the cost of replacing it when spoiled. I'd have nothing in the house too good for the sun, or me, to shine on; and even that should be selected by myself, or—somebody I loved as well! That is all I have to say about *that*.

New York Ledger
Dec. 10, 1859

SHALL WOMEN VOTE?

THE PRINCIPAL OBJECTION made by conservatives to their doing so, is on the score of their being thrown into rowdy company of both sexes. Admitting this necessity (though, by the way, I don't do it! because if incompetent men-voters are ruled out, it would follow incompetent women should be also), I cannot sufficiently admire the objection; when a good-looking woman, wife or sister, whom husbands and brothers allow, without a demur, to walk our public thoroughfares unattended, can scarcely do it without being jostled, and ogled at street corners, by squads of gamblers, and often times followed whole blocks, and even spoken to by well-dressed villains; when these ladies often have their toes and elbows nudged by them in omnibusses and cars, or an impertinent hand dropped on their shoulder or waist as if by accident. When two ladies, though leaning on the arm of a gentleman, cannot return from the Opera late at night, to a ferry-boat, without being insulted by the wretched of their own sex, or the rascals who make them such. I admire that, when a husband thinks it quite the thing for his wife to explore all sorts of localities, in search of articles needed for family consumption, because "he has not time to attend to it." I like that, when he coolly permits his wife and daughters to waltz at public places, with the chance male acquaintance of a week or a day. I admire that, when his serenity is undisturbed, though Tom, Dick and Harry, tear the crinoline from their backs, in the struggle to secure seats for an hour's enjoyment of the latest nine-day, New York wonder.

Pshaw! all such talk is humbug, as the men themselves very well know. We are always "dear—delicate fragile creatures," who should be immediately gagged with this sugar plum whenever we talk about that of which it is their interest to keep us ignorant. It won't do, gentlemen; the sugar-plum game is well nigh "played out." *Women will assuredly vote some day*; meanwhile the majority of them will "keep up a considerable of a thinking." The whole truth about the male creatures' dislike to it, is embodied in a remark of "Mr. Tulliver's,"[1] in a late admirable work. This gentleman, with more honesty than is usual with the sex, having admitted that from out a bunch of sisters, he selected his milk-and-water wife "*because he was not going to be told the right of things by his own fireside*!" I take particular pleasure in passing this sentiment round, because editors who have quoted largely and approvingly from this book, somehow or other, have never seemed to see *this* passage!

New York Ledger
June 30, 1860

A REASONABLE BEING

IF THERE'S ANYTHING I hate, it is "a reasonable being." Says the lazy mother to her restless child whom she has imprisoned within doors and whose active mind seeks solutions of passing remarks, "Don't bother, Tommy; do be *reasonable*, and not tease with your questions." Says the husband to his sick or overtasked wife, when she cries from mere mental or physical exhaustion, "How I hate tears; do be a reasonable being." Says the conservative father to his son, whom he would force into some profession or employment for which nature has utterly disqualified him, "Are you wiser than your father? do be a reasonable being." Says the mother to sweet sixteen, whom she would marry to a sixty-five-year old money-bag, "Think what a thing it is to have a fine establishment; do be a reasonable being."

As near as I can get at it, to be a reasonable being, is to laugh when your heart aches; it is to give confidence and receive none; it is faithfully to keep your own promises, and never mind such a trifle as having promises broken to you. It is never to have or to promulgate a dissenting opinion. It is either to be born a fool, or in lack of that to become a hypocrite, trying to become a "reasonable being."

New York Ledger
Feb. 16, 1861

A BIT OF INJUSTICE

AS A GENERAL THING there are few people who speak approbatively of a woman who has a smart business talent or capability. No matter how isolated or destitute her condition, the majority would consider it more "feminine" would she unobtrusively gather up her thimble, and, retiring into some out-of-the-way-place, gradually scoop out her coffin with it, than to develop that smart turn for business which would lift her at once out of her troubles; and which, in a man so situated, would be applauded as exceedingly praiseworthy. The most curious part of it is, that they who are loudest in their abhorrence of this "unfeminine" trait, are they who are the most intolerant of dependent female relatives. "Anywhere, out of this world," would be their reply, if applied to by the latter for a straw for the drowning. "Do something for yourself," is their advice in general terms; but, above all, you are to do it quietly, unobtrusively; in other words, die as soon as you like on sixpence a day, but don't trouble *us!* Of such cold-blooded comfort, in sight of a new-made grave, might well be born "the *smart business woman*." And, in truth, so it often is. Hands that never toiled before, grow rough with labor; eyes that have been tearless for long, happy years, drop agony over the slow lagging hours; feet that have been tenderly led and cared for, stumble as best they may in the new, rough path of self-denial. But out of this bitterness groweth sweetness. *No crust so tough as the grudged bread of dependence.* Blessed the "smart business woman" who, in a self-sustained crisis like this, after having through much tribulation reached the goal, is able to look back on the weary track and see the sweet flower of faith and trust in her kind still blooming.

New York Ledger
June 8, 1861

A VOICE FROM BEDLAM

IS MY ARTICLE for the *Ledger* ready? No, sir, it is not. With my hair standing on end, I tell you, it is NOT! Have I not been beset, since I left my bed this morning, with cook, chambermaid and sempstress? Have not butcher, baker, and grocer been tweaking that area-bell unceasingly, about matters which must be referred to my unpostponable decision? Have not whole rows of them been sitting in the kitchen sucking their thumbs, or standing on their hind legs awaiting it? Is not my head as woolly inside as out, with butter and meat, and vegetables, and—spools-and-needles! the sudden breaking of the sewing-machine, to the horror of the sempstress—and the settling up the thousand and one little matters which take up, and *must take up*, the precious morning hours, which, alas! show for nothing, and yet which no housekeeper may dodge, even with her coffin or a prospective article for the *Ledger* in sight? I don't speak in the connection of a married daughter's cook, who don't do as she "oughter," and whom I am telegraphed to run up after breakfast and Rar-ey-fy. I don't speak, when I have arisen in a heavenly and sprightly frame of mind, equal to the *Ledger*, or any of the papers which abuse it because they envy its circulation, of being after the experience above related, at ten o'clock in the morning, as exhausted as a squeezed sponge. I don't speak of my agony, after having, with much forethought on such carnal matters, laid in a store of "goodies" for several days, discovering this morning that a "surprise party," under pretense of being for my children, came in last evening while I was out, and rifled my refrigerator and—"*left their love*!" I don't speak, while I sit contemplating all this at ten o'clock in the morning, of Mr. Fern's coming down stairs, inked up to the knuckles, with three-precious-uninterrupted-hours-of-writing-the-biography-of-the-great-Zoo-Foo, and asking with uplifted inky paws of horror, in tones of innocent and tantalizing surprise, if I haven't begun writing *yet*? I don't speak of this, because man being in a primeval state of idiocy on all such matters, and being likely on account of his natural stupidity forever to remain so, one feels only sublime contempt at such imbecile queries. Nor do I speak of turning heroically away in this injured frame of mind from the sight of the tempting blue sky through my window, to gaze into a dark, clotted pool of an inkstand.

Moreover, I scorn to allude to any goneness about my belt, or any throbbing in my temples, or any disposition to kick in my heels at any miscreant of an organ-grinder under my window murdering poor Annie Laurie. I don't speak of Mr. Fern's catching up from my desk an *unanswered* invitation to "lecture on my own terms," at the Farmtown Insti*toot*; everybody knows it was very wise and judicious and humane, and just like a man, to go and pile up the agony at such a demented moment.

Also, I turn away disgusted from the Solomon who inquires majestically why I do not write at night, like the great Scriblio, who does the same through an amanuensis. I simply inquire if he thinks any husband would be pleased to have his wife spend her nights promulgating "thoughts that breathe and words that burn" for the *New York Ledger* in company with a-man-uensis? Now Mr. Fern, of course, will ask if I consider this article the thing for the public. If it is egotistical, haven't I the shining example of the exquisite Adolphus Fitz-Curly, well known in the field of letters, who informs us every week how often his horse sneezes, or his dog Towzer takes a nap? Am I to presume to be better than my betters? Besides, haven't I been told from my youth up, which, by the way, is a long distance, that it was an "*indulgent* public," and was there ever a bigger lie?

New York Ledger
Oct. 26, 1861

STORY READING

AT A CERTAIN AGE, children of both sexes delight in stories. It is as natural, as it is for them to skip, run and jump, instead of walking at the staid pace of their grandparents. Now some parents, very well meaning ones too, think they do a wise thing when they deny this most innocent craving, any legitimate outlet. They wish to cultivate, they say, "a taste for solid reading." They might as well begin to feed a new-born baby on meat, lest nursing should vitiate its desire for it. The taste for meat will come when the child has teeth to chew it; so will the taste for "solid reading" as the mind matures—*i.e.*, if it is not made to hate it, by having it forced violently upon its attention during the story-loving period. That "there is a time for all things," is truer of nothing more, than of this. Better far that parents should admit it, and *wisely* indulge it, than, by a too severe repression, give occasion for *stealthy* promiscuous reading.

New York Ledger
Apr. 26, 1862

GOSSIPS, AND HOW THEY ARE MADE

I AM INCLINED TO THINK that gossips, male and female, do not *begin* by being malicious. This is the way it happens. Their minds being uninformed and uncultivated, and their own lives meagre and barren of interest, they naturally fall to watching those about them, to see if they cannot extract a little pleasurable excitement from the contemplation of their neighbors. This taste "grows by what it feeds on;" and lacking the element of the marvellous, at any time, what easier than for them to supply it and make the story a round one, at any sacrifice. In proportion as the mind is cultivated, *things*, not persons, engage its attention. Had women as many resources as men, female gossips would be scarce in proportion.

Mothers, not only for this, but for other obvious reasons, should early cultivate a taste for *reading* in their daughters. A young girl has then a resource against the corroding rust of unemployed hours, not only in youth but in her old age, if unsurrounded by domestic ties. She need not then be agape for every bit of scandal, or employ her time running about to collect material for its manufacture. She can select her company *then* of the best, and dismiss them and recall them at her pleasure, without offence. Above all, she will be dignified, and be independent of excitement and vacuity.

New York Ledger
Aug. 30, 1862

NEW ENGLAND

NEW ENGLAND, all hail to thy peerless thrift! Thou art cranky and crotchety; thou art "sot," uncommon "sot," in thy ways, owing doubtless to the amiable sediment of English blood in thy veins. Thou wilt not be cheated in a bargain, even by thy best friend; but, in the meantime, that enableth thy large heart to give handsomely when charity knocks at thy door. Thy pronunciation may be peculiar, but, in the meantime, what thou dost not know, and cannot do, is rarely worth knowing or doing. Thou never hast marble, and silver, and plate glass, and statuary, in thy show-parlors, and shabby belongings where the world does not penetrate. Thou hast not stuccoed walls, with big cracks in them, or anything in thy domiciles hanging as it were by the eyelids. Every nail is driven so that it will stay; every hinge hung so that it will work thoroughly. Every bolt and key and lock perform their duty like a martinet, so long as a piece of them endures. If thou hast a garden, be it only a square foot, it is made the most of with its "long *saace*," and "short *saace*," and "wimmin's notions," in the shape of flowers and caraway seed, to chew on Sunday, when the minister gets as far as "seventeenthly," and carnal nature will fondly recur to the waiting pot of baked beans in the kitchen oven. O! New England, here could I shed salt tears at the thought of thy baked beans, for Gotham[1] knows them not. Alluding to that edible, I am met with a pitying sneer, accompanied with that dread word to snobs—"*provincial!*" It is ever thus, my peerless, with the envy which cannot attain to the perfection it derides. For you should see, my thrifty New England, the watery, white-livered, tasteless, swimmy, sticky poultice which Gotham christens "baked beans." My soul revolts at it. It is an unfeeling, wretched mockery of the rich, brown, crispy, succulent contents of that "platter"—yes, *platter*—I will say it!—which erst delighted my eyes in the days when I swallowed the Catechism without a question as to its infallibility. The flavor of the beans "haunts memory still;" but as to the Catechism, the world is progressing, and I am not one to put a drag on its wheels, believing that

Truth is sure
And will endure,

and it is best to let "natur" caper, especially as you can't help it; and after the dust it has kicked up has cleared away, we shall see what we shall see, be it wheat or chaff. Beside, the most conservative must admit, that though Noah's Ark was excellent for the flood, the "Great Eastern" is an improvement on it; and *'tisn't* pretty, *so they say who oftenest practise it!* to stand with the Bible in your hand in 1862, and clamor for a private latch-key to heaven.

But I have wandered from my baked beans. I want some. Some New England baked beans. Some of "mother's beans." But, alas, mother's oven is fast disappearing. Mother's oven, where the beans stayed in all night, with the brown bread. Alas! it has given way to new-fangled "ranges," which "don't know beans." Excuse the vulgarity of the expression, but in such a cause I shan't stand for trifles. If you want rose-leaf sentimental-refinement, together with creamy patriotism, you may look in the columns of the Whip-Syllabub-Family-Visitor. This is a digression.

When I started for a New England tour, it was my intention to get some of those beans; but the hotels there are getting so "genteel" with their paper-pantalettes on the roast-chicken's legs, and their paper frills on the roast-pigs'-tails, that I was convinced, that only at a genuine unsophisticated farmhouse, where I could light down unannounced on Sarah-Jane—could this edible in its native and luscious beauty be found.

Next summer, if "strategy" and the rebels don't chew us up, I start on a tour for those beans; nor am I to be imposed upon by any "genteel" substitutes or abortions under that name!

New England! another thing! Gotham don't know "mulled wine." It *thinks* it does, but it don't. You should see the messes that have been offered me in marble halls, where ignorance was inadmissable. Oh, land of "mulled wine" and "baked beans!" my tombstone will never stay down comfortably till I have tasted both once more.

New York Ledger
Oct. 4, 1862

JOB'S PATIENCE

NOW if there *is* a proverb that needs re-vamping, it is "*The patience of Job.*" In the first place, Job *wasn't* patient. Like all the rest of his sex, from that day to the present, he could be heroic only for a little while at a time. He *began* bravely; but ended, as most of them do under annoyance, by cursing and swearing. Patient as Job! Did Job ever try, when he was hungry, to eat shad with a frisky baby in his lap? Did Job ever, after nursing one all night, and upon taking his seat at the breakfast-table the morning after, pour out coffee for six people, and second cups after that, before he had a chance to take a mouthful himself? Pshaw! I've no patience with "Job's patience." It is of no use to multiply instances; but there's not a faithful house-mother in the land who does not out-distance him in the sight of men and angels, every hour in the twenty-four.

New York Ledger
Aug. 8, 1863

A CHAPTER FOR PARENTS

THERE IS one great defect in the present system of family education. Not that there is only one; but we wish to call attention at present to the practice of obliging the *girls* of a family, in almost every instance in which self-denial is involved, to give way to the boys. "Remember he is your brother," is the appeal to tender little hearts, which, though often swelling under a sense of injustice, naturally give way under this argument. This might be all very well, were the boys also taught reciprocity in this matter, but as this unfortunately is not often the case, a monstrous little tyrant is produced whose overbearing exactions and hourly selfishnesses are disgusting to witness. As years roll on, Augustus's handkerchiefs are hemmed at half a wink from his lordship that he wishes it done, and his breakfast kept hot for him, though he change his breakfast hour as often as the disgusted cook leaves her place; while his sister's faintest intimation of her desire for his escort of an evening is met with a yawn, and an allusion to "the fellows" who are always "expecting him." It is easy to see what delightful ideas of reciprocity in mutual good offices Augustus will carry into the conjugal state, if he ever marries. His bride soon finds this out to her dismay, and half a dozen babies, and her wakeful nights and careworn days, are no excuse for not always placing his clean linen on a chair by his bed when needed, "to save him the trouble of opening his bureau drawers." "Before he was married" his handkerchiefs were always laid in a pile in the north-east corner of his drawer, duly perfumed, and with the exquisite word "*Augustus*" embroidered in the corner.—And *now*! "Before he was married" he was always consulted about the number of plums in his pudding.—And *now*! "Before he was married" he was never bothered to wait upon a woman of an evening unless he chose.—And *now*! "Before he was married" he had his breakfast any time between seven in the morning and three in the afternoon.—And *now*!

And so the poor weary woman hears the changes rung upon the newly-discovered virtues and perfections of his family, till she heartily wishes he had never left them. It never once occurs meanwhile to the domestic Nero to look at the *other* side of the question. How should it? when all his life at home was one ovation to his vanity and selfishness. "He could never bear contradiction! dear Augustus couldn't;" so he must never be contradicted. His friends must either agree with him or be silent, "because a contrary course always vexed him." Now we beg all mothers, who are thus educating domestic tyrants in their nurseries, to have some regard for the wife of his future, waiting for him somewhere, all unconscious, poor thing! of her fate; even if they have none on his sisters and themselves.

The most interesting story we read, was one which did *not* end as usual, with the marriage of the children of the family, but followed them into homes of their own, where the results of affectionate and at the same time *judicious* home-training manifested themselves in their beautiful, unselfish lives. It would do no harm, if mothers would sometimes ask themselves, when looking at their boys, what sort of *husband* am I educating for somebody? It is very common to think what sort of *wife* a *daughter* may make. Surely the former question, although so seldom occurring, is no less important.

New York Ledger
Aug. 29, 1863

THOSE FEW MINUTES

EXECUTIVE PEOPLE have generally the reputation, from their opposites, of being ill-tempered people. Self-trained to the observance of the admirable old maxim, that "whatever is worth doing at all, is worth doing well," they are naturally disgusted with dawdling inefficiency and sloth in any shape. Chary of the precious flying moments, the most intolerable of vexations to them is to have their time trespassed upon, and wasted, in a million petty and unnecessary ways, by the stupidity or culpable thoughtlessness of those about them. Now what is called "an easy person," i.e., a person who is not self-contained, on whose hands time hangs heavily, cannot be made to understand why a person of an opposite description need make a fuss about a few minutes. Why, "what is a few minutes?" they ask. Much—much in the course of a life-time to those who carefully husband them.

Those "few minutes" may make all the difference between an educated and an uneducated person; between a man independent in his circumstances, and a man always under the grinding heel of want; all the difference between intelligence, thrift and system on one hand, and ignorance, discomfort and disaster on the other. Those "few minutes," carefully improved as they occur, have filled libraries with profound and choice volumes; those "few minutes," saved for mental cultivation, have enabled men, and women too, to shed over a life of toil a brightness which made even monotonous duty a delight. Such can ill afford to be robbed of them by those unable to appreciate their value. Like the infinitesimal gold scrapings of the mint, they may not be purloined, or carelessly brushed away by idle fingers; but conscientiously gathered up and accounted for; to be molten and stamped with thought, then distributed to bless mankind.

New York Ledger
Feb. 27, 1864

WHOSE FAULT IS IT?

NO. SO AND SO ——— street. I have lived in New York twelve years, but I never heard of *that* street. However, I hunted it up, and piloted by different policemen on the route, finally reached it. It was a warm day; there were slaughter-houses, with pools of blood in front, round which gambolled pigs and children; there were piles of garbage in the middle of the street, composed of cabbage stumps, onion-skins, potato-parings, old hats, and meat-bones, cemented with cinders, and penetrated by the sun's rays, emitting the most beastly odors. Uncombed, unwashed girls, and ragged, fighting lads swarmed on every door step, and emerged from narrow, slimy alleys. Weary, worn-looking mothers administered hasty but well-aimed slaps at draggled, neglected children, while fathers smoked, and drank, and swore, and *lazed* generally.

It was a little piece of hell. I grew sick, physically and mentally, as I staggered, rather than walked along. How *can* human beings sleep, and eat, and drink in this pestiferous atmosphere? I asked. How *can* those children ever get a chance to grow up anything but penetentiary inmates? How *can* those tired mothers take heart, day by day, to drag along their miserable existence? And yet this horrible street is only one of many to be seen in New York.

There must be horrible blame somewhere for such a state of things on this beautiful island. How far these poor creatures are responsible for the moral deterioration consequent upon such a state of things, is a question I could not solve with all my thinking. For one, I cannot believe self-respect to be possible where cleanliness of person and habitation is wholly unknown. No wonder that on the warm days these little bare-legged children, the color of whose skins is a matter of mystery, so many layers of dirt conceal them, swarm up into our parks, and lay trespassing but delighted hands on the dandelion and clover blossoms. I thank God that every ragged, dirty child I see there has unchallenged *his* share at least of the blue sky and the sunshine in those places, all too few as they are. Alas! if some of the money spent on corporation-dinners, on Fourth of July fireworks, and on public balls, where rivers of champagne are worse than wasted, were laid aside for the cleanliness and purification of these terrible localities which slay more victims than the war is doing, and whom nobody thinks of numbering.

New York Ledger
June 25, 1864

THE DAY OF REST

SUNDAY, "the Day of Rest," so called, to many mothers of families, is the most toilsome day of the whole week. Children, too young to go to church, must of course be cared for at home; domestics on that day, of all others, expect their liberty. The father of the family, also, in many cases, thinks it hard if, after a week's labor, he too cannot roam *without* his family; never remembering that his wife, for the same reason, needs rest equally with himself, instead of shouldering on that day a double burden. Weary with family cares, she remembers the good word of cheer to which she has in days gone by listened from some clergyman, not too library-read to remember that he was *human*. The good, sympathetic word that sent her home strengthened for another week's duties. The good word, which *men* think they can do without; but which *women*, with the petty be-littling every day annoyances of their monotonous life, long for, as does a tired child to lay its head on its mother's breast. A mother may feel thus and yet have no desire to evade the responsible duties of her office. Indeed, had she not often her oratory in her own heart, she would sink discouraged oftener than she does, lacking the human sympathy which is often witheld by those upon whom she has the nearest claim for it. To such a woman it is not a mere form to "go to church;" it is not to her a fashion exchange; she *really* desires the spiritual help she seeks. *You* may find nothing in the words that come to her like the cool hand on the fevered brow. The psalm which is discord to your ear, may soothe her, like a mother's murmured lullaby. The prayer, which to you is an offence, brings her face to face with One who is touched by our infirmities. If an "undevout astronomer is mad," it seems to me that an undevout woman is still more so. Our insane asylums are full of women, who, leaning on some human heart for love and sympathy, and meeting only misappreciation, have gone there, past the Cross, where alone they could have laid down burdens too heavy to bear unshared. A great book is unwritten on this theme. When men become less gross and unspiritual than they now are, they will see the great wrong of which they are guilty, in their impatience of women's keenest sufferings because they "are only mental." The only "day of rest" to many of them is the day of their death.

New York Ledger
Mar. 11, 1865

SOMETHING TO COME HOME TO

IT IS VERY STRANGE that men, as a general thing, should be proud of that, of which they should be ashamed, and ashamed of that, which ennobles them. Now, to my eye, a man never looks so grand, as when he bends his ear patiently and lovingly, to the lisping of a little child. I admire that man whom I see with a baby in his arms. I delight, on Sunday, when the nurses are set free, to see the fathers leading out their little ones in their best attire, and setting them right end up, about fifty times a minute. It is as good a means of grace as I am acquainted with. Now that a man should feel ashamed to be seen doing this, or think it necessary to apologize, even jocularly, when he meets a male friend, is to me one of the unaccountable things. It seems to me every way such a lovely, and good, and proper action in a father, that I can't help thinking that he who would feel otherwise, is of so coarse and ignoble a nature, as to be quite unworthy of respect. How many times I have turned to look at the clumsy smoothing of a child's dress, or settling of its hat, or bonnet, by the unpractised fingers of a proud father. And the clumsier he was about it, the better I have loved him for the pains he took. It is very beautiful to me, this self-abnegation, which creeps so gradually over a young father. He is himself so unconscious that he, who had for many years thought first and only of his own selfish ease and wants, is forgetting himself entirely whenever that little creature, with *his* eyes and *its mother's lips*, reaches out coaxing hands to go here or there, or to look at this or that pretty object. Ah, what but this heavenly love, could bridge over the anxious days and nights, of care and sickness, that these twain of one flesh are called to bear? *My* boy! *My* girl! There it is! *Mine!* Something to live for—something to work for—*something to come home to;* and that last is the summing up of the whole matter. "Now let us have a good love," said a little three-year older, as she clasped her chubby arms about her father's neck when he came in at night. "Now let us have a good love." Do you suppose that man walked with slow and laggard steps from his store toward that bright face that had been peeping for an hour from the nursery window to watch his coming? Do you suppose when he got on all fours to "play elephant" with the child, that it even crossed his mind that he had worked very hard all that day, or that he was not at that minute "looking dignified?" Did he wish he had a "club" where he could get away from home evenings, or was that "*good love*" of the little creature on his back, with the laughing eyes and the pearly teeth, and the warm clasp about his neck, which she was squeezing to suffocation, sweeter and better than anything that this world could give?

Something to come home to! That is what saves a man. Somebody there to grieve if he is not true to himself. Somebody there to be sorry if he is troubled or sick. Somebody there, with fingers like sunbeams, gliding and brightening whatever they touch; and all for him. I look at the business men of New York, at nightfall, coming swarming "up town" from their stores and counting-rooms; and when I see them, as I often do, stop and buy one of those tiny bouquets as they go, I smile to myself; for although it is a little attention toward a wife, I know how happy that rose with its two geranium leaves, and its sprig of mignonette will make her. He thought of *her* coming home! Foolish, do you call it? Such folly makes all the difference between stepping off, scarcely conscious of the cares a woman carries, or staggering wearily along till she faints disheartened under their burthen. *Something to go home to!* That man felt it, and by ever so slight a token wished to recognize it. God bless him, I say, and all like him, who do not take home-comforts as stereotyped matters of course, and God bless the family estate; I can't see that anything better has been devised by the wiseacres who have experimented on the Almighty's plans. "There comes *my* father!" exclaims Johnny, bounding from out a group of "fellows" with whom he was playing ball; and sliding his little soiled fist in his, they go up the steps and into the house together; and again God bless them! I say there's one man who is all right at least. That boy has got him, safer than Fort Lafayette.

New York Ledger
Nov. 18, 1865

BOGUS INTELLECT

THERE IS ONE CLASS of women that in my opinion need extinguishing. I think I hear some male voice exclaim, *One?* I wish there were not a great many! Sir! I know that the foolishest woman who was ever born is better than most men; but I am not treating of that branch of the subject now. As I was about to remark, there is a class of sentimental women who use up the whole dictionary in speaking of a pin, and circumlocute about the alphabet in such a way, every time they open their mincing lips, that nobody but themselves can know what they are talking about, and truth to say, I should have been safe not to admit even that exception. Their "*ske-iy*" must always be heavenly "*ble-u*;" to touch household matters with so much as the end of a taper finger would be "beneath them," and that though Astor may have considerable more money in the bank than themselves. To sweep, to dust, to make a bed, to look into a kitchen-closet, to superintend a dinner—was a woman made for that? they indignantly exclaim. Now, while I as indignantly deny that she was born with a gridiron round her neck, I repudiate the idea that any one of these duties is beneath any woman, if it be necessary or best that she should perform them. I could count you a dozen women on my fingers' ends, whom the reading world has delighted to honor, who held no such flimsy, sickly, hot-house views as these. Because a woman can appreciate a good book, or even write one or talk or think intelligently, is she not to be a breezy, stirring, wide-awake, efficient thorough, capable housekeeper? Is she not to be a soulful wife and a loving, judicious mother? Is she to disdain to comb a little tumbled head, or to wash a pair of sticky little paws, or to mend a rent in a pinafore or little pair of trousers? I tell you there's a false ring about women who talk that way. No woman of true intellect ever felt such duties *beneath* her. She may like much better to read an interesting book, or write out her own thoughts when she feels the inspiration, than to be *much* employed this way, but she will never, never disdain it, and she will faithfully stand at her post if there can be no responsible relief-guard. You will never find her sentimentally whining about moonshine, while her neglected children are running loose in the neighbors' houses, or through the streets. You may be sure she is the wrong sort of woman who does this; she has neither head enough to attain to that which she is counterfeiting, nor heart enough really to care for the children she has so thoughtlessly launched upon the troubled sea of life. I sincerely believe that there are few women with a desire for intellectual improvement, who cannot secure it if they will. To be honest, they find plenty of time to put no end of embroidery on their children's clothes; plenty of time to keep up the neck-and-neck race of fashion, though it may be in third-rate imitations. They will sit up till midnight, but they will trim a dress or bonnet in the latest style, if they cannot hire it done, when the same energy would, if they felt inclined, furnish the *inside* of their heads much more profitably; for mark you, these women who are above household cares will run their feet off to match a trimming, or chase down a coveted color in a ribbon. *That* isn't "belittling!" *That* isn't "trivial!" *That* isn't "beneath them!"

It is very funny how such women will fancy they are recommending themselves by this kind of talk, to persons whose approbation they sometimes seek. If they only knew what a sensible, rational person may be thinking about while they are patiently but politely listening to such befogged nonsense; how pity is dominant where they suppose admiration to be the while; how the listener longs to break out and say, My dear woman, *I* have washed and ironed, and baked and brewed, and swept and dusted, and washed children, and made bonnets, and cut and made dresses, and mended old coats, and cleaned house, and made carpets, and nailed them down, and cleaned windows, and washed dishes, and tended the door-bell, and done every "menial" thing you can think of, when it came to me to do, and I'm none the worse for it, though perhaps you would not have complimented my "intellect," as you call it, had you known it. Lord bless me! there's nothing like one's *own* hands and feet. Bells are very good institutions when one is sick, but I never found that person who, when I had the use of my feet, could do a thing as quick as myself, and as a general thing the more you pay them the slower they move; and as I'm of the comet order, I quite forget it is "*beneath me*" to do things, till I've done them. So you see, after all, so far as I am concerned, it is no great credit to me, although it *is* very shocking to know that a woman who writes isn't always dressed in sky blue, and employed in smelling a violet.

New York Ledger
Dec. 30, 1865

A GRANDMOTHER'S DILEMMA

I WISH some philosopher would tell me at what age a child's naughtiness *really* begins.[1] I am led to make this remark because I am subject to the unceasing ridicule of certain persons, who shall be nameless, who sarcastically advise me "to practice what I preach." As if, to begin with, anybody ever did *that*, from Adam's time down. You see before I punish, or cause to be punished, a little child, I want to be sure that it hasn't got the stomach-ache; or is not cutting some tooth: or has not, through the indiscretion, or carelessness or ignorance of those intrusted with it, partaken of some indigestible mess, to cause its "naughtiness," as it is called. Then—I want those people who counsel me to such strict justice with a mere baby, to reflect how many times a day, according to this rule, *they* themselves ought to be punished for impatient, cross words; proceeding, it may be, from teeth, or stomach, or head, or nerves; but just as detrimental as to the results as if they came from meditated, adult naughtiness.

Scruples of conscience, you see—that's it. However, yesterday I said: Perhaps I *am* a little soft in this matter; perhaps it *is* time I began. So I stiffened up to it.

"Tittikins," said I to the cherub in question, "don't throw your hat on the floor; bring it to me, dear."

"I san't," replied Tittikins, who has not yet compassed the letter *h*. "I san't,"—with the most trusting, bewitching little smile, as if I were only getting up a new play for her amusement, and immediately commenced singing to herself:

"Baby bye,
Here's a fly—
Let us watch him,
You and I;"

adding, "Didn't I sing that pretty?"

Now I ask you, was I to get up a fight with that dear little happy thing, just to carry my point? I tell you my "government" on that occasion was a miserable failure; I made up my mind, after deep reflection, that if it was not quite patent that a child was really malicious, it was best not to worry it with petty matters; I made up my mind that I would concentrate my strength on the first *lie* it told, and be conveniently blind to lesser peccadilloes. This course is just what I get abused for. But, I stood over a little coffin once, with part of my name on the silver plate; and somehow it always comes between me and this governing business. I think I know what you'll reply to this; and in order that you may have full justification for abusing me, I will own that the other day, when I said to Tittikins, "Now, dear, if you put your hands inside your cup of milk again, I must really punish you," that little three-year-older replied, in the *chirp-est* voice, "No, you won't! I know better." And one day, when I *really* shut my teeth together, and with a great throb of martyrdom, spanked the back of that dear little hand, she fixed her great, soft, brown, unwinking eyes on me, and said, "I'm brave—I don't mind it!" You can see for yourself that this practical application of the story of the Spartan boy and the fox, which I had told her the day before, was rather unexpected.

Tittikins has no idea of "the rule that won't work both ways." Not long since, she wanted my pen and ink, which, for obvious reasons, I declined giving. She acquiesced, apparently, and went on with her play. Shortly after, I said, "Tittikins, bring me that newspaper, will you?" "No," she replied, with Lilliputian dignity. "If you can't please me, I can't please you." The other day she was making an ear-splitting racket with some brass buttons, in a tin box, when I said, "Can't you play with something else, dear, till I have done writing?" "But I like this best," she replied. "It makes my head ache, though," I said. "You poor dear, you," said Tittikins, patronizingly, as she threw the obnoxious plaything down, and rushed across the room to put her arms around my neck—"you *poor* dear, you, of course I won't do it, then."

I have given it up; with shame and confusion of face, I own that child *governs me*. I know her *heart* is all right; I know there's not a grain of *badness* in her; I know she would die to-day, if she hadn't those few flaws to keep her alive. In short, she's *my grandchild*. Isn't that enough?

New York Ledger
June 30, 1866

WHAT SHALL WE DO?

"*IF YOU WANT* to be happy and tranquil, you must care for nothing but yourself." This was said to me with a thumb on my pulse. But what if you doubt whether happiness and tranquility are the most desirable things on earth? What if you are so constituted that injustice and wrong to others rouses you as if it were done to yourself? What if the miseries of your fellow beings, particularly those you are powerless to relieve, haunt you day and night? What if your spirits rise, or fall, at every move of our national chess players, in the game of ambition, baptized patriotism? What if you cannot help groaning over the wretched women who are imprisoned and punished for infanticide, and the injustice which allows the guiltier party free to come and go unquestioned? What if you fret daily over the unwisdom of philanthropists who make virtue so unsmiling, and monotonous, and dismal, that those whom they fain would help, give one shuddering look at its uninviting aspect, and go swiftly back to the old downward road of excitement and moral death? What if you are appalled at the few who stop to bind up and pour oil into the wounds of the suffering, and the multitude of the unthinking who pass carelessly by on the other side? What if you feel like rolling up your sleeves and engaging in deadly combat with every disgusting sham and humbug that comes in your way? What if your patience gives out at "bores," whose time hangs so heavy on their own hands, that they can never understand that their case is not precisely yours? What if the more you look into the world and its affairs, the more it seems such "a muddle" to you, and you such a powerless pigmy to right anything, that you almost long to get out of it?

What then, I say? What if you are not happy, although *you personally* have clothes and shelter and bread and meat? What if the stomach-ache do not comprise your list of human ills? What if you really *cannot* carry out the practically atheistic creed of so many of the present day? Of so many *young men*—to their shame be it said—who with a man's chances fold their supine hands over all these abuses, turn a deaf ear to all these cries of distress, put up their heels, light their meerschaums, and know no anxiety unless their tobacco gives out. Nations may rise and fall, at their leisure.

What interest have they in it? Congress and the President may settle questions to their liking, or leave them unsettled. What to them is the future of others, if *their selfish present* be undisturbed?

Well, rather than be *that* torpid thing, and *it a man*, I would rather be a woman tied hand and foot, bankrupt in chances, and worry over what I am powerless to help. At least I can stand at my post, like a good soldier, because it *is* my post; meantime—I had rather be taken off that by a chance shot, than rust in a corner with ossification of the heart.

New York Ledger
Feb. 2, 1867

HOW I READ THE MORNING PAPERS

IF THERE IS A TIME when I sigh for the "Cave of Adullam,"[1] whatever that may be, it is when, my coffee swallowed, my fingers clutch my precious, damp morning papers, for a blessed, quiet read.

I just begin an editorial, which requires a little chewing, when up comes Biddy with, "Ma'am, there's a hole in the biler." The "biler" settled, I go back to the place indicated by my forefinger, where the Editor was saying "that Congress—" when somebody upsets the coffee-pot in an attempt to burlesque last night's public performance. The coffee-pot set right end up, and the coffee pond drained off the table-cloth, I return to my beloved editorial;—when Biddy again appears with, "Ma'am, the man has come to mend the door-handle as is broke." That nuisance disposed of, I clutch my paper and retreat in self-defence to the top of the house, and commence to read again, "that Congress—" when I am interrupted with loud shouts of "Where's mother? Mother? where are you?" I disdain to answer. "Mother?" In despair, I cry, in tragic tones, "Well, what *is* it?" "A poor soldier is at the door with pictures at thirty cents a piece, and he has but one arm." "Well, I have but one life—but for mercy's sake take his pictures, and don't let in anything else, man, woman or child, till I read my paper through." I begin again: "If Congress—" when Biddy, who is making the bed in the next room, begins howling "Swate Ireland is the land for me." I get up and very mildly request—in view of a possible visit to an Intelligence Officer—that she will oblige me by deferring her concert till I get through my morning paper. Then I begin again: "If Congress—" when up comes paterfamilias to know if it is to be beef, or chicken, or veal, that he is to order at the market for that day's dinner. "Possum, if you like," I mutter, with both fingers on my ears, as I commence again. "If Congress—" Paterfamilias laughs and retreats, exclaiming, "Shadracks! vot a womansh!" and I finish "Congress" and begin on the book reviews. A knock on the door. "Six letters, ma'am." I open them—three for an "autograph," with the privilege of finding my own envelope and stamp, and mailing it afterward. One with a request for me to furnish a speedy "composition" to save a school-boy at a dead-lock of ideas, from impending suicide. One from a man who has made a new kind of polish for the legs of tables and chairs and wants me to write an article about it in the *Ledger* and send him an early copy of the same. One from a girl "who never in her life owned a dress bonnet," and would like, with my assistance, to experience that refreshing and novel sensation.

Foaming at the mouth, I begin again my postponed list of "book reviews;" when in comes paterfamilias to know "if I haven't yet done with that paper." That's the last ounce on the camel's back! Mind you, *he* has just read *his* morning paper through, and it contains a different stripe of politics from mine, I can tell you that. Read it in *peace*, too—with his legs on the mantel, smoking his beloved pipe. Read it up and down; backwards and forwards; inside out, and upside down; and disembowelled every shade of meaning from live and dead subjects; and then coolly inquires of me—me, with my hair on end in the vain effort to retain any ideas through all these interruptions—"if I haven't *yet* done with that paper?" Oh, it's *too* much! I sit down opposite him. I explain how I never get a chance to finish anything except himself. I tell him my life is all fragments. I ask him, with moist eyes, if he knows how the price of board ranges at the different Lunatic Asylums. What is his unfeeling answer? "Hadn't I better take some other hour in the day to read the papers?"

Isn't that just like a man?

Hasn't bother and worry "all seasons for its own," as far as women are concerned? Would it make any difference what "hour in the day" I took to read the papers? *Can* women *ever* have any system about anything while Biddy or a male creature exists on the face of the earth to tangle up things? Haven't I all my life been striving and struggling for that "order" which my copy-book told me in my youth "was Heaven's first law"? And is it my fault if "chaos," which I hate, is my unwilling portion?

I just propounded to paterfamilias these vital questions. With eyes far off on distant, and untried, and possible fields of literature, he absently replies: "Well, as you say, Fanny, I shouldn't wonder if it *does* rain to-day." Great heavens!

New York Ledger
Apr. 27, 1867

TYRANTS OF THE SHOP

THERE ARE PERSONS who can regard oppression and injustice without any acceleration of the pulse. There are others who never witness it, how frequent soever, without a desperate struggle against non-interference, though prudence and policy may both whisper "it's none of your business." I believe, as a general thing, that the shopkeepers of New York who employ girls and women to tend in their stores, treat them courteously; but now and then I have been witness to such brutal language to them, in the presence of customers, for that which seemed to me no offence, or at least a very trifling one, that I have longed for a man's strong right arm, summarily to settle matters with the oppressor. And when one has been the innocent cause of it, merely by entering the store to make a purchase, the obligation to see the victim safe through, seems almost imperative. The bad policy of such an exhibition of unmanliness on the part of a shopkeeper would be, one would think, sufficient to stifle the "damn you" to the blushing, tearful girl, who is powerless to escape, or to clear herself from the charge of misbehavior. When ladies "go shopping," in New York, they generally expect to enjoy themselves; though Heaven knows, they must be hard up for resources to fancy this mode of spending their time, when it can be avoided. But, be that as it may, the most vapid can scarcely fancy this sort of scene.

The most disgusting part of such an exhibition is, when the gentlemanly employer, having got through "damning" his embarrassed victim, turns, with a sweet smile and dulcet voice, to yourself, and inquires, "what else he can have the pleasure of showing you?" You are tempted to reply, "Sir, I would like you to show me that you can respect womanhood, although it may not be hedged about with fine raiment, or be able to buy civil words with a full purse." But you bite your tongue to keep it quiet, and you linger till this Nero has strolled off, and then you say to the girl, "I am sorry to have been the innocent cause of this!" and you ask, "Does he often speak this way to you?" and she says, quietly, as she rolls up the ribbons or replaces the boxes on the shelves, "Never in any other!" It is useless to ask her why she stays, because you know something about women's wages and women's work in the crowded city; and you know that, till she is sure of another place, it is folly for her to think of leaving this. And you think many other things as you say Good-morning to her as kindly as you know how; and you turn over this whole "woman-question" as you run the risk of being knocked down and run over in the crowded thoroughfare through which you pass; and the jostle, and hurry, and rush about you, seem to make it more hopeless as each eager face passes you, intent on its own plans, busy with its own hopes and fears—staggering perhaps under a load either of the soul or body, or both, as heavy as the poor shop-girl's, and you gasp as if the air about had suddenly become too thick to breathe. And then you reach your own door-step, and like a guilty creature, face your dressmaker, having forgotten to "match that trimming;" and you wonder if you were to sit down and write about this evil, if it would deter even one employer from such brutality to the shop-girls in his employ; not because of the brutality, perhaps, but because by such a short-sighted policy, he might often drive away from his store, ladies who would otherwise be profitable and steady customers.

New York Ledger
June 1, 1867

FASHIONABLE INVALIDISM

I HOPE TO LIVE to see the time when it will be considered a *disgrace* to be sick. When people with flat chests and stooping shoulders, will creep round the back way, like other violators of known laws. Those who *inherit* sickly constitutions have my sincerest pity. I only request one favor of them, that they cease perpetuating themselves till they are physically on a sound basis. But a woman who laces so tightly that she breathes only by a rare accident; who vibrates constantly between the confectioner's shop and the dentist's office; who has ball-robes and jewels in plenty, but who owns neither an umbrella, nor a water-proof cloak, nor a pair of thick boots; who lies in bed till noon, never exercises, and complains of "total want of appetite," save for pastry and pickles, is simply a disgusting nuisance. Sentiment is all very nice; but, were I a man, I would beware of a woman who "couldn't eat." Why don't she take care of herself? Why don't she take a nice little bit of beefsteak with her breakfast, and a nice *walk*—not *ride*—after it? Why don't she stop munching sweet stuff between meals? Why don't she go to bed at a decent time, and lead a clean, healthy life? The doctors and confectioners have ridden in their carriages long enough; let the butchers and shoemakers take a turn at it. A man or woman who "can't eat" is never sound on any question. It is waste breath to converse with them. They take hold of everything by the wrong handle. Of course it makes them very angry to whisper pityingly, "dyspepsia," when they advance some distorted opinion; but I always do it. They are not going to muddle my brain with their theories, because their internal works are in a state of physical disorganization. Let them go into a Lunatic Asylum and be properly treated till they can learn how they are put together, and how to manage themselves sensibly.

How I *rejoice* in a man or woman with a chest; who can look the sun in the eye, and step off as if they had not wooden legs. It is a rare sight. If a woman now has an errand round the corner, she must have a carriage to go there; and the men, more dead than alive, so lethargic are they with constant smoking, creep into cars and omnibuses, and curl up in a corner, dreading nothing so much as a little wholesome exertion. The more "tired" they are, the more diligently they smoke, like the women who drink perpetual *tea* "to keep them up."

Keep them up! Heavens! I am fifty-five, and I feel half the time as if I were just made. To be sure I was born in Maine, where the timber and the human race last; but I do not eat pastry, nor candy, nor ice-cream. I do not drink tea! I walk, not ride. I own stout boots—pretty ones, too! I have a water-proof cloak, and no diamonds. I like a nice bit of beefsteak and a glass of ale, and anybody else who wants it may eat pap. I go to bed at ten, and get up at six. I dash out in the rain, because it feels good on my face. I don't care for my clothes, but I *will* be well; and after I am buried, I warn you, don't let any fresh air or sunlight down on my coffin, if you don't want me to get up.

New York Ledger
July 27, 1867

THE WOMEN OF 1867

A WOMAN WHO WROTE used to be considered a sort of monster. At this day it is difficult to find one who does not write, or has not written, or who has not, at least, a strong desire to do so. Gridirons and darning-needles are getting monotonous. A part of their time the women of to-day are content to devote to their consideration when necessary; but you will rarely find one—at least among women who *think*—who does not silently rebel against allowing them a monopoly.

What? you inquire, would you encourage, in the present over-crowded state of the literary market, any more women scribblers? Stop a bit. It does not follow that she should wish or seek to give to the world what she has written. I look around and see innumerable women, to whose barren, loveless life this would be improvement and solace, and I say to them, write! Write, if it will make that life brighter, or happier, or less monotonous. Write! it will be a safe outlet for thoughts and feelings, that maybe the nearest friend you have, has never dreamed had place in your heart and brain. You should have read the letters I have received; you should have talked with the women I have talked with; in short, you should have walked this earth with your eyes open, instead of shut, as far as its women are concerned, to indorse this advice. Nor do I qualify what I have said on account of social position, or age, or even education. It is not *safe* for the women of 1867 to shut down so much that cries out for sympathy and expression, because life is such a maelstrom of business or folly, or both, that those to whom they have bound themselves, body and soul, recognize only the needs of the former. *Let them write* if they will. One of these days, when that diary is found, when the hand that penned it shall be dust, with what amazement and remorse will many a husband, or father, exclaim, I never knew my wife, or my child, till this moment; all these years she has sat by my hearth, and slumbered by my side, and I have been a stranger to her. And you sit there, and you read sentence after sentence, and recall the day, the month, the week, when she moved calmly, and you thought happily, or, at least, contentedly, about the house, all the while her heart was aching, when a kind word from you, or even a touch of your hand upon her head, as you passed out to business, or pleasure, would have cheered her, oh so much! When had you sat down by her side after the day's work for both was over, and talked with her just a few moments of something besides the price of groceries, and the number of shoes Tommy had kicked out, all of which, proper and necessary in their place, need not of necessity form the staple of conversation between a married pair; had you done this; had you recognized that she had a *soul* as well as yourself, how much sunshine you might have thrown over her colorless life!

"Perhaps, sir," you reply; "but I have left my wife far behind in the region of thought. It would only distress her to do this!" How do you know that? And if it were so, are you content to leave her—the mother of your children—so far behind? *Ought* you to do it? Should you not, by raising the self-respect you have well nigh crushed by your indifference and neglect, extend a manly hand to her help? *I* think so. The pink cheeks which first won you may have faded, but remember that it was in your service, when you quietly accept the fact that "you have left your wife far behind you in mental improvement." Oh! it is pitiable this growing apart of man and wife, for lack of a little generous consideration and magnanimity! It is pitiable to see a husband without a thought that he might and should occasionally, have given his wife a lift out of the petty, harrowing details of her woman's life, turn from her, in company, to address his conversation to some woman who, happier than she, has had time and opportunity for mental culture. You do not see, sir—you will not see—you do not desire to see, how her cheek flushes, and her eye moistens, and her heart sinks like lead as you thus wound her self-respect. You think her "cross and ill-natured," if when, the next morning, you converse with her on the price of butter, she answers you listlessly and with a total want of interest in the treadmill-subject.

I say to such women: Write! Rescue a part of each week at least for reading, and putting down on paper, for your own private benefit, your thoughts and feelings. Not for the *world's* eye, unless you choose, but to lift yourselves out of the dead-level of your lives; to keep off inanition; to lessen the number who are yearly added to our lunatic asylums from the ranks of misappreciated, unhappy womanhood, narrowed by lives made up of details. Fight it! oppose it, for your own sakes and your children's! Do not be *mentally* annihilated by it. It is all very well to sneer at this and raise the old cry of "a woman's sphere being home"—which, by the way, you hear oftenest from men whose home is only a place to feed and sleep in. You might as well say that a man's sphere is his shop or his counting-room. How many of them, think you, would be contented, year in and year out, to eat, drink, and sleep as well as to transact business there, and *never desire* or *take*, at all costs, some let-up from its monotonous grind? How many would like to forego the walk to and from the place of business? forego the opportunities for conversation, which chance thus throws in their way, with other men bent on the same or other errands? Have, literally, *no* variety in their lives? Oh, if you could be a woman but one year and try it! A woman—but not necessarily a butterfly—not necessarily a machine, which, once wound up by the marriage ceremony, is expected to click on with undeviating monotony till Death stops the hands.

New York Ledger
Aug. 10, 1867

TO MOTHERS AND TEACHERS

THE PAPERS ARE FULL of "school advertisements," of every kind.[1] "*Which is the best?*" ask the bewildered parents as they look over the thousand-and-one Prospectus-es and read the formidable list of "branches" taught in each, between the hours of nine and three, for each day, Sundays excepted. They look at their little daughter. "It is time," they say, "that she learned something;" and that is true; but they do not consider that is not yet time for her to learn *everything;* and that in the attempt she will probably break down before the experiment is half made. They do not consider, in their anxiety, that she should be educated with the railroad speed so unhappily prevalent; that to keep a growing child in school from nine till three is simply torture; and to add to that lessons out of school, an offence, which should come under the head of "Cruelty to Animals," and punished accordingly by the city authorities; who, in their zeal to decide upon the most humane manner in which to kill calves and sheep, seem quite to overlook the slow process by which the children of New York are daily murdered. That "everybody does so;" that "all schools" keep these absurd hours; that "teachers want the afternoons to themselves,"—seem to me puerile reasons, when I meet each day, at three o'clock, the great army of children, bearing in their bent shoulders, narrow chests and pale faces, the unmistakable marks of this overstrain of the brain, at a critical age. And when I see, in addition, the piles of books under their arms, effectually to prevent the only alleviation of so grave a mistake, in the out-door exercise that their cramped limbs, and tired brains so loudly call for, after school hours, I have no words to express my sorrow and disgust of our present school system.

It is not teachers, but *parents*, who are to right this matter. The former but echo the wishes of the latter. If parents think physical education a matter of no consequence, why should teachers love those children better than the parents themselves? If parents are so anxious for the cramming process, which is filling our church-yards so fast, why should teachers, who "must live," interfere? Now and then, one more humane, less self-seeking, than the majority, will venture to suggest that the pupil has already quite as much mental strain as is safe for its tender years; but when the reply is in the form of a request from the parent that "another branch will not make much difference," what encouragement has the teacher to continue to oppose such stupidity? Not long since, I heard of a mother who was boasting to a friend of the smartness and precocity of her little daughter of seven years, "who attended school from nine till three each day, and studied most of the intervening time; and was so fond of her books *that all night, in her sleep, she was saying over her geography lessons and doing her sums in arithmetic*." Comment on such folly is unnecessary. I throw out these few hints, hoping that one mother, at least, may pause long enough to give so important a subject a moment's thought. That she may ask, whether it would not be wise occasionally to visit the school-room where her child spends so much of its time; and examine the state of ventilation in the apartment, and see if the desk, at which the child sits so long, is so contrived that it might have been handed down from the days of the Inquisition, as a model instrument of torture. I will venture to say, that her husband takes far better care, and expends more pains-taking thought, with his favorite horse, if he has one, than she ever has on the physical well-being of her child. What *right*, I ask, has she to bring children into the world, who is too indolent, or too thoughtless, or too pleasure-loving to guide their steps safely, happily, and above all, *healthily* through it?

New York Ledger
Nov. 2, 1867

THE WORKING-GIRLS OF NEW YORK

NOWHERE more than in New York does the contest between squalor and splendor so sharply present itself. This is the first reflection of the observing stranger who walks its streets. Particularly is this noticeable with regard to its women. Jostling on the same pavement with the dainty fashionist is the care-worn working-girl. Looking at both these women, the question arises, which lives the more miserable life—she whom the world styles "fortunate," whose husband belongs to three clubs, and whose only meal with his family is an occasional breakfast, from year's end to year's end; who is as much a stranger to his own children as to the reader; whose young son of seventeen has already a detective on his track employed by his father to ascertain where and how he spends his nights and his father's money; swift retribution for that father who finds food, raiment, shelter, equipages for his household; but love, sympathy, companionship—never? Or she—this other woman—with a heart quite as hungry and unappeased, who also faces day by day the same appalling question: *Is this all life has for me?*

A great book is yet unwritten about women. Michelet has aired his wax-doll theories regarding them.[1] The defender of "woman's rights" has given us her views. Authors and authoresses of little, and big repute, have expressed themselves on this subject, and none of them as yet have begun to grasp it: men—because they lack spirituality, rightly and justly to interpret women; women—because they dare not, or will not tell us that which most interests us to know. Who shall write this bold, frank, truthful book remains to be seen. Meanwhile woman's millennium is yet a great way off; and while it slowly progresses, conservatism and indifference gaze through their spectacles at the seething elements of to-day, and wonder "what ails all our women?"

Let me tell you what ails the working-girls. While yet your breakfast is progressing, and your toilet unmade, comes forth through Chatham Street and the Bowery, a long procession of them by twos and threes to their daily labor. Their breakfast, so called, has been hastily swallowed in a tenement house, where two of them share, in a small room, the same miserable bed. Of its quality you may better judge, when you know that each of these girls pays but three dollars a week for board, to the working man and his wife where they lodge.

The room they occupy is close and unventilated, with no accommodations for personal cleanliness, and so near to the little Flinegans that their Celtic night-cries are distinctly heard. They have risen unrefreshed, as a matter of course, and their ill-cooked breakfast does not mend the matter. They emerge from the doorway where their passage is obstructed by "nanny goats" and ragged children rooting together in the dirt, and pass out into the street. They shiver as the sharp wind of early morning strikes their temples. There is no look of youth on their faces; hard lines appear there. Their brows are knit; their eyes are sunken; their dress is flimsy, and foolish, and tawdry; always a hat, and feather or soiled artificial flower upon it; the hair dressed with an abortive attempt at style; a soiled petticoat; a greasy dress, a well-worn sacque or shawl, and a gilt breast-pin and earrings.

Now follow them to the large, black-looking building, where several hundred of them are manufacturing hoop-skirts. If you are a woman you have worn plenty; but you little thought what passed in the heads of these girls as their busy fingers glazed the wire, or prepared the spools for covering them, or secured the tapes which held them in their places. *You* could not stay five minutes in that room, where the noise of the machinery used is so deafening, that only by the motion of the lips could you comprehend a person speaking.

Five minutes! Why, these young creatures bear it, from seven in the morning till six in the evening; week after week, month after month, with only half an hour at midday to eat their dinner of a slice of bread and butter or an apple, which they usually eat in the building, some of them having come a long distance. As I said, the roar of machinery in that room is like the roar of Niagara. Observe them as you enter. Not one lifts her head. They might as well be machines, for any interest or curiosity they show, save always to know *what o'clock it is*. Pitiful! pitiful, you almost sob to yourself, as you look at these young girls. *Young?* Alas! it is only in years that they are young.

Folly As It Flies
1868 and
New York Ledger,
Jan. 26, 1867

THE HISTORY OF OUR LATE WAR

MANY ABLE WORKS have already appeared on this subject, and many more will doubtless follow. But *my* History of the War is yet to be written; not indeed *by* me, but *for* me. A history which shall record, not the deeds of our Commanders and Generals, noble and great as they were, because these will scarcely fail of historical record and prominence; but *my* history shall preserve for the descendants of those who fought for our flag, the noble deeds of our *privates*, who shared the danger but missed the glory. Scattered far and wide in our remote villages—hidden away amid our mountains—struggling for daily bread in our swarming cities, are these unrecognized heroes. Travelling through our land, one meets them everywhere; but only as accident, or chance, leads to conversation with them, does the plain man by your side become transfigured in your eyes, till you feel like uncovering your head in his presence, as when one stands upon holy ground. Not only because they were brave upon the battle-field, but for their sublime self-abnegation under circumstances when the best of us might be forgiven our selfishness; in the tortures of the ambulance and hospital—quivering through the laggard hours, that might or might not bring peace and rest and health. Oh! what a book might be written upon the noble unselfishness *there* displayed; not only towards those who fought *for* our flag; but *against* it. The coveted drop of water, handed by one dying man to another, whose sufferings seemed the greater. The simple request to the physician to pass *his* wounds by, till those of another, whose existence was unknown to him a moment before, should have been alleviated. Who shall embalm us these?

Last summer, when I was away in the country, I was accustomed to row every evening at sunset on a lovely lake near by. The boatman who went with me was a sunburnt, pleasant-faced young man, whose stroke at the oar it was poetry to see. He made no conversation unless addressed, save occasionally to little Bright-Eyes, who sometimes accompanied me. One evening, as the sun set gloriously and the moon rose, and the aurora borealis was sending up flashes of rose and silver, I said, "Oh, this is too beautiful to leave. I *must* cross the lake again." I made some remark about the brilliance of the North Star, when he remarked simply, "That star was a good friend to me in the war." "Were you in the war?" asked I; "and all these evenings you have rowed a loyal woman like me about this lake, and I knew nothing of it!" Then, at my request, came the story of Andersonville,[1] and its horrors, told simply, and without a revengeful word; then the thrilling attempt at escape, through a country absolutely unknown, and swarming with danger, during which the North Star, of which I had just spoken, was his only guide. Then came a dark night, when the friendly star, alas! disappeared. But a watch, which he had saved his money to obtain, had a compass on the back of it. Still of what use was that without a light? Our boatman was a Yankee. He caught a glowworm and pinched it. It flashed light sufficient for him to see that he was heading for one of our camps, where, after many hours of travel, he at last found safety, sinking down insensible from fatigue and hunger, as soon as he reached it. So ravenously did he eat, when food was brought, that a raging fever followed; and when he was carried, a mere skeleton, to his home on the borders of the lovely lake where we were rowing, whose peaceful flow had mocked him in dreams in that seething, noisome prison pen, he did not even recognize it. For months his mother watched his sick-bed, till reason and partial health returned—till by degrees he became what he then was.

When he had finished, I said, "Give me your hand—*both of 'em*—and God bless you!"—and—then I *mentioned* his jailers! Not a word of bittterness passed his lips—only this: "I used to gasp in the foul air at Andersonville, and think of this quiet, smooth lake, and our little house with the trees near it, and long so to see them again, and row my little boat here. But," he added, quietly, "*they* thought they were as right as we, and they *did* fight well!"

I swallowed a big lump in my throat—as our boat neared the shore, and he handed me out—and said, penitently, "Well, if *you* can forgive them, I am sure I ought to; but it will be the hardest work I ever did."—"Well, it is strange," said he: "I have often noticed it, since my return, that you who stayed at home feel more bitter about it, than we who came so near dying there of foul air and starvation."[2]

New York Ledger
Feb. 15, 1868

THE TWO O'CLOCK TELEGRAM

Or, Who Would Be an Author?

WHAT IS THAT? The question was asked by Smith of his wife at two in the morning. Both had sprung from their pillows at a violent ringing of the front door bell, at that unusual hour. In the day time they were used to a perfect carnival of bells. The postman often sent in his bill for boots worn out in their especial service. Then everybody who had an ax to grind, took a turn, either at the front or back door bell. When the class just mentioned gave it a short respite, little boys pulled it for fun. Collectors of old hats, old umbrellas, and old clothes, exercised it without stint or limit; also venders of furniture polish, and excelsior soap, and blueing and whiting, and "superior black sewing silk," and sample needles and pins, and tea, and coffee, and tidys, and door-mats. I mention these things to show you that only an unusual circumstance in connection with their tintinnabulations would have roused the Smiths to take any interest in the subject.

"What's that?" ejaculated Smith again, as he and his wife confronted one another, with staring eyes and rampant hair, and, in the language of dressmakers, "short suits," in the middle of the floor. Ting-a-ling—ting-a-ling, louder than before, again went the door bell. Now appeared the chambermaid in the entry, also in a "short suit." At the head of the chamber stairs another "short suit," over which streamed a quantity of brown hair, and from the owner of which came feebly, "Heavens, who's dead?" Meanwhile Smith put his hands into everything but the match-box, and his legs everywhere but into his trousers, and finally, with that exemplary patience born of masculinity, rushed down stairs, *in statu quo*, without either. A blast of cold out-door air on bare feet, resting upon cold marble, is not the pleasantest sensation on emerging from a warm bed. But when one holds in his hand a telegram, at two in the morning, and death, and pestilence, and whatever else contained in the "seven vials," may be condensed in its two or three words, one does not mind cold feet. At this time the cook and the chambermaid, and the maiden of the brown curling locks who was seated on the top chamber stair, were holding their breath in dread suspense, while Smith felt round for the match-box. This done, and the envelope broken open, again the dread question was levelled at him by trembling voices, "Who's dead?" Smith ejaculating "devil!" rushed round for his eye-glass before answering. By this time the *little* Smith roused from her crib, joined the chorus, the telegram man frightening her out of a year's growth by his violent slamming of the door as he departed; and as *yet* the name of the deceased was an untold mystery. "Speak!" screamed the executive Mrs. Smith, "or give that telegram to me. Do anything but stand there looking like an idiot in that 'short suit.'" At this juncture Smith dropped to the floor in a limp heap, with a paper in his hand. Mrs. Smith, leaving him to have his fit or spasm out all by himself in any posture convenient, seized the fatal telegram, and to the horrified and listening audience in the entry, read;

"On consultation with Boston, we conclude not to have the table of contents abridged."

New York Ledger
Apr. 25, 1868

LADIES EXCLUDED FROM PUBLIC DINNERS

QUEEN VICTORIA—how glad I am she had such a good, loving husband, to compensate her for the misery of being a queen—tried her best to abolish the custom, prevalent in England at dinner, of the gentlemen remaining to guzzle wine after the ladies left. I am aware that guzzle is an unladylike word; but, as no other fits in there, I shall use it. Well—she succeeded only in shortening the guzzling period—not in abolishing it; so those consistent men remained, to drink toasts to "lovely women," whose backs they were so delighted to see retreating through the door.

What of it? Why, simply this, that Queen Victoria did what she could to civilize her own regal circle; and that she set a good precedent for American women of to-day to follow. I fail to see why, when a hostess has carefully watched the dishes and glasses come and go, at her husband's dinner-party, to the obstruction of all rational conversation, save by agonized spasms,—I fail to see why, when the gentlemen guests have eaten to satiety, and conversation might be supposed to be at last possible, why, at that precise, enjoyable period, the lady of the house should be obliged to accompany the empty plates to regions unknown and uncared for. This seems to me a question well worthy of consideration in this year of our Lord, 1868. It strikes me, rather an inglorious abdication for a woman of intelligence, who may be supposed to understand and take an interest in other things than the advance and retreat of salad, and ragouts, oysters, and chicken. I call it a relic of barbarism, of which men of intelligence should be ashamed. Then what advantage has the woman who cultivates her mental powers, over the veriest fool? It is an insult to her. But you say, all women are not thoughtful or intelligent. Very true: and why should they be—save that they owe it to their own self-respect—when gentlemen thus offer premiums for insipidity?—why should they inform themselves upon any subjects but those of dressing well and feeding well?

It is a satisfaction to know that there are gentlemen, who endorse the other side of the question. There was lately a dinner given in New York to a literary gentleman of distinction.[1] One of the gentlemen invited to attend it, said to his wife: "It is a shame that ladies should not attend this dinner. *You* ought to be there, and many other ladies who are authors." Acting upon this impulse, he suggested to the committee that ladies should be invited. The answer was: First—"It would be so awkward for the ladies. Secondly—there were very few literary ladies compared to the number of literary gentlemen." Now as to the question of "awkwardness," the boot, I think, was on the other foot; and if the ladies were awkward,—which was not a complimentary supposition,—why should the gentlemen be to blame for it? And if there were "few lady authoresses," why not ask the wives of the *editors* who were to be present?

No—this was not the reason.

What was it? *Tobacco*—yes, sir, tobacco! I don't add wine—but I might. In short, these men would be obliged to conduct themselves as gentlemen were ladies present; and they wanted a margin left for the reverse. They preferred a bar-room atmosphere to the refining presence of "lovely woman," about whom they wished to hiccup at a safe distance.

Perhaps, in justice, I should add, that it was suggested that they might perhaps see the animals feed from the "musicians' balcony," or listen to the speeches "through the crack of a door," with the servants, or in some such surreptitious and becoming and complimentary manner, which a woman of spirit and intelligence would, of course, be very likely to do.

To conclude, I trust those gentlemen who are in the habit of bemoaning "the frivolity of our women, and their sad addictedness to long milliner's bills," will reckon up the cost of cigars and wine at these dinners, from which ladies are excluded; and while they are on the anxious seat, on the economy question, ask themselves whether, putting other reasons out of the question, the presence of ladies, on these occasions, would not contribute greatly to *reduce their dinner expenses?*

I lately read an article in a London paper, in which "the woman-question" was treated in the following enlightened manner: The writer avowed his dislike to the cultivation of woman's intellect; since men had enough intellect, in their intercourse with each other; and wanted only with woman that charming, childish prattle and playfulness, which was so refreshing to the male creature, when he needed relief and amusement!

The author of these advanced ideas didn't state whether he considered these *childish*, *prattling* women fit to be mothers and heads of families; probably that was too puerile a question to consider in the same breath with the amusement they might afford men by the total absence of intelligence.

New York Ledger
May 16, 1868

"DELIGHTFUL MEN"

ISN'T HE a delightful man? This question was addressed to me by a lady in company concerning a gentleman who had rendered himself during the evening, peculiarly agreeable. Before I answer that question, I said, I would like to see him at home. I would like to know if, when he jars his wife's feelings, he says, "Beg pardon" as willingly and promptly as when he stepped upon yonder lady's dress. I would like to know if, when he comes home at night, he has some pleasant little things to say, such as he has scattered about so lavishly since he entered this room this evening; and whether if the badly cooked dish, which he gallantly declared to the hostess at the table, "could not have been improved," would have found a similar verdict on his own table, and to his own wife. *That is the test.* I am sorry to say that some of the most agreeable society-men, who could, by no possibility, be guilty of a rudeness abroad, could never be suspected in their own homes of ever doing anything else. The man who will invariably meet other ladies with "How very well you are looking!" will often never, from one day to another, take notice of his own wife's appearance, or, if so, only to find fault. How bright that home would be to his wife with one half the courtesy and toleration he invariably shows to strangers. "Allow me to differ"—he blandly remarks to an opponent with whom he argues in company. "Pshaw! what do *you* know about it?" he says at his own fireside and to his wife. Children are "angels" when they belong to his neighbors; his own are sent out of the room whenever he enters it, or receive so little recognition that they are glad to leave. "Permit me," says the gallant male *vis-à-vis* in the omnibus or car, as he takes your fare; while *his* wife often hands up her own fare, even with her husband by her side. No wonder she is not "looking well" when she sees politeness is for every place but for home-consumption.

"Oh, how men miss it in disregarding these little matters," said a sad-eyed wife to me one day. And she said truly; for these little kindnesess are like a breath of fresh air from an open window in a stifled room; we lift our drooping heads and breathe again! "Little!" did I say! *Can* that be little which makes or mars the happiness of a human being? A man says a rough, rude word, or neglects the golden opportunity to say a kind one, and goes his selfish way and thinks it of no account. Then he marvels when he comes back,—in sublime forgetfulness of the past,—that the familiar eye does not brighten at his coming, or the familiar tongue voice a welcome. Then, on inquiry, if he is told of the rough word, he says: "O-o-h! *that's* it—is it? Now it isn't possible that you gave *that* a second thought? Why, *I* forgot all about it!" as if this last were really a palliation and a merit.

It would be ludicrous, this masculine obtuseness, were it not for the tragic consequences—were it not for the loving hearts that are chilled—

the homes that are darkened—the lives that are blighted—and the dew and promise of the morning that are so needlessly turned into sombre night.

"Little things!" There *are* no little things. "Little things," so called, are the hinges of the universe. They are happiness, or misery; they are poverty, or riches; they are prosperity or adversity; they are life, or death. Not a human being of us all, can afford to despise "the day of *small* things."

New York Ledger
Jan. 16, 1869

A POSTSCRIPT TO A SERMON

"*MIDDLE AGE* is inevitable routine, but keep your *souls* above it," I heard a clergyman remark the other night. He "knew that it was difficult," he said, "not to merge one's self at this crisis in the shop, in the store, in the office; difficult *not* to become a mere drudge and a machine; but still, avoiding it was the only hope for this life." Oh, how my heart echoed these words—not for men, but for my own sex, of whose routine life the clergyman said nothing. I wanted to get up and say to him, "My dear sir, your address is eloquent, and true, scholarly, and sound, so far as it goes. It *is* the only hope for this life that these men of business should not become mere tools." But I wanted to ask him if men, with their freedom of action—men who, out in the world, inevitably come into collision with *stirring*, not *stagnant* life—find this difficult, what of their wives? With twenty nerves where men have one to be jarred and agonized, with the pin and needle fret, of every minute, which they may never hope to escape or get away from; tied hand and foot, day and night, week after week, with the ten thousand cords, invisible often to the dull eye of husband and father, who accepts at evening the neat and pleasant result, without a thought of how it was accomplished—without a thought of the weariness of that inexorable grind of detail necessary to it—without a thought that a change of scene is either necessary or desirable for the wife and mother who is surely under its benumbing influence, merging *her* "soul" till she is a mere machine.

I wanted to hear this clergyman say something about that. I wanted to know of him whether these women were doing God and their husbands service, by so sinking the spiritual part of them that one could hardly tell that it had existence. I wanted to ask him whether, if their husbands, through indifference or selfishness, or both, gave no thought to this matter, if he—set in a high place to teach the people—had no word of advice to such men, that they look as well to the spiritual deterioration of the *mothers* of their children as to their own—the fathers. Nay, I insist that for the mother it is of *more* consequence, as having infinitely more to do with the forming years of these children. And what time, pray, have many of these "routine" mothers for "thought," properly so called? What time for reading even the daily papers, to keep up intelligently with the great issues of the day, of which it is a shame and disgrace for any American wife and mother to be ignorant? How can they in this way be fit companions for their children's future? How can they answer their questions, on this subject and on that, while their vision is for ever bounded by the horizon of the physical wants of the household? You may preach "woman's duty" to me till you are hoarse; and I will preach to you the lust and the selfishness, which is ever repeating the dilemma of "the old woman in the shoe," till she has not an interval to think whether she or her brood *have* souls. "Routine life" of *men!* Men can and do get out of it—"business takes them away from home on journeys." "Business" takes him out pleasant evenings; on rainy ones, he never has "business;" then he goes early to bed, to prepare for a long evening of "business" when the sky clears.

His wife—well, "she don't seem to need it; or if she does, she don't say so;" and I might add, in the language of Dickens's nurse, Sary Gamp,[1] "it is little she needs, and that little she don't get," at least from him.

Routine men! Oh, bah! "Routine men" have a result to show for their "routine." They have clerks—not from Intelligence-offices[2] either—who have to do as they bid them. They also lock up shop at dark. They also walk or ride home in the fresh air, and talk with their male friends while doing it. They also are not dependent on the whim or caprice of any man to take them out for a breath of fresh air at night, after an exhaustive day of indoor stifling detail. And so, though the sermon to which I listened was excellent *from a man to men*, I made up my mind to add this little Appendix to women, from a woman, on the routine-woman's side of the question. You may talk of the selfishness of women till your head is white; there never lived that selfish woman so execrably selfish as a selfish man can be. I don't say *you* are so, sir: though at this distance, I venture to inquire whether, were you in your wife's place, you wouldn't occasionally like to climb up on the edge of the peck-measure in which she daily revolves, and look about outside, even if it should tip over on the whole brood of young ones in the process?

New York Ledger
Mar. 20, 1869

A VISIT TO WASHINGTON

I'VE BEEN TO WASHINGTON, and I didn't want office either. Had I, I think my patience would soon have oozed out, in the stifling atmosphere of that room in the White House, where clamorous lobbyists sat with distended eyes, watching the chance of their possible entrance to the President's presence—sat there, too, for weary hours, a spectacle to gods and men; of human beings willing to sacrifice self-respect and time, and what little money they had left in their purses, for the gambler's chance. Anything, everything, but the open and above-board, and sure and independent, and old fashioned way of getting a living!

So I thought as the living stream poured in, and I went out, thankful that I desired nothing in the gift of the President of the United States of America. How any man living can wish to be President passes my solving, I said, as I stepped out into the clear, fresh, bracing air, and shook my shoulders, as if I had really dropped a burden of my own under that much-coveted roof. I can very well conceive that a pure patriot might wish the office, because he sincerely believed himself able to serve his country in it, and *therefore* accepted its crown of thorns; but lacking this motive, that a man in the meridian of life, or descending its down-hill path, and consequently with the full knowledge of this life's emptiness, should stretch out *even one hand* to grasp such a distracting position, I can never understand.

The good dame "who went to sleep with six gallons of milk on her mind" every night, was a fool to do it. A step-mother's life under the harrow were paradise to it; only the life of a *country* clergyman who writes three sermons a week, and attends weddings at sixpence a piece, and hoes his own potatoes, and feeds the pigs, and is on hand for church and vestry meetings during the week, and keeps the run of all the new-born babies and their middle names, and is always, in a highly devotional frame of mind, is a parallel case.

I should like to have taken all those lobbyists I saw in the White House with me the afternoon of that day to "Arlington Heights," and bade them look there at the thousands of head-stones, gleaming white like the billows of the sea in the sunlight, far as the eye could reach, labelled "unknown," "unknown," telling the simple tragic story of our national struggle more effectually than any sculptured monument could have done. I would like to have shown them this, to see if for one moment it had power to paralyze those eager hands outstretched for bubbles.

"Unknown?" Not to him, in whose book every one of those names is written in letters of light! Not to him, in whose army of the faithful unto death, there are no "privates"!

My eyes were blind with tears, as I signed my name in the visitor's book at the desk of the Freedman's Bureau there, once General Lee's residence. All *was* "quiet on the Potomac," as its blue waters glittered in the sunlight before us. Yet the very air was thick with utterances. The place on which I stood is now indeed holy ground. And far off rose the white dome of the Capitol, crowded with men, some of them, thank God, not forgetting these white head-stones, in their efforts to keep inviolate what these brave fellows died for; and some, alas! willing to sell their glorious birthright for a "mess of pottage."

The sharp contrast of luxury and squalor, in Washington, even exceeding New York,—the carriages and their liveries, and the sumptuous dames inside; the pigs which run rooting round the streets; the tumble-down, shambling, rickety carts, with their bob-tailed, worn-out donkeys, so expressive of lazy unthrift,—must be regarded with the eye of a New Englander, trained to thoroughness and "faculty," to be properly appreciated. I avow myself, cursed or blessed, as you will, with the New England "bringing up," to which anything that "hangs by the eyelids" is simple crucifixion, whether it be in a cart or a statute-book, an unhinged door, or a two or a four-legged dawdle.

"Oh, you'd come into it, and be as lazy as anybody," said my companion, "if you lived here a while."

Shade of the Pilgrim Fathers!—Assembly's Catechism!—baked beans—fish-balls—"riz" brown bread! Never!

I didn't see Vinnie Ream's statue of Lincoln.[1] It was boxed for Italy, Congress having made the necessary appropriation. But I saw Vinnie. She has dimples. Senators like dimples. And in case the statue is not meritorious, why—I would like to ask, amid the crowd of lobbying *men*, whose paws are in the national basket, after the loaves and fishes—should not this little woman's cunning white hand have slily drawn some out?

New York Ledger
Apr. 10, 1869

THE MODERN OLD MAID

SHE DON'T shuffle round in "skimpt" raiment, and awkward shoes, and cotton gloves, with horn side-combs fastening six hairs to her temples; nor has she a sharp nose, and angular jaw, and hollow cheeks, and only two front teeth. She don't read "Law's Serious Call,"[1] or keep a cat, or a snuff-box, or go to bed at dark, save on vestry-meeting nights, nor scowl at little children, or gather catnip, or apply a broomstick to astonished dogs.

Not a bit of it. The modern "old maid" is round and jolly, and has her full complement of hair and teeth, and two dimples in her cheek, and has a laugh as musical as a bobolink's song. She wears pretty, nicely fitting dresses too, and cunning little ornaments around her plump throat, and becoming bits of color in her hair, and at her breast, in the shape of little knots and bows; and her waist is shapely, and her hands have sparkling rings, and no knuckles; and her foot is cunning, and is prisoned in a bewildering boot; and she goes to concerts and parties and suppers and lectures and matinees, and she don't go alone either; and she lives in a nice house, earned by herself, and gives jolly little teas in it. She don't care whether she is married or not, nor need she. She can afford to wait, as men often do, till they have "seen life," and when their bones are full of aches, and their blood tamed down to water, and they have done going out, and want somebody to swear at and to nurse them—then marry!

Ah! the modern old maid has her eye-teeth cut. She takes care of herself, instead of her sister's nine children, through mumps, and measles, and croup, and chicken-pox, and lung fever and leprosy, and what not.

She don't work that way for no wages and bare toleration, day and night. No, sir! If she has no money, she teaches, or she lectures, or she writes books or poems, or she is a book-keeper, or she sets types, or she does anything but hang on to the skirts of somebody else's husband, and she feels well and independent in consequence, and holds up her head with the best, and asks no favors, and "*Woman's Rights*" has done it!

That awful bugbear, "Woman's Rights"! which small souled men, and, I am sorry to say, narrow *women* too, burlesque and ridicule, and won't believe in, till the Juggernaut of Progress knocks them down and rides over them, because they will neither climb up on it, nor get out of the way.

The fact is, the *Modern* Old Maid is as good as the Modern Young Maid, and a great deal better, to those who have outgrown bread and butter. She has sense as well as freshness, and conversation and repartee as well as dimples and curves.

She carries a dainty parasol, and a natty little umbrella, and wears killing bonnets, and has live poets and sages and philosophers in her train, and knows how to use her eyes, and don't care if she never sees a cat, and couldn't tell a snuff-box from a patent reaper, and has a bank-book and dividends: yes, sir! and her name is Phœbe or Alice; and Woman's Rights has done it.

New York Ledger
June 5, 1869

DULL HOMES IN BRIGHT PLACES

WHEN I LIVE in the country, the front door of my house shall be made for use, and not for show; and the blinds and windows shall be thrown wide open from sunrise until sunset; and I will issue invitations to the bees and birds and butterflies to come in and out at their own convenience, without fear of molestation from me, or of danger to my furniture or belongings. If a few mosquitoes follow suit, I will accept them as a necessary evil, and not to be compared, in the way of annoyance, with that air of sepulchral gloom which, like a wet blanket of mist, surrounds the exterior of most country dwellings, where the men, women, and children skulk round like burglars to the *back* of the house to effect an entrance, and the closed door and blinds are suggestive of a corpse awaiting burial. And yet I think I understand how this bad custom came about. It was from many babies and much darning and baking, and the dread of impending fly-specks on the gilt frame encircling General Washington and the large looking-glass. But, dear friends, put a mahogany frame round the General, and banish the looking-glass, which will, in a few years, if you neglect all that makes home cheerful, reflect only the imprint of life's cares, instead of its pleasures and contents. "*They* are so very few," you say. Well, then the more necessity for letting in the sunshine. As I walk about, I notice the careworn, pallid faces of the wives and mothers about many of these country homes, and the careless untidiness of dress which, in a woman, means that she has given the whole thing up, either from overwork or lack of sympathy from the one person for whom the shining hair was once neatly combed, and the strip of white collar carefully pinned, although it might be late in the day before time was found to do these things. When I see these women at nightfall, in this neglectful dress, sitting alone upon the back door-step, while the husband and father has strolled off to some neighbor's, and lies flat on his stomach on the grass, with half a dozen other husbands and fathers, browsing like so many cattle, without a thought of those weary women, I fall to thinking how much life would be worth to me reduced to this utilitarian standard of cow and cabbage. Then I wonder if those women were to throw open the blinds and doors and windows of the front of the house, and smooth their hair a bit, and let one of the children pick some grasses and wild flowers for the mantel, and then tell their respective Johns and Toms to bring into the house the men they like to talk to at that hour, so that all could be jolly together, whether it wouldn't change things for the better. If that plan didn't work, do you know what I would do? I would shoulder my baby, and trot down the road to the nearest neighbor's, and let the old coffin of a house take care of itself. I *wouldn't* rust, anyhow.

Now, it may be that these women wouldn't know how miserable they were, if I didn't tell them of it. So much the worse, then. I only know that if life were *all work* to me, it should go hard but I would try to catch a sunbeam now and then, if it were only that the children might not be demoralized by growing up to look at me in the light of a dray-horse; if it were only that my boys need not expect *their* wives to close their eyes and ears to the beauty and harmony which God had scattered so lavishly about them. Because there are rocks, shall there be no roses? Because there is dust, shall there be no dew?

Do you do well, my sisters, to make your houses so gloomy that your husbands would rather roost outside upon the stone fences, than stay in them? Don't *have* a "best carpet;" don't *have* a "best sofa." Let in the sun, and the birds, and the children, though it involve bare floors and wooden chairs, and the total banishment of General Washington and that best looking-glass. *Eat* in your "best parlor," and laugh in it; don't save it up to be laid out in! Try it now, and see if life isn't a different thing to you all. As to your "work," a great deal of it is unnecessary. John and the children would be much better without pies, cakes, and doughnuts. Make it your religion to give them wholesome bread and meat, and then stop and take a little breath. Nobody will thank you for turning yourself into a machine. When you drop in your tracks, they will just shovel the earth over you, and get Jerusha Ann Sombody to step into your shoes. They won't cry a bit. You never stopped to say a word to them except "*get out of my way*." To be sure, you were working hard for them all the while, but that won't be remembered. So you just take a little comfort yourself as you go along, and look after "No 1." Laugh more and darn less; they will like you twice as well. If there is more work than you can consistently do, *don't do it*. Sometimes there is a little blossom of a daughter in a family who makes everything bright with her finger-tips; if there is none in yours, do *you* be that blossom. Don't, even for John, let your children remember home as a charnel-house, and you as its female sexton.

New York Ledger
Sept. 4, 1869

WOMEN'S SALARIES

> "Miss Marianna Thompson, now a student at the Theological school, received during her summer vacation two invitations to settle with good societies, each of which offered her twelve hundred dollars per year. Pretty good for a school-girl, I think."
>
> Yes, that is very good; and we trust Miss Thompson will accept one of these (or a better) and do great good to her hearers. And, should some excellent young man ask her to "settle" with him as wife, *at no salary at all*, we advise her to heed that "call" as well. —*N. Y. Tribune.*

WELL, NOW, Mr. *Tribune*, I don't. I have seen too many women, quite as capable as Miss Thompson of being self-supporting individuals, exhausting the last remnant of their strength in the family, and carefully saving every penny for a husband, who never doled out twenty-five cents, without asking the purpose for which it was needed, and reiterating the stale advice to spend it judiciously. I have seen such women, too proud to complain or remonstrate, turn away with a crimson cheek, and a moist eye, to dicker, and haggle, and contrive for this end, when the husband who gave this advice, had effectually blotted out the word self-denial from his own dictionary.

No, Mr. *Tribune*, I differ from you entirely. I advise no woman to refuse twelve hundred independent dollars a year for good, honest labor, to become such a serf as this.

And while we are on this subject, I would like to air the disgust with which I am nauseated, at the idea of any decent, intelligent, self-respecting, capable wife, ever being obliged *to ask* for that which she so laboriously earns, and which is just as much hers by right, as the money that her husband receives from his customers is *his*, instead of his next-door—dry-goods—neighbor's.

No man should thus humiliate a woman; no woman should permit herself to be thus humiliated. I am not now speaking of those foolish women, to whom a ribbon, or a necklace, is dearer than their husband's strength, life, or mercantile honor. I put such women entirely out of the question; only remarking, that if a man marries a fool in the hope of her being pliant, and easily ruled by him, he will find too late that he is mistaken. But that's his affair. Men always have, and always will keep on admiring their own perspicacity in reading female character, when not one in ten knows any more what his wife is spiritually made of, than what sheep furnished the coat for his own back.

Sary Gamp advised her comrade—nurse—to put the mutual bottle on the shelf, and "*look the other way!*"

That's just what I would advise the husbands of intelligent wives to do with regard to the money which they "allow" them, and which one would imagine was rightly theirs, by virtue of risking their lives every Friday to become the mother of twins; by virtue of, when lying faint and weak beside them, giving out orders for the comfort and well-being of the family down-stairs before they are able to get about; by virtue of *never* being able for one moment, day or night, sick or well, to drop, or to shake, off the responsibility which a *good* wife and mother must always feel, whether present or absent from her family.

Oh! treat such a woman generously. Make up your mind what in justice she should receive in the money way, and don't above all things, wait for her to *ask* you for it, and never, never be mean enough to charge a woman of this kind "to spend it carefully."

I daresay you have done it, and *you*, and *you;* I daresay you are real good fellows too, and *mean* to do what is right. And I know you "love" your wives—*i.e.*, as *men* love—thus—wounding a sensitive spirit, without the least notion you are doing it; thus—charging the tear that follows to a coming toothache or stomach-ache! Great blundering creatures! I sometimes don't know whether to box your ears or hug you. Because the very next minute you will say, or do, some such perfectly lovely thing, that, woman fashion, I exclaim, "Well—well;" but I won't tell you what I do say, because you'll hop right off the stool of repentance, and go to your normal occupation of crowing and bragging.

But, seriously, I do wish you would consider a little this same money question, and when the time comes for payment, don't, as I tell you, open your pocketbook, heave a deep sigh, as you spread a bill on your knee, and give it a despairing glance of love, as you dump it in your wife's outstretched hand. No, sir! follow Sary Gamp's advice: "Put it on the shelf, and look the other way, and don't trouble yourself to tell her to '*make it go as far as she can*,'" because she will naturally do that, and there's where you are a fool again. I should think you'd know by this time, that it will go so far *you* wont see it again your natural lifetime. And why shouldn't it? Does she require to know whether you pay fifteen cents apiece for your cigars; whether you couldn't buy a cheaper kind, and how many a day you smoke! Come now, be honest—would *you* like that?

New York Ledger
Dec. 18, 1869

LEGAL MURDERS

I WOULD LIKE to write a book on this subject; that is if really *good* people had not such moonshine notions about "delicacy." This class are really the drags on the wheel of reform. I don't say that sometimes it is not necessary, and even right, to drive rough-shod right over them, if they will persist in walking in such a narrow path; but one does it after all with regret, because they so sincerely believe themselves to be in the "path of duty," as they call it. Dear me! if there ever was a perverted phrase, this is one! It makes me sick to hear it.

What do I mean by "legal murders"? Well, if a woman is knocked on the head with a flat-iron by her husband and killed, or if arsenic is mixed with her food, or if a bullet is sent through her brain, the law takes cognizance of it. But what of the cruel words that just as surely kill, by constant repetition? What of the neglect? What of the diseased children of a pure, healthy mother? What of the ten or twelve, even healthy children, "who come," one after another, into the weary arms of a really good woman, who yet never knows the meaning of the word *rest* till the coffin-lid shuts her in from all earthly care and pain? Is the self-sacrifice and self-abnegation all to be on one side? Is the "weaker" always to be the stronger in this regard? I could write flaming words about "the inscrutable Providence which has seen fit to remove our dear sister in her youth from the bosom of her young family," as the funeral prayer phrases it.

Providence did nothing of the sort. Poor Providence! It is astonishing how busy people are making up bundles to lay on *His* shoulders! I imagine Providence meant that women, as well as men, should have a right to their own lives. That they, equally with men, should rest when they can go no further on the road without dying. That while the father sits down to smoke the tobacco which "Providence" always seems to furnish him with, although his family may not have bread to eat, his wife should not stagger to her feet, and try to shoulder again her family cares and expenses.

Sometimes—nay, often—in view of all this, I rejoice in regarding the serene Mrs. Calla-Lily. *She* goes on just like a man. When she is tired she lies down, and stays there till she is rested, and lets the domestic world wag. If she don't feel like talking, she reads. If the children are noisy, she sweetly and cunningly gets out of the way, on that convenient male pretext, "putting a letter in the post-office." She don't "smoke," but she has her little comforts all the same, and at the right time, although the heavens should fall, and little Tommy's shoes give out. She looks as sleek and smooth and fair as if she were *really* a lily; and everybody says, "What a delightful person she is! and how bright and charming at all times!"

Now this spectacle soothes me, after seeing the long procession of bent, hollow-eyed, broken-spirited women who are *legally* murdered.

I exclaim, Good! and think of the old rhyme:

> "Look out for thyself,
> And take care of thyself,
> For nobody cares for thee."

Of course this is very "unamiable" in me, but amiability is not the only or the best quality in the world. I have seen people without a particle of it, as the phrase is often understood, who were the world's real saviours; and I have seen those human oysters, "amiable" people, till sea-sickness was not a circumstance to the condition of my mental and moral stomach.

New York Ledger
Mar. 12, 1870

HOW I LOOK

A CORRESPONDENT inquires how I look? Am I tall? have I dark, or light complexion? and what color are my eyes?

I should be very happy to answer these questions, did I know myself. I proceed to explain why I cannot tell whether "I be I."

First—one evening I was seated at the opera, waiting patiently for the performances to begin. In two orchestra chairs, directly in front of me, sat a lady and gentleman, both utter strangers to me. Said the *gentleman* to his companion, "Do you see the lady who has just entered yonder box?" pointing, as he did so, to the gallery; "well, that is Fanny Fern."—"You know her, then?" asked the lady.—"Intimately," replied this strange gentleman—"*intimately*. Observe how expensively she is dressed. See those diamonds, and that lace! Well, I assure you, that every cent she has ever earned by her writings goes straightway upon her back." Naturally desiring to know how I did look, I used my opera-glass. The lady was tall, handsome, graceful, and beautifully dressed. The gentleman who accompanied me began to grow red in the face, at the statement of my "intimate" acquaintance, and insisted on a word with him; but the fun was too good to be spoiled, and the game too insignificant to hunt; so, in hope of farther revelations, I laughingly observed my "double" during the evening, who looked as I have just described, for your benefit.

Again—in a list of pictures announced to be sold lately, was one labelled "Fanny Fern." Having lost curiosity concerning that lady myself, I did not go on a tour of inspection; but a gentleman friend of mine who did, came back in high glee at the manner in which the purchaser thereof, if any should be found, would be swindled—as "I was *not* I" in that case either.

Some time ago "Fanny Fern" was peddled round California, or at least, so I was informed by letter. In this instance they had given her, by way of variety, black eyes and hair, and a brunette complexion. I think she was also taken smiling. A friend, moreover, informed me that he had seen me, with an angelic expression, seated upon a rosy cloud, with wings at my back. This last fact touched me. Wings are what I sigh for. It was too cruel a mockery.

You will see from the above, how impossible it is, for such a chameleon female, to describe herself, even to one "who likes my writings." If it will throw any light on the subject, however, I will inform you that a man who got into my parlor under cover of "New-Year's calls," after breathlessly inspecting me, remarked, "Well, now, I *am* agreeably disappointed! I thought from the way you *writ*, that you were a great six-footer of a woman, with snapping black eyes and a big waist, and I *am* pleased to find you looking so soft and so femi-*nine!*"

I would have preferred, had I been consulted, that he should have omitted the word "soft;" but after the experiences narrated above, this was a trifle.

New York Ledger
Apr. 9, 1870

LADY LECTURERS

AS I HAVE always declined all requests to lecture, or to speak in public, I may be allowed to make a few remarks on the treatment of those who do.

To begin with, can anybody tell me why reporters, in making mention of lady speakers, always consider it to be necessary to report, fully and *firstly*, the dresses worn by them? When John Jones or Senator Rouser frees his mind in public, we are left in painful ignorance of the color and fit of his pants, coat, necktie and vest—and worse still, the shape of his boots. This seems to me a great omission. How can we possibly judge of his oratorical powers, of the strength or weakness of his logic, or of his fitness in any way to mount the platform, when these important points are left unsolved to our feeble feminine imaginations? For one, I respectfully request reporters to ease my mind on these subjects—to tell me decidedly whether a dress, or a frock-coat, or a bob-tailed jacket was worn by these masculine orators; whether their pants had a stripe down the side, and whether the dress lapels of their coats were faced with silk, or disappointed the anxious and inquiring eye of the public by presenting only a broadcloth surface. I have looked in vain for any satisfaction on these points.

I propose that the present staff of male reporters should be remodelled, and that some enterprising journal should send to Paris for the man-milliner Worth, in order that this necessary branch of reportorial business be more minutely and correctly attended to.

Speaking of reporters, I was present the other night at a female-suffrage meeting, where many distinguished men made eloquent speeches in favor thereof. At the reporters' table sat two young lady reporters side by side with the brethren of the same craft. Truly, remarked I to my companion, it is very well to plead for women's rights, but more delicious to me is the sight of those two girls *taking them!* But, rejoined my cautious male friend, you see, Fanny, a woman couldn't go to report a rat-fight, or a prize-fight, or a dog-fight. *But*, replied I, just let the women go "marching on" as they have begun, and there will soon *be* no rat-fights, dog-fights, or prize-fights to report. It will appear from this, that I believe in the woman *that is to be*. I do—although she has as yet had to struggle with both hands tied, and then had her ears boxed for not doing more execution. Cut the string, gentlemen, and see what you shall see! "Pooh! you are afraid" to knock that chip off our shoulder.

How strange it all seems to me, the more I ponder it, that men can't, or don't, or won't see that woman's enlightenment is man's millennium. "My wife don't understand so and so, and it's no use talking to her."—"My wife will have just so many dresses, and don't care for anything else."—"My wife won't look after my children, but leaves them to nurses, she is so fond of pleasure." So it would seem that these Adams and the "wife thou gavest to be with me," even now find their respective and flowery Edens full of thorns, even *without* that serpent, female suffrage, whose slimy trail is so deprecated.

Put *this* in the crown of your hats, gentlemen! *A fool of either sex is the hardest animal to drive that ever required a bit. Better one who jumps a fence now and then, than your sulky, stupid donkey, whose rhinoceros back feels neither pat or goad.*

New York Ledger
June 18, 1870

ONE SORT OF WOMAN

THERE IS a great deal of "cussedness" in inanimate things; else why do water pipes always break loose of a Sunday?

Plumbers are Christians; at least one can never be found till Monday morning, though a second deluge be imminent.

It is sufficiently agonizing to state the case thus; but when you superadd, that the master of the house has gone off lecturing for the enlightenment of the human race, thus neglecting his "domestic sphere," the situation becomes complicated.

"I knew something of the sort would turn up the minute his back was turned," I remarked to my Monday morning plumber. "I never knew it to fail," said I, pointing to the wet ceiling.

Setting his hat upon one side, with a quizzical look, he answered:

"Why, ma'am, I judged from your writings that you were three-quarters a man yourself, and wouldn't need one of us to tell you what to do!"

Now what do you think of that blow, flat between the eyes?

"Sir," said I, "at the boarding-school I attended, gas-fitting and plumbing were branches that were, unfortunately, neglected. In the good time coming, women will know lead pipes like the alphabet, and your occupation will be gone; therefore prepare yourself to be a milliner or a chambermaid."

One Sort of Woman

"Three-quarters a man!" I sat down with my needle to think of it. How could he get such an impression from anything I ever wrote? May not a woman be earnest as the Lord made her, and express herself correspondingly, without this imputation? If you, Mr. Plumber, had a fit in my house, I should be enough of a "man" not to faint or to scream, but to stand by you, and do my best to get you out of it, and see you safely home after it. If your leg or your arm needed amputation, I could stand by you, if need be, and hold the instruments and see it done. If you were my husband, and your health failed, and you could not work, I could go out into the world and earn your living and mine too. So far I *am* "three-quarters a man."

But after that, I'd have you, and others who have made the same mistake, to know that there's considerable of a woman left. I like a man's arm to lean on. I like a man's counsel and advice about things of which he knows better than I; and I know how to accept it too, without a pout—provided it is given as he would like it given were he a woman. I could be very "nervous" also, which is one womanly qualification, I believe, if I would let myself; as it is, it sometimes "whistles itself," as the boy said when he was thumped at school for this accomplishment. I love babies too, and flowers, and all pretty and sweet things, as few men could do. I can make a pudding or cake, or I can roast meat; I can trim and make a bonnet, and cut a dress, and mend stockings, and "clean house," and attend to the "kitchen cabinet," in true, thorough, New England fashion, as a man could never do. I can earn my living, and not whine about it, as many men *don't*! and I can be an egotist, as you see, if I get stirred up and when I am misunderstood.

Isn't it the funniest thing in life, that a woman can't be vital and energetic, without being thought masculine?

There are some flowers which, if nipped, go off with a pop-gun noise; but they are none the less flowers—are they?

New York Ledger
Nov. 19, 1870

THEOLOGICAL NUTS

I WONDER is it necessary for clergymen to keep preaching on "the doctrines"? I can't help thinking that to teach men and women how to live, is much more important in this brief life than to define doctrines. I can't help thinking that the time spent in telling how the adherents of every denomination but our own are going to the "bad place," had better be spent in teaching those about us how to get to the good place. If you reply that it is necessary to put up these doctrinal fences to keep intruders off our territory, I say if you are wiser than anybody else in the world, it would be a more Christian act to leave wide open the hospitable gates, that outsiders might come in and profit by it. If you had anathematized a visitor on your front door-step, he wouldn't be likely to accept your after invitation to come in and sit down with you at your table, would he?

Now there are the great army of the weary-hearted, who, look up to their "minister," with eyes wistful, like those of a dumb animal in pain, hungering for the hopeful, cheering word that shall give them strength to shoulder another week's burdens; why, instead of the bread of heaven, give them the stone of an indigestible doctrine?

I hope what I say will be taken in all kindness, as it is meant. I have so many times, under such circumstances, gone away without having my burden lifted, not so much as by a finger, from the above causes, that I cannot but deplore it; no more than I can help being grateful for the fitting words, that have been to me like "apples of gold in pictures of silver."

The misery that may not be spoken to human ears! The cross worn close to the tender heart, of which there is no outward sign! Oh, if clergymen would oftener deal with these! Creeds!—I don't know them. I know God's love, and our exceeding needs. I know His infinite pity, and our outreached, groping fingers. I don't ask what my neighbor believes. I want to know *how he lives*.[1]

New York Ledger
Feb. 10, 1872

SAUCE FOR THE GANDER

EVERY WRITTEN or spoken sentence, not calculated to benefit mankind, carries with it, I verily believe, its own antidote in the shape of narrowness and bigotry.

This comforting thought occurred to me on leaving a lecture hall the other evening, where the speaker, in saying some very good things, had mentioned all female employments, save housekeeping, especially those of writing and lecturing, with utter contempt, averring that the education and training of children were the only things worthy their notice. He did not stop to explain what was to become of all the old maids and single women generally; or whether they might be excused for earning an honest support by pen and ink, or even stepping upon the platform, when they had no "home," and consequently no "home duties" to attend to; and whether, if the lecture they should deliver were as narrow and illogical as his own, the patient public might not, as in his case, be willing to *pay* and *listen*. Also, while insisting upon every woman being a mother, and desiring nothing beyond her nursery walls, not even her own intellectual progression, to qualify her to meet the questioning *youth*, as well as the dependent *infancy* of her children, I heard not one syllable from him upon the home duty devolving on the *father* and *the husband*, as to his share in their government and *home* education, which, in my opinion, is more important than that of school; nor of the cultivation of his companionable qualities, to assist in making home pleasant. Not a word did he say on this head, no more than as if these things were not binding equally on him as on the wife. As if that *could* be "home," in any true sense, where *both* did not know and practise these duties. He told us it was "of course more pleasant for women to be like the noisy cascade, and to mount the platform, than to imitate the gentle, silent rivulet, and stay quietly at home out of the public eye." As the lecturer had a home himself, and was a husband and father, and not particularly in need of any emolument from lecuring, it occurred to me that the propriety of his own absence from the "gentle rivulet" of home duties might admit of a doubt. It could not be possible that he who could map out a wife's home duty by such strict latitude and longitude, should himself have wearied of their tameness, and "mounted the platform to keep in the public eye."

What nonsense even a male lecturer may utter! said I, as I left his presence. As if there were no women, good and earnest as well as gifted, who neglected no duties while mounting the platform, but who honored it with their womanly, dignified presence, and made every large-souled, large-brained man who listened to them rejoice that they were there.

This "vine and oak" style of talk is getting monotonous. There is more "oak" to the women of to-day than there was to those of the past. Else how could the great army of drunken, incompetent, unpractical, idle husbands be supported as they are by wives, who can't stop to be "gentle, silent rivulets," but have to "keep in the public eye" as business women? Our lecturer didn't mention this little fact—not he!

New York Ledger
Mar. 30, 1872

END OF THE SUMMER SEASON

THERE IS NOTHING more absurd than the hot haste with which people hurry from a watering-place at the first crisp breath of Autumn, when "the season" is closed. The definition of "the season" has been for many years changed; the season closing now, not when ladies can no longer wear gauze dresses in riding, but very near the time when Jack Frost's hieroglyphics may be read upon the window pane. The upstart rich do not seem to know this, anymore than they can understand that most of our fashionable people of solid foundation have built unto themselves beautiful villas in the neighborhood of great hotels, so perfect as to gastronomic and equestrian arrangements, to say nothing of extensive bath-rooms of their own, as to monopolize all the party giving under the privacy of their own roofs. This the new people do not know, and cannot therefore account for the chance of an audience on the occasion of the unloading of their numerous trunks, for the crowded promenade corridor of half-dress, instead of the crowded ball-room in full dress.

"It don't pay," says mamma, looking at her daughter's new diamonds, purchased with the gongings of many years in avenue groceries.

"It's all humbug," says papa, mopping his face with his handkerchief, as he thinks of his slippers and easy chair at home.

"Where are the men?" asks Angeline, giving her curls an extra twirl. "I shall be an old maid before I am brought out. Matilda will never be married off at this rate."

This is the exposition of the whole matter. This is why the hotels are closed at the end of the "fashionable season." This is why our solid families remain in pretty villas, enjoying their horseback rides at noon and their evening drives, and their social parties, and the genuine hospitality which is born not of eating and drinking, but of good feeling and good taste.

There are people of refined nature but limited means, who would prefer to remain till winter sets in, and enjoy the lovely autumn days, were it not for unhealthy stoves and the absence of gas, so necessary at this season, to which their eyes have become accustomed in the long, bright city evenings. But, as it is acknowledged for years past by all physicians, that city life has too much friction, perhaps this going to bed at hen-roost is the best preparation for the coming winter.

As for me, whether I go early or late, whether my eyes are open or shut, memory will always make pictures for me of dear, blessed Newport, full of sparkle and sunrise, eastern gems and sunset splendors, dog-carts and donkeys, phaetons and four-in-hand, long-haired literary people and close-cropped dandies, all moving in that crisp air, which makes me say with Festus,[1] "Oh, God, I thank thee that I live."[2]

New York Ledger
Oct. 12, 1872

EXPLANATORY NOTES TO NEWSPAPER ARTICLES

THE MODEL HUSBAND

1. "The Model Husband" is the first of seven clearly identifiable articles published by Fanny Fern in the *Olive Branch* before she began using the Fanny Fern signature in September 1851. These early articles were either unsigned or were signed "Tabitha" or "Clara."

THOUGHTS ON DRESS

1. Benedict: probably a reference to Benedick in Shakespeare's *Much Ado about Nothing*, who was an inveterate railer against women and a confirmed bachelor until he was tricked into believing Beatrice was in love with him.

2. Peggoty is David Copperfield's kind nurse in Dickens's novel. As a child, Copperfield always sees her with her sewing, and he remembers that her finger was "roughened by needlework, like a pocket nutmeg grater."

DEACONS' DAUGHTERS AND MINISTERS' SONS

1. "Deacons' Daughters and Ministers' Sons" contains a number of autobiographical references. Fern's father was a deacon of the Park Street (Congregational) Church in Boston. He was commonly referred to as the "Deacon," and, having undergone a religious conversion after his marriage, he became strictly devout, renouncing dancing and other "ungodly" pursuits. As a child and young girl, Fern was spirited and merry, and, although she dutifully learned her catechism and shared her mother's love of God, she was not sufficiently pious for her sober father. She refused to be converted or to be frightened by stories of hell (see EP 22–42, *New Story Book* 7–25). The Willises had nine children, though not all daughters. The episode of pie stealing at boarding school took place when Fern was at Catharine Beecher's Female Seminary and is recorded in a letter from Harriet Beecher Stowe to James Parton (SSC).

AUNT HETTY ON MATRIMONY

1. The lucifer-match, the first practical friction match, was manufactured in 1829 by Samuel Johnes of London, who called the matches "Lucifers" because when ignited, they gave off a shower of sparks and noxious fumes.

FAMILY JARS

1. California widow was the term given to the wives of men who had gone to California in search of gold and adventure after the Gold Rush of 1849 and had not returned.

MISTAKEN PHILANTHROPY

1. The parable of Dives and Lazarus, Acts 16, tells of the rich man who goes to hell and suffers torment while the beggar Lazarus goes to heaven.

WOMAN'S WICKEDNESS

1. Kit North is the pseudonym under which Professor John Wilson contributed to *Blackwood's Magazine*.

A WHISPER TO ROMANTIC YOUNG LADIES

1. Araminta is the young cousin of Belinda in William Congreve's play *The Old Bachelor*, first produced in 1693, and the beloved of the character Vainlove, who plans to marry her.

2. "Receive the mitten": an expression referring to a man's proposal to a woman and its subsequent refusal.

ALL ABOUT SATAN

1. Jane Grey Cannon Swisshelm (1815–84), an American newspaper editor who from 1847 to 1857 edited the *Pittsburgh Saturday Visiter* [sic], a paper which she had founded. The baby Fern refers to did not prevent her from continuing her work. In 1857 she sold the paper and, taking her daughter with her, permanently separated from her husband and established a new paper in Minnesota. Writing primarily on abolition, temperance, and the rights of women, Swisshelm was known for her audacious, stinging, and humorous invective.

A LITTLE BUNKER HILL

1. *Sigh*-acruse, a reference to the third National Woman's Rights Convention held in Syracuse, New York, in 1852.

PRAISE FROM A WOMAN

1. This article was occasioned by comments from Harriet Marion Stephens (1823–58) in her article "Town-Talk" for the Boston *Times*. Stephens published two works, *Home Scenes and Sounds* (1854), a book of short stories and poems, and a novel, *Hagar the Martyr* (1855), which is one of the few novels of the period to portray a happy ending for a fallen woman.

CHILDREN'S RIGHTS

1. Ananias and Sapphira in the Bible, Acts 5, pretend that the money they give to the church treasury is the whole payment for land they have sold, whereas it is only a part. They are struck dead because of their lie.

"I CAN'T."

1. The car of Juggernaut is a reference from Hindu ritual involving the movement of a massive car during the Puri festival. The term came to mean the movement of an inexorable force crushing anything in its path.

DON'T DISTURB HIM!

1. This article was published in *Fern Leaves*, Second Series (1854), under the title "Sober Husbands." The April 9, 1853 issue of the *Olive Branch* is missing from the Antiquarian Society, but a copy is located in the Library of Congress.

MRS. STOWE'S UNCLE TOM

1. Harriet Beecher Stowe (1811–96) published her famous antislavery novel, *Uncle Tom's Cabin*, as a serial in 1851 and 1852. It came out in book form in 1852, and 100,000 copies were sold in one week. Soon after the book appeared, Stowe went to England where she was loudly acclaimed and honored.

THE CHARITY ORPHANS

1. This article provided the germ for Fanny Fern's novel *Rose Clark* (1856), the opening scenes of which take place in an orphanage and probe beneath the outward appearance of order.

APOLLO HYACINTH

1. This is a satirical portrait of Fern's brother N. P. Willis, who had refused to help her when she was destitute. Willis (1806–67) was quite a dandy, urbane and fastidious in his tastes. In 1874 the *New York Herald* noted that when Fern's sketch of her brother appeared, it "created a fervor greater than any of Macaulay's vivid pictures were capable of creating" (Derby 220). This sketch is the basis for the character of Hyacinth in *Ruth Hall*.

"WHO LOVES A RAINY DAY?"

1. Coelebs is the protagonist of Hannah More's 1808 novel, *Coelebs in Search of a Wife*.

2. Di (Diana) Vernon is the spirited, outspoken heroine of Sir Walter Scott's *Rob Roy* (1818).

MRS. ADOLPHUS SMITH SPORTING THE "BLUE STOCKING"

1. I have been unable to locate an earlier printed version of this article. It may have been written originally for *Fern Leaves*, Second Series.

A BROADWAY SHOP REVERIE

1. Honiton was a lace made in Devon, England. Queen Victoria's wedding gown in 1840 was made of Honiton lace.

2. I have been unable to locate an earlier printed version of this article. It may have been written originally for *Fern Leaves*, Second Series.

PEEPS FROM UNDER A PARASOL

1. Richard Grant White (1821–85) was the music critic for the *Morning Courier* and wrote for other periodicals on various subjects. He was six feet two, with erect posture and an athletic build.

2. Edwin Hubbell Chapin (1814–80) was pastor of the Fourth Universalist Society in New York. A powerful speaker, he preached to a steadily growing congregation and was cofounder of the Chapin Home for indigents. George Washington Bethune (1805–62) was a Dutch Reformed clergyman and, at the time of Fern's article, pastor of a church in Brooklyn.

3. Horace Greeley (1811–72) was a journalist and political leader who had founded the *New York Tribune* in 1841. He took a strong antislavery position which in the 1850s led to his leaving the Whigs for the newly formed Republican party and made him a widely discussed figure.

4. George Ripley (1802–80) succeeded Margaret Fuller as literary editor for the *New York Tribune* in 1849 and remained in this post for thirty-one years. The *Tribune* was the first daily to establish a regular book review department. In 1850 Ripley founded *Harper's New Monthly Magazine*. He had been one of the organizers of the Brook Farm experiment of 1841–47.

5. Colonel Hiram Fuller (1814–88) had joined N. P. Willis and George Pope Morris on the New York *Evening Mirror* in 1843 and after their withdrawal continued to own it for fourteen years. He wrote gossipy, diverting correspondence under the pseudonym "Belle Brittan."

6. The *Albion* was a weekly eclectic magazine founded in 1822. It printed

pirated material from British periodicals mostly, but also had theater reviews and other original matter.

7. Richard Storrs Willis was Fanny Fern's younger brother (1819–1900) and at this time was editor of the New York *Musical World and Times*. An accomplished musician, Willis is most widely known as the composer of the Christmas carol "It Came upon a Midnight Clear."

8. Charles A. Dana (1819–97), New York journalist, became city editor of the *Tribune* in 1847 and then its managing editor until 1862. He later was part owner of the New York *Sun*. At the time of Fern's article, Dana was in sole charge of the *Tribune* while Horace Greeley was in Europe in 1855 and 1856.

9. Bayard Taylor (1825–78) was a poet and traveler on the *Tribune* staff. He wrote and lectured extensively and was known for his cosmopolitan taste.

10. Henry Ward Beecher (1813–87), son of Lyman Beecher and brother of Harriet Beecher Stowe and Catharine Beecher, became pastor of Plymouth Congregational Church in Brooklyn in 1847. One of the most popular preachers of all time, Beecher was a friend of Fern's in his youth (see, e.g., Derby 219).

11. James Parton (1822–91) was Fanny Fern's third husband. He was called the Father of American Biography because he was the first to portray his subjects realistically and with the abundant and intimate detail that recreated the living person. His first biography, *The Life of Horace Greeley*, was published the same year as *Ruth Hall* (1855) by the same publishers, Mason Brothers. Parton had begun writing for N. P. Willis's *Home Journal* in 1848 and although he left it a few years later because of Willis's refusal to allow him to continue to clip and print Fanny Fern's articles, he continued to write for other periodicals, including the *New York Ledger*, and he published numerous biographies, most notably *The Life of Andrew Jackson* (1859–60) and the *Life and Times of Ben Franklin* (1864).

12. John Lester (1820–88), son of James William Wallack, until 1861 acted professionally under the name John Lester so as not to rely on his famous father's name.

13. Laura Keene (1826–73) was the stage name of Mary Moss, the English actress who came to New York with James William Wallack in 1852. She toured the United States and Australia and returned to New York in 1855, where she became the first woman theater manager of any scope and power in the United States, and the first producer to give dignity to light comedy. In 1856 the Laura Keene Theatre was built, and for seven years she was its manager and leading actress. She was imperious as a manager and stories were told of quarrels with actors, but she was known for her integrity. Her most famous role was in *Our American Cousin*, in which she was playing in Ford's Theater in Washington when President Lincoln was shot in 1865.

14. James William Wallack (1795–1864), American actor and theater manager, was the head of a famous theater family.

15. Potiphar (George William) Curtis (1824–92), author and orator who, after four years travel in Europe, Egypt, and Syria as a correspondent for the *New York Tribune*, published two collections of his letters to the *Tribune*: *Nile Notes of a Howadji* (1851) and *The Howadji in Syria* (1852). In 1853 he published *The Potiphar Papers*, a gentle satire of the social life of New York in the style of Washington Irving.

16. Dr. Lowell Mason (1792–1872) was a compiler of church music, hymn writer, and musical educator. He used methods derived from Pestalozzi in Zurich to teach singing before teaching how to read music and introduced his technique into the Boston public schools in 1837. In 1851 he came to New York City.

17. Dr. Thomas Harvey Skinner (1791–1871), Presbyterian clergyman, was noted for his vigorous preaching. He helped to found Union Theological Seminary, where he was endowed with a chair.

18. Thomas Hood (1799–1845) was an English poet and humorist, whose best-known poems express love and pity for humankind.

19. "Peeps from under a Parasol" as printed here consists of material from three separate articles published in 1856. Although the other articles in this volume have been printed in their entirety as they appeared in the original newspaper texts, I have had to edit this selection in order to combine the three articles.

"LEAVES OF GRASS"

1. Fanny Fern was the first woman to praise Whitman's *Leaves of Grass* in print. Whitman had had the poem printed the previous year, setting about ten pages of the type himself. James Parton had introduced Fern to him soon after their marriage, and he visited them often. After he borrowed money from James Parton under false pretenses and was unable to repay the debt as promised, however, Parton threatened to sue. Although Whitman had no money, Parton's lawyer called at his house on June 17, 1857, and the debt was settled out of court. Whitman turned over certain items (books, a painting) in lieu of the promised money. The Partons, disenchanted with Whitman, considered him a scoundrel because of his behavior, and the friendship ended. (For a summary of the Whitman debt, see Oral S. Coad, "Whitman *vs.* Parton," *The Journal of the Rutgers University Library* 4 (December 1940): 1–8). Whitman blamed Fern for her husband's pursuit of the debt and soon afterward referred to her contemptuously in

an article criticizing intellectuality in women: "One genuine woman is worth a dozen Fanny Ferns," he wrote in an editorial in the *Brooklyn Daily Times* on July 9, 1857. This was shabby treatment indeed for the woman whose daring and courageous review had given him a boost at a time when the press was generally so critical.

2. Catholic-hating Know-nothing: The influx of nearly three million immigrants between 1845 and 1854, the majority of whom were Catholic, caused many Protestant Americans to fear that America's values and institutions would be corrupted. This fear lead to the formation of the Native American party, or American party, which came out of a secret patriotic society whose members customarily replied to any questioners, "I know nothing." Hence the term Know-Nothing came to be applied to the American party which, in 1854, was able to capture several state governorships and seventy-five seats in Congress on a platform of nativism, nationalism, and anti-Catholicism. The Know-Nothings soon became embroiled in the slavery issue, however, and the party disintegrated in 1856, with most of the Northern Know-Nothings going into the newly formed Republican party, which had been wooing them with pledges of "No Popery and No Slavery."

3. Ralph Waldo Emerson wrote a letter to Whitman praising *Leaves of Grass* on July 21, 1855. Whitman, without asking Emerson's permission, had the letter printed in the *New York Tribune* in October 1855 and included it in the 1856 edition of *Leaves of Grass*. William Howitt, reviewer for the *London Weekly Dispatch*, influenced by Emerson's letter, wrote a favorable review which was reprinted on April 19, 1856, in *Life Illustrated*, the periodical published by the phrenologists, Fowler and Wells, distributors of Whitman's book. *Life Illustrated* also reprinted Fern's review one week after it appeared.

4. Although Whitman's *Leaves of Grass* received some favorable comments, many reviewers—even those who praised the work—criticized Whitman's "vulgar" language and imagery. R. W. Griswold wrote in the New York *Criterion*, "It is impossible to imagine how any man's fancy could have conceived such a mass of stupid filth." The Boston *Intelligencer* said the author was "below the level of a brute," and the London *Critic* predicted that the "depth of his indecencies will be the grave of his fame." Charles A. Dana of the *Tribune*, although he praised Whitman's "bold, stirring thoughts," labeled the work "uncouth," "coarse," and "indecent."

HAS A MOTHER A RIGHT TO HER CHILDREN?

1. In cases of divorce or separation, the courts automatically awarded custody of the children to the father. This practice was consistent with the patriarchal system in which all property belonged to the father, with children considered as property. In 1880, the concept of the "tender years" was introduced into the legal system, and it was conceded that an infant might be better off with its mother during its early years. Not until the 1920s, however, did the mother replace the father as preferred guardian.

FRESH LEAVES *BY FANNY FERN*

1. Fern's satirical review of her own book was printed without any introduction; readers might well have taken it seriously as a very critical review until they arrived at the end of the column and saw Fern's signature.

WHERE HAVE I BEEN, AND WHAT HAVE I SEEN?

1. Harriet Hosmer (1830–1908), American sculptor, studied and worked in Rome; her works were world famous. Her *Beatrice Cenci* in 1857 was made for and is still located at the Mercantile Library in St. Louis.

2. Fern used the term Miss Nancy to mean a prudish, very proper person, here hypocritically so.

3. Rosa Bonheur (1822–1908), French painter and sculptor of animals, was an energetic and eminently successful artist who sought to be accepted on the same level as male artists. Her most famous painting, *The Horse Fair*, is in the Metropolitan Museum of Art in New York.

THE CHILD WHOM NOBODY CAN DO ANYTHING WITH

1. "The Song of the Shirt" is the title of a poem by Thomas Hood published in *Punch* in 1843; the poem tells compassionately of the weary, poorly recompensed labor of the seamstress. Fern, who had done such work before she began writing, wrote often of the poor working conditions and poor pay of seamstresses. Her 1854 article in the *Saturday Evening Post*, January 7, 1854, begins with a line from Hood's poem, "Stitch! stitch! stitch!"

A LAW MORE NICE THAN JUST

1. In addition to custom prohibiting women from wearing pants, there were municipal laws against breeches for women. Fern wrote on this subject again on October 8, 1859, in response to a newspaper report of a woman arrested for working as a seaman to support her ailing husband. Fern asks if the law would have been so concerned if the woman had earned her living as a prostitute, and points out that women do not have the earning power of men, that they are paid one-third of a man's wages for the same work. No wonder, she said, women wish they were men. On June 11, 1866, Fern wrote again on this subject when the newspaper reported the arrest of a woman in San Francisco for wearing men's clothes.

2. She is referring to her brother Richard Storrs Willis.

BLACKWELL'S ISLAND

1. On Blackwell's Island in the East River off New York City was located the prison that Fern visited. In 1921 the island was renamed Welfare Island.

BLACKWELL'S ISLAND NO. 3

1. Mrs. Grundy comes from Thomas Morton's play, *Speed the Plough* (1798), in which a character constantly worries about what her neighbor, Mrs. Grundy, will say. The term has come to stand for conventional censorship in everyday life.

AMIABLE CREATURES

1. This article appeared in the *New York Ledger* under the title "A Pickle for Those Who Are Fond of Sugar." Because I was not able to locate the newspaper article until after this volume went to press, I have used the text from *Folly As It Flies* (1868). The original article was stronger in its criticism of women. The words "the majority of" are missing from line one, and there is an additional section describing the hypocrisy of women who, though unpleasant to each other, act "angelic" when men are around. Also missing from the 1868 text is a section describing why male visitors are preferable to female visitors—deleted perhaps because of the possible sexual connotations.

INDEPENDENCE

1. Lantern was a famous trotting horse belonging to Robert Bonner, editor of the *Ledger*, and one of the first horses Bonner acquired for his stable.

2. At the time of Fern's writing, books published in one country could be copied and republished in another without any payment to the author. Thus Dickens's novels were printed in the United States with no recompense to him, and Harriet Beecher Stowe's *Uncle Tom's Cabin* was published all over the world without her receiving a penny. It was not until 1886 that an international copyright agreement was signed and books published in one country were protected in other countries. On November 28, 1857, Fern wrote an article in the *Ledger* on the need for an international copyright law, which was occasioned by the recent publication of *Ruth Hall* in German, for which she was to receive nothing. James Parton wrote in the *Atlantic Monthly* in October 1867 urging that such a law be enacted and referred to Stowe's situation. Stowe's letter thanking him was the first of several letters between her and Fanny Fern (SSC).

SHALL WOMEN VOTE?

1. Mr. Tulliver is the father of Tom and Maggie Tulliver in George Eliot's *Mill on the Floss*. Tulliver tells his friend, whom he has asked for advice on a school for Tom (bk. 1, ch. 3), that although Maggie is clever, Tom "unfortunately" takes after his mother—an unforeseen outcome of Tulliver's planning: "I picked the mother because she wasn't o'er 'cute—. . . . I picked her from her sisters o' purpose, 'cause she was a bit weak, like; for I wasn't a-goin' to be told the right o' things by my own fireside."

NEW ENGLAND

1. Throughout her writings Fern used the term Gotham to refer to New York City, and Frogtown to mean Boston—an allusion to the frog pond in Boston Common. Historically, Gotham was a village in Nottinghamshire in England, whose residents, when threatened by an unwanted visit from King John, feigned imbecility so that after the king's scouts reported that the inhabitants of Gotham were all fools, he decided to go elsewhere. The term Gotham has come to mean a "city of fools." It was used by Washington Irving as an ironic name for New York City.

A GRANDMOTHER'S DILEMMA

1. Fanny Fern's eldest daughter, Grace—who had married Mortimer Thomson, a journalist who wrote under the name Q. K. Philander Doesticks—died in childbirth in 1862. Fern and James Parton brought up her child, Ethel—"Effie." After Fern's death in 1872 Fern's daughter Ellen took Ethel with her to Newburyport, Massachusetts. Four years later, Ellen and her stepfather, James Parton, were married, and when Ethel came of age she legally changed her name to Parton.

HOW I READ THE MORNING PAPERS

1. Cave of Adullam refers to a fortified cave in the ancient city in Israel where David and his followers took refuge in their flight from King Saul. See I Samuel 22:1–4.

TO MOTHERS AND TEACHERS

1. This is one of Fern's many articles decrying the conditions in the schools. A *Ledger* editorial in 1860 gives us an idea of those conditions: "Here is one classroom, where you see assembled one hundred and twenty little girls, from four to seven years of age. They are ranged upon seats, one above another, like flower pots in a conservatory. . . . At the base of the mountain stands the young lady, aged nineteen, salary one hundred dollars per annum, whose duty it is to watch these human buds and keep them quiet (with short intermissions) for the space of six hours. . . . The atmosphere? Why, what must it be? The art of ventilation has yet to begin to exist." Fern applauded the new kindergartens which permitted young children to sit at small tables (NYL 11/28/63), and throughout her career she urged reforms that have become accepted practice today.

THE WORKING-GIRLS OF NEW YORK

1. Jules Michelet (1798–1874) was a French historian, who wrote his monumental *Histoire de France* between 1833 and 1867. His method was to describe the past by immersing his own personality in his narrative. His ideas on women were

expressed primarily in his works *L'amour* (1858) and *La femme* (1859), in which he described the ideal woman as childlike, docile, and ignorant. Since she was inferior to her husband, he said, she aided the marriage by being submissive and obedient. She stayed at home while he went out into the world, and her role was to love her husband, raise her children, and take care of the house.

2. I cannot locate this in the *New York Ledger*. It may have been written originally for *Folly As It Flies,* or may have appeared in one of the issues of the *Ledger* from which Fern's column has been cut out of the only remaining copy. A longer version of this article first appeared in the *New York Ledger* on January 26, 1867. It was signed Sara P. Parton and appeared in Bonner's editorial column.

THE HISTORY OF OUR LATE WAR

1. Andersonville was the Confederate prison in Georgia during the Civil War, where conditions were so bad that within a period of three months in 1864, 8,589 men died of disease and starvation. The commandant of the Andersonville prison, Major Henry Wirtz, was the only Confederate leader executed for "war crimes" after the war.

2. Fern had taken a very strong position during the Civil War, urging that the North continue the fight until the South was thoroughly beaten. In 1862, she wrote, for example: "If ever there was a righteous fight ours is, and whoever needlessly withdraws his services or drawls 'peace' because war affects his business—is a traitor." See also *New York Ledger*, September 17, 1864, and May 27, 1865.

LADIES EXCLUDED FROM PUBLIC DINNERS

1. At the end of his tour of the United States, Charles Dickens was to be honored at a farewell dinner in New York by the Press Club, an all-male organization, on April 18, 1868. Three women, all writers who were married to Press Club members, applied for membership, but they were laughed at and refused. They were Fanny Fern, Mrs. David Croly (Jennie June), and Mrs. Charlotte B. Wilbour. At the last minute they were told that they could attend the dinner, but under certain conditions—which they rejected. Afterward, they started the first women's club in America, Sorosis, of which Fanny Fern was a vice-president.

A POSTSCRIPT TO A SERMON

1. Sary Gamp is Sarah Gamp, a character in Charles Dickens's *Martin Chuzzlewit*. An unprofessional nurse, she made herself available for any job—from lying-in to laying-out.

2. Intelligence Office was a term that designated an employment agency for domestic help.

A VISIT TO WASHINGTON

1. Vinnie Ream (1847–1914) was an American sculptor who, though she had little training, had at the age of seventeen modeled a clay bust of President Lincoln during several sessions with him in 1864. When Lincoln died in 1865, Congress authorized $10,000 for her to make a full-scale marble statue of him for the Capitol rotunda. She was the first woman to receive such a federal commission. Much criticism arose because of her youth and inexperience, and it was suggested, by Jane Swisshelm for example, that Congress had been influenced by her feminine charms. Ream went to Italy to complete the statue and it was formally unveiled in January 1871. It has been criticized, but is also considered to be an accurate likeness and an impressive achievement for an essentially untrained artist.

THE MODERN OLD MAID

1. "Law's Serious Call" refers to the book *A Serious Call to a Devout and Holy Life* (1728) by English clergyman William Law.

THEOLOGICAL NUTS

1. The editor of the *Ledger* apparently considered this a dangerous position to take, and although he allowed it to be printed, he appended a long Editor's Note, pointing out Fern's error in not recognizing the importance of doctrine.

END OF THE SUMMER SEASON

1. Festus is the principal character in Philip James Bailey's dramatic poem *Festus*, a version of the Faust legend first published in England in 1833. It was a best seller in the United States in 1852. The quotation to which Fern refers appears in the last scene of the poem: "My Maker! let me thank Thee, I have lived / And live a deathless witness of Thy grace."

2. This is Fanny Fern's last article and appeared two days after her death. The *Ledger* continued to run her column for two weeks. On October 19, it printed a short piece entitled "To Be Read by Those Who Are Selecting Schools for Their Children," which was a reiteration of her criticism of the conditions in the schools, and on October 26 it reprinted "Our First Nurse," Fern's first article for the *Ledger* in January 1856. The *Ledger* announced her death on November 2, 1872.